A Cumulative Index
to New Testament
Greek Grammars

A Cumulative Index to New Testament Greek Grammars

Timothy Lawrence Owings

Baker Book House
Grand Rapids, Michigan 49506

To
my Greek professors,
with gratitude

Naymond Keathley

R. Alan Culpepper

Frank Stagg

James Blevins

Contents

Preface

In the process of earning the Ph.D. degree in New Testament at The Southern Baptist Theological Seminary, I became acutely aware of the need for a tool that would aid students in using the major New Testament grammars. During a Greek seminar on Romans, I found myself spending too much time in the indices of the grammars and too little with the issues they raised. Thus *A Cumulative Index to New Testament Greek Grammars* was conceived in the labors of personal study.

The *Index* is a tool for scholars of the Greek New Testament. It exhaustively includes the indices of eight major advanced and intermediate grammars used in colleges and seminaries today. It is in no way selective. The indices have been reproduced exactly as they appear, by book, chapter, and verse in the New Testament. The order of verses in the *Index* does not reflect textual decisions. These and other critical matters must be the work of the scholar in dialogue with the text.

The *Index* is also an ideal tool for students who have had

at least one semester of New Testament Greek. The student can soon discover that the comments found in an intermediate grammar only scratch the surface of grammatical details in a given text. The advanced student will find the *Index* invaluable for locating and using material in the grammars quickly and accurately.

A word is in order regarding the *Index's* format. Five of the eight grammars indexed are listed by page number. Three, BDF, RD, and Zer, are listed by paragraph numbers. The paragraph symbol is, for economy's sake, used for only the first reference in each listing.

A project like this is never done successfully without contributions from others. My professors and colleagues in the New Testament department of The Southern Baptist Theological Seminary gave to me their faithful support and insight. Members of Dr. James Blevins's Greek seminar on the Book of Revelation were particularly helpful in this project's early stages. A special word of thanks is due to Allan Fisher and Dan Van't Kerkhoff of Baker Book House, who dared to support an unknown scholar with their personal encouragement and professional expertise. Members of Hillcrest Baptist Church in Frankfort, Kentucky, supported their pastor with prayer and affirmation during the long months of production: God bless you! Mary Nell and Ernie Moulton shared this dream in the early stages and lent patient and productive help by making accessible to me their word processor. The *Index* would not be a reality had it not been for their contribution to the typing and editing of the manuscript.

Finally, a tribute is due to my family. During the past year my wife Kathie has been a never-ending source of strength and encouragement. She has agonized with me over every page of this book. In the late hours of the evening, she stayed up to help me check and correct the thousands of references in the text. On top of her aid in this project, she kept our family warm and close, giving birth two months ago to our third child. No person could ask for companionship any dearer or more precious.

It is my prayer that the *Index* will provide students of the Greek New Testament an opportunity to understand better the great message contained within its covers.

Abbreviations

BDF Blass, F., and Debrunner, A. *A Greek Grammar of the New Testament and Other Early Christian Literature.* Translated by Robert W. Funk. Chicago: University of Chicago, 1961.

BW Brooks, James A., and Winbery, Carlton L. *Syntax of New Testament Greek.* Washington, D.C.: University Press of America, 1979.

DM Dana, H. E., and Mantey, Julius R. *A Manual Grammar of the Greek New Testament.* Toronto: Macmillan, 1957.

Moule Moule, C. F. D. *An Idiom Book of New Testament Greek.* Cambridge: Cambridge University, 1959.

MHT I Moulton, James Hope. *A Grammar of New Testament Greek: I, Prolegomena.* 3d ed. Edinburgh: T. & T. Clark, 1978.

MHT II Moulton, James Hope, and Howard, Wilbert Francis. *A Grammar of New Testament Greek: II, Accidence and Word-Formation.* Edinburgh: T. & T. Clark, 1979.

MHT III   Moulton, James Hope, and Turner, Nigel. *A Grammar of New Testament Greek: III, Syntax.* Edinburgh: T. & T. Clark, 1963.

MHT IV   Turner, Nigel. *A Grammar of New Testament Greek: IV, Style.* Edinburgh: T. & T. Clark, 1976.

Rob   Robertson, A. T. *A Grammar of the Greek New Testament in the Light of Historical Research.* 4th ed. Nashville: Broadman, 1923.

RD   Robertson, A. T., and Davis, W. Hersey. *A New Short Grammar of the Greek Testament.* New York: Harper & Brothers, 1931. Reprint. 10th ed. Grand Rapids: Baker Book House, 1977.

Zer   Zerwick, Maximillian. *Biblical Greek.* Edited and translated by Joseph Smith. Rome: Pontificii Instituti Biblici, 1963.

Matthew

13

23 BDF §157(2); DM 107; Moule 17;
    MHT II 30, 447; MHT IV 34; Rob
    505, 611, 713, 881; Zer §6

24 MHT II 453; Rob 541

25 BDF §157(2); Rob 459, 975; Zer
    §6

34 MHT II 424

Chapter 2

1   BW 16; DM 141; MHT I 48; MHT
    III 26, 172; Rob 255, 263,
    408bis, 575, 760, 762, 791

2   BDF §253(5); BW 104; DM 214;
    Moule 140; MHT I 138, 204;
    MHT II 129; MHT III **26**, 134,
    172, 189; Rob 234, 366, 370,
    419, 540, 542, 840, 915, 990,
    1062, 1088, 1428; RD §347(g),
    455(a)

3   BDF §56(4), 275(2); DM 138;
    Moule 94; MHT I 48; MHT II 147;
    MHT III 317; Rob 253, 263, 760,
    772, 774; RD §387(e); Zer §190

4   BDF §323(2); BW 78; DM 186;
    Moule 7; MHT I 120; MHT III 63,
    65; Rob 517bis, 627, 773, 795,
    866, 1043, 1045; RD §387(e),
    452(b)

5   BW 71; DM 105; Rob 695, 1186;
    RD §379

6   BDF §264(6); MHT II 60, 108;
    MHT III 31, 48, 151, 170; Rob
    255, 559, 587, 652, 669, 729,
    1106, 1109, 1165; RD §360; Zer
    §219

7   BW 69; DM 141, 224; Rob 530,
    762, 1106

8   BDF §420(2); MHT III 112, 154,
    156, 335; Rob 366, 479, 860,
    971, 986; RD §419(c), 430(b)

9   BDF §215(2), 253(5); DM 109,
    125, 278, 281; MHT III **26**, 172,
    279; Rob 408, 642, 714, 840,
    969, 975; RD §423(b); Zer §69

10 BDF §153(1); BW 47; DM 227;
    Moule 32, 178; MHT I 117;
    MHT II 129, 445; MHT III **160**,
    242; MHT IV 33, 48; Rob 258,
    477, 484, 1122; RD §174 a; Zer
    §62

11 Moule 68, 106; MHT II 106; Rob
    593

12 DM 110; MHT III 52; Rob 561,
    747, 800, 816

13 BDF §321; BW 159; DM 284; Moule
    128; MHT II 453; MHT III 141,
    142; MHT IV 33, 43; Rob 313,
    476, 513, 828, 868, 882, 990,

1060, 1088; RD §349, 420(c),
432, 455(d); Zer §383

14 DM 249; MHT III 235; Rob 1112

15 Moule 66, 145; MHT I 138;
    MHT III 151; Rob 299, 636, 1428

16 BDF §62; MHT III 72, 154, 227;
    Rob 231, 297, 298, 834, 1112,
    1126; RD §410(b); Zer §363n

17 Rob 255, 1428

18 Rob 475, 1159; RD §445

19 Zer §7

20 BDF §141; Moule 206; MHT I 58;
    MHT II 453; MHT III **25**, 75, **81**,
    154, 293; Rob 392, 406, 892bis,
    996, 1111; RD §462(b); Zer §7

21 Rob 559

22 BDF §177, 324; BW 19, 28; DM
    81, 100; MHT III 26, **64**, 226;
    Rob 299, 510, 574, 1029; RD
    §343(1), 434(c); Zer §133

23 MHT I 17; MHT II 149; MHT III
    7, 26; MHT IV 43, 74; Rob 593;
    Zer §7, **417**

Chapter 3

1   BW 80; DM 185, 228; Rob 587,
    697, 868, 1185; RD §387(d)

2   Rob 408, 609, 652, 762, 895; RD
    §365

3   DM 127, 141; MHT III 44; Rob
    255, 697, 1428

4   BDF §209(4), 277(3); DM 130;
    Moule 62; MHT I 91, 102; MHT II
    431; MHT III **41, 66**; MHT IV 36;
    Rob 231, 577, 620, 686bis, 709,
    883; RD §376; Zer §205

5   MHT II 147; MHT III **16, 66**; Rob
    255, 624, 652, 773, 883

6   BW 24; DM 116, 187, 227;
    MHT III **66**; Rob 271, 525bis,
    586, 636, 651, 760, 791, 883;
    RD §332, 345(e), 402(b)

7   BDF §149; DM 106, 132; MHT I
    116, 138; MHT III **66**; Rob 213,
    602, 735, 848, 883, 916, 1176;
    RD §381, 448(c)

8   BW 13; DM 256; Rob 504, 835,
    1192; RD §343(j), 425

9   BDF §392(1a); DM 252; Moule
    186; MHT I 15, 124; MHT III 42,
    168; Rob 598, 834, 853, 1035

10 DM 256; Moule 53, 107 n.1; MHT III 62, **199**, 200; MHT IV 43; Rob 418, 423, 771, 881; Zer §236

11 BW 21, 25, 56, 87; DM 83, 104(2), 123, 261; MHT I 208; MHT II 10, 458; MHT III **252, 266**; Rob 418, 428, 516, 520, 586, 590, 645, 658, 679, 889, 1076, 1148, 1153, 1186; RD §303, 337, 344(d), 345(b), 360, 472(d)

12 DM 107, 162; MHT II 10, 434; MHT III 325; MHT IV 21, 36; Rob 260, 355, 533, 562, 575, 581, 606, 683, 722; RD §346(f), 364; Zer §201

13 Moule 52; MHT III 141; MHT IV 43; Rob 575

14 BDF §326; BW 85, 128; DM 189, 219; Moule 9; MHT I 129; MHT II 302; MHT III 39, 65, 139, **334**; Rob 235, 677, 682, 885, 1076, 1148, 1183, 1392; RD §102 G, 402(b); Zer §273, 455a

15 BW 126, 131; DM 217; Moule 94; MHT III 88, 149, 200; Rob 221, 309, 315, 393, 491, 772, 881, 1058, 1086, 1110, 1119, 1126; RD §402(a)

16 DM 101, 276; Moule 92; MHT III 25, **259**; Rob 538, 561, 575, 578, 968, 1025, 1213; RD §362, 424(b), 442; Zer §**87**

17 BW 22, 93; DM 198; Moule 7, 69; MHT I 104; MHT II 50, 458; MHT III 25, 44, 186; Rob 372, 460, 597, 697, 837, 842, 1097; RD §458

25 RD §342(o)

Chapter 4

1 MHT III 134; MHT IV 39; Rob 635, 820, 880, 990; RD §372

2 BDF §474(1); MHT II 172; Rob 349, 860, 1112; Zer §149

3 BW 112; DM 294; MHT I 208; MHT III 183; MHT IV 36, 38; Rob 329, 781, 993; RD §387(b)(2); Zer §303

4 BW 105; Rob 604, 649, 889; Zer §226

5 Rob 756

6 Moule 91; MHT III 183; Rob 221, 548, 625, 781; RD §377, 387(b)(2), 410(b); Zer §84

7 Rob 311, 319, 874, 883, 895

8 MHT II 202; MHT III 227; MHT IV 32; Rob 311, 419

9 Rob 705

10 DM 191; Moule 90; Rob 391

11 BW 86; DM 208; MHT III **67**; Rob 540, 838, 847, 883

13 DM 108; MHT II 112, 149, 158, 191; Rob 219, 273, 593, 613, 759; RD §208 c

14 DM 249; Moule 145; Rob 1428

15 BDF §161(1); BW 21; MHT II 332, 459; MHT III 175, **212, 247**; Rob 469, 500, 646; RD §342(d)

16 BDF §466(4); Moule 206; MHT II 424; MHT III 39, 316

17 DM 113; MHT II 455; MHT IV 32; Rob 576; RD §461(b)

18 Rob 269, 615, 656, 1190; RD §425

19 BW 21; Rob 480, 517, 645, 949; RD §353

20 Rob 770

21 BW 9, 46, 141; DM 77, 92; Moule 38; Rob 263, 501, 586, 747, 770, 780; RD §342(h), 368; Zer §149

23 BDF §150; MHT III 51, 211; Rob 428, 477, 499, 562, 617, 655

24 DM 155; MHT II 405; Rob 412, 428, 799

25 BDF §479(1); MHT III **275**; MHT IV 43; Rob 28, 428, 788; RD §344(d)

30 Zer §149

32 Zer §149

Chapter 5

1 BDF §423(1); BW 68; MHT III **173**, 322; MHT IV 39; Rob 561, 593, 597, 756, 1132; RD §361, 386(a); Zer §48, 167

2 MHT II 454; Rob 885; Zer §272, 363n

3 BDF §462(2); BW 38, 66; DM 145; Moule 46; MHT III 220, 239; Rob 417, 443, 523, 757, 762, 945; RD §334, 345(d), 386(b), 474(i); Zer §53

4 BDF §462(2); DM 145; Rob 443, 533, 757, 764, 872, 945; RD §334

5 BDF §462(2); MHT III 232; Rob 443, 757, 945; RD §334; Zer §67, 236

6 BDF §462(2); MHT III 177, 232; Rob 443, 474, 508, 757, 945; RD §334; Zer §67, 236

7 BDF §462(2); Rob 443, 757, 945; RD §334; Zer §236

8 BDF §462(2); DM 88; MHT III 220, 239; Rob 395, 443, 523, 757, 871, 945; RD §334, 345(d); Zer §53, 236

9 BDF §462(2); MHT III 208; Rob 394, 443, 485, 757, 945; RD §334, 342(j); Zer §42, 236

10 BDF §462(2); Moule 14; MHT III 85; Rob 443, 757, 945; RD §334, 353; Zer §242

11 BDF §462(2); BW 67; Rob 234, 392, 443, 473, 505, 551, 945; RD §334

12 BDF §462(2); BW 20, 144; Moule 74; MHT I 129, 174; MHT III **76**; Rob 443, 621, 855

13 BDF §273(1), 390(3), 462(2); BW 141; MHT II 132, 402, 408; MHT III 183; Rob 269, 534, 590, 739, 751, 768, 1019, 1024; RD §442; Zer §84, 174

14 BDF §462(2); BW 13; MHT III 279; Rob 505, 642; RD §343(k), 353

15 BDF §5(1), 442(2), 462(2); BW 50; Moule 28, 65; MHT II 30, 447; MHT III **150**, 292; MHT IV 32, 33; Rob 221, 263, 428, 491, 633, 635, 757, 766, 1183; RD §320, 342(o), 372; Zer §455g

16 BDF §462(2); MHT III 72, **150**; Rob 640, 710, 782; RD §353; Zer §250

17 BDF §445(2), 462(2); BW 108, 121; DM 214, 240, 284; MHT I 138; MHT III **77**, 134; Rob 231, 427, 789, 833, 834, 853, 857, 858, 932, 990, 1080, 1088, 1187, 1188; RD §401(a), 406(a), 410(a), 457(c)

18 BDF §247(2), 474(1); Moule 92; MHT I 58, 191; MHT II 433; MHT III 96; MHT IV 33; Rob 186, 405, 406, 561, 677, 751, 933, 1062, inset, 1430

19 BDF §107, 488(1c); BW 111; DM 273; Moule 103; MHT III 31, 45, **107**; Rob 660, 669, 698, 712, 959bis; RD §408, 416

20 BDF §185(1), 246; BW 25, 109; DM 172, 267; MHT II 165; MHT III 96, **216**; MHT IV 33; Rob 516, 666, 667, 854, 933, inset

21 BDF §362; BW 88, 105; MHT I 138, 140, 186; MHT III 86; Rob 212, 342, 349, 504bis, 538, 541, 658, 844, 850, 889, 957,

1035, 1042, 1157, 1162; RD §308, 337, 402(c), 410(a); Zer §280, 286

22 DM 127, 244; MHT II 152, 460; MHT III 151; Rob 219, 502, 535, 537, 541, 677, 744, 772, 866, 1107, 1148, 1153, 1186; RD §343(b), 374, 382, 460(b)

23 Rob 849, 1393, 1420

24 BDF §336(3); BW 21; MHT III **75**; Rob 428, 470, 529, 621, 640, 657, 690, 882, 949

25 BDF §353(1), 369(3); MHT I 174, 226; MHT III 88, 89, **110**; Rob 375, 488, 573, 729, 890, 975, 976, 1415; RD §288 a, 308, 348, 407, 419(b), 420(c)bis; Zer §236, 473

26 BDF §5(1); MHT I 191; MHT III 96; MHT IV 33; Rob 255, 976, inset; RD §420(c)

27 MHT I 138; Rob 889; Zer §280

28 BDF §333(2), 402(5); DM 123, 145, 284; MHT I 65, 140, 218; MHT III **73**, **144**, 151, 232; Rob 474, 508, 573, 842, 866, 1003, 1060, 1075bis, 1153, 1186; RD §343(1), 410(a), 435(d); Zer 67, **391**

29 BDF §442(1); BW 20; MHT I 210; MHT III 32, 42, 115, 139; Rob 502, 539, 575, 681, 687, 779, 834, 992, 1009, 1018; RD §344(d), 358, 434(a); Zer §236, 329

30 Rob 779; Zer §329

31 BDF §130(1); MHT I 138, 186; Rob 850

32 BW 21; Moule 103; MHT III **107**, 151; Rob 348, 517, 646, 764bis, 773, 1153, 1186, 1391; RD §344(d), 353, 410(a); Zer §128n, 442

33 MHT I 138; MHT II 99, 236, 315; Rob 224, 333, 889; RD §470(h); Zer §280

34 BDF §445(1); Moule 21, 183; MHT I 126; MHT II 450; MHT III 149; Rob 475, 588, 594, 1060, 1084, 1094, 1153, 1189, 1424; RD §410(a), 455(b)

35 DM 112, 248; Moule 183; MHT II 464; MHT III 255; Rob 633, 1189; RD §372, 410(a)

36 Moule 21, 183; MHT I 126; MHT II 129; MHT III 75; Rob 853, 1189, 1214; RD §174 a, 302, 410(a)

37 BDF §60(3), 185(1), 432(1); BW
    25; Moule 42; MHT II 154; Rob
    279, 516, 618, 660, 947,
    1150bis; RD §465, 472(c)

38 BDF §480(5); BW 28; DM 100; MHT
    I 138

39 BDF §337(2), 380(2); MHT I 79,
    174; MHT II 450; MHT III 48,
    77, 149, **197**; Rob 727, 746,
    747, 1084, 1153, 1181; RD §380,
    410(a); Zer §28

40 BDF §466(4); Moule 199; MHT I
    69; MHT II 424; MHT III 39,
    316; Rob 437, 529, 538, 683,
    802, 1181; Zer §27, 28

41 BDF §380(2); MHT II 67; MHT III
    48; Rob 183, 562, 1181; Zer §28

42 MHT I 129, 174; MHT III 76; Rob
    311, 809, 855, 943, 1181; RD
    §407; Zer §28, 246

43 BDF §362; BW 88; DM 299; MHT I
    138; MHT III 86; Rob 330, 547,
    646, 889, 943, 1181; RD
    §402(c); Zer §279

44 BW 144; DM 175; MHT III **86**; Rob
    630, 889, 941, 943, 947, 1153;
    RD §407, 410(a)

45 BDF §129, 182(4), 309(1), 492;
    DM 156; Moule 27 n.1; MHT III
    52, 53, 208, 291; Rob 392, 757,
    764, 799, 801, 1200; RD
    §386(b); Zer §42, 424

46 Moule 122; Rob 735, 1019, 1181;
    Zer §278

47 MHT I 186; Rob 687, 850,
    1019bis, 1387

48 BDF §362; BW 88; DM 277; MHT II
    458; MHT III 86; Rob 429, 678,
    889

Chapter 6

1   BW 45, 121; DM 110, 215, 284;
    Moule 140, 164; MHT II 471;
    MHT III **144**; Rob 244, 394, 542,
    626, 818, 820, 858, 991, 1003,
    1075bis, 1080, 1088, 1148,
    1148-49, 1173; RD §347(g),
    457(d), 472(a); Zer §278

2   BW 82; DM 276; MHT I 159, 186;
    MHT III 42, **77**, 112; Rob 349,
    429, 577, 633, 687, 853,
    866bis, 969, 972, 986, 1154; RD
    §424(b), 430(b), 472(c); Zer
    §246

3   BDF §423(3); MHT I 174;
    MHT III 17, 39; Rob 652, 662,
    856, 943, 1131, 1170, 1202,
    1405; Zer §278

4   MHT II 422; MHT III 39, 334;
    Rob 437, 471, 653, 764, 986,
    1402, 1413; Zer §278

5   BDF §98, 362; BW 110; DM 283,
    299; MHT II 458; MHT III 86,
    112, **226**; Rob 552, 828, 874
    bis, 942, 963, 968, 986,
    1157, 1420; RD §425(b); Zer
    §424, 443

6   BW 115; DM 175, 244; MHT II
    419; MHT III 77, 112; Rob 204,
    777, 835, 855, 947, 1186; RD
    §401(a)

7   BDF §219(2); BW 41; Moule 77;
    MHT II 68, 272, 463; MHT III
    253; Rob 184, 589, 591, 969,
    1035; RD §424(b); Zer §119,
    236, 246

8   BDF §293(5); MHT III 49, 144;
    Rob 452, 482, 720, 726, 857,
    881, 895, 978, 1061, 1075,
    1091, 1392; RD §342(i), 421(b);
    Zer §221

9   BDF §277(1); BW 144, 149; DM
    124; Moule 135; MHT III 35; Rob
    422, 459, 464, 779, 852, 855;
    Zer §236

10 Moule 135; MHT III **75, 77**; Rob
    334, 350, 396, 422, 600, 818,
    852, 855, 1181; RD §311, 363,
    401(a); Zer §236

11 BDF §123(1); BW 116; Moule 135;
    MHT I 129, 174; MHT II 313; Rob
    159, 422, 779. 852, 855; Zer
    §242

12 BDF §453(2); BW 116; Moule 135;
    MHT I 137, 140; MHT II 202;
    MHT III 37; MHT IV 33; Rob 422,
    538, 677, 852, 963, 967, 852;
    RD §347(g)

13 BDF §263(1); BW 67, 116; DM
    171; Moule 135, 207; MHT I 125;
    MHT III **14**, 77; Rob 422, 518,
    575, 593, 652, 653, 852, 853,
    932; RD §333; Zer §89

14 DM 244; MHT IV 31; Rob 1186; RD
    §366

15 BDF §445(2); Rob 1185

16 BW 136; DM 228; MHT I 186; MHT
    III 76, 112; Rob 395, 427, 854,
    1040, 1102, 1121; RD §461(b)

17 BDF §277(1); BW 133; MHT I 85,
    236; MHT III 37, 54, 154; Rob
    683, 779, 811, 1035, 1102,
    1126; Zer §233

18 BDF §414(3); MHT III 106, 159;
    Rob 589, 891, 1115, 1121, 1185;
    RD §430(b)

19   BW 116; DM 124, 131, 278; MHT I 58, 240; MHT III **42, 76**; MHT IV 36; Rob 231, 286, 405, 687, 853, 875, 1186; RD §348, 407

20   DM 124, 244; Rob 792; RD §377

21   Rob 523

22   MHT III **183**; Rob 284, 768, 849, 1018

23   DM 244, 273; Moule 148; Rob 740, 849, 917, 1027, 1186

24   MHT II 419; MHT III 36; Rob 251, 573, 748, 749, 751, 890, 1052, 1188, 1191; RD §383, 457(a)

25   BDF §131, 337(3); BW 33; DM 101, 171; MHT III 24, **76, 99, 117**; Rob 539, 564, 738, 853, 917, 935, 1028, 1031, 1044, 1176; RD §347(g), 406(a), 452(a); Zer §254, 348

26   BDF §246; Moule 92; MHT II 165; Rob 561, 581, 1035, 1183, 1185; RD §344(e); Zer §455a

27   BDF §247(2), 417; BW 135; DM 228; Moule 92; MHT I 230; MHT II 173; MHT III 209; Rob 515, 561, 733, 891, 1115, 1128; RD §380, 460(c), 462(a)

28   BDF §476(2); DM 132; MHT I 117; MHT II 195; MHT III **76**, 179, 313, 325; Rob 341, 606, 619, 799, 1185; RD §474(j), Zer §242, 221n

29   Rob 502, 515, 746, 807, 1164, 1185; RD §344(b)

30   BDF §372(1a); MHT II 10, 68, 202, 294; MHT III **115**; Rob 532, 1107, 1115; RD §348, 354

31   BW 108; Rob 738, 934, 935, 1028, 1031, 1044; RD §406(a), 452(a)

32   DM 252; Moule 41; MHT III 313; Rob 404, 419, 705, 771

33   Rob 542; RD §350; Zer §236

34   BDF §176(2), 337(3); BW 108; DM 171; MHT II 313; MHT III **72, 76**, 77, 311; Rob 411, 509, 547, 594, 765, 853, 1202; Zer §254

37   BDF §366(2)

Chapter 7

1   DM 248, 283, 301; MHT I 191; Rob 853, 890, 947, 983; RD §430(a); Zer §236

2   BDF §130(1); Moule 27, 33, 130; MHT II 464; MHT III **291**; Rob

534, 590, 718, 721; RD §380; Zer §236

3   DM 130, 132; MHT II 419; MHT III 191; Rob 471, 685bis, 738, 782; RD §375, 381

4   BW 107; DM 171; Moule 22; MHT I 175, 176; MHT III 94; Rob 234, 286, 430, 596, 931; RD §406 a, 430(a); Zer §279

5   MHT III 139; Rob 582, 659, 1088

6   BDF §111(3), 214(6), 369(2); MHT II 75, 464; MHT III 77, **346**; Rob 203, 538, 763, 853, 875, 988, 1185, 1200, 1415; RD §401(a)

7   MHT II 83, 419, 421; Rob 357, 1023, 1213

8   MHT III 151; Rob 773, 866, 1213

9   BDF §469; MHT I 193; MHT II 60; MHT III 55, 325; MHT IV 35; Rob 439, 482, 917, 1177; RD §342(i), 448(f)

10   Moule 89; Rob 231, 1023, 1188

11   MHT III 157; Rob 740, 1053, 1062, 1103, 1129, 1417

12   MHT III **107**, 108, **138**; MHT IV 36, 43; Rob 427, 704, 732, 733, 959, 1180, 1402; RD §380, 416, 455(d)

13   BDF §492; MHT I 174; MHT II 419; Rob 800, 1200

14   BDF §299(4); Rob 730, 739

15   BDF §293(2); DM 275; MHT II 460; MHT III 48; Rob 272, 477, 548, 589, 727, 729, 800, 966; RD §332, 427; Zer §217

16   Moule 28; MHT I 59; MHT II 447; MHT III 293; Rob 392, 566, 576, 917, 1172

17   BW 79; DM 183; Moule 8; MHT III 63; Rob 221

19   Rob 402; Zer §236

20   DM 242, 260; Moule 164; MHT II 452; Rob 425, 1148bis, 1190; RD §472(a)

21   MHT III 196; Rob 752ter, 1107; RD §383

22   DM 144; MHT I 138; MHT II 208; Rob 367, 524, 525, 708, 917, 1157, 1175, 1213; RD §387(e)

23   BDF §187(4), 412(5); DM 250, 252; MHT I 174; MHT II 469; MHT III 153, 177; Rob 548, 559, 575, 1028, 1035, 1165

24 BDF §293(2), 466(3); DM 116; Moule 50, 106, 124; MHT II 424; MHT III 48, 189, **233**, 316; MHT IV 35; Rob 468, 479, 602, 727, 772, 905, 957, 1105bis, 1107; RD §363, 380, 387(e), 414; Zer §69, 218

25 BDF §126(3), 202, 492; MHT II 190; Rob 361, 366, 606, 905, 1157; RD §275, 364, 403(b)

26 MHT III 151, 221; MHT IV 35; Rob 727, 752, 772, 957, 1105, 1107; RD §380, 387(e), 414; Zer §218

27 BDF §126(3), 492; MHT III 207; Rob 1100

28 DM 280; Moule 133; MHT II 426; MHT III 66; Rob 350, 532, 835, 883, 966, 970, 1043, 1207; RD §419(f); Zer §389n

29 Rob 394, 656

Chapter 8

1 BDF §423(1); DM 124; MHT I 74; MHT III 39, 322; MHT IV 39; Rob 597, 683, 1132

2 BDF §372(1a); MHT III 65; Rob 391, 1018, 1019, 1214, 1418; Zer **§309**

3 BW 90; DM 131, 148, 196; MHT II 67; Rob 183, 391, 684, 770, 1028, 1216; RD §320, 375, 449

4 BDF §336(3); DM 104; MHT II 209; MHT III 40, 78; Rob 330, 338, 430, 595, 683, 849, 854, 932, 949; Zer §489

5 DM 108; MHT III 322; MHT IV 39; Rob 258, 932

8 BDF §442(2), 473(1); Moule 65; MHT I 208; MHT II 327, 421; MHT III 139, 189; Rob 258, 329, 635, 653, 657, 658bis, 681, 819, 992, 1076; RD §372; Zer §410

9 BDF §101, 336(1); DM 112; Moule 135; MHT III 75; MHT IV 35; Rob 391, 817, 1180bis, 1182; RD §410(a)

10 MHT I 140; Rob 710, 844; RD §379

11 MHT III 26; Rob 334, 357, 408, 819

12 BDF §62; MHT II 448; MHT III 29, **173**; Rob 278, 298, 803; Zer §178, 400

13 Rob 818, 968

14 BDF §471(5); Rob 1026

15 MHT IV 39; Rob 367; RD §387(e)

16 DM 89; MHT III **241**; Rob 392, 533, 653, 773

17 MHT III 40; Rob 1428

18 DM 109; Rob 491, 646; RD §342(o)

19 BDF §107, 247(2); DM 136; Moule 125; MHT I 97; MHT II 432; Rob 282, 292, 674, 675, 796, 969, 1411; RD §384; Zer §155

20 BDF §368; DM 144; MHT II 347; Rob 737, 757bis, 800; RD §386(b), 396; Zer §348

21 MHT II 422; MHT III 334; Rob 748, 1152

22 BDF §488(1c); Rob 690, 858; RD §377

23 Moule 92; Rob 525, 560, 585, 683

24 BW 25, 83; DM 286; MHT III **66**; Rob 679, 883; RD §374

25 BW 76; DM 182; MHT I 114; MHT II 206; Rob 828, 879, 941; RD §402(a)

26 MHT II 61; Rob 738, 813

27 BDF §298(3), 444(3), 456(2); MHT II 436; MHT III **318**; Rob 292, 507, 543, 741, 917, 1001, 1176; RD §381, 435(b), 448(c); Zer §420, 420n

28 BDF §291(3), 423(1); Moule 141; MHT III 322; MHT IV 39; Rob 597, 634, 708, 1171

29 Moule 74; MHT III 156, 179; MHT IV 17; Rob 348, 621, 702, 1136; RD §344(d)

30 MHT II 452; Rob 499

31 Rob 948, 1009; Zer §329

32 BDF §225; BW 116; DM 176; Moule 60, 94; MHT I 172; MHT II 208; Rob 339, 570, 607; RD §364

34 BDF §328; DM 104; Moule 70, 94; MHT I 14; MHT III 65, 106; Rob 528, 609, 628, 771, 995, 1046; RD §387(e), 434(b)

Chapter 9

1   DM 131; MHT I 90; Rob 691, 692, 770

2   DM 74; MHT II 206; MHT III **64**, 292; MHT IV 33; Rob 315, 603

3   MHT II 16; MHT III 43, 209

4   DM 249; MHT III 23; Rob 244, 395, 739bis, 916, 1176; RD §381, 448(e)

5   BDF §320; DM 133, 243; MHT II 70, 206; MHT III 32; Rob 186, 617, 737, 916, 917, 1176, 1177, 1190; RD §448(c), 448(f)

6   BDF §470(3), 483; MHT III 344; Rob 119, 319, 434, 443, 562, 907, 1203, 1388; RD §403(a), 474(f)

7   MHT II 453

8   MHT I 58; Rob 409, 710; RD §387(e)

9   BDF §308; DM 300; Moule 92; MHT II 453; MHT IV 35; Rob 215, 314, 602, 800

10   BDF §423(1); MHT I 16, 17; MHT II 426; MHT III 322; MHT IV 35; Rob 316bis, 529, 1043, 1131, 1423

11   Moule 159; Rob 244, 916, 1176, 1396; RD §448(c)

13   MHT III 282; Rob 261, 844, 1163, 1164, 1166, 1429

14   Rob 402

15   BDF §382(3); DM 113, 282; MHT II 419, 441; MHT III 208; Rob 300, 497, 559, 722, 733, 978; RD §419(d); Zer §43

16   MHT III 65; Rob 214, 278, 604, 1378

17   BDF §73; MHT II 206; MHT III 292; MHT IV 35; Rob 251, 292, 342, 352, 745, 880, 1025, 1220; RD §111

18   BDF §247(2), 423(1), 448(3); BW 93; MHT I 74, 140; MHT II 129, 432; MHT III 65, 196, 322, 330; MHT IV 39; Rob 433, 842, 1109, 1132; RD §320; Zer §226

19   MHT II 453

20   MHT II 171; Rob 212, 1115

21   BW 110; DM 290; MHT III 43; Rob 1019

22   BDF §291(3); DM 72, 128; MHT III 35, **69**; MHT IV 32; Rob 264, 433, 462, 517, 575

24   Moule 90; Rob 512; RD §343(1), 402(b)

25   MHT IV 39; Rob 300, 508; RD §343(1)

26   MHT III 312; Rob 708bis

27   BDF §147(3), 308; MHT III 51; Rob 463

29   Rob 609

30   DM 295; Rob 368, 430, 932, 949, 996, 1213; RD §278, 407

31   Rob 708; RD §409

32   MHT IV 35

33   DM 80

34   BDF §219(1); Moule 77; MHT I 104

35   BDF §150; Rob 477, 655, 773; RD §387(e)

36   BDF §229(2); DM 276; Moule 62f.; MHT II 192, 193; Rob 211, 212, 364bis, 619, 968

37   Rob 1153

38   BW 163; DM 294; MHT III 106; Rob 995, 1413; RD §434(b)

Chapter 10

1   BDF §390(3); BW 122; Moule 140, 144; MHT III 136, 139; Rob 500, 809, 990, 1089, 1090, 1414; RD §432; Zer §352

2   DM 142; MHT III **168**; Rob 657, 767, 1397

4   BDF §339(1); DM 225; MHT III **80**; Rob 760, 859, 1114; Zer §267

5   Moule 38; MHT I 138; MHT III 169, **212**; Rob 495, 500; RD §343(d)

6   MHT IV 49; Rob 358, 800, 881

7   MHT II 469

8   BW 156; DM 93, 154; MHT I 139; Rob 488, 799; RD §342(k), 348

9   DM 99, 300; MHT I 125; Rob 810, 852bis; RD §470(n)

10   BDF §445(1); DM 99, 248; MHT I 38; MHT II 100; Rob 395; RD §410(a)

11 BDF §466(2); MHT II 424, 434; MHT III 316; MHT IV 21, 36; Rob 1185; Zer §27

13 BDF §362; MHT II 204, 430; MHT III **86**; Rob 849, 874, 948, 1019

14 BDF §107; BW 21; MHT III 48; Rob 437, 517, 642, 813, 959; RD §344(d), 353; Zer §69, 84

15 Moule 98; MHT II 147; MHT III 213, 216; Rob 214, 257, 587, 663, 666

16 BDF §60(1); MHT III **38**; Rob 648, 653; RD §387(c)

17 BDF §187(1); MHT II 460

18 Rob 1180, 1185; RD §343(k)

19 BDF §368; DM 133; MHT I 93; MHT II 204, 432, 447; MHT III 49, 117; Rob 738bis, 739, 972, 1045; RD §381; Zer §236

20 Rob 401; Zer §278, 445

21 MHT III 313; Rob 403

22 DM 161; MHT III 45, 89; Rob 357, 437, 584, 792, 871, 889, 891, 1110; RD §460(c)ter

23 BDF §306(2); Moule 18; MHT III 112, **197**; Rob 748bis, 776, 976, inset; RD §420(c)

24 BW 57; DM 112; Moule 64; Rob 632

25 BDF §157(2); MHT I 140, 208, 210; MHT II 377; MHT III 139; MHT IV 33; Rob 393, 537, 740, 992, 1417; RD §347(e)

26 DM 258; MHT I 191; MHT II 29, 436; MHT III **77**, 286; Rob 334, 472, 473, 485, 575, 577, 726, 816, 853, 960, 1001, 1158, 1164, 1200; RD §342(j), 358, 398, 435(e), 470(j); Zer §246, 425

27 Rob 603, 705

28 BDF §444(3); MHT I 102; MHT II 245, 460; MHT III 335; Rob 352, 472bis, 473, 577bis, 1046, 1170, 1213; RD §342(j) bis

29 BDF §252; BW 11, 21; Moule 39, 82, 182; MHT I 236; MHT II 430, 433; MHT IV 42; Rob 355, 356, 510, 515, 603, 637, 638, 751; RD §344(b), 353, 383; Zer §446, 455a

30 DM 251; MHT III 24; Zer §236

31 Rob 473, 519, 853, 1170; RD §342(j), 401(a)

32 BDF §220(2), 380(2), 466(3); BW 34; DM 256, 273; Moule 83, 183; MHT I 104; MHT III 48, **110**, 316; Rob 108, 436, 475, 524, 541, 588, 956, 957, 959, 961

33 BDF §380(4); DM 127; MHT II 29; MHT III 108, **110**; Rob 727, 951, 956, 957, 959, 968

34 MHT I 138; Rob 603

35 BW 27; Moule 143f.; Rob 284, 581, 607

36 MHT II 377

37 BW 56, 130; DM 112, 225; Rob 633, 956, 1108; Zer §445

38 BDF §445(3); Rob 956, 962, 1158; RD §412, 414, 417, 470(d)

39 Rob 859, 1108, 1109, 1111, 1112

40 Rob 859, 1108, 1115

41 Moule 79; MHT III 266; Rob 356, 389, 525, 593, 595, 649, 956, 1108; RD §361, 380; Zer §98, 106

42 BDF §107; DM 119; Moule 79; MHT I 188; MHT III **18**; Rob 484, 653, 1108, 1202, inset, 1405; RD §380

Chapter 11

1 BDF §414(2); BW 136; MHT I 17; MHT II 171, 426; MHT III 141, 159; MHT IV 43; Rob 683, 1102, 1121; RD §461(b); Zer §389n

2 BDF §418(4), 420(2); MHT II 29, 462

3 BDF §323(1), 366(1); MHT I 185; MHT III 63; Rob 748, 934, 1107, 1116; RD §378

4 MHT II 453; Rob 194, 258, 726

5 BW 66; DM 161; MHT III 58; Rob 652, 816

6 DM 260; MHT I 104; MHT II 464; MHT III 253; Zer §65

7 BW 25; MHT II 455; MHT III 134; Rob 765, 820, 1088, 1166, 1396

8 BDF §448(4); DM 284; Moule 96; MHT II 68; MHT III **17**; MHT IV 35; Rob 364, 589, 653, 1088, 1166

9 Moule 98; Rob 1150, 1166; RD §472(c)

10 BDF §378; MHT II 436, 466; MHT III **37**, 45; Rob 698, 703, 960, 1193

11 BDF §61(2); BW 23; MHT II 459; MHT III 29; Rob 516, 587, 668

12 Moule 73; MHT II 365, 419; MHT III 58; Rob 548, 816

13 Rob 367

14 DM 292; Rob 1026; RD §303, 402(c)

16 BW 89; Moule 92; MHT II 69, 70; MHT III **86**, 179; Rob 186, 477, 748

17 MHT I 139

19 MHT II 433, 461; MHT III 258; MHT IV 35; Rob 204

20 BDF §60(2), 245(1); Moule 95, 98; MHT I 79; MHT II 455; MHT III **31**; Rob 279, 670, 1078

21 BW 107; DM 290; MHT II 50; MHT III **91**; Rob 269, 302, 923, 1014, 1015, 1193; RD §413, 438, 448(h); Zer §314

22 Rob 646

23 Moule 75; MHT III **17**, 37; Rob 505, 643, 653, 792bis, 975; RD §353, 420(d)

24 Rob 1036

25 DM 252; MHT I 91, 136, 139; MHT II 215, 432, 453; Rob 337, 419, 523, 682, 696, 709, 965; Zer §366n, 452

26 BDF §214(6); BW 59, 73; Moule 32; MHT II 465; Rob 461, 465, 769; RD §341(c)

27 BDF §107, 380(3); MHT I 140; MHT II 10; MHT III **107**, 108, **110**, 286; Rob 682, 742, 752, 842, 878, 1024, 1164; RD §382

28 Rob 235, 625, 682, 873bis, 915, 924, 1193

29 DM 88; MHT II 436; MHT III 42, 220; Rob 200, 523, 537, 687, 1023, 1182

30 Rob 262

Chapter 12

1 MHT II 128, 455; MHT III 27; Rob 262, 696

2 Rob 392, 523, 587, 1159

3 MHT I 140; Rob 726, 844

4 Moule 27; MHT II 440, 468; MHT III **137**; MHT IV 92; Rob 491, 611, 714, 776, 1016, 1025, 1032, 1039, 1084-85, 1119, 1130, 1188; RD §410(a), 462(c); Zer §468

5 MHT III 27; Rob 1035

6 MHT III **21**

7 BW 98; MHT I 148; Rob 261, 904, 923, 1015, 1417

8 BDF §472(1b)

9 Rob 683

10 BDF §369(2); DM 138, 246: MHT III **100**, 195, 333; Rob 511, 512, 916, 1024, 1176; RD §448(d); Zer §401

11 MHT IV 35

12 DM 256; Moule 144; MHT II 128; MHT IV 33; Rob 262, 292, 740, 999; Zer §350n

13 MHT II 189; MHT III **197**; Rob 401, 656, 746

14 Moule 192; Rob 119, 994, 1413; RD §434(b)

15 Rob 994

16 Rob 541, 993

17 Moule 145; Rob 1428

18 BDF §148(2); Moule 145; MHT II 458, 475; MHT III 43; Rob 474, 842

19 Moule 145; Rob 752; Zer §226

20 Moule 145; MHT II 106, 126, 189; Rob 365, 1212; RD §320

21 BDF §187(6); DM 165; Moule 145; MHT III 238; Rob 889; RD §303, 402(c)

22 DM 286

23 Rob 292, 697, 917

24 BDF §219(1); BW 43; MHT III **152**; MHT IV 37; Rob 590

25 MHT III 43; MHT IV 37; Rob 319, 406, 413, 817, 1105, 1106, 1116

26 BDF §73, 366(1); Rob 452, 602, 750, 842, 847, 876, 1008; Zer §306

27 DM 106; Rob 1008; RD §437

28 DM 106; MHT I 140; MHT III 347; Rob 425, 429, 847, 1008, 1190bis; RD §410(a), 437

29 Rob 742, 757, 1018

30 Rob 607, 611, 956, 1172

31 BW 15; DM 79; Rob 494, 500, 655, 779, 873bis, 1379; RD §343(b), 343(f)

32 Rob 594, 607, 956, 1165, 1179, inset, 1405; RD §470(n)

33 DM 248; MHT II 421

34 Rob 880, 924

35 MHT III **14, 22**; MHT IV 33; Rob 408, 757, 776, 1397; RD §387(b)(1)

36 BDF §466(3); BW 6; Moule 30; MHT II 424; MHT III 48, 316; Rob 436, 439, 459, 718

38 MHT II 453; Rob 515, 579, 742, 923; Zer §366n

39 MHT II 468; MHT III **214**; Rob 255, 411; Zer §45

40 Rob 429

41 BDF §207(1); DM 104; Moule 204; MHT III **21, 255, 266**; MHT IV 35; Rob 453, 525, 561, 593, 828; RD §361; Zer §98, 106

42 BDF §173(1), 253(5); Moule 177; MHT I 236; MHT II 146, 430; MHT III 172; MHT IV 31, 33; Rob 268

43 DM 151; Moule 55, 91; MHT IV 35; Rob 418, 560, 582; RD §354

44 BDF §471(3); BW 159; DM 278; MHT III 162, 319; Rob 300, 548, 1041

45 MHT II 431; MHT III **41**, 43; Rob 516, 611, 749, 1396; Zer §204

48 MHT III **183**

49 MHT II 129

50 DM 260; MHT III 41; Rob 679, 957; RD §374, 415

Chapter 13

1 Moule 51, 92; Rob 314, 367, 615, 813; RD §366

2 Moule 94; MHT I 230, 241; MHT III 154; Rob 602, 979, 1126

3 BW 30, 142; DM 84; MHT III 141; Rob 512, 652, 757, 764, 1088; RD §343(m)

4 DM 105, 138, 216; Moule 77; MHT II 450; MHT III 36, 145; Rob 107, 490, 564, 606, 695, 747, 765, 1073ter; RD §364

5 BDF §369(3); DM 216; MHT I 79; MHT III 142; Rob 746, 749, 891, 1071, 1091, 1159, 1171; RD §457(d)

6 BW 125; MHT I 79; MHT III 142, 172, 345; Rob 746, 749, 794; RD §388

7 MHT I 79; Rob 746, 749

8 MHT I 79; MHT II 202; MHT III 36, **67**; Rob 746, 749, 838, 883

9 Rob 956; RD §414

11 MHT III 45, 135; Rob 707

12 BDF §380(1); BW 153; MHT III **110**, 282, **292**; Rob 727, 957, 1156; RD §415

13 BDF §369(2); Moule 207; MHT II 60, 202; Rob 233, 315, 993; RD §302, 320, 426(c); Zer §413, 426

14 BDF §422; MHT I 75; MHT II 443, 444; MHT III 97, 157, 238; Rob 94, 531, 539, 1004bis, 1110, 1127, inset; Zer §226, 369

15 Moule 155; MHT I 140; MHT II 74, 470; MHT III 23; Rob 201, 376, 533, 844, 988, 1173, 1415

16 MHT II 437; Zer §424

17 MHT I 139; Rob 339, 367

18 Rob 501

19 BDF §250, 466(3); MHT II 205, 424; MHT III 151, 200; MHT IV 37; Rob 315, 744, 773, 1105; RD §382

20 MHT IV 37

21 DM 110; Rob 623, 1136

22 BDF §468(3); MHT II 424; Zer §375

23 BDF §250, 451(4), 468(3); DM 261; MHT II 205, 424; MHT III 36, 333; Rob 695bis, 1149; RD §320

24 BDF §488(1a); MHT I 140; MHT III **179**; MHT IV 33; Rob 835, 1392; Zer §65, 256

25 BW 124; DM 99, 282(2); Moule 67, 77; MHT II 450; MHT III 145; Rob 244, 550, 571, 762, 1070, 1073, 1385

26 MHT III 72; MHT IV 43; Rob 348, 762, 799

27 BDF §488(1a); DM 267; Rob 418, 917, 1157, 1176

28 BDF §366(3); Moule 139, 158; MHT I 140; MHT II 421, 433, 452; MHT III **99**, 154, 195; MHT IV 35; Rob 418, 430, 878, 924, 935, 1175, 1399

29 BDF §194(3); BW 44, 71; DM 147; Moule 81; MHT III 276; Rob 534, 637, 638, 1157, 1164, 1174; RD §346(h), 353, 470(j)

30 BDF §158, 493(2); BW 121; Moule 82; MHT I 97; MHT II 439; MHT III 144, 187; Rob 479, 482, 626, 639, 645, 974, 1075

31 MHT II 419; MHT IV 35; Rob 656, 713, 836, 1126

32 MHT I 53; Rob 194, 343, 372bis, 1000, 1205; RD §474(k)

33 BDF §474(4); Rob 503, 1110, 1126; RD §420(c)

34 BDF §255(1); BW 21; Rob 517, 648; RD §344(d), 353

35 Moule 145; Rob 791, 1106, 1428

36 MHT II 453

37 BDF §488(1a); Moule 116; MHT III **183**; Rob 233; Zer §175

38 MHT II 424, 441; MHT III 208; Rob 233, 394, 698; Zer §42

39 MHT III 183; Rob 233, 768

40 Rob 969

41 Rob 598

42 Zer §178

44 BDF §255(1), 291(3); Moule 13; MHT I 139; MHT II 461; MHT III 73, 179; MHT IV 35; Rob 562, 580, 715, 837, 868

45 MHT II 433; MHT III 195; MHT IV 35; Rob 847; Zer §65

46 BDF §343(1), 344; BW 97; DM 204; Moule 13, 14; MHT I 142, 143, 145; MHT II 452; MHT III **70**, 73, 154; Rob 735, 837, 844, 897, 1110, 1126

48 BDF §263(4); Moule 13; MHT III **14**, 73, 154; Rob 561, 715, 763, 837; Zer §256

49 Moule 92; Rob 550, 578, 648, 775

51 BDF §95(1); DM 262; Rob 310, 1150, 1175; RD §448(a), 448(b), 472(c)

52 BDF §148(3); Moule 91; MHT II 400, 433; MHT III 195; MHT IV 35; Rob 399, 475, 539, 559,
656, 727, 1206; RD §474(o)

53 MHT II 426; MHT III 52; Zer §389n

54 Rob 1091

55 DM 265; Rob 757, 917, 1157

56 Moule 52; MHT II 467; MHT III **273**; Rob 625

57 MHT II 464; MHT III 253

Chapter 14

1 MHT III 167; Rob 760

2 BW 71; MHT I 140; MHT III 180; Rob 694, 840, 842

3 DM 138; Moule 16; Rob 508, 585, 840

4 DM 188; Rob 485

5 BDF §157(3); Rob 481, 817, 1129

6 BDF §200(3); Moule 44f.; MHT III 27, 243; Rob 648, 1392

7 BDF §187(4), 350; Moule 61; MHT III 135; Rob 611, 877, 963, 1028, 1031, 1039, 1047

8 BW 36; Moule 145 n.2; MHT III 64; Rob 233, 360, 434, 604, 866

9 BDF §142, 442(16); MHT III **26**; Rob 1129; Zer §7n

11 MHT II 430; MHT III 40

13 MHT III 18; Rob 520, 550, 609; RD §345(b), 351

14 DM 282; MHT III **40**; Rob 568, 1430

15 MHT I 140, 247; Rob 546, 613, 842

16 Moule 127

17 Rob 265

18 RD §385

19 BDF §421; MHT I 107; MHT III **158**; Rob 350, 367, 561, 1136; RD §356

20 MHT III 316; Rob 392, 1109

21 BDF §474(7); BW 21; Rob 419, 648, 674; Zer §291

22 BDF §383(2); Rob 477, 857, 891, 975, 976bis, 1048, 1081; RD §420(c)bis, 454

23 MHT III 28; Rob 224, 656, 657

24 BW 13; Moule 85; Rob 469, 644, 775

25 BW 37, 49; Moule 49f.; Rob 523, 603; RD §345(c); Zer §123

26 Moule 49f.; MHT II 461, 469; Rob 580

28 MHT III 27; Rob 601

29 BDF §336(1); MHT III **75**; Rob 601

30 MHT II 455; MHT IV 32

31 DM 113; MHT II 458; MHT III **266, 267**; MHT IV 33; Rob 508, 739; RD §343(1)

32 DM 282

33 MHT III 183; Rob 546

34 Rob 219

35 Rob 546, 827; RD §349

36 MHT IV 38; RD §415, 416; Rob 732, 956, 958, 993

Chapter 15

2 MHT III 38, 112; Rob 564, 739, 811, 972

3 Rob 477, 739

4 MHT II 443; Rob 531; RD §461(d); Zer §60

5 BDF §360(1); MHT I 177; MHT III **91, 309**; MHT IV 33; Rob 485, 789, 875, inset

6 BDF §365(2); MHT I 140; MHT II 419; MHT III 96, 97; Rob 845, 874; RD §470(k)

7 Moule 47

8 MHT III 23

9 Rob 482

11 MHT II 424; MHT IV 37; Rob 559, 1166, 1172, 1187

13 MHT I 139; MHT II 339; MHT III 48

14 MHT II 71; Rob 488, 849

15 MHT II 453

16 Rob 488, 546

17 BDF §111(6); MHT II 448; Rob 773, 1035

18 Moule 92; Rob 561

19 MHT III 28; Rob 408bis, 427

20 BDF §399(1); MHT II 193; MHT III 140; Rob 1058, 1082, 1424

22 MHT III 195; Rob 261, 463, 464

23 BW 21; MHT II 195; MHT III 156; Rob 341, 484, 645, 1135; RD §302, 353

24 DM 79; MHT I 138

25 BW 34; MHT III 65; Rob 541; RD §347(g)

26 Rob 757

27 MHT II 345, 461; Rob 519, 577, 1116; RD §344(e); Zer §68

28 BDF §146(1b); DM 71; Moule 32; MHT III 33; MHT IV 32; Rob 463, 464, 1193; RD §424(b), 448(h); Zer §35

29 BW 50; Moule 51; MHT IV 33; Rob 615; RD §366

30 BDF §306(2); Moule 141; MHT III 43, **154**, 197; Rob 212, 615, 749, 1127

31 Moule 141; MHT III 161

32 BDF §144, 368, 445(4); BW 58, 158; DM 110; Moule 31; MHT I 70; MHT II 132; MHT III 49, 135, 231; Rob 266, 275, 460, 602, 623, 726, 737; RD §340(d)

33 Rob 710, 990, 1089, 1414; RD §379

34 BDF §111(3); Rob 740, 1176; RD §381

35 MHT III 236; Rob 491, 561, 602; RD §342(o)

36 Rob 311

37 MHT III 316; Rob 219, 502

38 BDF §474(7); BW 66; Zer §291

Chapter 16

1 Rob 1182; RD §386(b)

2 BDF §108(4); MHT II 101, 405; Rob 147, 213, 460

3 BDF §108(4); MHT III 27; Rob 1062bis

4 BDF §454(5); MHT II 453, 468

5 Rob 812

6   BDF §149; Rob 472, 949, 1047, 1183; MHT II 460

7   BDF §480(6); MHT I 139; MHT III **49**; Rob 1028bis

8   Rob 1028

9   Rob 506, 1045bis; RD §343(1); Zer §447

10   Rob 1164

11   DM 109; MHT II 460; Rob 1047, 1160; RD §470(i)

12   MHT II 450, 460; Rob 1029, 1035, 1047, 1060, 1160

13   BW 104; DM 168, 171; Rob 781bis, 1103

14   BDF §306(2), 480(1); MHT III 36, **197**; Rob 695, 749bis, 1103, 1394

16   MHT III 183; Rob 235, 678, 768, 781; RD §387(b)(2)

17   MHT I 140; Rob 255, 419, 682, 842

18   Moule 50, 90; MHT III **22**, 27, 189; MHT IV 38; Rob 174, 255, 408, 457, 510, 562, 604, 682, 780, 791, 875, 889, 1028, 1029, 1185, 1201; RD §340(b), 388, 451(a), 474(d)

19   Moule 18; MHT II 131; MHT III 89; Rob 231, 265, 361, 907, 1387; RD §176 C.d., 270, 403(c)

20   MHT I 208; Rob 485, 679, 983, 993bis, 1046, 1049

21   Moule 72; MHT II 205, 455; MHT III 258; Rob 311, 579, 587, 1035, 1082

22   BDF §128(5), 189(3), 365(1); Moule 157; MHT I 190, 191, 240; MHT II 455; MHT III 97, 240, 282, **309**; MHT IV 33; Rob 260, 272, 396, 541, 942, 1157, 1175, inset, 1405; RD §162(b), 470(h) and (k); Zer §444

23   Rob 174, 498, 562

24   DM 300; MHT II 421; Rob 690, 742, 878, 890; Zer §440n

25   MHT III 43, **107**, 108; Rob 425

26   BDF §159(2), 366(1); Moule 185; MHT I 230; MHT III **98**, 199; Rob 485, 501, 935, 1023, 1129

27   DM 101; Rob 576, 745, 882; RD §358

28   BDF §198(2); MHT II 464; MHT III 96, 233, 241; Rob 489,

743, 794, 955, 957, 962, 1116, 1123, inset; RD §415

Chapter 17

1   MHT III 18; Rob 224, 787, 788, 1398

2   BDF §343(3), 466(4); MHT III 316

3   Moule 92; Rob 405, 562

4   BDF §372(1a, 2c); MHT II 453; MHT III **115**, 149; Rob 425, 490, 538, 661, 750, 1009bis; Zer §309, **366n**

5   DM 152; Moule 69; Rob 367, 396, 697, 776, 837; RD §448(h)

6   Rob 409

8   Rob 657

9   BDF §423(1, 6), 466(4); BW 17; MHT I 125; MHT III 316, 322; Rob 596, 597

10   Rob 487

11   BDF §323(1), 447(6); MHT III 63; Rob 870; Zer §149

12   BW 32; Moule 76; MHT I 138, 140; MHT III **53**, 264; Rob 484, 588bis, 815

14   BDF §426(3), 466(4); BW 17; Moule 203; MHT I 74; MHT II 424; MHT III 316; MHT IV 35; Rob 513, 1132; RD §343(m); Zer §27, 50

15   MHT II 405; MHT III 189; Rob 802

16   DM 109; Rob 334, 350, 368, 817

17   BDF §146(2); Moule 85; MHT III 33, 35, 234; Rob 300, 548, 643, 917, 1101, 1176, 1394; RD §448(d)

18   MHT IV 32

19   MHT II 467; MHT III 18, 37; Rob 224, 487, 739

20   BDF §104(1); DM 172; MHT II 210; Rob 268, 300, 308, 328, 548, 849, 889

22   Moule 90; MHT III 24; Rob 594, 681, 870, 1132

24   Moule 173; Rob 580

25   BDF §101; Moule 173; MHT III 159; Rob 551, 748, 1102, 1120; RD §461(b)

26   BDF §423(6); Moule 173, 203;

Rob 513, 1132, 1148, 1190bis

27 BDF §283(2), 315; DM 100; Moule
    71, 103, 139, 173; MHT II 369,
    448; MHT III 42, 43, 53, 152,
    258, 292, 344; MHT IV 32, 36;
    Rob 425, 573, 593, 687, 792;
    Zer §93

Chapter 18

1   DM 242; MHT I 78; MHT III 29,
    183; Rob 668, 916, 1176

2   MHT III 65; Rob 216

3   MHT III 321; Rob 551, inset

4   BDF §380(2); MHT III 29; Rob
    244, 281; RD §335

5   MHT II 179; Rob 525, 710

6   Moule 62; MHT I 208; MHT II
    442, 463; Rob 317, 594, 620,
    992

7   BDF §176(1); MHT II 461; Rob
    537, 577, 580; RD §347(f); Zer
    §475

8   BDF §245(3); DM 120; MHT III
    31, 42, 149; Rob 406, 537, 593,
    658, 661bis, 687, 1084, 1188;
    RD §347(e), 455(b); Zer §329,
    394

9   BDF §245(3); MHT III 149; Rob
    276, 496, inset; Zer §329

10 DM 113; MHT III 78; Rob 995,
    996

11 MHT I 137

12 MHT II 172; MHT III 63; Rob
    213, 541bis, 870, 1019; RD
    §347(b)

13 DM 106; MHT I 17; Rob 1019,
    1043, 1058, 1423

14 BDF §214(6); BW 112; DM 294;
    MHT II 465; MHT III 139;
    MHT IV 36; Rob 993

15 BDF §333(2); BW 21, 94; Moule
    184; MHT I 140; MHT III 42, 43,
    73; MHT IV 36; Rob 339, 348,
    428, 505, 562, 645, 687, 842,
    846, 949, 1019bis, 1020, 1419

16 BDF §234(4); Moule 149 n.1;
    MHT II 467; MHT III 42, 57; Rob
    604, 649, 846; Zer §231

17 BDF §190(1); BW 70; Moule 89;
    MHT III 239; Rob 231, 539, 757,
    846, 1019, 1027, 1419; Zer §489

18 DM 233; Moule 18; MHT III 89;
    Rob 362, 375, 733, 907; RD

§403(c)

19 BDF §373(2); DM 109; MHT II 75;
    MHT IV 32, 33; Rob 715, 716,
    1010, 1421; Zer §16

20 MHT II 434; MHT III 344;
    MHT IV 32, 36; Rob 593, 656,
    685, 776

21 BDF §471(2); BW 89; MHT II 422;
    MHT III 342; Rob 281, 333, 356,
    548, 674, 889, 917, 934, 1176;
    RD §402(c); Zer §453

22 BDF §248(2); MHT I 98; MHT II
    175; MHT III 188; Rob 673bis;
    Zer §159

23 MHT I 140, 160; MHT II 433;
    MHT III 47, 56, 185, 195;
    MHT IV 30, 35; Rob 109, 611,
    837; RD §401(a)

24 BDF §423(1); MHT II 432, 455;
    MHT III 322; MHT IV 32, 35, 39;
    Rob 233, 283, 674

25 BDF §324, 423(2); DM 275; MHT I
    219; MHT III 64, 138, 322; Rob
    514, 735, 1048, 1068, 1132,
    1172; RD §454

26 BW 30, 142; DM 84; MHT III 65;
    Rob 538, 568, 570, 605, 949; RD
    §347(f), 355, 363

27 BDF §176(1); MHT III 234; Rob
    509

28 BDF §376; DM 247; MHT II 298;
    MHT III 321; Rob 538, 883, 1025

30 BDF §327; MHT II 452; Rob 309,
    834, 885, 976

31 Rob 689, 690; RD §377bis

32 BDF §328; DM 247; Rob 464, 708

33 BW 86; MHT III 90; Rob 886,
    919, 968, 1181

34 Rob 773

35 DM 108; MHT III 23; Rob 746bis

Chapter 19

1   DM 280; MHT II 426; MHT III 52;
    Rob 517, 763; Zer §389n

2   Rob 774

3   Moule 59; MHT III 268, 333;
    MHT IV 40; Rob 609, 916bis,
    1176

4   MHT II 104, 160; Rob 574

5   BDF §208(1); BW 59, 89; DM 14;
    Moule 71, 183; MHT II 67, 462;

MHT III 253; Rob 458, 595, 819;
RD §340(b); Zer §32

6   Moule 144; MHT I 140; Rob 314,
    845, 1165; RD §410(a)

7   Rob 1416; Zer §458

8   BDF §239(8); DM 110; Moule 53;
    MHT II 469; Rob 626

9   Rob 646, 649, 747, 1028; Zer
    §128, 442

10 BDF §5(3b), 434(1); Moule 192;
    MHT III 115, 226; Rob 545, 1008

11 Rob 706, 720, 752, 1163

12 BW 57; DM 102; MHT I 139; Rob
    233, 312, 367, 727, 1190, 1214

14 BW 127; Rob 710, 1061bis, 1094,
    1425; RD §379, 468

16 BDF §247(2); Moule 125, 173;
    Rob 675, 735

17 DM 109; MHT III 183; Rob 653,
    661, 738, 768

18 MHT III 182; Rob 766; RD
    §387(a)

20 BDF §154; Moule 24 n.1; MHT III
    246; Rob 419, 476, 478, 1216

21 MHT III 146; Rob 949, 1023,
    1038, 1083; RD §460(a)

22 BW 136; DM 228; Moule 18;
    MHT II 452; MHT III 154;
    MHT IV 31; Rob 110, 1127; RD
    §462(a)

24 BDF §24; DM 276; Moule 98;
    MHT II 72; MHT III 216; Rob
    192, 666

25 BDF §440(2)

26 Rob 1096

27 BDF §440(2); Moule 173; MHT I
    140; Rob 309bis;

28 MHT II 103, 171, 424; MHT III
    214; Rob 314, 565, 601; Zer §41

29 BDF §460(3); MHT I 140;
    MHT III 48, 232, 316; Rob
    673bis

30 Rob 280, 669

Chapter 20

1   Moule 82; MHT II 433; Rob 548,
    638, 658, 728, 809; RD §337

2   BDF §161(2), 252; Moule 34, 39,
    92; Rob 470, 510, 562, 599,

611, 769

3   BW 35; DM 109; Moule 62; Rob
    320, 586, 620

4   MHT III **107**, 108; Rob 190

5   DM 109, 276

6   BW 48; DM 93, 109; MHT III **179**;
    Rob 320, 470, 738; RD §342(f)

7   MHT I 140

8   Moule 181; MHT II 454;
    MHT III 155; MHT IV 32; Rob
    643, 1126bis, 1203

9   DM 99, 109; Moule 67; MHT III
    179; Rob 673

10 BDF §266(2), 349(2); MHT III
    14; Rob 766, 876, 1028, 1029;
    RD §451(a)

12 MHT I 140; MHT III 220; Rob
    530, 658, 842; RD §346(c)

13 BDF §495(2); BW 11; Moule 39;
    Rob 472, 510, 881

15 BDF §440(1); Rob 1430

16 Rob 769

17 MHT II 467; MHT III 18; Rob 224

18 BDF §195(2), 323(3); MHT III
    63, 240; Rob 532, 794

19 BW 37; DM 87; MHT III 143; Rob
    349, 522, 595, 1072; RD §345(c)

20 MHT I 160; MHT III 87; Rob 482,
    805; Zer §274, **284**

21 DM 102; MHT II 438; MHT III 36;
    MHT IV 38; Rob 597, 750; Zer
    §156

22 BDF §293(5); DM 132; MHT I 45,
    160; MHT II 89; Rob 291, 343,
    805; RD §381

23 BDF §399(1), 448(8); DM 102,
    240; MHT I 241; MHT II 468;
    MHT III 140; Rob 685, 721, 765,
    1153, 1187, 1424

24 BDF §480(1); Moule 63; MHT III
    178; Rob 619

25 Rob 1100

26 BDF §362; MHT II 458; MHT III
    86, **107**; Rob 190, 874, 943; Zer
    §443

27 MHT III 108

28 BDF §62, 208(2), 283(4), 308,
    369(3); DM 100; Moule 71; MHT I
    105; MHT III 31, 43, 51, 57,
    134, 258; Rob 175, 567, 573,

1088; RD §343(k); Zer §92, 94, 381

29 Moule 92; Rob 561

30 BDF §147(3); MHT III 167; Rob 463, 464, 491, 615; RD §342(o)

31 BDF §147(3); MHT II 165

32 MHT II 421; Rob 994

33 MHT II 83; MHT III **94**; Rob 1213

Chapter 21

1 DM 280; MHT III 72; Rob 267, 834, 971; Zer §97

2 MHT II 465; Rob 644; RD §353; Zer §280

3 BDF §362; MHT II 458; MHT III 86; Rob 742, 874, 943; Zer §320

4 BDF §343(3); Moule 15; MHT III 70; Rob 1123, 1428

5 BDF §192; Moule 91; MHT III 239; Rob 536, 560, 633

6 MHT III 154; Rob 968, 1126

7 BDF §141(8); Moule 173; MHT III **26**; Rob 409, 477; Zer §84

8 BDF §60(2), 134(1c); Moule 98; MHT II 203; MHT III **31**, 312; Rob 279, 318, 404, 660, 690, 774, 779, 838; RD §326, 377

9 MHT II 194; MHT III 174; Rob 525, 670

10 Moule 94; Rob 697; RD §379

11 BDF §209(3); MHT II 112, 149; MHT III 210, 259; Rob 219

13 MHT III 86; Zer §280

15 Rob 1122

16 MHT I 138, 140; Rob 649, 845

17 MHT II 453; Zer §84

18 MHT III 51

19 BDF §247(2), 365(2); BW 49; MHT I 179; MHT II 108, 432; MHT III 96; MHT IV 33, 35; Rob 594, 603, 674, 943, 1024-25, inset; RD §447

20 Moule 207; MHT I 139

21 MHT III **16**; Rob 767, 849, 1018, 1026; RD §387(a), 416

22 MHT II 247; MHT III 316; Rob 959

23 MHT II 419; MHT III 322; MHT IV 35, 39; Rob 653, 740, 1188; RD §381

24 BDF §247(2); Moule 33; Rob 482, 740

25 DM 102, 113; MHT II 464; Rob 300, 613

26 BDF §157(3), 470(3); Moule 35, 70; MHT III 246; Rob 443, 481

27 Rob 1185

28 BDF §62; MHT III 32; MHT IV 35; Rob 949, 1411; Zer §151

29 BDF §441(2); Rob 1157

30 RD §365

31 BDF §62, 245a(3); MHT III 32; Rob 291, 737; Zer §151

32 MHT I 216; MHT II 464; MHT III 136, 141; MHT IV 43; RD §455(d); Rob 334, 996, 1060, 1066, 1090; RD §455(d); Zer §383, 392

33 MHT II 191, 212, 433; MHT III 55; Rob 308, 340, 367, 399bis, 575, 617, 727, 1214

34 MHT III 135; RD §381

35 DM 147; MHT III 36; Rob 696

36 Rob 516, 667

37 Rob 473, 485, 819, 873; RD §342(j), 401(c); Zer §149, 151

38 Rob 330, 697; RD §448(h)

39 Rob 1213; Zer §84

40 Moule 43 n.1; Rob 484, 880

41 BDF §488(1a); DM 272; Moule 139; MHT III 27, 55; MHT IV 38; Rob 119, 355, 727, 873, 960, 989, 1201, 1214; RD §303, 474(q); Zer §343

42 BDF §138(2), 220(1), 295; BW 24; Moule 182; MHT I 59, 138, 139, 140; MHT II 423, 462; MHT III **21**, 45, 253; Rob 254, 410, 458, 587, 615, 655, 704, 718; RD §431; Zer §19, 32

43 BW 87; Rob 873

45 BDF §324; MHT III 64; Rob 787, 1029, 1035, 1041

46 BDF §157(5); DM 247; Moule 35, 70; MHT II 462; MHT III 246, 247, **266**; Rob 334, 481, 965; RD §342(i); Zer §70

Chapter 22

1   DM 230; MHT I 131; Rob 409, 860

2   MHT I 140; MHT II 433; MHT III 27; MHT IV 33; Rob 408, 957; RD §415

3   DM 284; Rob 885, 919

4   MHT III **309**; MHT IV 32; Rob 788

5   BDF §286(1); Moule 121; MHT I 88, 90; MHT III 36, 192; Rob 399, 691, 695, 1395; RD §379

7   MHT III **26**, 72; Rob 834, 835; Zer §7n

8   MHT III 27; Rob 1153

10   Rob 424

11   BDF §416(1), 430(1); Moule 105; MHT I 231, 232; MHT III **161**, 285; MHT IV 35; Rob 485, 818, 1138bis, 1139bis, 1172; RD §463; Zer §440n

12   BDF §495(2); Rob 1138; RD §463

13   BDF §62; MHT III 232; Rob 486, 828

14   Zer §475

15   Rob 148; RD §434(b)

16   Moule 28; MHT II 464; MHT III 87, 257; Rob 392, 550, 619; RD §312; Zer §284

17   BDF §5(1); MHT II 419; Rob 269, 1158bis, 1177

21   MHT III 47

22   MHT II 453

23   Rob 891, 1081

24   Zer §7n

25   MHT IV 31; Rob 348

27   BDF §62; MHT III 316; Rob 488, 668

28   BDF §164(1); MHT II 419; MHT III 209; Rob 833, 1378; Zer §289n

30   BDF §101; MHT II 410; MHT III 57, 321; Rob 392

31   MHT III 180

32   BDF §128(2)

34   DM 200; Rob 840

36   BDF §245(2); Moule 97f.; MHT II 30, 442; MHT III **31**; Rob 660,

740; Zer §146

37   BDF §275(4); MHT III **39**, 199; Rob 774bis

38   MHT II 442; Rob 411, 661, 669

39   MHT II 60; MHT III 42; Rob 232, 530

40   Rob 317

42   Rob 760

43   Rob 480

44   Rob 310, 314

Chapter 23

1   MHT II 454; RD §322

2   BDF §342(1); Moule 11; MHT II 458; MHT III 72; MHT IV 33; Rob 758, 786, 837, 866; Zer §256

3   MHT III 316; Rob 733, 866, 1128

4   DM 244; Rob 560, 1184, 1186

5   BW 55; MHT III 144; Rob 542, 1075; RD §432

7   BDF §493(1); MHT II 245

8   Moule 135; MHT III 183, 189; Zer §175

9   Moule 135, 166; MHT IV 32

10   Moule 135; MHT III **184**; Rob 1128

11   Zer §280

12   BDF §380(2); Rob 957

13   BDF §339(3); MHT II 465; MHT III **81**; Zer §274

14   Rob 892, 1116

15   BDF §61(2), 102(4), 150; Moule 174; MHT II 166, 441; MHT III **16**; Rob 204, 278, 299, 652, 763, 1202; RD §332

16   Moule 60, 183; MHT II 464; MHT III 48, **51**; Rob 424, 475, 720

17   Rob 737, 1177; RD §381

18   Moule 183; MHT II 464; MHT III 48, **51**; Rob 720, 1146; RD §320

19   MHT II 161; Rob 737

20   Moule 183; MHT II 464; Rob 859

21   Moule 183; MHT I 104; Rob 317

22   Moule 183

23 BDF §407; Moule 149; MHT I 140, 185, 248; MHT II 126, 215; MHT III 90, 148; Rob 261, 309, 310, 337, 347, 845, 886, 919, 944, 1080, 1084, 1092; RD §438

24 Moule 186; Rob 205, 606

25 BDF §184; Moule 72; MHT II 471, 479; MHT III 216, **260**; Rob 642, 765

26 BDF §184; Moule 83, 106, 186; MHT III **14**; Rob 517, 640, 641, 642, 765, 1391

27 MHT II 121, 405; Rob 203, 260, 267, 506, 530, 548, 1102; RD §343(1)

28 BDF §157(5); Rob 505, 633, 1102, 1153, 1378

30 BW 164; MHT I 201; MHT III 215; Rob 312, 340, 394, 922, 1015; RD §438; Zer §316

31 BW 32; DM 85; Moule 144; MHT II 472; MHT III 42; MHT IV 32; Rob 538; RD §347(g)

32 BW 117; Rob 948, 1198, 1220; RD §474(1)

33 BDF §149, 366(1); MHT I 116, 185; MHT III 99; Rob 476, 929, 934, 1399

34 MHT II 433, 438; MHT III 209; MHT IV 32; Rob 266, 333, 356, 515, 599

35 Moule 206; Rob 213, 255, 645, 715, 789; Zer §274

36 MHT II 471

37 DM 277; Moule 34; MHT II 10, 133, 148; MHT III 42; Rob 120, 204, 486, 531, 689, 718, 917; RD §176 C.b., 342(k)

39 DM 113; MHT I 191; Rob 548, inset

Chapter 24

2 Moule 159; MHT II 424, 438; MHT III 96; Rob 565, 601, 828, 960, 1001, 1158, 1164, inset; RD §435(e), 470(j), 470(k)

3 BDF §423(1); Moule 92; MHT III 18, 322; Rob 224bis, 787

4 DM 294; Rob 430, 933, 995; RD §434(c)

5 Rob 604

6 BDF §163, 461(1); Rob 430, 500, 889, 932, 949, 996; Zer §475

7 Rob 1405

9 MHT II 447; MHT III 89; Rob 353, 593, 889

10 RD §378

12 MHT III 142, 345; Rob 357, 660, 858, 966, 1428

13 MHT II 424; MHT III 45; Rob 698

15 BDF §465(1); MHT II 144, 160; Rob 320, 434

16 BW 149

17 BDF §437; Moule 74; MHT I 174; Rob 231, 307, 328, 599, 856

18 Moule 86; MHT I 174; Rob 453, 548, 586, 645, 856, 1405; RD §345(f), 361

20 BW 10, 37; Moule 39; MHT III 235; Rob 495, 522, 523; RD §343(e), 345(c)

21 BDF §343(3), 431(3); BW 153; Moule 157; MHT II 419; MHT III **14**, 70, 96, 286; Rob 207, 244, 731, 793, 1175, inset

22 BDF §428(2); MHT II 434; MHT III 196, 199, **268**, 282; Rob 752, 772, 1016, 1163; RD §383 bis; Zer §112, 317, 446

23 MHT I 124; Zer §278

24 Moule 143; Rob 990, 1428; Zer §352

26 MHT II 89; Rob 409

27 MHT III 26, 172; Rob 792

28 BW 111; DM 278; Rob 871, 969, 1411

29 Moule 18; MHT II 451

30 BW 18, 87; MHT I 150; MHT III 161, **214**; Rob 334, 356bis, 603, 611, 819, 873, 891; Zer §**46**

31 BDF §141(1), 270(2), 474(4); MHT III **25**, 218, **225**, 234; Rob 611, 775; Zer §47

32 MHT II 60, 264; Rob 232, 341, 443, 640, 1401

33 BW 36, 111; DM 281; Moule 50; MHT III 27, 179; Rob 443, 525, 604, 792, 972; RD §345(e), 419(f)

34 MHT III 96; Rob 443, inset

35 BDF §365(1); MHT I 190; MHT III 96, 97; Rob 443, 757, inset

36 MHT IV 92; Rob 443, 776

37   Rob 443

38   BDF §101; BW 158; DM 279; Moule 18 n.1; Rob 443, 621, 639, 717, 974, 1406, 1412

39   BW 159; Rob 443, 975; RD §420(c)

40   MHT II 438; MHT III 36, 319; MHT IV 36; Rob 443, 675, 750, 869

41   BDF §418(2); MHT II 60, 136, 356; MHT III 36; Rob 154, 231, 233, 443, 675

42   Rob 292, 443, 522, 740bis

43   BDF §291(5), 323(2); Moule 34, 149; MHT I 201; MHT II 252; MHT III 46, 63; Rob 349, 443, 708, 740, 870, 922, 1014, 1015, 1417; RD §438; Zer §317

44   BDF §98; Moule 34; Rob 433, 718

45   BDF §269(5), 273(1); MHT I 140; MHT II 339; MHT III 141, 183, 186; MHT IV 34; Rob 443, 768, 777, 783, 792, 845, 916, 1065, 1176; RD §448(c)

46   MHT III 162; Rob 443, 891

47   Rob 443, 604

48   MHT I 142; Rob 443

49   MHT II 455; Rob 443, 849, 1420

50   Rob 443, 715, 716, 718; Zer §16

51   MHT II 472; MHT III 226; Rob 443

Chapter 25

1   Moule 70; MHT III 154; Rob 727, 1127; Zer §65

2   BDF §265; MHT III **178**; Rob 272

3   Rob 611

4   MHT III **13**; Rob 272, 611

5   BW 16, 84; DM 80; MHT III **67**; Rob 349, 367, 838, 883; RD §401(a), 402(b)

6   BDF §186(2), 343(3); BW 97; DM 77; Moule 14; MHT I 14, 146; MHT III 225, 235; Rob 495, 522, 775, 793, 897; RD §343(e), 387(c)

8   DM 182; Moule 7; MHT II 106, 206; MHT IV 32; Rob 318, 879; RD §402(a)

9   BDF §336(1), 370(4), 428(6), 431(3); Moule 139; MHT I 184, 189, 192; MHT III 42, 75, **98**, **99**, 155; Rob 244, 272, 334, 689, 818, 929, 933, 934, 995, 1127, 1159, 1161, 1174, inset; RD §466, 470(j); Zer §444

10   MHT II 157; MHT III 27; Rob 272, 763

11   BDF §493(1); Rob 1200

14   BDF §453(4), 482; MHT III 87, 192; MHT IV 31; Rob 969, 1153, 1203; RD §472(d); Zer §283

15   MHT II 114; MHT III 36; Rob 282, 696, 969

16   MHT I 116; MHT III 154; Rob 746, 813, 969

17   Rob 747, 969

18   MHT II 452; MHT III 154; Rob 969, 1118, 1125

19   Moule 56; MHT I 160; MHT III 56; Rob 652

20   BDF §342(1); MHT I 140, 238; MHT III 69; Rob 835, 910, 1111, 1118, 1125; RD §403(a), 460(c)

21   BDF §102(3), 233(2); Moule 49; Rob 299, 337, 601, 604; Zer §124

22   MHT I 140; MHT IV 31

23   BDF §102(3); Moule 49; Rob 299, 604

24   BDF §342(1), 437; BW 157; MHT I 138, 238; MHT III 226; MHT IV 33, 35, 69; Rob 548, 718, 909, 910, 1034, 1111, 1116, 1118, 1125; RD §403(a), 460(c); Zer §16, 207

25   MHT I 238; MHT II 452; MHT III 154; Rob 1045

26   BDF §437; MHT I 138; MHT III **38**, 226; Rob 548

27   BW 105; DM 169; MHT III 90; Rob 886, 919, 922, 1014, 1015

28   RD §448(d)

29   Moule 173; MHT II 424; Rob 873

30   BDF §62

32   Moule 92; MHT III 313; Rob 559, 873

33   Rob 408, 1153

34   BDF §183; BW 23; Moule 73; MHT II 459; MHT III 152, 234; Rob 504, 516, 777, 793, 1106

35 BDF §390(2), 492; MHT III 135; Rob 340, 347, 915, 1087, 1200; RD §310

36 Moule 90; MHT III 39; Rob 234, 915

37 BDF §492; MHT III 155; Rob 334, 339, 357, 819, 915

38 BDF §416(1); Moule 90; MHT III 161; Rob 915, 917, 1123, 1176

39 Rob 234, 915

40 DM 113, 274; MHT I 138; MHT III 31; Rob 733, 963; RD §427; Zer §125

41 BDF §336(1); MHT I 221; Rob 777, 792, 1096

42 Rob 1157

43 Moule 90; Rob 312, 1157

44 MHT III 155

45 DM 113; MHT III 31; Rob 963, 1157, 1159; RD §427; Zer §125

46 BW 66; Rob 272, 1153; RD §332, 334

54 Zer §16

56 BDF §343(3)

Chapter 26

1 MHT II 426; Zer §389n

2 BDF §323(2); BW 54; DM 185; Moule 7; MHT I 120; MHT III 63, 135, 143; Rob 595, 612, 869, 870, 1072, 1090; RD §365

4 BW 103, 162; DM 132, 160; Moule 203; MHT I 157; MHT III **54**; Rob 263, 693, 811, 993

5 BDF §481; Rob 1202

6 BDF §423(1); Rob 263, 595

7 Rob 512, 1399

8 Rob 739

9 BW 86; Moule 149; MHT III 90; Rob 510, 886; RD §343(1)

10 Moule 69; MHT I 116, 140; MHT III 256; Rob 484, 842, 1393

11 Zer §278

12 MHT II 445; MHT III 144; Rob 603, 1075, 1428

13 MHT I 140; MHT III 199; Rob 842, 873, 969, 1411

14 MHT II 91, 420; Rob 934

15 BDF §442(2); DM 291; MHT II 88; MHT III 27, 334; Rob 951, 1023, 1183bis; RD §410(a), 442

16 Moule 72; Rob 674

17 Moule 199; MHT II 421; MHT III 27, 135; Rob 400, 935, 989; RD §432

18 BDF §64(5), 141(3); BW 81; Moule 7, 52f.; MHT II 179; MHT III 27, 63; Rob 234, 292, 491, 625, 744, 870; RD §226 a, 342(o), 379, 387(e)

20 Rob 316

22 MHT II 455; Rob 675, 743, 746, 917; RD §378, 383

23 DM 105; Moule 24 n.1, 91; MHT II 424; MHT IV 37; Rob 525, 559, 585, 698, 707bis; RD §345(f), 360

24 BDF §360(1), 428(2); DM 289; Moule 149; MHT I 200; MHT III **90, 91**, 284; Rob 707, 886, 887, 920, 1014, 1015, 1160, 1169, 1417; RD §405, 438, 470(c); Zer §440n

25 BDF §427(2); DM 144, 265, 267; MHT I 140; MHT III 87, **283**; MHT IV 45; Rob 842, 859, 915, 917, 1028, 1114, 1168; Zer §283

26 Rob 768

27 Rob 519

28 BDF §229(1); BW 72; DM 109, 148; Moule 63, 206; MHT III 269; Rob 213, 352, 567, 595, 618, 768, 1106, 1116, 1118; Zer §96

29 BDF §12(3), 247(2), 382(3); MHT III 96, 112; Rob inset

31 MHT II 464; Rob 523, 1397

32 BW 124; DM 216; MHT I 212; MHT III 143, 148; Rob 490, 563, 858, 1039, 1074, 1092, 1397

33 BDF §372(1c); MHT II 464; MHT III 115; Rob 1008, 1026, 1397, 1417; RD §378, 437

34 BDF §123(1), 395; BW 123; DM 282; MHT III 78, 140; Rob 873, 1091, 1397

35 BDF §365(2); Moule 81; MHT I 190, 191; MHT III 96, 97, 265; Rob 208, 628, 849, 875, 1026bis, inset, 1405; RD §470(k); Zer §444, 444n

36 BDF §103; Rob 976

37 MHT II 455

38 BDF §336(1); BW 11; DM 109; MHT III **75, 77,** 175; Rob 617, 643, 856

39 BDF §211; BW 48; MHT III 338; Rob 469, 653, 737, 1187

42 MHT II 468; Rob 1012, 1019, 1020, 1160bis; RD §444

43 DM 232; Moule 19; Rob 906; RD §269

44 DM 129; Moule 122; Rob 597

45 BDF §442(4), 451(6); DM 176; MHT II 421; Moule 161; MHT III 24, 334; Rob 807, 882, 890, 948, 1183; RD §407

46 DM 154; MHT II 205; MHT III 51, 151; Rob 312, 428, 439, 799bis

47 Rob 774, 1127

48 MHT III **77**

50 BDF §300(2), 495(2); MHT I 93; MHT III **50;** Rob 602bis, 696, 725, 917; RD §448(c); Zer §**223**

51 BDF §310(1); BW 8; DM 76; Moule 24 n.1; MHT I 157; MHT III 55, **56,** 167; MHT IV 35; Rob 496, 805, 810, 1205; RD §343(g)

52 Rob 524, 534, 859, 1191; Zer §133

53 BDF §185(4), 328, 440(1), 471(2); MHT I 50; MHT II 76, 161, 422; MHT III 65, 334, 342; Rob 276, 312, 666, 681, 1214; RD §387(e)

54 BDF §366(1); BW 154; MHT III 99; Rob 851, 934, 1399

55 BW 57; Moule 173; Rob 602, 813, 884; RD §363

56 Moule 15; MHT III 70; Rob 705; Zer §415

57 Moule 123; Rob 694, 1395

58 MHT III 66; Rob 883

59 Rob 505, 883, 986

60 MHT III 66; Rob 1129; Zer §149

61 BDF §223(1); Moule 56; MHT III 267; Rob 581, 697; Zer §115

62 BDF §298(4), 299(1); Moule 90; MHT III 49, 154; Rob 562, 738, 1126

63 BDF §149; BW 18, 83; MHT III 64, **66,** 183, 268; MHT IV 38; Rob 475, 607, 781, 865, 883, 993, 1045

64 BDF §12(3); MHT I 86, 140; MHT III 37; Rob 678, 679, 842

65 BDF §173(1); MHT I 140; MHT II 193, 469; MHT III 56, 233; Rob 212, 802, 842

66 Rob 504bis, 658, 1392

67 BDF §250; DM 128; Moule 92; MHT II 193; MHT III 37; Rob 212, 561, 694, 1395

69 Moule 92, 125; MHT II 432; MHT III 166; Rob 313, 337, 674

70 MHT III 156; Rob 517, 1136, 1182; RD §344(d)

71 BW 74; MHT III 39; Rob 547, 697; RD §379

72 MHT II 469; Zer §64

73 MHT II 25; Rob 28, 103, 653, 1182

74 MHT II 205, 455, 469; MHT III 137; Rob 1028, 1035; RD §320

75 BDF §123(1); MHT II 11; MHT III 140; Rob 910, 1028, 1091, 1113

Chapter 27

1 BDF §391(3); DM 284; Moule 140; MHT I 207; MHT III 136; Rob 653, 990, 1089bis, 1414; Zer §352

3 Rob 609, 817, 858, 859, 860, 1112, 1113, 1128; Zer §133

4 BDF §127(3), 299(3), 339(1), 362, 414(5); DM 299; MHT I 140, 177; MHT III 80, **86, 154;** Rob 109, 290, 339, 626, 736, 859, 860, 874, 942bis, 1121, 1428; RD §310, 407

5 DM 158; Moule 24; MHT I 155; MHT III 27, 54; Rob 409, 807, 860; RD §397; Zer §232

6 DM 247; MHT II 153

7 BDF 190(3); Moule 73; MHT III 238; Rob 510, 537, 599

8 BW 10; DM 245; Moule 14; MHT III 71; Rob 643, 848, 962, 1202

9 MHT II 419; MHT III 208; Rob 1201

10 MHT III 320; Rob 967; RD §424 (a)

11 BDF §277(1); BW 105; Moule 83;
    MHT I 86; MHT III 37, 183; Rob
    678bis, 768, 769, 915; Zer §175

12 MHT II 450; MHT III 58, 145,
    148; Rob 473, 484, 1073, 1388;
    Zer §229

13 MHT III 50; Rob 512, 741, 1177;
    RD §381

14 MHT IV 36; Rob 473, 738, 751

15 Moule 59; MHT III 268; Rob 606,
    608, 884, 888

17 BDF §423(1); MHT III 166, 322;
    MHT IV 39; Rob 330, 737, 1177;
    RD §381, 402(c)

18 Rob 583, 841, 888bis, 898,
    1029; RD §359, 403(b)

19 Moule 92; MHT I 140, 183; Rob
    396, 707, 842

20 MHT III 72; Rob 805, 835, 993;
    Zer §252

21 DM 80; MHT I 77, 102; MHT III
    209; Rob 515, 577, 737; RD
    §344 (b)

22 Moule 35, 43 n.1; MHT III 166,
    246; Rob 484

23 BDF §60(3), 452(1); DM 243;
    MHT I 140; Rob 279, 845, 1149,
    1190; RD §410(a), 472(a)

24 BDF §182(3), 362; BW 21, 105;
    DM 169; Moule 82; MHT I 90;
    MHT II 461, 465; MHT III 38,
    86, 215; Rob 516, 576, 639,
    644ter, 678, 770, 810, 874,
    942; RD §374, 387(e)

25 BDF §480(5); MHT I 183; Rob
    1202

26 MHT III **135**

27 Rob 562, 593

28 Moule 91; MHT II 129; Rob 483

29 BDF §147(3); MHT III 24; Rob
    465, 474, 598

30 MHT III 256; Rob 593, 884

31 BW 47; Moule 16, 33; MHT III
    143; Rob 483bis, 840

32 MHT I 14; MHT III 220; MHT IV
    35; Rob 528, 993

33 BDF §132(2), 465(2); DM 231;
    Moule 17; MHT II 105, 149; Rob
    411, 714, 881, 1087, 1105

34 MHT II 90; Rob 611

35 MHT I 157; Rob 690, 811

37 MHT III 183; Rob 604, 697; Zer
    §175

38 MHT II 438; Rob 675, 750, 792

39 Rob 473

40 BDF §339(3), 412(5); MHT I 127;
    MHT II 210; MHT III **81**, 151,
    153, 183; Rob 308, 465, 581,
    781, 892, 1107, 1116; Zer §274

41 Rob 374, 891

42 BDF §187(6); Moule 49; MHT III
    183, 237; MHT IV 37; Rob 307,
    419, 746

43 BDF §148(2); MHT II 469;
    MHT III 174; Rob 317, 1028bis,
    1029

44 BDF §152(1), 154; Moule 34;
    MHT I 58; MHT III **26**, 246;
    MHT IV 43; Rob 409, 473, 480,
    482, 487, 1106; Zer §7

45 BW 10; MHT III 178; Rob 602,
    643, 772

46 BDF §36, 147(3), 192; DM 144;
    Moule 11 n.1, 32, 62, 185;
    MHT I 140; MHT III 45, 72, 179;
    Rob 29, 95, 215, 219, 261, 412,
    463, 705, 739, 842; RD §341(c)

47 MHT III 195; Rob 235, 697, 1136

48 BDF §421; DM 80; MHT IV 35; Rob
    1392

49 BDF §351(1), 418(4); DM 226,
    285; MHT I 175, 230; MHT III
    87, 94, 157; Rob 430, 877, 931,
    991, 1045, 1118, 1128, 1399; RD
    §406(a), 433; Zer §282

51 BDF §104(2); Rob 297, 300, 580,
    643bis

52 Rob 1213

54 BDF §5(1); Moule 116; MHT III
    183; Rob 258, 697, 780, 781; RD
    §387(b)(2), 388

55 BDF §390(1); MHT III 134; Rob
    548, 727, 957, 1406; RD §380,
    415

56 MHT II 146; MHT III 168; Rob
    263

57 BDF §148(3), 160; DM 23; MHT II
    63, 400; MHT III 44, 53, 220;
    MHT IV 35; Rob 208, 263,
    475bis, 487, 697, 800; Zer §53,
    66, 74

58 Rob 697, 1078

60 MHT III 190; MHT IV 39; Rob
    542, 681, 715

61 Moule 82; MHT II 465; Rob 405, 505, 639, 747, 1104, 1406; RD §344(d), 353

62 MHT I 91; MHT III **17**; Rob 653, 728, 765, 957

63 BDF §323(1); BW 81; Moule 7; MHT III 63; Rob 816, 870, 1035; Zer §278

64 BDF §62; MHT III 32; Rob 280, 669, 775, 794; Zer §151, 231

65 Rob 949

66 Rob 611

Chapter 28

1 BDF §164(4); BW 10, 21; Moule 86; MHT I 72, 73; MHT II 439, 471; MHT III 27, 135, 187, 278; Rob 517bis, 519, 522, 622, 646, 775, 841; RD §353; Zer §154

2 Rob 841-42

3 Rob 197

4 MHT II 461

5 DM 230; MHT II 453; Zer §366n

6 Rob 430, 845, 931, 949

7 MHT I 140; Rob 842, 889

9 BDF §260(1); MHT III **26, 167**; Rob 1391; Zer §7

10 MHT IV 36, 38; Rob 949, 993

11 Rob 223

12 MHT III 27

13 Moule 56

14 Moule 152; Rob 871, 1019

15 BW 10; Moule 14; MHT I 139; MHT III 72, 169; Rob 614

17 BDF §250; MHT III 37; Rob 694, 1395

18 Moule 94; MHT I 140; MHT II 454; MHT III 175; Rob 772, 842

19 BDF §148(3); DM 135; MHT II 400; MHT III 40, **255**; Rob 475, 525, 592, 649, 684, 1128; Zer §66, **106**

20 MHT I 139; Moule 34, 43

Mark

Chapter 1

1 MHT III 166, 211, **307**; Rob 781, 793, 795

2 BDF §378; DM 272, 284; MHT II 466; MHT IV 16; Rob 606, 621, 956, 960; RD §414

3 MHT III 151; Rob 774, 1106

4 BDF §413(1); DM 76; Moule 70; MHT II 452; MHT III **87**, 151, **211, 214**; Rob 496, 595, 782, 891, 892, 1127; RD §343(b), 361

5 DM 102; MHT III 172; Rob 592, 791, 1127

6 MHT II 104; Rob 118, 204, 485

7 BDF §418(5); BW 129, 137; DM 126, 219(2); MHT I 95, 237; MHT II 10, 434; MHT III **67**, 154, 325; MHT IV 21; Rob 231, 656, 722, 961, 1052, 1126; RD §457(b); Zer §201

8 MHT II 458; MHT III 41; MHT IV 16; Rob 524; RD §345(d), 360, 374

9 BDF §205; Moule 68; MHT II 426; MHT III **166**, 210, **254**; MHT IV 16; Rob 497, 525, 592, 1423; RD §360; Zer §87

10 DM 101, 103; Moule 92, 102; MHT III 25; Rob 517bis, 561, 577, 597, 1393; RD §344(d), 362

11 Moule 11, 69; MHT I 134; MHT II 458; MHT III 25, 72; MHT IV 16; Rob 532, 768, 837

12 BW 140; MHT II 452; Rob 880

13 BW 18; DM 108; Moule 61; Rob 255, 611; RD §343(k), 365

14 BW 70; Moule 60, 134; MHT III 143; Rob 1074; RD §421(d)

15 BDF §187(6); Moule 80, 80 n.4; MHT I 67; MHT II 464; MHT III **75, 82, 237, 263**; MHT IV 16; Rob 119, 453, 536, 540, 601; RD §347(a)

16 Rob 188; RD §354

17 DM 291; MHT I 45; Rob 996, 1023, 1391

18 RD §346(a)

19 BDF §442(9); BW 67; DM 119; MHT II 423; Rob 659, 1379; Zer §377

37

20 DM 108

21 BDF §339; BW 80, 86; Moule 7,
    9; MHT II 446; MHT III 27; Rob
    262, 559, 880; RD §163 B.b.,
    422

22 BW 40, 136; Rob 1127, 1140

23 BDF §198(2), 203, 219(4), 272;
    MHT II 446, 464; MHT III **159**,
    221, 241, **250, 252**; MHT IV 22;
    Rob 589, 784

24 BW 104; DM 146, 168; Moule 154;
    MHT II 83; MHT III 149, 166,
    240, 325; MHT IV 16; Rob 118,
    263, 395, 488, 738, 762, 916;
    RD §347(c), 381, 448(c)

25 MHT I 176

26 MHT III 312

27 BDF §456(2); DM 285; Rob 334,
    540, 1181

28 BDF §103

29 DM 108; MHT II 446; Rob 255,
    611

30 BW 80; Moule 7; MHT II 446

31 MHT III 67, 79; MHT IV 26; Rob
    860; RD §401(a)

32 MHT II 194, 209; Rob 341,
    348, 1109, 1214bis, 1406

33 Moule 53

34 BDF §466(4); BW 161; Moule 72;
    MHT II 114, 189; MHT IV 21; Rob
    195, 315, 319, 367, 546, 1034,
    1216, 1421; RD §302, 320; Zer
    §27

35 Moule 72; MHT II 453

36 DM 108; MHT I 116; Rob 606, 766

37 BW 161; Rob 1028

38 BDF §103; MHT II 276; Rob 299,
    424, 477, 595

39 BDF §205; Rob 118, 593

40 BDF §470(1); MHT II 206; Rob
    474, 849ter, 1214, 1418; Zer
    §327

41 MHT II 129; MHT IV 26

42 Moule 72; MHT II 67, 242; Rob
    183, 559

44 BDF §64(1), 229(1); DM 109,
    295; MHT I 124; MHT II 181,
    420; MHT III 40, 78; MHT IV 26;
    Rob 118, 430, 619, 932, 949

45 BDF §392(2); MHT II 446, 455;
    Rob 300, 604, 1186

Chapter 2

1-12 MHT IV 11

1 BDF §205, 223(1), 405(2); Moule
   75; MHT I 82; MHT III 261; Rob
   119, 525, 559, 581, 586, 593,
   1120; RD §343(e), 345(f), 359,
   361; Zer §115

2 Moule 27, 53; MHT III **291**;
   MHT IV 26; Rob 119, 625

3 MHT I 222; Rob 392, 1097

4 DM 278; MHT II 324, 461, 470;
   Rob 604, 969, 1393; RD §423(c)

5 BDF §320; BW 81; MHT I 119;
   MHT II 206; MHT III **64**; Rob
   866; Zer §236

6 Moule 75; MHT II 452; MHT III
   23

7 BDF §300(2); MHT I 231;
   MHT II 16; MHT IV 22; Rob
   118, 221, 697, 705, 1025, 1129

8 Moule 75; MHT II 432; MHT III
   23; MHT IV 22

9 MHT II 206; Rob 737, 1215

10 BDF §470(3); BW 12; Moule 50,
    138; Rob 119, 434, 907, 999,
    1203, 1388; Zer §415

11 DM 300; MHT IV 58; Rob 428, 855

12 BDF §434(2); DM 285; Moule 83;
    MHT III 226; Rob 1028

13 BDF §207(1); Moule 68; Rob 119,
    596

14 BW 144, 145; Moule 92; MHT II
    453

15 BDF §393(5), 471(4); MHT I 16,
    17; MHT II 427; MHT III **342**,
    348; MHT IV 26; Rob 316, 393,
    1043, 1190, 1423

16 BDF §300(2); DM 252; Moule 43,
    159; MHT III **49**, 209; Rob 730,
    917, 1028, 1029, 1035, 1396,
    1421; RD §448(d)

17 Rob 990; RD §432

18 BW 33; DM 104; MHT II 452;
    MHT III **292**; Rob 786, 787,
    1186

19 DM 282; Moule 174; MHT II 419,
    441; Rob 528, 587, 718, 733,
    879bis, 978bis; RD §419(a),
    419(d)

20 BDF §382(3); BW 153; MHT III 27; Rob 118

21 DM 247; MHT III 41, **209**; MHT IV 14; Rob 212, 1025, 1392

22 BDF §65(3); DM 247; MHT II 206; Rob 214, 373

23 MHT I 16, 17, 159; MHT II 389, 427, 455; MHT III 56; MHT IV 29; Rob 523, 720, 763, 1043, 1423; RD §410(a); Zer §228, 376

24 MHT IV 22; Rob 523, 738, 1045, 1159, 1396

25 MHT III 41, 49; Rob 679, 1392; Zer §289n

26 DM 107; MHT II 440; MHT III 137, 149; Rob 603, 628, 714

27 BW 57; DM 102; Moule 55; MHT III **268**; Rob 584; Zer §112

28 BDF §472(1b); Moule 144; Rob 439

32 Rob 1406

Chapter 3

1 MHT II 223; Rob 656, 789, 902, 1123, 1389; RD §387(c)

2 Rob 1024, 1045

3 Rob 775

4 BDF §245(3); MHT II 442; MHT III 32

5 Moule 192; MHT II 189, 325; MHT III 23; Rob 368, 813; RD §278

6 BDF §94(1); BW 163; MHT II 202; MHT III **56**; MHT IV 29; Rob 994, 1214, 1413; RD §434(b)

7 BDF §207(1); DM 165; Moule 68; MHT IV 21; Rob 596, 611, 624, 838, 1183bis

8 Moule 62; Rob 28, 620, 733, 898, 1390; RD §353, 380

9 MHT I 208

10 Moule 90

11 DM 280; MHT I 168; MHT III 93, 125, 183, 313; Rob 118, 404, 884, 922, 958, 973, 1385; RD §419(f); Zer §358

12 MHT II 446

13 MHT III **179**; MHT IV 14; Zer §133

14 BDF §392(1e); BW 146; MHT III **78**, 135; Rob 611, 1088; RD §415

16 BDF §143; MHT I 69, 235; Rob 434, 441, 459, 488, 1413

17 BDF §162(6); MHT II 441; MHT III 208; Rob 411, 434, 713

18 Rob 530

19 MHT II 145

20 BDF §445(2); MHT IV 26; Rob 627, 792

21 BDF §237(2), 342(1); Moule 52; MHT I 106, 134; MHT II 420; MHT III **16**, 273, **292**; Rob 614bis, 842, 845; Zer §3, **4**

22 MHT II 105; MHT III 152; Rob 210, 778, 1106

23 Rob 1036

24 BDF §372(1b); Rob 817, 879; Zer **§306**, 325

25 BDF §372(1b)

26 BDF §372(1b); MHT I 187; MHT II 430; Rob 602, 1417

27 MHT IV 26; Rob 1019

28 BDF §296; DM 252; MHT II 430; MHT III **110**; Rob 479, 732, 733

29 MHT IV 16; Rob 504ter; RD §343(j)

30 Rob 589

31 BDF §73; BW 140; DM 285; MHT III 82; Rob 991, 1115; RD §460(c)

32 MHT II 206; Rob 404

34 BW 7, 35; DM 71; Rob 521, 524, 617; RD §345(b), 348

39 Zer §278

Chapter 4

1 DM 110; Moule 51, 92, 94, 98; MHT I 241; MHT II 110, 455; MHT III **31**; Rob 525, 615, 625, 670

2 MHT III **292**

3 Rob 431

4 BDF §447(3); BW 50; Moule 51, 77, 125; MHT II 18, 426, 450, 451; MHT III 36, 145; Rob 107, 339, 1073, 1152, 1153, 1183, 1395, 1423

5 BW 159; DM 278; MHT I 79;
   MHT III 142; Rob 747, 749

6 DM 213; MHT I 79; MHT III 142,
   345

7 BW 104; MHT I 79; Rob 915

8 BDF §207(2), 248(3); BW 43;
   Moule 68, 77, 78, 187; MHT I
   79, 103; MHT II 176, 202, 439;
   MHT III 188, **265**, 266; Rob
   232, 589, 592; Zer §158

9 MHT II 205; Rob 720, 956; RD
   §380, 414

10 BDF §228; MHT II 195; MHT III
    16, 18, 21, **26, 270**; Rob 244,
    341, 482, 550, 653, 765; Zer
    §7n

11 Moule 77; MHT III 45

12 BDF §369(2), 471(3); Moule 142,
    187, 207; MHT II 204, 444,
    470; MHT III **102**; Rob 233,
    315, 1173, 1413, 1415; RD §320,
    426(c); Zer **§413, 426, 414n**

13 BDF §275(3); MHT II 438;
    MHT III **200**; Rob 876; Zer
    §444, 459

14 BDF §488(1a)

16 DM 250

17 DM 250; MHT III 63; Rob 300,
    880, 1131

20 BDF §248(3); Moule 187;
    MHT II 60, 439; MHT III 188;
    Rob 232; Zer §158

21 BDF §5(1); DM 265; MHT II 448;
    Rob 789, 883, 917, 1028bis

22 BDF §382(1), 488(8); DM 240;
    MHT I 191, 241; MHT II 436,
    468; MHT III 330; MHT IV 13,
    14; Rob 653, 764, 960, 999,
    1020, 1185, 1187; Zer §425,
    469, 470

23 BW 164; DM 247, 289; Rob 956,
    1009, 1087; RD §414

24 Moule 33; Rob 392, 471, 718,
    883

25 BDF §380(1); MHT III **110**; Rob
    392, 720, 956, 957, 1158; RD
    §415

26 BDF §380(3, 4); BW 111, 160; DM
    277; Moule 23, 50; MHT I 185;
    MHT III 320; Rob 603, 883,
    928, 968, 974, 987, 1402; RD
    §424(b)

27 Moule 34; MHT II 231, 423; Rob
    470, 1213; RD §320

28 DM 119(2); MHT I 46, 50;
    MHT II 61, 68, 158, 162;
    MHT III 225, 316; Rob 160,
    183, 273, 275, 276, 549, 687;
    RD §208(c); Zer §11

29 MHT II 211; Rob 309, 800,
    972, 1214

30 BDF §280; MHT II 319, 419; MHT
    III 28, 257; MHT IV 22; Rob
    407, 678, 736, 883, 1392; Zer
    §65

31 DM 83, 152; Moule 208; Rob 516,
    782, 1104, 1129; RD §344(c)

32 Moule 65f.; MHT I 53; Rob 343,
    371, 635

33 Rob 710, 884; Zer §413

34 MHT III 18; Rob 224

35 BDF §423; MHT III 322

36 BW 80; MHT II 420, 453;
    MHT III **321**; Rob 549, 1399

37 Moule 92; MHT III 52; Rob 231,
    561, 800, 868, 1000; RD §435(c)

38 DM 294; Moule 28, 49; MHT II
    206; MHT III **271**; Rob 427,
    602, 623, 879, 965, 1034, 1422;
    RD §369

39 BDF §346, 461(1); MHT I 176;
    MHT III **85**; Rob 330, 360,
    428, 908, 950; RD §308, 403(a)

40 MHT IV 22

41 BDF §153(1), 444(3), 456(2); BW
    46; DM 94, 286; MHT I 58;
    MHT II 436, 445; MHT III 318,
    335; MHT IV 15, 29; Rob 405,
    468, 699, 1001, 1182; RD
    §342(g), 379; Zer §420, 424,
    447

Chapter 5

1 MHT IV 21

2 BDF §219(4); MHT II 464;
   MHT III 39, **252**; MHT IV 22; Zer
   §116

3 Moule 157; MHT IV 26; Rob 223,
   1165

4 BW 39; DM 89, 216; MHT III **143**,
   241; Rob 231, 581, 636, 765,
   828, 909, 966, 1070bis,
   1071bis, 1079, 1081, 1091,
   1407, 1428; RD §346(f), 354,
   359

5 Moule 39; MHT II 452; MHT III
   235; Rob 244, 582, 793

6 Rob 300

7   DM 95, 121; Moule 46, 203;
    MHT III 156, 166; MHT IV 17;
    Rob 279, 475, 483, 670; RD
    §342(i)

8   BDF §347(2); Zer §290

9   Rob 656

10 MHT I 208; MHT II 446; MHT III
    65; Zer §84, 252, 272

11 BW 36; DM 110; Moule 54;
    MHT II 12, 452; MHT III 274;
    Rob 624bis

12 MHT III **65**; Zer §252, 272, 415

13 BW 22; DM 107; MHT I 172;
    MHT III 67, 313; Rob 283,
    580, 607, 674, 884, 968; RD
    §402(b), 424(b)

14 BW 167; DM 298; Rob 1043; RD
    §452(c)

15 BDF §343(2); MHT I 145;
    MHT II 76, 195; MHT III **21, 41**,
    70, 83; MHT IV 27; Rob 868,
    900, 910, 1099, 1117bis, 1136;
    Zer §204, 289, 371

16 Moule 176; MHT II 431; Rob 1032

17 BDF §328; MHT II 455

18 BDF §423(2); MHT II 204;
    MHT III 322; MHT IV 27; Rob
    1117; Zer §371

19 MHT I 143; MHT III 69, 83;
    MHT IV 27; Rob 624, 733, 901,
    1045, 1177; Zer §460

20 MHT II 455; Rob 625, 733

21 MHT III 166, **229**

22 Moule 46; MHT II 432; Rob 1383;
    RD §369

23 BDF §369(3), 387(3); BW 138; DM
    229, 249, 302; Moule 144; MHT I
    179; MHT II 446, 452; MHT III
    40, **95**; MHT IV 23; Rob 297,
    299, 324, 546, 933, 943, 986,
    994, 1387; RD §349, 430(a); Zer
    §250, 273, 415

24 BW 146; DM 165; Rob 774, 838,
    1390

25 Moule 78; MHT III 152; MHT IV
    26; Rob 779, 892, 1105, 1115,
    1136; Zer §116

26 BDF §488(1a); Moule 51;
    MHT III **15**, 43; Rob 615, 635,
    '1110-11, 1136

27 MHT II 92, 420; MHT III **15**,
    166, 257; MHT IV 22; Rob 619,
    1105, 1136

28 MHT III 321; Rob 208, 1018,
    1025, 1027, 1060

29 MHT II 60; MHT III 58, 161; Rob
    232, 524, 1041bis, 1216

30 BDF §416(2), 474(5b); MHT III
    27, 189; Rob 508, 599, 1042,
    1110, 1123, 1136; Zer §268

31 MHT III 161

32 BW 86; DM 190; MHT III **66**, 139;
    Rob 838, 883, 1088, 1136

33 BDF §5(3b), 345; MHT III 70,
    83; Rob 542, 726, 858, 897,
    1118

34 BDF §206(1); BW 51; Moule 70;
    MHT I 174, 226; MHT II 463;
    MHT III 35, 83; Rob 264, 462,
    596; RD §172(c), 341(a)

35 Rob 502, 845

36 BDF §416(1); Moule 89; MHT I
    124; MHT III **75**, **161**; Rob 845;
    Zer §242

37 MHT II 433; MHT IV 26

38 MHT II 446; Zer §97

39 DM 240; Rob 1166

40 BDF §277(3); Rob 1119

41 BDF §147(3), 493(1); Moule 17,
    32; Rob 29, 104, 465, 684, 714,
    866, 881, 1119, 1215; RD §25,
    341(c), 387(f); Zer §34

42 MHT II 443; MHT III 242; Rob
    497, 531, 1190; RD §410(a); Zer
    §62

43 BDF §392(4), 409(2); MHT II
    211, 446, 450; MHT III 138,
    149; MHT IV 29; Rob 308,
    1079, 1085, 1214; RD §456

Chapter 6

1   BDF §321; Rob 880

2   BDF §298(2), 474(5b); MHT II
    455, 462; MHT III **31**; MHT IV
    23; Rob 262, 705, 710bis, 735,
    771; RD §387(e)

3   BDF §273(1); Moule 52; MHT II
    146, 464, 467; MHT III 183;
    MHT IV 13; Rob 255, 263, 697,
    768, 785

4   MHT II 138, 350; MHT III **306**;
    Rob 269, 1420

5   BDF §376; MHT III 39, 321;
    MHT IV 26; Rob 212, 368, 682,
    751, 1011, 1013bis, 1169, 1429;
    Zer §470

6　BDF §150; Moule 108f.; MHT III 221; Rob 797

7　BDF §248(1); Moule 67, 182; MHT II 420, 439, 455; MHT III 187; Rob 284, 673; Zer §157

8　BDF §470(2); BW 166; DM 298; MHT III 225, 326; Rob 438, 441, 657, 944, 950, 993, 1042, 1046, 1047bis, 1402; RD §453(b)

9　MHT III **317**; Rob 413, 438, 633; Zer §15n, 394

10　DM 278, 281; Rob 969, 1411

11　BDF §469; BW 21; MHT III 324, 325; Rob 257, 517, 647; RD §344(d), 353

12　MHT II 420; Rob 993

13　Rob 212, 483

14　BDF §413(1), 471(4); MHT I 127; MHT II 194, 447; Rob 694, 1029, 1111; Zer **§285**

15　BDF §306(5); MHT II 438; MHT III **306**, 320

16　DM 126; MHT II 424; MHT III 324; MHT IV 21; Rob 698, 719; Zer §285

17　BDF §277(3); Moule 176; MHT I 94; MHT II 431; MHT III **41**, 41; Rob 964; Zer §205, 290, 363n

18　Moule 10; MHT III **41**, 41, **67**

19　BW 32; MHT III 52; Rob 539, 542, 800, 1202; RD §347(g)

20　BDF §414(5); MHT II 445, 446; MHT III 162; Rob 1103, 1123

21　Moule 43; MHT II 112, 364; MHT III 27; Rob 408, 523, 786, 1392; RD §345(c)

22　BDF §277(3), 423(4); Moule 33; MHT I 160; MHT II 431; MHT III **41**, 41, 55, 108, 322; Rob 482, 805, 956, 1392; Zer §205, 485

23　BW 11; DM 79; MHT I 160; MHT II 177; MHT III 55, 210; Rob 275, 502, 643, 655, 729, 775, 805, 959, 1028, 1032, 1040, 1047; Zer **§234**

24　BDF §316(2), 413(1); MHT I 127, 160; MHT III 55, 151; Rob 805, 934

25　BDF §316(2), 387(3), 425(2); Moule 145 n.2; MHT I 160, 179; MHT III 55, 154, **229**; Rob 431, 611, 805, 933, 943, 993, 1139, 1214; RD §462(d)

26　BDF §442(16); Moule 54; MHT I 51; MHT III **26, 335, 350**; MHT IV 19, 21; Zer §460

27　BDF §392(4), 409(1); MHT II 109, 129; MHT III 149; Rob 1084

28　MHT III 40

29　Rob 310, 347

30　Rob 733

31　MHT III 18; Rob 224, 367, 488, 654, 1087; RD §342(k); Zer §198

33　BDF §150; Rob 530

34　BDF §155(1); BW 47; DM 94; MHT II 455; Rob 482, 1140, 1430

35　BW 72; DM 149

36　BDF §60(2), 368; Moule 109 n.1; MHT II 164; MHT III 117; MHT IV 22; Rob 279, 640, 670, 737, 1044, 1045; Zer §349

37　BDF §95(1), 366(2), 369(3); MHT II 75; MHT III 37, **98**; Rob 201, 309, 580, 876, 934, 1399

38　MHT I 170; Rob 916, 949; RD §448(c)

39　BDF §158, 392(4), 493(2); Moule 182; MHT I 97, 107; MHT II 439; MHT III 138, 231; Rob 284, 460, 487, 604, 673, 1084; Zer §157

40　BDF §158, 204, 248(1), 493(2); BW 49; Moule 59, 60, 67, 208; MHT III 187, **266**, 268; Rob 460, 487, 673bis, 1210; RD §340(d)

41　MHT II 204; MHT III 67; MHT IV 13, 27; Rob 613; Zer **§271**

43　MHT II 433; MHT III 209; MHT IV 15

45　BDF §383(1); BW 159; DM 281; MHT II 471; MHT III **40**, 321; MHT IV 13; Rob 259, 975, 976; RD §419(b), 420(c)bis; Zer §276

46　Rob 542, 684

47　Rob 550, 686, 775, 884

48　BDF §233(1), 404(3); BW 50; Moule 50, 62; MHT II 450; MHT III 146; MHT IV 22; Rob 400, 477, 528, 640, 1073; RD §347(e)

52   MHT III 23; Rob 604, 806

53   Rob 214, 623

55   Moule 90; MHT II 455; MHT III
     116; Rob 234, 477, 604,
     617bis, 884, 953, 1029, 1049;
     Zer §346n

56   BDF §367; DM 278; Moule 138;
     MHT I 167, 168; MHT II 202;
     MHT III **93, 100**, 125; MHT IV
     22, 39; Rob 318, 733, 806bis,
     922, 957, 958, 969, 973, 984,
     1025, 1385; RD §320, 408,
     416bis, 423(c), 424(c); Zer
     §336, 358

Chapter 7

1   Rob 562

2   MHT II 249; MHT III 45, 325;
     MHT IV 16; Rob 234, 399, 416,
     705

3   MHT II 352; Rob 439, 806

4   BDF §209(4); BW 101; DM 158;
     Moule 192; MHT II 420; MHT III
     135, 179, 259; MHT IV 32; Rob
     256, 791, 807, 1087, 1218

5   MHT III **185**; Rob 790; RD
     §386(b)

6   Moule 47; MHT II 189; MHT III
     23, 206; Rob 367, 546

9   BDF §495(2); MHT II 100; Rob
     1198; RD §474(1)

10   MHT II 443; Rob 793

11   BDF §360(1), 465(2), 470(3);
     Moule 131, 151; MHT II 85,
     153; MHT III **91**; Rob 233,
     270, 433, 599, 1023, 1203

12   MHT I 191; MHT IV 26; Rob
     484, 1162

13   MHT II 209, 419; Rob 715,
     716; Zer §16

14   RD §320

15   BDF §104(2), 273(3); BW 23;
     Moule 84; Rob 642

18   BDF §104(2); Rob 233, 300, 438,
     548; RD §328

19   BDF §111(6), 126(3), 137(3);
     MHT II 74, 448; MHT III **316**;
     Rob 118, 413, 438bis, 1130,
     1203; RD §328; Zer **§15**

20   BDF §291(4); MHT II 424;
     MHT III 46; MHT IV 21; Rob 707

21   BDF §104(2); Moule 72;
     MHT III 23, 28; Rob 300

22   Rob 408

23   BDF §104(2); Rob 300

24   BDF §429; MHT II 318, 453;
     MHT III 285; Rob 27, 156, 334,
     350, 368, 1094, 1162; RD §468

25   BDF §198(2), 297; DM 110; Moule
     91, 132, 176; MHT I 13, 94, 95;
     MHT II 420, 434, 452; MHT III
     241, 325; MHT IV 21; Rob 560,
     683, 722, 1205; RD §474(r); Zer
     §201, 485

26   DM 248; Moule 46; MHT I 75;
     MHT II 279, 349; MHT III 67;
     Rob 155, 487, 884, 993

27   Zer §485

28   BW 21; MHT I 139; MHT II 345,
     461; MHT III 156; Rob 633,
     634, 647

30   MHT II 129; Rob 1123, 1429

31   BDF §207(1); BW 49; DM 99;
     Moule 67; MHT II 471; Rob 491,
     596, 775; RD §342(o)

32   BDF §34(6); MHT II 106, 129;
     Rob 210, 770

33   MHT III 18; Rob 231

34   MHT II 83; Rob 29, 215, 714

35   MHT II 83; Rob 349, 549, 835,
     838, 885, 1213

36   BDF §60(3), 154, 246; DM 121;
     MHT III 29, 246; Rob 278,
     279, 488, 546, 663, 680, 733,
     967; RD §349, 424(d)

37   MHT III **26**, 83; Rob 171, 297,
     546, 1391; Zer §7n

Chapter 8

1   MHT III 117; Rob 407, 696,
     708, 737, 1131; Zer §348

2   BDF §144, 203; BW 7; DM 70;
     MHT I 70; MHT II 447; MHT III
     243; MHT IV 17; Rob 460, 726;
     Zer §54

3   MHT I 53; MHT II 132, 221;
     MHT III 82; Rob 266, 275,
     337, 1215; RD §320

4   Moule 33; Rob 508, 1028, 1422

5   MHT III 65

6   MHT II 204; Rob 561, 983

7   BDF §111(3), 392(4); MHT I 52; MHT II 194, 450; MHT III 138; Rob 339, 1046-47; RD §302

10 MHT II 420

11 MHT II 209, 430, 455; Rob 529, 614

12 BDF §300(2), 372(4), 454(5); DM 246; Moule 151, 179; MHT II 468; MHT III 127, 333; Rob 94, 1004, 1024bis; RD §442

13 MHT II 453

14 Moule 16; MHT I 170; MHT II 212; Rob 190, 841, 1060

15 BDF §149; MHT II 31, 460; Rob 471, 541, 577, 949; RD §407

16 BDF §324; MHT II 194; MHT III 64

17 MHT II 202; MHT III 23, 185; Rob 360, 409, 789, 1389; Zer §447

18 Rob 902; Zer §51

19 BW 139; MHT I 50; MHT II 162; MHT III **236**, 316; Rob 535; Zer §11

21 MHT II 202

22 Rob 259, 807

23 BDF 170(2); MHT III 65, 232, 256; Rob 508bis, 916, 1027

24 DM 154; MHT I 94; MHT II 436; Rob 423, 1041bis; Zer §268

25 BDF §119(4); MHT II 189; Rob 170, 368; Zer §455g

26 BDF §445(2); MHT I 125

27 Moule 28; MHT III 65, 212, 293

28 MHT II 454; MHT III **306**; Rob 747, 1028, 1036

29 BW 140; MHT III 65, 80; Rob 861, 1186

31 BW 161; MHT II 455; MHT III 258; MHT IV 22; Rob 350, 579, 1035

34 BDF §293; DM 247; MHT II 421; Rob 727, 956; RD §414

35 BDF §380(3); MHT III 43, 108, **110**; Rob 193, 956, 957, 959, 961, 1385; RD §414, 416; Zer §336

36 Moule 28; MHT I 87; MHT IV 16; Rob 472, 485, 689

37 BDF §366(1); MHT II 211; Rob 309, 573, 935, 1214, 1399; RD §306

38 MHT III 257; MHT IV 22; Rob 472, 485, 523; RD §342(j); Zer §205

Chapter 9

1 BDF §474(5c); Moule 18; MHT II 88, 464; MHT III 82, 96, 233; Rob 742, 957, 962, 1041, 1116, 1123, inset; RD §415; Zer §268

2 Moule 109 n.3; MHT III 18; Rob 428, 1398

3 MHT II 435, 452; MHT III 46, 88, 89; Rob 375, 723, 890, 903; Zer §201

4 BDF §471(4); MHT II 452; Rob 268, 529

5 MHT II 453; MHT III 149; Rob 750; Zer §366n

6 BDF §330; BW 167; DM 297; MHT III **67, 117**; Rob 473, 738, 1028, 1031, 1044; RD §452(a), 452(c); Zer §348

7 MHT II 452; MHT III 88; Rob 1383; RD §343(1)

8 BDF §448(8); MHT II 468; MHT IV 13, 26; Rob 657, 809; Zer §235, 470

9 MHT II 209; Rob 1025, 1065; RD §470(c)

10 BDF §5(3b), 239(1), 399(1); BW 127; Moule 110; MHT III 140, **182**; Rob 1058, 1065, 1424

11 BDF §300(2); DM 252; Moule 132, 159; MHT III 49; Rob 244, 730, 917; RD §448(d); Zer §222

12 BDF §233(2), 442(8), 447(6); BW 154; MHT II 99, 111, 396; Rob 149, 219, 224, 316, 342, 602, 993, 1152; RD §347(g); Zer §459

13 BDF §233(2); Rob 732

14 Moule 62; Rob 620

15 Rob 407, 597

17 Rob 624

18 BDF §101, 148(1); MHT I 186; MHT II 71, 257, 403, 409; Rob 184, 318, 850, 969, 1411

19 BDF §146(2); Moule 52; MHT II 467; MHT III 33, 35, 39;

MHT IV 13; Rob 264, 464; Zer §35

20 BDF §134(3), 466(4); MHT III **66**, 312, 316; MHT IV 28; Rob 436, 603bis, 883, 1139; RD §347(g)

21 BDF §455(3); DM 281; Moule 73, 133; MHT II 164; MHT III 70; Rob 300, 740, 741, 963, 974bis; RD §419(g)

22 BDF §448(3); BW 116, 144; DM 176, 240; MHT II 206; MHT III 69, 330; Rob 312, 340, 472, 948, 1214, 1430; RD §302, 407

23 BDF §267(1); DM 145; Moule 110; MHT III 182; Rob 118, 491, 766; RD §387(a)

24 BDF §420(2); MHT III 156, 189

25 MHT I 125; Rob 465, 769, 1173

26 BDF §134(3), 155(1); DM 215; Moule 35; MHT II 446; MHT III 31; Rob 412, 968, 1091; RD §336

28 BDF §300(2), 423(2); BW 16; DM 80, 252; Moule 45, 159; MHT II 195, 467; MHT III 18, 39, **49**, 243, 322; Rob 224, 244, 514, 730, 917; Zer §222

29 DM 247

30 BW 12; Moule 55; MHT II 211; MHT III **129**, 282; Rob 308, 983, 994, 1055, 1156, 1214

31 BDF §323(1); BW 81; Moule 7; MHT III 24, 63; Rob 815, 870

33 MHT II 209; Rob 118

34 Moule 97; MHT II 195; MHT III 30; Rob 334, 529, 668, 811, 818

35 MHT II 458; MHT III 86; Rob 775, 874, 961, 1416; Zer §280

36 MHT II 406, 430; Rob 800

37 DM 240; MHT II 75; MHT III 107, 209, 282, **287**; MHT IV 15; Rob 710, 771, 954, 1163, 1187; Zer §445

38 BDF §326; Moule 9; MHT I 129; MHT III 65; MHT IV 27; Rob 964, 1123, 1396

39 MHT I 125, 174; Rob 726, 1164

40 BDF §380(1); BW 152; Moule 64; Rob 630

41 BDF §397(3); Moule 33, 79; MHT I 100, 188; MHT III 96, 246; Rob 484, 795, 1033, 1034, inset; RD §342(i), 406(a)

42 BDF §245(3), 360(4), 372(3); DM 120; MHT II 442, 463; MHT III **31, 92**; Rob 663, 997, 1011, 1416, 1417; RD §367; Zer §**311**

43 BDF §245(3); MHT II 106, 442, 448; MHT III 31, 149; MHT IV 22; Rob 218, 661, 849, 1019

44 MHT III 292; Rob 849

45 BDF §245(3); MHT II 442; MHT III 31, 149; Rob 231, 661, 849, 850, 1418; Zer §145

46 Rob 849

47 BDF §245(3); MHT II 442; MHT III 31, 149; Rob 849, 1084, 1418

48 MHT II 206; Rob 318

49 MHT II 132, 408; Rob 269, 534; RD §182 f

50 MHT II 132; MHT III 43, 44; Rob 145, 269ter, 534; RD §182 f, 314

Chapter 10

1 BW 99; MHT II 92, 453; MHT III 82, 154; Rob 801, 904, 968

2 MHT II 195; Rob 794, 916

3 Zer §458

4 Rob 1028

5 BDF §239(8); DM 110; Moule 53; Zer §98

6 MHT II 104, 160, 205

7 BDF §208(1); Moule 71; MHT I 91; Rob 574

8 DM 103; Moule 144, 183

9 Rob 314

10 BDF §205; MHT II 195; Rob 593

11 MHT III **272**; Rob 747

12 BDF §101; Rob 747

13 BW 30; Moule 28; MHT I 59; MHT II 447; MHT III 293; Rob 392, 538; RD §347(g)

14 MHT III **214**; RD §374

15 Rob inset

16 MHT II 406: MHT III 39; Rob 318

17 BDF §247(2), 423(2); Moule 43 n.1, 125, 173; MHT II 432; MHT III 322; Rob 418bis, 474, 675;

RD §382

18 BW 66; DM 95; MHT IV 22; Rob
    176, 276, 298, 479, 480, 656,
    661, 916, 1176bis; RD §335,
    448(c)

19 BDF §368; MHT III 51

20 Moule 24 n.1; MHT I 159; MHT
    III 55; Rob 597, 842; Zer §235

21 BDF §180(5); BW 156; MHT III
    72; Rob 302, 476, 541, 834,
    1193

22 DM 225; MHT II 420, 452; Rob
    888

23 BDF §396; Moule 207; MHT III
    137; Rob 741

24 MHT III 82, 137; Rob 302

25 BDF §24; Moule 177; MHT II
    430, 441; MHT III 31; Rob 780

26 BDF §442(8); MHT IV 29; Rob
    1182; Zer §459

27 Rob 542, 1096

28 BDF §95(1); Moule 173; MHT II
    455; Rob 309

29 BDF §460(3); MHT I 191; Rob
    427, 726, 955, 961; RD §416

30 Moule 61, 76; MHT II 157; MHT
    III 193; Rob 611, 673, 727,
    1020

32 DM 232; MHT I 227; MHT II 452,
    455; MHT III **37**; Rob 376, 541,
    888

33 BDF §195(2); MHT III 240; Rob
    533, 539, 882

34 Rob 333, 356

35 Moule 7; MHT I 160, 179; Rob
    405, 501, 805, 933, 994

36 MHT II 421; Rob 430, 994

37 MHT III 36; Rob 750, 993,
    1065; RD §378

38 BDF §153(2); MHT I 160; MHT II
    89; MHT III 245; Rob 426, 478,
    485, 715, 717, 805, 879; RD
    §342(j)

39 Rob 312, 356, 1214

40 MHT II 468; MHT III 324;
    MHT IV 13; Rob 721, 1058,
    1065, 1076, 1424; RD §387(a)

41 BDF §480(1); MHT II 455;
    MHT III **178, 255**

42 Rob 510

43 DM 260, 272, 273; MHT II 458;
    MHT III 108; Rob 961

44 MHT II 458

45 BDF §283(4); DM 100, 155; Moule
    64, 71, 139; MHT I 105; MHT III
    57, 258; Rob 573, 632, 815; Zer
    §91

46 Moule 51; Rob 1204, 1397

47 MHT II 455; MHT III 166; Rob
    760

48 BW 43; RD §346(g)

49 BDF §392(4); MHT II 104;
    MHT III **138**

51 BDF §366(3); Moule 145; MHT I
    179; MHT II 421; MHT III **95**;
    MHT IV 23; Rob 933; Zer §415

52 BW 95; MHT III 83

Chapter 11

1 BDF §321; MHT II 148, 149;
   MHT IV 22; Rob 259, 624, 971;
   Zer §97

2 BDF §343(1); MHT II 420, 465;
   MHT III 70; Rob 505, 1165; RD
   §343(k)

3 BDF §299(1); MHT II 458; Rob
   738, 874, 943

4 Moule 53; MHT II 123

5 BDF §414(5); MHT III 82, **154**;
   Rob 1121

6 Rob 309

7 Moule 173

8 MHT II 76, 81, 375; MHT III
   115; Rob 198, 593

9 Rob 620, 786

10 Moule 107; Rob 279

11 BDF §129, 241(3); MHT I 72;
    MHT III 17

12 Zer §88

13 BDF §351(1), 368, 416(1),
    425(3); MHT III 87, 116, 161;
    Rob 877, 1024bis, 1027, 1043,
    1045, 1190; Zer §403

14 BDF §384; Moule 136; MHT I
    165, 179; MHT II 453; MHT III
    121, **122**; MHT IV 26; Rob 854,
    913, 939bis, 940, 943, 1170,
    1173, 1215; RD §308, 406(b),
    447; Zer §366n

15 MHT II 455; Rob 787

16 BW 162; MHT I 176; MHT II 189; MHT III 138; Rob 315, 431, 993, 1216; RD §320

17 MHT III 83

18 Rob 786, 838, 995

19 BDF §367; MHT I 168, 248; MHT III **93**, 226; Rob 392, 922, 958, 973bis; RD §408bis, 419(f); Zer §336, 358

20 MHT II 105, 223; Rob 362

21 Rob 473

22 BW 15; Rob 500; RD §343(f)bis

23 MHT III 63; Rob 880, 1048bis

24 BDF §333(2); BW 94; MHT III 73; Rob 732, 1023, 1029; RD §451(a); Zer §460

25 BDF §73, 382(4); DM 280; Moule 133; MHT I 168; MHT II 73, 204; MHT III 112; Rob 150, 188, 351, 958, 972, 1393; RD §419(f)

27 BDF §423(2)

28 MHT II 419, 464; MHT IV 23; Rob 292, 740, 916, 999; Zer §410

29 BDF §247(2); Rob 1177; Zer §155

30 MHT II 423; MHT III **217**

31 BDF §470(3); DM 102; MHT II 464; MHT III 326; MHT IV 29; Rob 613

32 BDF §330, 408, 476(1); MHT III **67**, 149, 325; MHT IV 16; Rob 295, 443, 551, 887, 1029, 1034, 1203

Chapter 12

1 BDF §123(1); MHT II 212, 455; MHT III 55; Rob 190, 308, 409; RD §301

2 BDF §386(3); BW 29; MHT III **128**, 129, 209; MHT IV 15; Rob 519, 614

4 BDF §108(1); MHT II 384, 395; MHT III 135; Rob 149, 551

5 MHT II 245; MHT III 36; Rob 213, 394, 694, 696, 1213

6 MHT II 430; MHT IV 29; Rob 334

7 MHT III 94; MHT IV 28; Rob 430, 768, 789, 931; RD §406(a)

8 Rob 339

10 MHT II 423; MHT III 324; MHT IV 21; Rob 718

11 BDF §138(2); Moule 182; MHT I 59; MHT III **21**; Rob 234, 254, 410, 655, 704

12 BDF §239(6), 324, 442(1); DM 217; Moule 53; MHT II 453; MHT III 64, **342**; MHT IV 29; Rob 858, 1060, 1078, 1183; Zer §455b

13 Rob 233, 786

14 BDF §5(1); BW 108, 133; DM 171; Moule 22, 28; MHT I 185; MHT II 315, 419, 464; MHT III 99, **286**; MHT IV 26; Rob 792, 850, 928, 934bis, 1158, 1170, 1177, 1399; Zer §416

15 BW 143; Moule 145; Rob 1395; RD §406(a), 466, 488(g); Zer §415

17 Rob 597; RD §343(g), 387(a)

18 BW 128; MHT II 195; Rob 1046, 1082, 1171; RD §451(b), 457(f), 468

19 BDF §470(1); Rob 309, 348; Zer §415

20 Rob 669

23 BDF §164(1); MHT I 145; MHT II 419; MHT III 209; Rob 497, 587

24 Rob 700; RD §470(j)

25 BDF §101; MHT II 410

26 BDF §128(2); MHT II 79, 123, 454; MHT III 137, 217; Rob 199, 253, 603, 1032bis; RD §163 A

28 BDF §164(1); DM 82; Moule 97f., 113; MHT II 442; MHT III 31, 161, **210**, 316; Rob 410, 516, 669, 740, 1042, 1123; RD §398; Zer §12

29 BDF §462(1); Moule 113; MHT II 103, 454; Rob 1422

30 BDF §275(4); MHT III 199; Rob 774

31 MHT III 42; Rob 667, 688

32 MHT II 208; Rob 1187

33 BDF §275(4), 399(1); MHT III 140, 181, 199; Rob 774, 789, 890, 1058, 1081, 1394, 1424

34 DM 294, 295; MHT II 271;
MHT III 325; MHT IV 16, 26; Rob
297, 546, 551

35 MHT II 453; Zer §366n

36 MHT III 41; Zer §205

37 DM 151; MHT III 41; Rob 660,
774, 775

38 BDF §425(2); MHT II 460;
MHT III 154, 227; Rob 441,
458, 589, 1106, 1199

39 Rob 458

40 MHT I 50; MHT II 60; MHT III
45, **317**; Rob 233, 413, 458,
1106, 1130; Zer §15n

41 BDF §332(2); BW 13; DM 187,
199; Moule 82; MHT II 465;
MHT III 67, 137; Rob 838, 839,
844, 883, 884, 1032; RD
§402(b)

42 DM 199; MHT II 432, 452; Rob
411, 674, 713, 838

43 DM 199; MHT II 165; Rob 700,
838

44 BDF §332(2); DM 199; Rob 838

Chapter 13

1 BDF §423(1); MHT I 74; MHT III
322; Rob 413, 741; RD §381

2 Moule 82; MHT I 189, 191;
MHT II 190, 424, 438; MHT III
96; Rob 638, 960, 962, 1174,
1175, inset; Zer §444

3 BDF §205, 423(2); BW 13; MHT II
465; MHT III 18, 322; Rob 224,
593, 644, 930

4 MHT III 89, 112; Rob 972

5 DM 294; MHT II 455; Rob 751,
995, 996

6 MHT I 175

7 BDF §382(4); Moule 21; Rob 972

8 Moule 58; MHT III **268**

9 BDF §205; MHT II 67; MHT III
37; Rob 593, 603

10 Moule 69, 204; Rob 535

11 DM 246, 281; Moule 133; MHT I
91; MHT II 424, 432; MHT III
112; MHT IV 21; Rob 233, 709,
738, 768; RD §379

12 MHT III 313

13 MHT I 150; MHT III 45; Rob
859, 889

14 BDF §134(3); MHT II 222;
MHT III **15**, 82, 312; Rob 320,
429

15 MHT II 210; MHT III **15**; Rob
308, 599, 1405; RD §308,
406(a)

16 BDF §205; MHT III **15**; Rob 453,
525, 536, 547, 548, 586, 593,
645, 1405; RD §345(f), 361

17 MHT III 51

18 MHT III 235

19 BDF §294(1), 297, 343(3),
431(3); Moule 176; MHT I 95;
MHT II 419, 435; MHT III 46,
70, 96, 324, 325; Rob 547, 710,
715bis, 722, 731, 1390, 1391,
inset; RD §379; Zer §202

20 BDF §428(2); BW 107; DM 290;
MHT II 434; MHT III 55; Rob
424, 584, 752, 818, 1015, 1417

21 Moule 21; Rob 1170, 1419

22 MHT III 144; Rob 891, 1075,
1428; Zer §352

23 MHT III 37

24 MHT I 150; Rob 873

25 BDF §353(7); DM 232; Moule 18;
MHT I 150; MHT II 451;
MHT III 89; Rob 353, 375, 782,
873, 889, 1116, 1180; RD
§460(c)

26 MHT I 150; MHT II 447; MHT III
257; MHT IV 22; Rob 873

27 MHT I 150; MHT III 25, 175,
225; Rob 599, 775, 873

28 MHT II 60, 264; Rob 232, 341,
350, 614, 827, 1401

29 Moule 53; MHT III 27; Rob 601

30 BDF §383(2); BW 111; DM 281;
Moule 85; MHT II 115; MHT III
96, 196; Rob 873, 975, inset;
RD §420(d)

31 BDF §365(1); MHT I 190, 191;
MHT III 97; Rob 873, inset,
1405; Zer §444n

32 MHT IV 13, 92

33 Rob 1177

34 BDF §453(4), 482; MHT II 73;
MHT III **75, 77**; Rob 993, 1203

35 BDF §123(1), 186(2); MHT II 73;
MHT III 235; Rob 185, 495,

1188; RD §410(a)

36 DM 248; Moule 139; MHT III 99; Rob 987; RD §430(d)

37 Rob 720

Chapter 14

1 BDF §323(4); MHT II 420, 464; MHT III 27, 252; MHT IV 22; Rob 408, 590; Zer §3, **5**, 117

2 BDF §370(2), 481; Rob 988, 1415; RD §430(d), 470(j); Zer §344

3 BDF §113(2), 181; MHT I 55, 176; MHT II 91, 122, 379; MHT III 154; MHT IV 14; Rob 253, 339, 342, 499, 512, 607, 1127, 1131

4 BDF §239(1), 412(4); MHT II 452; MHT III 70, **153**; Rob 739, 916, 1176; RD §448(c)

5 BDF §185(4); DM 169; MHT II 198; Rob 341, 368, 511, 538, 541, 642, 666, 674, 1406

6 BW 31; MHT I 175; MHT III 264; Rob 484, 564

7 BDF §102(3); MHT III 112; Rob 299, 473, 879; Zer §278

8 BDF §392(2); MHT I 176; MHT II 445; MHT III 138, 227; Rob 551, 845, 1120; RD 461(b); Zer §289n

9 BDF §206(4), 207(1); Rob 593, 969, 1407, 1411; Zer §247

10 BDF §247(2); BW 148; MHT I 97; MHT II 211; MHT III 129; Rob 309, 675, 983, 1394

11 Rob 1036

12 MHT II 421; Rob 522, 980, 989, 1399; RD §432; Zer §363

13 Rob 333, 356, 499, 573, 873

14 BDF §378; BW 159; DM 273; MHT I 151; MHT III **109**; Rob 234bis, 442, 737, 955, 960, 969, 989, 1045, 1049, 1177, 1399, 1411; RD §414, 423(c), 431, 448(d), 452(c); Zer §343

15 MHT II 121; Rob 185, 260, 538; RD §162 f

17 'DM 185

18 MHT I 111

19 BDF §305; DM 97; Moule 60; MHT I 105; MHT II 439, 455;

MHT III 198, 268; MHT IV 23; Rob 105, 282, 450, 460, 555, 568, 606, 675; RD §470(g); Zer §10

20 Moule 24 n.1, 92; MHT III 55; MHT IV 22; Rob 231, 525, 560; RD §345(f), 360

21 BDF §360(1, 4), 428(2); Moule 149; MHT I 171, 200; MHT II 448; MHT III **92**, 284; MHT IV 14, 22; Rob 432, 1016, 1169, 1417; RD §470(c); Zer §440n

23 MHT III 209; MHT IV 15

24 Moule 63, 64, 103; MHT III 152, **271**; Rob 213, 618, 629, 632

25 BDF §382(3), 431(3), 435(a); MHT II 445; MHT III 96, 112, 227, 286; MHT IV 15, 26, 48; Rob 708, 854, 930, inset; RD §470(j)

27 Rob 538

28 MHT I 149; MHT III 57, 143, **146**, 148; Rob 355, 681, 756, 871, 1070, 1074, 1083; Zer §231

29 BDF §372(1c), 448(5), 457, 479(1); MHT III 37, **115**, 330; Rob 394, 1008, 1026bis, 1203, 1417; RD §470(n)

30 BW 36, 123; DM 87, 215; MHT I 151; MHT III 140; Rob 522bis, 550, 873, 1091; RD §421(a)

31 BDF §60(3), 365(2); MHT I 190, 191; MHT III 96, 97; Rob 529, 819, 850, 875, 1019, 1026, inset, 1405, 1418; RD §470(k); Zer §444n

32 BDF §383(2); MHT I 169; MHT II 342; Rob 976; RD §420(c)

33 MHT II 455

34 BDF §336(1); Rob 856

35 BDF §211; MHT III 66; Rob 603, 883, 993

36 BDF §211, 298(4); DM 133; Moule 92; MHT I 93, 233; MHT II 70; MHT III 49, **330**; Rob 29, 186, 461, 465, 561, 737; RD §341(c), 387(f); Zer §34, 221

37 Rob 426, 1103

38 MHT I 178; Rob 933, 994, 1153, 1170

39 MHT III 80; Zer §261

40 MHT II 230, 452; Rob 319, 339, 1183, 1213; Zer §348

41 BDF §129, 451(6); Moule 27, 161; MHT II 462; MHT III 24, **291, 336**; MHT IV 14; Rob 391, 392, 470, 487, 577, 800, 842, 866; RD §322, 401(a)

42 MHT I 175; MHT II 205; MHT III 82; Rob 312, 931; RD §308

43 MHT IV 22; Rob 526, 786

44 BDF §277(3); MHT II 190; MHT III 41, 70, 83; Rob 679, 905

45 BDF §493(1); MHT II 452; Rob 606

46 Rob 339, 684, 1213

47 BDF §111(3); Moule 24 n.1; MHT I 157; MHT II 432; MHT III 55, 196; Rob 292, 564, 684, 742, 805, 810, 828, 1110; RD §375, 382

48 DM 106; Rob 526

49 BDF §448(7); Moule 52, 144, 173; MHT II 452, 467; MHT III **95**, 330; MHT IV 13, 66; Rob 550, 625, 1187, 1203; RD §351

50 MHT II 453

51 BDF §337(1); DM 91, 111; Rob 485, 529

54 BDF §184; Moule 85; MHT II 192, 452; MHT III 54, 266; Rob 314, 548, 625, 643, 807; RD §369, 397; Zer §232

55 BDF §327; Moule 60; MHT III 143, 166; Rob 367, 607, 883; RD §364

58 BDF §223(1); MHT III 161, 267; Rob 1042

60 BDF §298(4), 299(1); MHT III 49, **67**; MHT IV 26; Rob 550, 648, 738, 775, 792, 917, 1158

61 BDF §441(2); Moule 158; Rob 695, 917, 1388; RD §398, 405; Zer §229

63 MHT I 38; MHT II 420; MHT III 27; Rob 212

64 BDF §173(1); MHT III 233; Rob 1036, 1392

65 BDF §5(3b), 198(3); Moule 192; MHT II 455; MHT III **241**; MHT IV 29; Rob 391, 530, 617

66 MHT II 432

67 MHT III 166; MHT IV 26; Rob 118, 313

68 BDF §445(2); MHT IV 14; Rob 620, 1185, 1189; RD §368

69 MHT II 455

70 Rob 612

71 MHT II 205, 455; MHT III 137; Rob 317, 371; RD §320

72 BDF §308; BW 52; MHT I 131; MHT II 11; MHT III 52, **137**, 140; Rob 509bis, 550, 800, 861bis, 1091, 1109, 1127

Chapter 15

1 MHT I 159; MHT IV 29; Rob 787, 802, 812

2 BDF §273(1); MHT I 86; MHT III 183

3 MHT II 446; Rob 367, 511, 884

4 MHT III 50; Rob 292, 917; RD §448(h)

5 MHT IV 26; Rob 473, 484

6 BDF §64(3), 367; BW 84; DM 188; Moule 124; MHT II 319; MHT III 48, 67, 93, 268; Rob 291, 608, 710, 884, 905, 922, 1154; RD §402(b), 472(e); Zer §358

7 MHT II 190; MHT III 83; Rob 255, 339, 366, 727, 841, 905

8 MHT II 455; Rob 905

9 MHT III 155; Rob 905, 1205, 1399

10 BDF §345; MHT II 190; MHT III 83; Rob 366, 841, 905, 1029; RD §403(b)

11 MHT IV 40; Rob 255

12 BDF §273(1); MHT II 421; MHT III 183; Rob 484, 718, 720

14 RD §353

15 BDF §5(3b); Moule 192; MHT I 20; MHT III 135; MHT IV 29; Rob 1385

16 BDF §184; BW 13; DM 126; Moule 85; MHT III 216; Rob 232, 411, 505, 643, 712; RD §343(k), 380

17 BDF §101; Moule 33; Rob 318, 483; RD §342(i)

18 BDF §147(3); MHT I 71; MHT II 455; Rob 465, 898

19 BDF §5(3b); Moule 192; MHT IV 29

20 DM 94; Moule 33; MHT II 75; MHT III 191; Rob 203, 542

21 MHT II 67; Rob 183, 791

22 MHT II 148; MHT III **102**; Rob 259, 411, 483, 714

23 BDF §251; BW 85; DM 128; MHT II 202, 205, 407; MHT III 37, **65**, 178; MHT IV 27; Rob 311, 695, 885; Zer §273

24 BDF §298(5); MHT II 456; Rob 737, 916, 1044, 1176; RD §381, 448(c)

25 BDF §442(4); Moule 172; MHT I 12; MHT II 421; Rob 793, 1183; Zer §455d

27 Moule 28; MHT II 438, 447, 456; MHT III 179

29 MHT III 24; Rob 231, 1193; RD §448(h)

30 DM 156; Rob 307, 802, 861, 1113; RD §396

32 MHT II 210; Rob 308, 856

33 Rob 793, 794

34 BDF §36; Moule 11 n.1, 185; MHT II 153; MHT III 72, **267**; Rob 29, 205, 261, 714

35 Rob 320

36 MHT I 175; MHT II 109; MHT III 94; Rob 430, 742, 931, 1399

38 BDF §104(2); Rob 300bis, 548, 550

39 BDF §5(1); MHT III **16**, 183; Rob 597, 649, 652, 697

40 MHT II 146, 452; Rob 297, 300, 501, 780

41 BDF §412(4); MHT II 195; MHT III 153; Rob 529

42 BDF §395; MHT I 51; Rob 965, 1139

43 MHT II 452; MHT III 166; MHT IV 26

44 BDF §454(1); DM 246, 298; Moule 154; MHT III 5, **69**; MHT IV 27; Rob 430, 845, 916, 965, 1024, 1043, 1045, 1177; RD §442; Zer §404

45 Rob 579, 760

46 MHT II 191, 387; Rob 542

47 BDF §162(3); Moule 38; MHT II 146; MHT III **168**; Rob 501, 1043bis; RD §452(b)

Chapter 16

1 BDF §162(3); MHT II 452; MHT III **168**, 278; Rob 501

2 BDF §200(1), 423; DM 106; MHT II 439; MHT III 187, 227, 322; MHT IV 22; Rob 523, 602, 672

3 Moule 91, 92; MHT IV 28; Rob 596, 597

4 MHT III 135; Rob 1035, 1041, 1190

5 MHT III **17**; Rob 408, 485

6 BW 93; Moule 15; MHT I 135, 137, 163; MHT III 57; Rob 817, 842; Zer §231

7 MHT III **330**

8 MHT IV 26

9 BDF §247(1); MHT I 216; MHT II 190; MHT III 187, 259; MHT IV 11; Rob 578, 672, 905, 1406; Zer §7

10 BDF §291(6); Rob 708

11 Rob 1422

12 BDF §306(1); Rob 293, 749, 792

13 BDF §291(6); Zer §133

14 BDF §137(3); MHT II 420; MHT III 316; Zer §151

17 BDF §480(3); MHT III 193

18 MHT I 191; MHT III 52, 96; Rob 208, 472, 1026, 1405, 1419

19 Moule 162; MHT III 143; Rob 561, 1074

20 BDF §291(6); DM 229; MHT IV 11; Rob 891, 1127

Luke

Chapter 1

1 BDF §107, 456(3), 464, p.2 n.4; BW 91; DM 197; MHT III **33**, 318; Rob 107, 121, 367, 418, 432bis, 841, 965, 1154, 1208; RD §21, 25, 324, 410, 426(b), 472(e)

2 BDF §95(1), 453, 464, p.2 n.4; MHT II 98; MHT III 320; Rob 107, 121, 308, 347, 418, 432 bis, 687, 1208, 1214; RD §21, 257 A N, 324, 410

3 BDF §60(2), 146(1a), 410, 464, p.2 n.4; DM 72; Moule 31f.; MHT II 20; MHT III 31, 33, **199**; Rob 107, 121, 221, 244, 279, 392, 418, 432bis, 463, 464, 670, 771, 1039bis, 1084, 1085, 1208; RD §21, 324, 410; Zer §394

4 BDF §294(5), 464, p.2 n.4; DM 126; Rob 107, 121, 418, 432 bis, 719, 1208; RD §21, 324, 410

5 DM 134, 138; Moule 76; Rob 292, 395, 743, 760; RD §382

6 BW 13; Moule 45; MHT II 465; MHT III 181; Rob 505, 641; RD §353

7 BDF §197; DM 85; Moule 18 n.1; MHT I 75, 103; MHT III 220; Rob 523, 587, 906, 963

8 BDF §472(3); BW 13; Moule 76, 174; MHT II 426, 450, 465; Rob 148, 505, 640, 658, 979, 1072, 1423; RD §343(k), 353, 421(c)

9 BDF §171(2), 400(3); BW 127; DM 213; MHT III 141; Rob 231, 509, 1060, 1068, 1113; RD §455(b); Zer §393

10 DM 224; Moule 17, 18 n.1, 94; MHT II 452; Rob 888

12 BDF §472(2); Rob 418, 560, 602

13 BDF §157(2); BW 105; DM 169, 192, 245; Rob 480, 964; RD §426(a); Zer §246, 280

14 MHT III 233; Rob 356, 357, 541, 871, 889

15 BDF §365(3); BW 13; Moule 113, 203; MHT I 177, 191; MHT II 103; MHT III 96, 180; MHT IV 57; Rob 270, 505, 642, 871, 933, inset, 1405; RD §343(k), 353, 401(c); Zer §181n, 444, 473

16   Rob 679, 889

17   BDF §218; DM   224; Moule 76;
     MHT II 145, 171; MHT III 23,
     257; Rob 255, 477, 562, 679,
     683

18   BDF §197; Moule 18 n.1, 59; MHT
     I 75; MHT III 37, **268**; Rob 739,
     1412

20   BDF §206(1), 353(1), 383(2); BW
     10, 26; DM 100; Moule 18, 18 n.
     1, 68, 71; MHT I 92; MHT III
     48, 88, 89; Rob 208, 353, 594,
     714, 717, 721, 728, 889, 960,
     963, 975, 1173, 1412; RD §427;
     Zer §92, 219

21   BDF §404(3); BW 37, 124; DM
     216; Moule 17, 18 n.1, 76; MHT
     II 450, 452; MHT III 146; Rob
     260bis, 532, 979, 1073, 1092;
     RD §455(b)

22   Moule 17, 18 n.1; MHT II 452;
     Rob 582, 680, 888, 1029; RD
     §374, 402(b)

23   BDF   §472(3);   Moule   174;
     MHT II 426; Rob 658, 1423; RD
     §410(a), 419(g), 424(b)

24   MHT II 214, 245; Rob 351, 617,
     1217

25   Rob 224, 566, 721, 792

26   Moule 76; MHT II 149; MHT III
     258; Zer §**90**

27   MHT II 193; Rob 364

28   MHT I 183; Rob 611

29   BDF §386(1);   DM   123, 174;
     MHT III 123, 131; MHT IV 62;
     Rob 741, 938, 1031, 1044, 1045,
     1408, 1409; RD §381; Zer §339,
     346

30   DM   108; Moule 52; Rob 614,
     647; Zer §246

31   BDF §157(2); MHT III 86; Rob
     480, 1202; Zer §280

33   BDF §233(2); MHT III 25; Rob
     602; Zer §124

34   DM 14; Rob 1159; RD §426(b)

35   BDF §138(1), 339(2b), 451(5);
     DM   245; Moule 90, 91, 107,
     113; MHT III 21, 87; Rob 409,
     560, 764, 1181; Zer §181n, 283

36   MHT III 192; MHT IV 53; Rob
     256, 267, 272, 275, 701, 790;
     RD §179(a), 208 b

37   BDF   §302(1);   MHT II   434;
     MHT III 196; Rob 752

38   Moule 23, 96f.; MHT I 195;
     MHT III 185; MHT IV 62; Rob
     940, 1408

39   DM 119; Moule 96, 187; MHT II
     453, 471; MHT III **16**; Rob 255,
     652, 708

40   Rob 255

41   BDF §173(1); MHT II 426; Rob
     506, 1423; RD §343(1); Zer
     §181n

42   BDF §245(3); DM   14; MHT II
     443; MHT III **31**; Rob 417, 422,
     660, 1199; RD §474(p); Zer §146

43   BDF §189(3), 394; DM 286, 295;
     MHT I 208, 211, 217; MHT III
     45, 139, **240**; Rob 235, 398,
     422, 699, 992, 998, 1076, 1199;
     RD §379, 435(a); Zer §410, 459

44   BDF §205; MHT III 254; Rob 422,
     1199

45   BDF §237(1); BW 24; Moule 51;
     MHT III **35**, 42; Rob 422, 615,
     689, 1199; Zer §90, 416

46   BDF §4(2a), 74(1), 259(3),
     391(4), 442(6); MHT IV 50; Rob
     242, 422, 1199

47   BDF §4(2a), 74(1), 259(3),
     391(4), 442(6); DM 106; Rob
     242, 422, 532, 605, 1199, 1212;
     RD §363; Zer §**260**

48   BDF §4(2a), 74(1), 259(3),
     391(4), 442(6); Moule 91, 96f.;
     MHT III 185; Rob 242, 355, 422,
     547, 560, 1199

49   BDF §4(2a), 74(1), 259(3),
     391(4), 442(6); MHT III 296;
     Rob 242, 422, 1199; Zer §455e

50   BDF §4(2a), 74(1), 259(3),
     391(4), 442(6), 493(2); Rob
     242, 422, 594, 1199

51   BDF §4(2a), 74(1), 259(3),
     391(4), 442(6); DM 105; MHT II
     482; MHT III 23, **74**, **228**; MHT
     IV 50; Rob 242, 422, 590, 793,
     837, 1199; Zer §256, 259

52   BDF §4(2a), 74(1), 259(3),
     391(4), 442(6); MHT III **74**; Rob
     242, 422, 837, 1199

53   BDF §4(2a), 74(1), 259(3),
     391(4), 442(6); Moule 203;
     MHT III **74**; Rob 242, 422, 510,
     837, 1199

54   BDF §4(2a), 74(1), 259(3),
     391(4), 442(6); DM 285; Moule
     127; MHT I 210; MHT III 136;
     Rob 242, 422, 508, 1001, 1086,
     1199; RD §457(b); Zer §392

55 BDF §4(2a), 74(1), 259(3), 391(4), 442(6); MHT III **238**; Rob 242, 422, 1199; Zer §55

56 DM 111; Rob 535, 562, 628, 1199

57 BDF §472(2); BW 151; MHT II 417; Rob 1039, 1052, 1061, 1076; Zer §383

58 Moule 61, 183f.; MHT I 106, 246; MHT II 466; MHT IV 50; Rob 530, 610, 611

59 BDF §326; DM 94, 106, 189; Moule 9; MHT I 129; MHT II 426; MHT III **65**; Rob 480, 523, 605, 885, 1423; RD §402(b); Zer §273

60 DM 267; Rob 391bis, 1187; RD §322, 410(a), 464(b), 470(m)

61 DM 252; Moule 46; Rob 234, 726

62 BDF §386(1); BW 113; DM 174; MHT I 198; MHT III 39, 123, 130, 182; MHT IV 62; Rob 683, 739, 766, 884, 890, 938, 940, 1021, 1025, 1031bis, 1046, 1408; RD §406(b), 408, 440, 452(c), 452(d); Zer §346

63 BDF §420(2); MHT II 375; MHT III **156**; Rob 457; Zer §368

64 BW 136; DM 228; Rob 297, 550, 885, 1127, 1201, 1213; RD §474(t)

65 BDF §472(2); Moule 96; MHT III **16**

66 BDF §299(2); Moule 208; MHT III **23**, 23; Rob 409, 736, 739

67 BDF §472(2); Rob 422; Zer §181n

68 BDF §4(2a), 259(3), 391(4), 400(6); MHT III 174; Rob 422, 1199

69 BDF §4(2a), 259(3), 391(4), 400(6); Rob 422, 1199

70 BDF §4(2a), 259(3), 269(6), 391(4), 400(6); MHT III 25, 187; MHT IV 55; Rob 107, 422, 762, 783, 1199

71 BDF §4(2a), 259(3), 391(4), 400(6); MHT III 24; Rob 422, 649, 1199

72 BDF §4(2a), 206(3), 259(3), 310(1), 391(4), 400(6); Moule 127; MHT I 210; MHT II 466; MHT III 56, 136; MHT IV 50; Rob 422, 509, 1001, 1086, 1199; Zer §19, 392

73 BDF §4(2a), 153(2), 259(3), 295, 391(4), 400(6), 400(8); Moule 127; MHT III 141, 324; Rob 422, 475, 479, 488, 718, 1199; RD §342(g); Zer §385

74 BDF §4(2a), 259(3), 391(4), 400(6); MHT III 24; Rob 422, 540, 1039, 1061, 1076, 1199

75 BDF §4(2a), 201, 259(3), 391(4), 400(6); Moule 43; MHT III 243; Rob 422, 470, 527, 1199

76 BDF §4(2a), 259(3), 391(4), 400(6), 484; MHT I 217; MHT II 466; Rob 422, 560, 678, 694, 990, 1001, 1149, 1185, 1199; RD §455(d), 472(b)

77 BDF §4(2a), 259(3), 391(4), 400(6); DM 214; MHT III 142; Rob 422, 1199; Zer §385

78 BDF §4(2a), 259(3), 391(4), 400(6); MHT III 142; Rob 422, 1001, 1199; Zer §385

79 BDF §4(2a), 259(3), 391(4), 400(6); Moule 127; MHT I 217; MHT III 52; Rob 231bis, 341, 349, 371, 422, 1086, 1199

80 BDF §165; MHT III 123; Rob 497

Chapter 2

1 BDF §5(3a), 317, 472(3); BW 151; DM 219; Moule 92; MHT I 47, 162; MHT II 87, 426, 471, 474; MHT III 57, 139; Rob 185, 417, 561, 708, 793, 809, 1076, 1086, 1423; RD §25

2 BDF §292; MHT II 60, 72; MHT III **32**, 192; Rob 82, 510, 657, 669, 701, 704, 790; RD §379; Zer §**152**

3 BDF §317; MHT I 162; MHT III 57; MHT IV 55; Rob 417, 746

4 BDF §209(3); BW 102; DM 160, 275; Moule 38; MHT I 91, 212; MHT III **47**, 142, 148; Rob 417, 578, 728bis, 729, 966, 1039, 1071, 1428; RD §428; Zer §216

5 BW 102; DM 160; MHT I 162; MHT II 105, 193; MHT III 57; Rob 216, 364, 804, 807, 809, 1080, 1214

6 MHT II 426, 450; Rob 1061, 1076, 1423; Zer §388, 389n

7 DM 245; Rob 541, 1210; RD §347(b)

8 BDF §153(3), 353(2); Moule 17; MHT III 235, 245; Rob 376, 477; RD §342(g)

9   Moule 90; MHT IV 47; Rob 542

10   Rob 538; Zer §246

11   MHT III 239; Rob 350; Zer §416

12   MHT III 192; Rob 701

13   BDF §134(1b), 472(1d); MHT II 157; MHT III 312; Rob 272, 404, 407, 412, 655, 656, 1390; RD §208(b), 346(h)

14   BDF §165; DM 106; Moule 114, 175; MHT III **213**, **264**; Rob 242, 792bis; RD §388; Zer §120

15   BW 13, 107; DM 261; Moule 22; MHT II 426; MHT III 94, 175; Rob 393, 714, 1149, 1423; RD §472(b)

16   Rob 759, 760, 861, 1109, 1113; RD §410(a)

17   MHT II 232

18   DM 82, 102; Rob 532, 619, 838

19   DM 111; MHT II 144; Rob 828, 884

20   Rob 429, 716, 717

21   BDF §157(2), 400(2), 442(7); BW 5; DM 70, 95; Moule 74; MHT II 422; MHT III 40, 141, 144; Rob 457, 480, 621, 858, 978, 1039, 1075, 1076, 1091; Zer §457

22   BDF §400(6); BW 121; Moule 128; MHT III 142, 217; Rob 491, 561, 609, 990, 1088; RD §342(o)

23   MHT II 104

24   BDF §400(6); Moule 128; MHT III 142; Rob 204, 990, 1088

25   Moule 113; Rob 395, 602, 770; RD §387(e); Zer §123, 181n

26   BDF §312(1), 383(3), 405(2), 407; BW 159; DM 232, 282; Moule 19, 133; MHT I 169; MHT III 113, 140, 148, 149, 176; MHT IV 52, 59; Rob 362, 816, 858, 977bis, 1030, 1036, 1047, 1080, 1084, 1085, 1091; RD §420(e)bis

27   BDF §183, 229(2), 404(2); Moule 63; MHT II 450, 459; MHT III **145**, 151, 176, 234, **336**; Rob 47, 490, 504, 619, 858, 979, 1039, 1065, 1073, 1081, 1109; RD §342(1), 343(j), 451(b); Zer §390, 457

28   BDF §277(3); MHT II 406; Rob 473, 593

29   BDF §259(3); Rob 1199

30   BDF §259(3); Moule 96; MHT III 14; Rob 1199; Zer §206

31   BDF §140, 259(3); DM 107; MHT II 466; MHT III 25; MHT IV 49; Rob 1199

32   BDF §259(3); Rob 210, 1199; RD §474(p)

33   Moule 17; MHT II 452; Rob 405, 412, 605; RD §326

34   BDF §339(2b); MHT III 87; Zer §283

35   Moule 138; MHT III **105**; Rob 687, 986, 1413; RD §430(b)

36   BDF §197; Moule 34; MHT I 75; Rob 723

37   BW 148; Moule 45; MHT II 60, 172; Rob 232, 495, 518, 559, 576, 680bis; RD §343(e), 344(e)

38   MHT II 432; MHT III 194; MHT IV 53; Rob 523, 541, 574, 686; RD §345(c), 376

39   MHT I 130; Rob 766, 800, 841

41   BW 37; DM 107; MHT III **22**, 67; Rob 224, 270, 523, 608, 884; RD §345(c); Zer **§276**

42   Moule 101, 101 n.1; MHT III **81**, 154; Rob 497

43   Moule 76, 101; MHT II 450; MHT III **145**, 166

44   DM 82; MHT II 138, 350; MHT III 212; Rob 269, 469, 479, 496, 1036, 1060; RD §342(e)

45   Zer §284

46   MHT II 426; Rob 491, 1423; RD §342(o)

47   BDF §442(16); MHT III 66; Rob 883

48   Moule 8; MHT III 62; Rob 402, 879; RD §326

49   BDF §162(8); BW 84; DM 188, 252; Moule 75; MHT I 103; MHT III 261; Rob 502, 586, 739, 767, 884, 1034, 1176; RD §381, 448(c), 448(e)

50   BDF §347(2); Rob 680bis; Zer **§290**

51   MHT II 452; Rob 828, 884; Zer **§360**

Chapter 3

1 BDF §111(2); MHT II 175; Rob
   189, 255, 510, 523, 788, 793

2 BDF §162(1); BW 10; DM 107;
   MHT III 174, 207; Rob 255bis,
   501, 603

5 MHT II 462; MHT III **16**, 253;
   Rob 458, 595, 652

6 Moule 96; MHT III 14; Rob 772

7 BDF §149

8 MHT I 15; MHT II 455; MHT III
   168; Rob 853

9 DM 185, 251; MHT III 63, **199**;
   Rob 870

10 BW 108; DM 171, 188; Rob 850,
   916, 934, 1176; RD §448(c)

11 DM 227; Moule 62; MHT II 100

12 Rob 243, 996

13 Moule 51; MHT II 165; MHT III
   151, 216; Rob 187, 667

14 MHT II 74; MHT III 27, 57, 151;
   MHT IV 47, 152; Rob 409, 532,
   541, 582, 626, 853, 1173

15 BDF §370(3), 386(2); BW 114; DM
   297; MHT I 194, 199; MHT III
   23, 123, 130; MHT IV 62; Rob
   939, 940, 988, 996, 1031, 1044,
   1045, 1177, 1408, 1409, 1415;
   RD §448(d), 452(c)

16 BDF §195(1d); DM 261; MHT I
   95, 237; MHT II 434, 458;
   MHT III 240; Rob 355, 521, 722,
   828; RD §342(j), 345(b), 360;
   Zer §201, 229

17 MHT II 10, 434; Rob 260, 503;
   Zer §201

18 BDF §451(1); DM 251(2); Moule
   45, 162; MHT III 197, 337; Rob
   474, 749bis, 1181

19 BDF §260(1), 294(5); Rob 258,
   512, 619, 717, 719; RD §343(m)

20 BDF §235(3), 461(2); MHT II
   438; Rob 605bis; Zer §128

21 BDF §404(2); MHT II 427, 438,
   450; MHT III **145**; Rob 371, 771,
   1073, 1423; RD §387(e), 451(a);
   Zer §390

22 Moule 69; MHT II 458; Rob 795,
   837bis

23 BDF §162(2), 453(3); MHT I 227,
   236; MHT III **168**, 321; Rob 236,
   761, 1102

24 Rob 215, 236, 263, 761

25 MHT II 144; Rob 215, 236, 761

26 MHT II 144; Rob 236, 761,
   1413bis

27 Rob 214, 236, 761

28 Rob 236, 761, 1413

29 Rob 215, 236, 761

30 Rob 236, 761

31 Rob 236, 761

32 Rob 214, 236, 761

33 Rob 236, 255, 761

34 Rob 236, 761

35 Rob 236, 761

36 Rob 236, 761

37 Rob 184, 236, 761

38 Rob 236, 761

Chapter 4

1 BDF §218, 418(6); DM 244;
   Moule 205; MHT III **159**, 257;
   Rob 396, 880, 1185

2 RD §470(j)

3 BW 164; DM 294; MHT III 183;
   Rob 781, 1009bis; RD §437

4 Zer §226

6 Rob 701, 771; RD §387(e)

7 BDF §187(2); Rob 234, 540

8 Moule 178

9 MHT II 148; MHT III 183; Rob
   834

10 MHT I 116; MHT II 450;
   MHT III 141; Rob 582, 642, 762,
   1068; Zer §386

11 Rob 1415

12 Moule 179

13 BW 10; Rob 505, 576, 771, 791,
   974; RD §353, 387(e), 420(b)

14 BDF §225; BW 12; Moule 60; Rob
   607

15 BDF §277(3); BW 137; DM 229;
   Rob 1127

16 BDF §189(1); BW 33; DM 85;
   MHT II 149; MHT III 27, 151;

Rob 219, 299, 358, 523, 537, 881, 909

17 DM 278; MHT II 92; MHT III 173; Rob 29, 103

18 BW 26; Moule 83, 177; MHT I 143; MHT II 67; Rob 425, 641, 901; RD §353

19 Moule 40; MHT II 57; MHT III **211**

20 BDF §275(1); Moule 102, 109; MHT II 452; MHT III **158, 200**; Rob 757, 773; RD §386(a)

21 BDF §341; MHT II 455

22 BW 8, 41; Moule 50; MHT II 440; MHT III 213; Rob 418, 496, 532, 651, 697, 838, 1406; Zer §40

23 BDF §205; MHT III 161; Rob 402, 864, 1035, 1103, 1207

24 MHT III 89; RD §383

25 Moule 75; MHT I 60; MHT II 123, 145; MHT III **21**; Rob 253, 255, 410, 523, 602, 604; Zer §470

26 BDF §448(8); MHT I 241; MHT II 433, 468; MHT III **330**; Rob 219, 263, 399, 1016, 1187, 1203; RD §332

27 BDF §448(8); MHT II 67; Rob 214, 603

28 Moule 109; Rob 1127; RD §462 (a)

29 BDF §390(3), 391(3); BW 121; DM 215, 284; Moule 140; MHT II 191, 250, 453; MHT III 136; Rob 365, 603, 905, 990, 1000, 1089, 1414; RD §403(b), 435(c), 457(c); Zer §352

30 Rob 550, 565, 581, 648, 775, 791, 905

31 MHT II 452

32 BDF §198(2); Zer §386

33 MHT I 227

34 MHT II 150; MHT III **13**; Rob 391 bis, 488, 539, 738, 1193; RD §448(h)

35 BDF §443(1); Moule 32, 34; MHT III 246; Rob 230, 231, 472, 482, 484, 648, 860, 1172; RD §342(i)

36 BDF §456(2); MHT II 126; MHT III 318; Rob 735, 1001; Zer §420

37 Rob 261

38 BDF §260(2); MHT II 452, 453; Rob 619

39 MHT II 453

40 BDF §75; MHT II 194, 205; Rob 800

41 BW 98; DM 206; MHT II 448; MHT III 183, 292, 313; MHT IV 46; Rob 404, 1035, 1041, 1103, 1421; RD §326

42 Moule 9; MHT I 220; Rob 643, 1061bis, 1078, 1089, 1094, 1171, 1425; RD §455 (b)

43 BDF §306(2); MHT III **197**; MHT IV 53; Rob 474, 748, 776

44 MHT II 452

Chapter 5

1 BDF §442(5); Moule 76, 121; MHT II 426, 450, 452; MHT III 335; Rob 375, 393, 615, 1183; Zer §199n, 390, 455g

2 Moule 91; Rob 559

3 BDF §304; BW 29, 46; DM 76, 190; Moule 139; MHT II 270, 432, 442; MHT III **50**, 52, 154; Rob 597, 733

4 BW 160; MHT III 52, 159; Rob 431, 860, 891, 1102, 1121

5 BW 10; Moule 56, 120; MHT II 208; MHT III 199, 272; Rob 339, 582, 604, 774, 1186; Zer §126

6 MHT II 193, 206; Rob 212, 318, 885, 1219bis; Zer §273

7 BDF §236(4), 338(1); DM 107, 286; Moule 51; MHT III 141, 198, 273; Rob 529, 616, 745, 748, 769, 1039, 1068, 1425; Zer §274, 386, 394

8 BDF §474(6); Moule 72; Zer §88

9 BDF §294(2); DM 111; Rob 433, 628, 717

10 BDF §190(1); DM 145, 146, 232; Moule 18; MHT III 89, 239; Rob 353, 504, 528, 765, 889; RD §387(a)

11 Rob 1423

12 MHT II 426, 433, 450; MHT III 179; Rob 334, 393, 792, 817, 849, 1183, 1418, 1423; RD §344(e); Zer §390

13 BDF §420(2); MHT III 156

14 BDF §229(1), 470(2); MHT II 204; MHT III 40, 326; Rob 442, 537

16 Moule 17; MHT II 452; Rob 1406

17 DM 225; Moule 17; MHT II 426, 433; MHT III 143; Rob 323, 393, 788, 888, 906, 1183, 1379, 1423, 1425; RD §403(b), 410(a); Zer §199n

18 Zer §375

19 BDF §186(1); BW 12; Moule 39; MHT I 73; MHT III **16**, 235; Rob 494, 506, 550, 561, 636, 652, 740bis, 1029, 1044, 1202; RD §343(d), 452(c)

20 Rob 315, 342, 1216; RD §11, 304

21 BDF §142, 420(2); MHT II 16, 455; MHT III **26**, 156, **226**; Rob 703; Zer §7n, 368

22 MHT III 23; MHT IV 22

23 MHT I 119; Rob 315, 896

24 BDF §336(1), 470(3); MHT III 75; MHT IV 52, 58; Rob 434, 907, 1203, 1388

25 Rob 642, 1393

26 Rob 845

27 BW 50; DM 108; Moule 92; Rob 263, 612

28 MHT II 453

29 MHT II 452; Rob 263

30 Moule 159; Rob 611

32 Rob 844

33 BDF §154; Moule 35, 120; MHT III 56; Rob 478; Zer §227

34 DM 105, 113; MHT II 441; MHT IV 49; Rob 978, 1085, 1391

35 BDF §382(3)

36 BDF §272, 444(3); Moule 91; Rob 560, 1025, 1027, 1182, 1378

37 MHT III 41; Rob 356

38 BDF §65(3), 127(4); MHT I 222; MHT II 188, 224; Rob 157, 373, 486, 1097; RD §316(g), 342(j), 458

39 Moule 97; MHT II 442; MHT III 31

41 MHT IV 22

Chapter 6

1 BDF §115(2); BW 39; DM 89; Moule 91; MHT I 17; MHT II 175, 269, 427; Rob 168, 393, 533, 560, 1043, 1423

2 BW 149; MHT III 195; MHT IV 22; Rob 235, 425

3 BDF §107, 455(1); Moule 133; MHT I 168; Rob 300, 726, 971, 1045

4 BDF §372(2a), 409(3), 428(1); MHT I 171; MHT II 440; MHT III 137, 149; Rob 435, 714, 1032, 1039, 1084

6 MHT II 427; Rob 393, 684, 748, 1423; Zer §455e

7 MHT III 55; Rob 1103

8 Moule 109; MHT III 186; Rob 680, 800

10 MHT II 189

11 BDF §386(1); BW 114; MHT I 198; MHT II 216; MHT III 123, 130; MHT IV 62; Rob 327, 854, 885, 938, 940bis, 1021, 1408; RD §307, 406(b)

12 MHT II 427, 452; Rob 500, 582, 1040, 1049, 1058, 1085, 1423

13 BW 29; MHT I 65; Rob 428, 477, 577

14 BDF §444(4); Rob 428, 480

15 Rob 428

16 BDF §162(4); MHT II 145; MHT III **168**; Rob 428, 501, 767

17 MHT II 158; Rob 28, 273, 428, 579, 613, 714

18 Moule 73

19 Moule 94

20 DM 252; Rob 593, 681, 683, 770, 910, 1393; RD §320, 375, 410(b), 1393

21 Rob 333, 356

22 MHT II 67; MHT III 72, 285; Rob 641, 834; RD §353

23 MHT I 129, 174; Rob 208, 523, 687, 855; Zer §242

24 MHT III 206; Rob 1107, 1187, 1193; RD §410(a)

25 BDF §412(5); MHT III 35, 153; Rob 333, 355, 459, 466, 1107, 1193; RD §320

26   Rob 208

27   BDF §462(2); Rob 428, 473

28   Rob 473bis

29   BDF §180(1), 337(2); Moule 41;
     MHT I 79, 125, 174; MHT III
     235; Rob 518

30   MHT I 119, 129, 174; MHT III
     76, 151; Rob 855, 890, 1214

31   MHT III 293

32   BDF §372(3); DM 292; MHT III
     115; Rob 740, 1019, 1026

33   Rob 850, 1019, 1418

34   DM 172; Rob 576, 720, 721, 1010

35   MHT I 65; MHT II 62, 98; Rob
     223, 476; RD §33 b

36   MHT II 458

37   BW 109, 117; DM 172; Moule 33;
     MHT I 191; MHT III 96; Rob 930,
     948, 1164, 1182, inset

38   BDF §29(2), 101; BW 117; Moule
     27, 28, 33; MHT II 69; MHT III
     240, 291, 293; Rob 184, 213,
     718, 828, 1136; Zer §2

39   BDF §427(2); DM 265; MHT II 71;
     MHT III **283**; Rob 917ter, 1157,
     1175

40   Rob 1105

41   BDF §286(1); DM 131; MHT I 90;
     MHT II 103, 419; Rob 691

42   BDF §430(2); BW 107; DM 171;
     Moule 22; MHT I 175, 231, 232;
     MHT III 41, 94, 139; Rob 312,
     597bis, 686, 932, 980, 1138,
     1139, 1214, 1399; RD §308, 362,
     376; Zer §279, 440n

44   Moule 28; MHT II 447; MHT III
     293

45   MHT III **14**; Rob 676, 762, 763

47   MHT II 424; MHT III **79**, **233**;
     Rob 436, 1398; Zer §65, 69, 249

48   BDF §101, 153(3), 293(2),
     471(4); MHT II 101, 193, 250,
     403; MHT III **79**, 152; Rob 212,
     214, 232, 256, 365, 530, 551,
     712, 779, 909, 1071, 1081,
     1091, 1105, 1136, 1407; RD
     §155 c, 320; Zer §460

49   BDF §293(2); MHT III **79**; Rob
     212, 648, 785, 1105, 1114; Zer
     §249

Chapter 7

1   BDF §414(2), 455(1); DM 280;
     MHT III 159, 321; Rob 841,
     965bis, 971; RD §419(c)

2   MHT III 89; Rob 1383

3   DM 294; MHT III 106; Rob 582,
     995; RD §434(b); Zer §408

4   BDF §5(3b), 379; BW 111, 152;
     DM 273; Moule 92, 192; MHT II
     114; MHT III 139; Rob 724, 872,
     884, 961, 996, 1399; RD §349,
     414; Zer §343, 349

5   Rob 367; RD §434(d)

6   BDF §418(4); BW 83; MHT I 156;
     MHT III **66**, 139, 157, 216; Rob
     518, 807; Zer §410

7   DM 245; MHT II 421; Rob 1023

8   BDF §336(1); MHT III **64**; Rob
     767, 856, 865; RD §401(b)

9   Rob 290, 474

11   MHT II 426; Rob 523, 530, 547,
     660, 774, 1423

12   BDF §190(4), 442(7); BW 149,
     160; MHT II 60; MHT III 335;
     Rob 232, 536, 537, 680, 1116,
     1183, 1397; RD §347(e); Zer
     §199n, 457

13   Moule 53; MHT I 125; Rob 1430

14   DM 175; Moule 26

15   MHT II 455

16   MHT I 135; Rob 842

17   BDF §218; MHT III **257**; Rob 586

18   DM 134; MHT III **195**; Rob 194,
     258

19   BW 131; MHT I 80; Rob 742, 748,
     1108, 1116, 1118; RD §382

20   Moule 92

21   MHT II 432; MHT IV 53; Rob 818

22   MHT II 453; MHT III 58, 154,
     331

23   MHT II 464

24   BDF §448(4); MHT II 455; Rob
     857, 1080

25   Rob 364, 816

27   BDF §378; MHT II 466; Rob 872,
     960

28 Moule 42, 98; MHT II 459;
MHT III 30; Rob 234, 504

30 BDF §192; Rob 535, 594

31 Rob 1392; Zer §65

32 MHT I 82; MHT III 153, 179; Rob
778, 792, 1107; Zer §192

33 Rob 519, 1189

34 MHT II 433; MHT IV 49

35 BW 92; DM 197; Moule 13, 73,
178; MHT II 461; MHT III 73;
Rob 837; Zer §43

36 MHT III 209; Rob 742

37 Rob 586, 1035

38 BW 40; Moule 86; MHT II 127,
455; Rob 262, 525, 533bis, 645,
799; RD §163 B b, 346(f); Zer
§247

39 BW 106; DM 289; Moule 149;
MHT III 48; Rob 292, 727, 736,
741bis, 887, 923, 1012, 1014,
1048, 1049, 1177; RD §381ter,
405, 408, 438bis; Zer §368, 416

40 DM 218; Rob 742, 1087

41 Rob 201, 668, 749, 750, 920; RD
§378

42 BDF §164(1); Moule 98; MHT II
165; MHT III 209; Rob 515, 668,
737

43 Moule 98; Rob 393, 659, 720,
1034, 1048, 1379

44 DM 106; MHT II 127; Rob 262,
701; RD §163 B b

45 BDF §241(2); MHT III 17, 159,
226; Rob 581, 653, 717, 978,
1102, 1121

47 Moule 95, 147; MHT II 206;
MHT III 319; Rob 647, 720, 722,
774, 777, 962, 966; RD §410(a),
427; Zer §**422, 427**

49 MHT II 455; MHT III 312; Rob
703, 724, 735, 961

50 BDF §206(1); Moule 79; MHT II
463

Chapter 8

1 DM 107; MHT II 426; Rob 587,
608, 680, 1423

2 BDF §315; BW 99; DM 206; MHT II
448; MHT III **53**, 292; MHT IV 46

3 Moule 46; Rob 214, 215, 599,
749

4 BDF §99(1); BW 24; DM 102; Rob
313, 505, 583

5 BDF §250, 447(3), 488(1a); MHT
II 450; MHT III 36, 145; Rob
107, 478, 695, 749, 990, 1072,
1073, 1152, 1153; RD §457(d);
Zer §390

6 BDF §250, 306(2); DM 275; MHT I
79; MHT II 375; MHT III 197;
Rob 350, 749, 966; RD §311

7 Moule 75, 85; MHT I 79; Rob
216, 341, 350, 644, 749

8 MHT I 79; Rob 284, 350, 749,
777

9 BDF §386(1); MHT III 123, 131;
MHT IV 62; Rob 736, 938, 1031,
1408

10 BDF §369(2); MHT II 204;
MHT III **102**; Rob 993; RD §320,
426(c)

11 Rob 704

12 BDF §468(3); MHT II 434;
MHT III 23; MHT IV 21, 53; Rob
233; Zer §375

13 BW 50; Moule 53; Rob 625, 793

14 BDF §468(3); Moule 209; MHT II
424, 453; Rob 704, 708, 1164;
Zer §375

15 MHT II 424; MHT III 23; Rob
176, 1182, 1201

16 BDF §5(1); MHT II 202; MHT III
279; Rob 318, 634

17 BDF §365(3), 448(8); MHT II
436; MHT III 96; Rob 726, 764,
1001, 1158, 1164, inset; Zer
§425

18 BDF §380(1); MHT III 284; Rob
957, 962, 1170; RD §417

19 Rob 530

20 Rob 349, 881; RD §311

21 Rob 700

22 MHT II 426; Rob 675, 1379, 1423

23 MHT II 394; MHT III 72; Rob
834, 838, 884, 885

24 BDF §493(1); MHT II 206; Rob
787, 879, 1200; RD §474(h)

25 BDF §444(3), 456(2); MHT II
436; MHT III 318; MHT IV 45;
Rob 541, 697, 917, 1176; RD

§435(b), 448(d)

26 BW 12; Moule 82; MHT III 216;
    Rob 573, 638, 639, 728; RD §353

27 BDF §201; BW 42; DM 90; Moule
    16, 43; MHT I 75; MHT III 244;
    Rob 527, 528, 809, 841; RD
    §346(b); Zer §282

28 MHT III 156; MHT IV 17; Rob
    234, 463, 464, 519

29 BDF §201; DM 206; Moule 9, 10,
    43; MHT I 75, 113, 148; MHT II
    121, 386; MHT III 65, **67, 243**;
    Rob 212, 262, 318, 392, 527,
    543, 581, 827, 905; RD §163 A,
    346(b), 359; Zer §54

30 MHT II 76; MHT III 296, 313;
    Rob 404; RD §326

31 Rob 252

33 Rob 607; RD §364, 402(b)

34 Rob 339

35 BDF §164(2); Moule 72; MHT III
    208, 313; MHT IV 46; Rob 339

36 Rob 1043, 1045

37 BDF §328; MHT III 65; Rob 1186

38 BDF §392(1c), 409(5); MHT I 54;
    MHT II 90, 195, 199; Rob 203,
    342, 1214; RD §320

39 Rob 608, 733; Zer §7n

40 BDF §404(2); Moule 128; MHT II
    450, 452; MHT III 145; Rob 107,
    587, 891, 1073

41 BDF §277(3), 290(1); BW 5; Rob
    697

42 BDF §453(3); MHT I 114; MHT II
    60, 450; Rob 232, 680, 827; Zer
    §273, 390

43 MHT I 102; MHT II 171; Rob 367,
    1105, 1115

45 Rob 828

46 MHT I 229; MHT III **160, 161**;
    Rob 234, 742, 910, 1035, 1042,
    1103, 1109, 1118, 1123; RD
    §451(c); Zer §268

47 MHT III 137; Rob 718, 721,
    726bis, 966, 1045bis, 1032; RD
    §427

48 BDF §206(1); DM 103; MHT II
    463; MHT III 35; Rob 264, 462

49 Moule 7; MHT I 121, 125; Rob
    742, 827, 867, 890, 895

50 BDF §336(3); MHT III **75**; Rob
    549; RD §350; Zer **§242**

51 Rob 752

52 BDF §336(3); Moule 24, 33;
    MHT I 125; MHT III **76**; Rob 475,
    809, 853, 1166

53 MHT II 195; Rob 341, 827, 838

54 BDF §111(3), 126(3), 147(3); DM
    71; Moule 26, 32; MHT I 70;
    MHT III 52; Rob 264, 465, 769;
    RD §172(c)

55 Rob 1049, 1085

56 MHT III 151; Rob 1109

Chapter 9

1 MHT III 55; Rob 427

3 BDF §389; BW 126; Moule 52,
   126; MHT I 179; MHT II 100;
   MHT III **78**; Rob 571, 944, 1047,
   1092, 1189, 1409

4 Rob 1047

5 Rob 437, 733, 1047

6 MHT II 420; Rob 299, 608

7 DM 135; Rob 743, 750, 1049,
   1071, 1109

8 BDF §306(5); MHT II 438;
   MHT III **305**; Rob 233, 636, 747,
   1392

9 BDF §322; BW 82; MHT III 37,
   46, 62; Rob 710, 1186; RD §379

10 MHT III 18; Rob 691, 733, 1423;
    Zer §97

11 Rob 367

12 MHT II 171, 455; MHT III 52;
    Rob 800; RD §396

13 BDF §185(4), 376; MHT I 171,
    187; MHT II 75; Rob 201, 666,
    751, 762, 1016, 1017, 1025,
    1172, 1186, 1399; Zer §332

14 BDF §158; BW 51; Moule 35, 60;
    MHT III 187, 266; Rob 482, 487,
    968

15 Rob 771

16 MHT III 67; Rob 561; Zer **§271**

17 MHT II 171

18 Moule 17 n.1, 134; MHT II 426,
    450; MHT III **18**, 87, 89; Rob
    371, 375, 431, 891, 1035, 1036,
    1423; RD §456; Zer §390

19   Rob 695, 1047

20   Rob 1036

22   Rob 579, 762;   Zer §265n

23   MHT II 421; MHT III **76**; Rob
     681, 688, 690, 811; RD §397;
     Zer §242n

24   BDF §283(4); MHT III **43**; Rob
     641, 688, 689, 698; Zer §212

25   BW 134; MHT I 87, 230; MHT III
     43, 80, 157; Rob 816, 1023,
     1129

26   Zer §205

27   MHT III 96, 233; Rob 473, 743,
     inset

28   BDF §144, 442(5); DM 108; MHT I
     70; MHT II 426; MHT III 231,
     335; Rob 107, 434, 460, 968,
     1398, 1423

29   Moule 17 n.1, 134; MHT II 450;
     MHT III 87, **145**; Rob 163, 748,
     1073; Zer §390

30   Rob 957

31   MHT I 53; Rob 343, 884, 1423

32   BW 44; DM 111; Moule 13, 81;
     MHT II 301; MHT III **71**, 265;
     Rob 529, 533, 582, 628, 766; RD
     §370

33   MHT II 426, 450; MHT III 117,
     149; Rob 299, 720, 726, 750,
     931, 1030, 1048, 1423; Zer
     §348, 390

34   BDF §404(2); MHT II 103, 450;
     MHT III 148; Rob 885; Zer §390

35   Rob 507, 818

36   BDF §294(4), 343(3), 345,
     404(2); DM 126; MHT I 52, 144;
     MHT II 221, 450; MHT III 70,
     324; Rob 337, 364, 657, 680,
     720, 776, 834, 897bis; Zer §390

37   BDF §186(2), 223(1); MHT II
     426; MHT III 235, 267; Rob 393,
     529, 774, 1423

38   BW 33; MHT II 60; MHT III 149;
     Rob 232, 541

39   Rob 231, 296

40   BDF §134(3); MHT III 312; Rob
     993

41   BDF §146(2); DM 110; Moule 52;
     MHT III 35; Rob 264, 299, 463,
     464, 623

42   BDF §101, 423(2); MHT II 193,
     403; MHT III 322; Rob 212, 818

43   Rob 537, 716, 717, 883

44   MHT III 24; Rob 883; Zer §198

45   BDF §391(5); Moule 142, 142
     n.2; MHT I 210; MHT III **102**,
     234; Rob 509, 812, 883, 998,
     1212; RD §397; Zer §352, 353

46   BDF §202, 218, 386(1); BW 114;
     Moule 76; MHT I 198; MHT III
     123, 130, 182; MHT IV 62; Rob
     424, 491, 585, 739, 766, 890,
     938, 940, 1021, 1031, 1044,
     1046, 1176, 1408; RD §440,
     452(c)

47   BW 36; Moule 52; MHT II 319;
     MHT III 23; Rob 614

48   Moule 152; MHT III 30, **31**; Rob
     668, 698, 954; Zer §146

49   BDF §193(1), 326; Moule 9;
     MHT III **65**; Rob 611, 838, 864,
     885, 892, 964, 1030, 1034,
     1041, 1048

50   BDF §380(1); Rob 607, 720, 956,
     962, 1158

51   Moule 76; MHT II 259, 426, 450;
     Rob 349, 426, 951, 1002, 1042,
     1068, 1183, 1423; RD §435(d);
     Zer §389n, 390

52   BDF §390(3), 391(1, 3), 425(3);
     BW 122; DM 215, 284; Moule 140;
     MHT II 466; MHT III 134, 136,
     169; Rob 621, 967, 987, 990,
     1089, 1091, 1414; RD §424(b),
     432, 457(c); Zer §352

53   BDF §353(1); MHT II 452

54   BDF §366(3); MHT I 185; MHT II
     421, 450; MHT III **99**; Rob 561,
     858, 878, 935, 1046, 1080,
     1399; RD §329

55   BDF §300(1); MHT III 49; Rob
     731, 740bis

56   Rob 748

57   BW 111; DM 270, 278; MHT II
     422; Rob 969, 1411; RD §423(c)

58   BDF §368; Moule 139; MHT II
     347; MHT III **109**; Rob 969,
     1044, 1045; RD §452(c)

59   BDF §306(2), 410; MHT III 149,
     197; Rob 1039, 1084

60   BDF §488(1c); Rob 582, 1201

61   BDF §205, 306(2); MHT III **197**;
     Rob 536, 593; Zer §100

62   Rob 1097

Chapter 10

1 BDF §248(1); BW 49; DM 99, 108;
   Moule 67; MHT I 97; MHT II 439,
   466; MHT III 41, 187, 266, 311;
   MHT IV 50; Rob 284, 299, 571,
   655, 673bis, 749, 884, 969; RD
   §356, 378, 423(b)

2 Rob 1413; Zer §408

3 BDF §47(4); Moule 85; MHT II
   135; Rob 644; RD §188c

4 BW 49; DM 107, 300; MHT I 125;
   MHT III **77**; Rob 608, 853, 1172,
   1409

5 Rob 537;   RD §336

6 BDF §362, 480(6); MHT II 441;
   MHT III 52, 208; MHT IV 49; Rob
   334, 357, 394, 561, 819, 849,
   874, 948, 1025

7 BW 70; DM 129, 144, 301; Moule
   52, 93, 122; MHT I 91, 125;
   MHT III 15, 194; MHT IV 53; Rob
   408, 561, 615, 709, 757; RD
   §386(b); Zer §205

8 MHT II 429; Rob 437, 849, 959,
   1115, 1418

10 Rob 437, 849, 1418

11 BW 32; Rob 401, 539, 699

13 BDF §134(2); MHT II 50; Rob
   1417

14 MHT II 405; Rob 1409

15 Rob 643, 678; RD §353

16 Rob 418

17 Rob 543, 1181; RD §410(a)

18 Moule 206; MHT I 134; Rob 843,
   864, 883, 910, 1041, 1042,
   1114, 1116, 1123bis; RD
   §403(a), 451(c), 460(b),
   460(c); Zer **§269**

19 BDF §431(3); BW 13; MHT III 97;
   Rob 875, 890, 1061, 1076, 1165,
   1175, 1405, inset

20 MHT I 125; MHT III 25, 313; Rob
   965, 1035, 1173bis; Zer §445

21 Moule 76, 93, 122; MHT I 91;
   MHT II 432, 465; MHT III 194;
   MHT IV 53; Rob 464, 524, 709,
   764, 788; Zer **§180**, 452

22 Rob 845, 959

23 MHT II 437; MHT III 18, 38; Zer
   §424

24 DM 250; Rob 339, 678, 843

25 DM 136; Moule 103; MHT II 309;
   MHT III 157, 232; Rob 743, 796;
   RD §384

26 Rob 423, 917, 1176; RD §448(d)

27 BDF §275(4); MHT II 181;
   MHT III 199; Rob 765

28 MHT II 421; Rob 949; RD §407;
   Zer §226

29 DM 251; Moule 86, 102; MHT III
   157; Rob 234, 547, 646, 765,
   1182; RD §349; Zer §459

30 BDF §414(1); BW 35; Moule 125;
   MHT II 241; Rob 521, 524, 542,
   634, 1113; RD §345(b)

31 Moule 70, 71; Rob 165, 565,
   572, 613; RD §318(b), 357

32 Moule 70, 71

34 BDF §73; MHT II 108; Rob 219,
   508, 691, 817, 1220; RD §343(1)

35 BDF §404(2); BW 154; MHT II
   108, 450; MHT III **145**, 148; Rob
   107, 243, 291, 602, 681, 688,
   729, 959bis, 964, 1039; RD
   §380; Zer §390

36 DM 103; Moule 86, 92; MHT I
   146; Rob 501, 561, 585, 593,
   646, 765, 908

37 BDF 206(3), 310(1); Moule 61,
   103; MHT II 466; MHT III 56,
   152; MHT IV 50; Rob 611, 802

38 MHT II 450; Rob 633, 743; Zer
   §390

39 BDF §289, 290(1); DM 128;
   MHT II 145, 319; MHT III **44**;
   Rob 289, 613, 696

40 BDF §392(1f); BW 53, 129; DM
   218; Moule 28, 62; Rob 529,
   560, 565, 573, 618, 620, 627,
   816, 1087, 1090, 1422; RD
   §318(b), 346(h), 357, 367, 370

41 BDF §493(1); Moule 62; MHT II
   435; Rob 816

42 Moule 91; MHT I 92; MHT II 145;
   Rob 518, 559, 562, 728, 810,
   819; Zer §146, 218

Chapter 11

1 DM 280; MHT II 426, 450; Rob
   371, 375, 429, 742bis, 891,
   952, 1036, 1042, 1181, 1423;
   Zer §390

2   BDF §192, 382(4); Moule 135; MHT III 112; Rob 852

3   BDF §123(1), 337(4); DM 146; Moule 59, 135; MHT I 129, 173, 174; MHT II 313; MHT III **77**; Rob 159, 487, 766, 852, 855, 1214; Zer §74, 242

4   DM 302; Moule 135; MHT I 119; MHT III **77**, 151, 200; Rob 315, 335, 541, 744, 773, 852, 853, 880, 963, 1216; RD §320

5   BDF §366(1), 442(3); Moule 23; MHT II 73; MHT III 99, 320; Rob 185, 738, 875, 930, 934, 1399; RD §406(a); Zer §297, 321

6   BDF §379; DM 270; Moule 23, 139; MHT III **109**, 320; Rob 720, 726, 960, 965, 996; RD §410(b), 414, 434(d); Zer §343

7   BDF §104(2), 205; Moule 68; MHT I 125; MHT III 99; Rob 340, 362, 593, 853, 947, 1170, 1399; RD §465; Zer §100, 321

8   BDF §372(3), 428(1), 439(3); DM 292; MHT III 284, 330; Rob 244, 518, 733bis, 1012, 1026, 1027, 1070, 1071, 1148bis, 1149, 1417, 1428

9   DM 301; MHT II 83, 419, 421; MHT III **75**; Rob 357, 1213; Zer **§242**

10 MHT II 83; Rob 1213

11 BDF §469; DM 100; Moule 35, 92, 156 n.2; MHT III **247**, 258; Rob 436, 439, 490, 573, 738; Zer §92

12 Moule 156 n.2

13 BDF §437; MHT III 25; Rob 548, 599, 1045, 1204, 1417; Zer §242

14 BW 132; MHT II 426, 452; Rob 1119, 1423

15 MHT III 210; Rob 515, 749

16 Zer §80

17 MHT II 438; Rob 750

18 BDF §372(3), 408; DM 251; MHT III 116; Rob 750, 891, 1081; Zer §420

19 MHT II 430; MHT III 37

20 MHT III 180; Rob 1008, 1416

21 MHT III 43, 112; Rob 690, 779

22 Moule 98; MHT II 190; MHT III 112; Rob 231, 366, 580, 904, 971; RD §419(c)

23 BW 27; RD §343(k)

24 BDF §134(3); MHT III 312; Rob 969; RD §423(a)

26 MHT II 431; MHT III 313; Rob 775

27 MHT II 110, 426, 450; Rob 219, 1423; Zer §390

28 BDF §450(4); DM 261; Moule 163, 167; MHT III 338; Rob 1151; RD §472(d)

29 MHT II 455, 468; MHT III **214**; Rob 500

30 Rob 1190

31 BDF §173(1); Moule 177; MHT II 146, 165, 430

32 Moule 204; MHT III **266**; Rob 963

33 BDF §5(1), 138(2); MHT III **21**; Rob 231, 764

34 DM 281; MHT III 112; Rob 284, 971; RD §419(c)

35 BDF §370(3); DM 265; MHT I 192; MHT III 305; Rob 995, 1045, 1169; RD §434(c), 470(e)

36 MHT III 305; Rob 1397

37 BDF §404(2); BW 44; Moule 128; MHT II 450; Zer §390, 408

38 BDF §317; Rob 532, 621, 808, 965, 1035

39 BDF §184; MHT II 471; MHT III 35; Rob 399, 505, 642, 643, 786

40 Rob 547, 642

41 BW 51; Moule 34, 186; MHT I 15; MHT II 471, 479; MHT III **247**

42 MHT II 73, 256; MHT III 90, 211; Rob 315, 477, 499, 500, 800, 919, 1171, 1193; RD §320

44 Rob 642; Zer §455g

45 Rob 473

46 Moule 32, 33; MHT I 56; MHT II 433; MHT III 246; Rob 484, 751

47 MHT II 471; Rob 1153

48 Rob 529, 1153bis, 1190; RD §410(a), 425

49 MHT III 209; MHT IV 46; Rob 1181, 1202; Zer §462

50 Moule 73; Rob 213, 796

51 Moule 188; MHT III **182**; Rob 789

52 MHT II 131; Rob 265; RD §176 C d

53 MHT II 455; MHT III 52; Zer
    §150

54 MHT III **30**; Rob 474

Chapter 12

1   BW 123; DM 131, 215; Moule 76,
    197; MHT I 102, 157; MHT II
    455, 460; Rob 231, 577, 587,
    623, 696, 714, 722, 727, 802,
    818, 952, 953, 1091, 1192; RD
    §380

2   DM 111; MHT I 191; MHT II 436;
    MHT III 286; Rob 627, 818bis,
    1158

3   BW 26; DM 100, 113; Moule 71;
    MHT III 258; Rob 696, 722, 724,
    818, 952, 962; RD §380, 410(a);
    Zer §266

4   BDF §60(3); DM 108; MHT I 102;
    MHT II 245, 460; Rob 472, 577,
    704, 752, 935, 1046, 1087,
    1213; RD §453(c)

5   BW 124, 166, 167; DM 216, 299;
    Moule 92; MHT III 143; Rob 232,
    560, 818, 858, 950, 979, 1046,
    1074, 1092; RD §453(c)

6   BDF §247(2); MHT III 58; Rob
    751, 818, 917, 1157, 1182, 1406

7   BW 25; Moule 42; MHT III 24;
    Rob 818bis, 1186

8   BDF §220(2), 380(3); BW 34;
    Moule 183; MHT I 104; MHT III
    110; Rob 108, 193, 439, 459,
    475, 524, 541, 588, 684, 955,
    956, 957bis, 959, 1114; RD §416

9   MHT III 58; Rob 642, 812, 818,
    819

10 BW 57; DM 103; MHT II 424; Rob
    436, 439, 459, 473, 594, 718,
    818, 957

11 BW 70; DM 281; Moule 92; MHT II
    447; MHT III 112; Rob 334, 561,
    739, 787, 1170; RD §419(f)

12 DM 129; Moule 93, 122; MHT I
    91; MHT II 432; MHT III **185**,
    194; MHT IV 53; Rob 523, 709,
    726, 776; RD §379

13 MHT II 450; MHT III 149; Rob
    742bis

14 DM 132; MHT II 365; MHT III 33;
    Rob 480, 1393

15 BDF §149; BW 101; DM 301; Moule
    128; MHT I 157, 178; MHT II
    450, 451, 460; MHT III 146; Rob
    472, 476, 543, 598, 772, 802,
    807, 933, 949, 979, 994, 1073,

1183bis, 1385

16 BDF §101, 473(1); MHT III 156;
    Rob 349

17 MHT III 117; Zer §348, 368

18 Rob 699

19 Moule 185; Rob 594, 902; RD
    §343(e)

20 BDF §189(2); Moule 28; MHT I
    58; MHT II 447; MHT III 239,
    293; MHT IV 46; Rob 264, 392,
    406, 463, 464, 523, 541, 816,
    820; RD §345(c), 398; Zer §1, 2

21 Moule 119 n.1; Rob 689

22 MHT III 24

23 BDF §131; MHT II 165; MHT III
    311; Rob 411, 516, 654

24 BDF §246; MHT I 117; Rob 606,
    1035, 1183; RD §410(a)

25 BDF §417; MHT II 173

26 MHT I 236; MHT III 31; Rob 669,
    670, 1012, 1024, 1160bis; Zer
    §368

27 MHT I 117

28 BDF §474(5c); MHT II 10, 68,
    202, 228, 294; MHT III **227**; Rob
    184, 352, 1212; RD §320

29 Rob 609

30 BDF §254(3); MHT III 181, 190,
    313; Rob 419, 705

31 BDF §449(1); MHT III 338; Rob
    1187

32 DM 104; Moule 11; MHT I 70;
    MHT II 346; MHT III **72**; Rob
    231, 261, 465; RD §341(c)

33 MHT II 108; MHT III 42, 151;
    Rob 215, 504, 1100, 1109, 1137,
    1172

34 MHT III 23; Rob 969; RD §423(c)

35 MHT I 176; MHT III 24, 89, 190;
    Rob 313, 314, 328, 330, 360,
    375, 890, 908; RD §308, 403(a),
    407

36 BDF §368, 423(6); MHT I 74;
    MHT II 83; MHT III 322; Rob
    597, 1044, 1045, 1110, 1132; RD
    §462(b); Zer §349

38 MHT III 321; Rob 158, 523, 794,
    1018, 1025, 1182; RD §443

39 MHT I 201; MHT II 252; Rob 471,
    740, 922, 1014, 1417; RD §438;
    Zer §317

40 BDF §294(5); Rob 718; Zer §278

41 BW 53; Rob 1180

42 DM 242; MHT II 339; Rob 604, 1393

43 MHT IV 21, 53; Rob 891

44 MHT III 64, 151; Rob 604, 866, 1393

45 MHT II 455; MHT III 139

46 MHT II 472; Rob 718

47 BDF §154; DM 110; Moule 32f.; MHT III **18**, **246**, 247; Rob 479, 485, 626, 653, 859, 1112, 1114; RD §342(j); Zer §72

48 BDF §154, 295, 466(3); Moule 29 n.1, 32f., 33, 173f., 176; MHT II 424, 447; MHT III 39, 293, 316, 324; Rob 436, 477, 479, 485, 659, 718, 720; Zer §2, 19, 29

49 BDF §299(4), 360(4); DM 133, 246; Moule 137, 187; MHT II 472; Rob 302, 739, 917, 1176, 1193; RD §381, 448(h); Zer §**405**

50 Moule 207; MHT III 138; Rob 302, 729

51 BDF §448(8); DM 240; Rob 1187, 1188

52 BDF §235(4); BW 32; DM 233; Moule 18; MHT III 89; Rob 361, 375, 605, 907; RD §270, 403(c)

53 DM 106

54 BDF §323(1); Moule 148; MHT III 63, 172; Rob 1180

55 MHT II 103

56 BDF §449(1); MHT III 193

57 MHT III 258; Rob 109, 686, 1180

58 BDF §5(3b), 342(1), 369(3), 455(2); DM 281; Moule 20, 23, 133, 192; MHT I 174; MHT II 191; MHT III 76, 99; Rob 559, 909, 967, 988, 1062, 1079, 1081, 1147, 1400, 1415, 1428; Zer §473

59 BDF §5(1); MHT I 55, 191; MHT II 210; MHT III 96; Rob 775, 976, inset

Chapter 13

1 DM 130; Moule 93; MHT III 194; MHT IV 53; Rob 290, 317, 611, 613, 686

2 BDF §245(3); BW 56; DM 120; Moule 51, 147; MHT II 438, 467; MHT III **31**; Rob 616bis, 661, 801, 1029, 1175; Zer §145, 420

3 Rob 849; RD §444

4 BDF §245(3), 297; DM 108; Moule 51; MHT II 171, 424, 438, 467; Rob 253, 283, 616bis, 724

6 DM 231; Rob 906, 1115, 1117, 1128

7 BDF §144, 322, 442(14); BW 77; DM 183, 249, 281; Moule 8; MHT II 447; MHT III 62; Rob 739bis, 879, 977, 1115; RD §420(a); Zer §459

8 BDF §383(2); BW 50; Moule 62; MHT I 169; Rob 528, 620, 976; RD §420(c)

9 BDF §206(1), 454(4), 480(6); BW 105; DM 291, 299; Moule 68, 151; Rob 208, 394, 594, 874, 924, 942, 1018, 1023, 1025, 1203

10 Moule 44; MHT II 452; Rob 1110; RD §461(a)

11 DM 111; Moule 164f.; MHT II 171, 172, 452; MHT III 266; Rob 627, 1119; RD §461(a)

12 Moule 90; Rob 264, 518

13 MHT II 190, 252; Rob 367, 770, 885

14 Moule 44; Rob 920, 965

15 Moule 44; MHT II 100; Rob 746

16 BDF §144; Moule 44, 183; MHT I 11; MHT II 171, 172, 447; MHT III 90, 231; Rob 283, 460, 518, 887, 919

17 DM 250; Rob 542, 605, 885

18 MHT II 419; Zer §65

19 MHT II 462; MHT III 253; Rob 458, 595, 690, 715, 791

21 Rob 656, 715

22 DM 107; MHT II 453; MHT III 56, 154; Zer §227

23 DM 246; MHT III 333; MHT IV 54; Rob 916, 1024; Zer §401

24 BDF §465(2); MHT I 174; Rob 434

25 BDF §476(2); Moule 154; MHT II
    179, 455; MHT III 149, 325; Rob
    188, 319, 324, 800, 978; RD
    §420(a)bis

26 MHT II 455; Rob 324; RD §306

27 MHT I 174; Rob 559, 773

28 BDF §382(4); MHT II 218, 251,
    448; MHT III 168, 226; Rob 188,
    324, 339, 348, 876, 972, 1218;
    RD §306, 320; Zer §376, 377

29 MHT III 26, 172; Rob 254

31 Moule 93; MHT III 194; MHT IV
    53

32 Moule 7, 44; MHT III 17, 63;
    Rob 653, 1202; RD §115

33 BDF §495(2); Moule 44; MHT III
    17; Rob 393, 652, 1198, 1202

34 BDF §47(4); DM 277; Moule 65,
    132, 180; MHT I 45; MHT II 10,
    130, 133, 148, 245; MHT III 42,
    43, 317; Rob 204, 219, 267,
    348, 635, 689, 718; RD §176 B
    c, 176 C b

35 BDF §382(2); MHT I 191;
    MHT III 96, 111, 112; Rob
    972bis, 976, inset; Zer §336

Chapter 14

1   BDF §404(2); Moule 174; MHT II
    426, 450, 452; MHT III 55, 145;
    Rob 613, 811, 1423; Zer §390

2   Rob 743

3   MHT II 454; Rob 787

4   BDF §170(2); MHT III 39, 232;
    Rob 818

5   BDF §164(1), 471(2); MHT II
    422; MHT III 209, 342

6   Moule 92; Rob 574

7   BW 103; DM 132, 160, 189; MHT I
    157; MHT III 137; Rob 477, 800,
    811, 883, 1032, 1202; RD
    §342(h)

8   BDF §337(3), 370(2); DM 302;
    MHT I 125; MHT III 89, 99; Rob
    907, 988, 1388, 1415; RD §306,
    403(a); Zer §452

9   MHT II 455; Rob 360, 910, 1415

10 BDF §369(2); Moule 23; MHT II
    70, 210, 453; MHT III 100, 154;
    Rob 186, 308, 328, 338, 561,
    910, 984, 988; Zer §340

11 Rob 1108

12 MHT I 125; MHT II 135;
    MHT III 112, 335; Rob 988,
    1409; RD §430(d)

13 MHT II 72; MHT III 112; Rob 192

14 Rob 574

15 Rob 356

16 MHT II 123; Rob 262, 743

17 MHT II 69, 70, 200; MHT III
    173; Rob 186, 656; Zer §168

18 BDF §157(3), 241(6), 471(1); DM
    231; MHT I 90; MHT II 28, 455,
    461; MHT III 18, 21, 162, 246;
    Rob 109, 360, 375, 480, 550,
    653, 809, 842, 1108, 1110,
    1122, 1389; RD §403(a), 461(a)

19 BDF §157(3), 323(3), 471(1);
    MHT III 63; Rob 748, 809, 818,
    842, 902, 1389

20 MHT I 135; Rob 842

21 BDF §460(3); MHT II 72; Rob
    427, 787bis; Zer §284

23 Moule 20; MHT III 76, 181; Rob
    789

24 MHT III 233; Rob 473, 506; RD
    §343(1)

25 Rob 774

26 MHT III 43; Rob 688, 789, 1012,
    1382, 1420; Zer §326, 329, 445

27 DM 243; Rob 1159

28 DM 243; MHT I 194; Rob 1024,
    1045; Zer §473

29 BDF §423(1); MHT III 322; Rob
    1173

30 BDF §414(2); DM 144, 153;
    MHT II 455; Rob 770, 1102; RD
    §387(e)

31 BDF §339(2b); Moule 49, 77 n.1,
    78; MHT III 87, 154, 241; Rob
    281, 531, 589, 748, 1045; Zer
    §117, 283

32 BDF §155(2); Moule 106; MHT II
    15, 339; Rob 546

33 DM 256; MHT III 43, 209; Rob
    515, 720, 744, 1158

34 DM 106, 253, 255; MHT II 132,
    402; Rob 269, 889, 934

35 Moule 29; MHT II 447; Rob 535

Chapter 15

1 MHT II 452, RD §474(a)

2 BW 44; Rob 529, 697; RD §370

3 Zer §368

4 DM 281; MHT II 172; Rob 213, 738, 976

5 Zer §197

6 BDF §316(1); Moule 90; MHT II 135; MHT III 55; MHT IV 55; Rob 562, 563, 786, 805, 1035

7 BDF §245(3); MHT II 442; MHT III 32; Rob 213, 661, 1188; Zer §145

8 BDF §5(1c); Rob 738

9 BDF §316(1); MHT III 55; Rob 787, 805, 1035

10 BDF §214(6)

11 Rob 743

12 BDF §308; Moule 103; MHT III 52, 152

13 BDF §433(3); BW 135; MHT III 282, **286**; Rob 771, 1163; RD §470(m)

14 Moule 58; MHT I 60; MHT II 123, 455; MHT III **21**, 268; MHT IV 60; Rob 253, 410, 608, 680; RD §163 A, 364, 374

15 BDF §247(2); MHT II 433; MHT IV 60; Rob 675, 817; RD §346(a)

16 BDF §18, 169(3); DM 187; MHT II 63; MHT III 66; MHT IV 60; Rob 208, 716, 883, 885; RD §374; Zer §252

17 BDF §172; BW 40; Moule 75; MHT I 114; MHT II 206; MHT IV 60; Rob 510, 532, 741, 828; Zer §221n

18 BDF §214(6); DM 103; MHT II 453; MHT III 154; MHT IV 60; Rob 594, 874

19 BDF §247(2); MHT I 208; MHT III 320, 321; Rob 658, 1061, 1076, 1080

20 BDF §423(2); MHT II 453; MHT III 42, 154, 322; MHT IV 60; Rob 1110; Zer §197, 208n

21 BDF §214(6); MHT IV 60; Rob 845, 1061

22 BDF §207(1); Moule 109; MHT III 256; MHT IV 60; Rob 483, 649; Zer §192, 489

23 BDF §420(3); Moule 135, 136; MHT III 80; MHT IV 55; Zer §261

24 MHT II 455; Rob 701, 904, 906; RD §403(b)

25 BW 19; DM 81; MHT II 452, 453; MHT III 154; Rob 507, 792

26 BDF §247(2), 299(1), 386(1); MHT I 198; MHT III 65, 123, 130; MHT IV 62; Rob 407, 411, 736, 890, 938bis, 940, 1031, 1408

27 BW 82; DM 182; MHT IV 55; Rob 881, 885, 893; Zer §284

29 BDF §322; BW 34, 77; Moule 8; MHT III 62; MHT IV 60; Rob 470, 477, 879; RD §342(f), 347(g), 402(a)

30 BDF §290(6); MHT II 92; MHT III 44; Rob 697

31 Moule 120; Rob 685; RD §375, 387(e)

32 Moule 10; MHT I 135; MHT III 71; Rob 834, 842, 887

Chapter 16

1 BDF §193(4), 290(1), 425(3); DM 275; MHT III 158; Rob 529, 652, 697, 703, 1140; RD §429, 462(d)

2 BDF §299(1); MHT II 206; Rob 312, 736, 916, 1164, 1176, 1214; RD §448(c)

3 DM 222; Moule 91; Rob 480, 483, 559, 600, 935, 1060, 1078, 1102; RD §434(e), 457(a), 461(b)

4 BDF §180(1); Moule 7, 11; MHT II 83; MHT III **74**, 235; Rob 308, 518, 827, 842, 893; RD §392, 401(a)

5 Rob 201

6 MHT III 154; Rob 499

8 BDF §176(1); DM 112, 115; Moule 64, 174; MHT II 440, 441; MHT III 43, 208, 213, 216, **250**; MHT IV 48; Rob 496, 633, 651, 667, 779; RD §371; Zer §40, 43

9 Moule 28, 38; MHT II 440, 447; MHT III 213, 260, 293; Rob 254, 510, 598; Zer §236

10 BDF §272; MHT III 31; Rob 658, 660, 782bis; RD §387(b)(3)

11   MHT III **98**; Rob 1009, 1012; Zer §303

12   Rob 288bis

13   MHT II 419; MHT III 36; Rob 251, 508, 748; RD §111, 343(1)

14   Rob 472, 705, 778

15   DM 156; MHT III 23, 305; Rob 1108; Zer **§166**

16   BW 13; DM 279; Moule 72; MHT II 113, 419; MHT III 58; Rob 221, 645, 975

17   MHT I 191; Rob 186, 921

18   Rob 579bis, 910bis

19   BW 51; MHT III 66, 247; Rob 485, 810, 883

20   BDF §347(1); MHT II 190, 192; MHT III 86; Rob 361, 364, 366, 905, 910; RD §403(b)

21   BDF §111(3); Rob 1186

22   MHT I 16; MHT II 427; Rob 1085, 1423

23   BDF §162(8); MHT III 27, 168; Rob 408, 502, 586; Zer **§199**

24   BDF §172; BW 29; DM 78; Moule 43; MHT III 225; Rob 495, 775; RD §343(d), 387(c)

25   BDF §289; Moule 123; MHT III **44**; Rob 341, 696, 1379; RD §293 b N., 310

26   BDF §104(1), 235(3), 437; DM 105; Moule 205; MHT II 464; MHT III **14, 226**; Rob 548, 561, 800, 896, 986; RD §353

27   Rob 1046

28   Rob 986

29   MHT II 146; Rob 268

30   Rob 791; Zer §306

31   BDF §101; MHT III 284; Rob 819, 871, 1012, 1210, 1382

Chapter 17

1   BW 127; Moule 27, 129; MHT I 217; MHT III 141, **292**; Rob 393, 720, 721, 996, 1002, 1040, 1059, 1060, 1068, 1094, 1171; RD §435(d), 455(d); Zer §386

2   BDF §159(4), 245(3), 372(3), 393(1); Moule 27, 91; MHT II 102, 193, 442; MHT III 32, **92**; Rob 212, 472, 485, 560, 661,

992, 997, 1417; Zer **§311**

3   MHT III 42; Rob 477, 542, 689, 802, 1202, 1419; RD §377

4   BDF §252, 266(2); MHT III **14**; Rob 505, 769

5   DM 176; Rob 310, 948; RD §320

6   BDF §372(1a); DM 291; MHT II 68; MHT III **92**; Rob 887, 921, 1015, 1022, 1416; RD §441; Zer **§310**, 329

7   BDF §448(4); MHT II 70; Rob 338

8   BDF §298(4), 383(2); DM 133; Moule 20, 135; MHT I 93; MHT III 49, **77**; Rob 340, 738, 869, 976, 1045, 1215, 1218; RD §293 b N., 303, 310, 401(c)

9   BDF §76(1), 427(2); Rob 349

10   BDF §76(1); Rob 920

11   BDF §222, 261(4); Moule 55, 67 n.2; MHT II 426, 450; MHT III 170, 267; Rob 550, 560, 562, 565, 581, 648, 791, 1042, 1423; RD §451(a); Zer §390

12   BDF §104(3), 423(1); MHT III 322; Rob 367

14   MHT II 67, 426, 450; Rob 1042, 1423; RD §451(a); Zer §390

15   BDF §198(3); Rob 611

16   Moule 51; Zer §199n

17   MHT II 67; MHT III 178; Rob 917, 1157; RD §470(g)

19   MHT II 453

20   MHT III 156

21   BW 13; Moule 75, 83f.; MHT III 216; Rob 505, 641; RD §343(k), 353

22   BDF §382(1); BW 153; MHT II 98, 100, 439; Rob 224

23   Moule 29; MHT I 59; MHT II 447; Rob 392; Zer §133

24   BDF §241(1); MHT II 438; Rob 652, 792, 1202

25   Rob 579

27   BDF §101; BW 83; Moule 18 n.1; MHT II 410; MHT III 66; Rob 717, 884, 975, 1412; RD §402(b), 409, 420(b)

28   Rob 968, 1412

29   BDF §129; Moule 27 n.1; Rob 522, 718, 791

30 Rob 208, 968

31 BDF §380(2), 469; MHT III 325; Rob 308, 440, 442, 708, 724, 957, 959, 1405

32 Rob 506; RD §343(1)

33 BDF §380(3); MHT III 110; Rob 193, 957

34 Rob 748, 749

35 BDF §418(2); Rob 602, 889

37 Rob 969, 1411

57 Rob 1411, 1412

Chapter 18

1 BDF §402(5); MHT I 218; MHT III 144; Rob 626, 997, 1003, 1049, 1060, 1075

2 BDF §445(4); MHT I 65; Rob 743, 1406

4 BDF §445(4); DM 106; Rob 688, 1012, 1026, 1027, 1398; RD §377, 444, 470(c)

5 BDF §207(3); MHT II 75; MHT III 266; Rob 201, 244, 1039, 1148bis, 1149, 1398; Zer §249

6 MHT II 440; MHT III 213; MHT IV 48; Rob 496, 651

7 BDF §365(4); BW 10, 49; DM 77; Moule 178; MHT I 159; MHT III 56, 96, 235; Rob 495, 802, 930, 934, 1158, inset; RD §343(e), 470(k)

8 Moule 78, 164; MHT III 56, 330; Rob 589, 916, 1176; RD §448(d); Zer §117

9 BDF §412(4); BW 38; MHT III 153; Rob 342, 540, 605, 778, 1107; Zer §192, 347

10 BDF §390(1); MHT I 205; MHT II 438; MHT III 134; Rob 748, 990, 1080, 1087, 1088

11 BDF §290(6); BW 29; Moule 32; MHT III 44, 57; Rob 502, 697, 700, 965, 1035, 1159, 1188; RD §379; Zer §231, 365

12 BDF §186(2); BW 10, 78; Moule 39; MHT II 394; MHT III 235; Rob 505, 646, 769, 880; RD §343(e), 402(a)

13 BDF §101, 314; BW 68; Moule 92; MHT III 57, 173; Rob 231, 561, 756, 858, 1423; RD

§320, 386(a)

14 BDF §185(3), 291(2); MHT II 467; MHT III 31, 45, 216; Rob 661, 703, 708; Zer §145

16 MHT I 124

17 MHT III 96; Rob inset

18 BDF §247(2), 473(1); Moule 173; Rob 675

20 Moule 179

22 BDF §189(3); Moule 91; Rob 541

23 Zer §284

25 BDF §24; Rob 192, 1058

26 Rob 1398

28 Moule 173; Rob 310

29 BDF §365(3), 460(3); MHT II 67; MHT III 96; Rob 234, 641, 726

30 MHT III 193; Rob 284, 673, inset

31 BW 33; MHT III 238; Rob 539

32 Rob 1190

33 MHT II 447; Rob 762

34 Rob 751

35 MHT II 426, 450; Rob 743, 1423; Zer §97

36 BDF §386(1); DM 298; MHT I 198; MHT III 65, 123, 131, 161; MHT IV 62; Rob 890, 938, 1022, 1031bis, 1042, 1044, 1408

37 MHT II 150; Rob 1035

38 Rob 463, 464

39 DM 121; MHT II 195; MHT III 41; Rob 532, 664, 800

40 BDF §423(2); MHT III 322

41 BDF §366(3), 465(2); Moule 145; MHT I 185; MHT II 421; MHT III 95, 99, 305; Rob 924, 935

42 BW 14

Chapter 19

1 Rob 472, 476, 563

2 BDF §277(3), 290(1); DM 70, 123; Moule 121, 176; MHT I 86; Rob 162, 457, 679, 723; Zer §199n, 455e

3 MHT II 461; Rob 423, 488, 580, 738, 1398

4 BDF §186(1), 484; BW 11; DM 77, 78; Moule 39, 90; MHT II 73; MHT III **16**, 235; Rob 186, 201, 472, 476, 494bis, 547, 652, 983, 1202, 1205; RD §343(d)

5 MHT II 210; Rob 328, 861, 1109, 1127; RD §401(a), 422

6 Moule 90

7 MHT III 273; Rob 614

8 DM 247; MHT II 79, 177; MHT III 63, 210; Rob 199, 275, 502, 742, 870, 880, 892, 1008

9 MHT III 305; Rob 963

10 Rob 411, 764, 1109

11 BDF §419(4), 435(b); BW 12; Moule 177; MHT II 445; MHT III 148, **227**; MHT IV 48; Rob 551, 640, 800, 1071, 1126, 1127, 1428

12 Rob 272

13 BDF §285(2), 383(1); Moule 76, 133; MHT I 35, 118; MHT II 69, 70, 200; Rob 690, 976, 978; RD §387(e), 419(a)

14 MHT II 339; Rob 879, 886, 919

15 BDF §298(5), 404(2), 442(5); MHT II 190, 211, 426, 450; MHT III **145**, 149, 335; Rob 107, 308, 737, 841, 1044, 1048, 1049, 1214, 1423; Zer §390

16 Rob 749

17 BDF §102(3); MHT I 174, 226; MHT III 31, 89, 345; Rob 299, 330, 375, 749, 890, 950

18 Rob 749; Zer §284

19 BDF §98; Rob 749, 1398

20 BDF §306(2); DM 231; Moule 192; MHT II 426; MHT III **197**; Rob 361, 375, 749, 776, 906bis, 1389

21 Moule 192; Rob 997; RD §434(c)

22 Moule 192; Rob 1423

23 BDF §360(2); MHT III **92**; Rob 922, 1014, 1023

26 BW 11; Moule 173

29 BDF §143; DM 70; MHT I 69; MHT II 60, 148, 152, 369; MHT III 230; Rob 154bis, 232, 259, 267, 458, 780; Zer §97

30 Moule 20; MHT III 76; Rob 644

31 MHT II 458; Rob 850

33 MHT III **22**

35 Moule 173; Rob 212, 799, 1392

36 MHT II 203; Rob 318

37 DM 110; Moule 54; MHT II 455; MHT III 274; Rob 154, 412, 619, 623, 624bis, 719, 1390

38 MHT IV 48

40 BDF §65(1b), 77, 373(2); DM 245; Rob 325, 333bis, 356, 361, 801, 873, 907, 1008, 1010, 1217, 1421; RD §270, 304, 403(c), 437; Zer §331, 336

41 MHT III 72; Rob 834; RD §401(a)

42 BDF §439(2), 482; MHT III 180, 331; Rob 483, 523, 793, 834, 835, 842, 1023, 1203, 1417; RD §442, 474(e); Zer §405

43 BDF §442(4); Moule 87, 173; MHT II 421; Rob 617, 873, 907, 1183; Zer §455d

44 BW 26; Moule 71; MHT II 423

45 MHT II 455

46 BW 48; MHT III 246; Rob 480

47 DM 232; MHT II 452; Rob 470, 487, 550, 888

48 BDF §392(1a); DM 145; MHT II 192, 206; MHT III 182; Rob 190, 317, 340, 766, 771, 1127, 1217, 1430; RD §320

Chapter 20

1 MHT II 426; Rob 523, 1379, 1423

2 BDF §101; MHT II 419; MHT III 156; Rob 1188; Zer §368, 489

3 BDF §247(2); Rob 1180

4 DM 248; Rob 1177

6 BW 132; DM 232; Moule 18; MHT III 137; Rob 163, 903, 1030, 1040, 1081, 1390; RD §403(a), 451(b)

7 BDF §406(2); MHT III 148; Rob 1036, 1038, 1171, 1422

9 MHT II 212, 455; MHT III 55; Rob 308, 470

10   BDF §369(2); DM 283; MHT III   40   Rob 1162
     100; Rob 324, 519, 522, 872,
     984; RD §430(a)   42   DM 102; MHT II 79; Rob 199, 686

11   BDF §435(a); Moule 177; MHT II   43   MHT II 204
     445; MHT III **227**; MHT IV 48;
     Rob 551, 748, 1078; RD §457(c)   44   BW 141

12   DM 14; MHT II 445; Rob 94, 822,   46   MHT II 460; MHT III 227
     1078
                                         47   MHT III 45; Rob 564
13   BDF §424; MHT III 322

14   BDF §260(1); Rob 497   Chapter 21

15   Rob 876
                                         1   MHT II 439; Zer §363
16   BDF §384; MHT I 194, 240; Rob
     939bis, 940, 1408; RD §406(b)   2   Rob 743

17   MHT II 423; Rob 718; Zer §19   3   MHT II 161, 165

19   BDF §239(6), 345; DM 129;   4   BW 33; DM 97
     MHT II 432; MHT IV 53; Rob 626,
     1183   5   BDF §109(3); Rob 153, 187

20   BDF §157(2), 391(3), 406(1); DM   6   BDF §466(1); DM 70, 74; MHT I
     215; Moule 140, 143; MHT III   69, 191; MHT II 424, 438;
     136, 147; Rob 481, 508, 787,   MHT III 316; Rob 416, 439, 459,
     990, 1036, 1039, 1040, 1089;   565, 601, 960
     Zer §352
                                         7   DM 256; MHT III 112
21   Moule 209; MHT II 464
                                         8   MHT I 125; Rob 932, 933, 996
22   BDF §5(1), 409(3); MHT II 419;
     MHT III 149; Rob 1158   11   BDF §443(1), 488(2); MHT II
                                              110, 364, 369; Rob 219, 1201;
23   MHT I 117   RD §474(q)

24   MHT III 136; Rob 393   12   Rob 622, 641

25   BDF §451(3); MHT III **16**, 340,   13   Moule 70, 89
     347; Rob 425, 767, 1154; RD
     §410(a), 472(f)   14   BDF §392(3); DM 258; Moule 209;
                                              MHT III 23, 139; Rob 334, 818,
26   BDF §170(2); BW 13; Moule 13;   1094, 1171; RD §320
     MHT II 465; MHT III 72; Rob
     508, 573, 1414; RD §343(k)   15   BDF §442(16); Rob 573

27   BDF §429; MHT III **286**, 316; Rob 16   MHT II 433; MHT III **7**, 209; Rob
     458, 1094, 1171; Zer §14   599; Zer §284

28   MHT II 204; Rob 849, 1418, 1420   17   DM 232; MHT III 89; Rob 375,
                                              636, 641, 878, 889
31   MHT II 208
                                         18   MHT III 24, 96; Rob 597, inset
32   BDF §62; Zer §151
                                         19   BW 14; DM 124; Rob 681, 683,
33   BDF §164(1); MHT III 209   871

34   BDF §101; MHT II 383, 441; Rob   20   Rob 1041
     150, 1213bis
                                         22   Moule 175; MHT I 217; Rob 1061,
35   BDF §101; MHT II 410; MHT III   1076, 1088
     193, 232; Rob 509, 598, 782,
     1189; RD §410(a)   23   MHT II 105; Rob 216

36   BDF §118(1), 445(1); MHT I 114;   24   BDF §383(2); DM 113, 232, 281;
     MHT II 292, 383, 441; MHT III   Moule 18; MHT III 27, 89, 240;
     79, 208; MHT IV 49; Rob 879;   Rob 534, 889, 974, 1412; RD
     Zer §43   §420(b)

37   BDF §234(3); Rob 253, 1034; RD   25   Moule 114; MHT II 126, 143;
     §163 A   MHT III 172, 175; Rob 262, 419,

794bis, 795; RD §163 B b, 186 a, 201 D

26   BW 35; MHT II 461; Rob 566

27   Rob 876

28   MHT III 24; Rob 1396

32   MHT III 96; Rob inset

33   BDF §365(1); MHT I 190, 191; MHT III 97; Rob 873, inset

34   MHT II 230, 379; MHT III 23, 225; Rob 186, 272, 400, 542, 550, 657, 708, 996, 1213bis

35   Moule 94; MHT II 466

36   BDF §97(1); BW 128; Rob 476

37   BDF §143, 205; DM 70; Moule 9; MHT I 69; MHT II 60, 152, 452; MHT III 67, **230**; Rob 154bis, 232, 267, 458, 470

38   MHT II 407

Chapter 22

1   MHT III 27, 215; Rob 416, 498

2   Rob 427, 766, 985, 1031; RD §452(d)bis

3   MHT II 145; Rob 1031

4   MHT II 211; MHT III 181; Rob 766, 1031, 1046; RD §387(a), 452(d)

5   Rob 350; Zer §282

6   BW 21; Moule 82; MHT I 220; Rob 517, 639, 1061, 1068, 1076; RD §344(d), 353

7   Rob 887

8   BDF §420(2); MHT III 156

9   Moule 139, 199; MHT II 421; Rob 1399

10   BDF §423(1); Rob 333, 356; Zer §278

11   BDF §378, 484; DM 283; MHT III **109**; MHT IV 19; Rob 934, 955, 969, 1045, 1205, 1399, 1411; RD §423(c); Zer §343

12   MHT II 121; Rob 185, 260; RD §162 f

14   Rob 219

15   BDF §198(6); BW 41; Moule 178; MHT II 443; MHT III 144, 148, 241; MHT IV 47; Rob 531bis, 621, 978, 1075; RD §457(d); Zer §60

16   DM 267; MHT III 96; Rob 976

17   MHT III 155

18   DM 267; MHT III 96; Rob 577, inset

19   BDF §339(2b); DM 111; MHT III 87, 191; Rob 685; Zer **§283**

20   DM 111; Moule 31 n.1, 63, 64, 78; MHT III 143, **301**; Rob 213, 1060, 1074; RD §457(d)

22   Rob 1152, 1153, 1390

23   BDF §386(1); BW 114; DM 174, 297; MHT I 199; MHT II 455; MHT III 89, 123, 131; MHT IV 62; Rob 427, 430, 739, 766, 890, 938, 1031bis, 1046, 1408; RD §387(a), 406(b), 452(c), 452(d)

24   Moule 75; Rob 739, 766, 938, 1031; RD §387(a), 451(c), 452(c), 452(d)

25   Rob 510

26   BDF §480(5); MHT II 458; Rob 1140, 1214, inset

27   Rob 737; RD §387(a)

28   Rob 1108

29   Rob 581

30   BDF §369(3); MHT II 60, 207, 238; Rob 232, 1216

31   MHT II 405

32   DM 263; Moule 63; MHT II 259, 420; Rob 300, 1139; RD §462(d)

33   Rob 659

34   BDF §383(3), 429; MHT I 239; MHT III 113; Rob 548, 908, 976bis, 977bis, 1036, 1094, 1171; RD §420(e)

35   BDF §154; BW 21; DM 134; Moule 82; MHT II 111; Rob 219, 639, 750; RD §383

37   BDF §145(2); DM 252; Moule 61; Rob 401, 611, 766, 818

38   Rob 411

40   BDF §336(1); MHT III 75; Rob 603, 853

41   BDF §5(3b); DM 93; Moule 34, 91, 192; MHT IV 29; Rob 469, 559

42   BDF §27, 211, 284(1), 482; MHT II 70, 197; MHT III 115; MHT IV 48; Rob 193, 339, 1023, 1203, 1214; RD §310, 320; Zer §303

44   MHT I 51; MHT II 213; Rob 231, 339

45   BDF §210(1); DM 133; Moule 73; MHT II 461; MHT III 258; Rob 580

46   BDF §336(1); MHT III 75

47   BDF §150; Rob 477

48   Rob 311, 533

49   BDF §228, 351(2), 366(2); BW 89; DM 246; Moule 62, 77, 151, 158; MHT I 12, 185; MHT III **16**, 86, **98**, **270**; MHT IV 54; Rob 374, 456, 502, 590, 620, 876, 878, 916, 934, 935, 1024bis, 1109, 1118, 1215; RD §360, 460(c); Zer §282, 401

50   BDF §111(3); Moule 125; MHT III 195, 196; Rob 156, 292, 675, 742; Zer §155

51   BDF §111(3); Moule 99

52   Moule 61; Rob 611; RD §365

53   BDF §423(2); Moule 173; MHT III 190; Rob 704

54   BW 100; DM 156; Rob 559; RD §301

55   Moule 89; MHT II 409; Rob 617, 644

56   Rob 697

57   Moule 32; MHT III 33

58   MHT III 33, 210; Rob 612, 653, 678

59   Rob 550, 697, 743, 746

60   MHT III 33

61   MHT II 11; MHT III **137**, 140; Rob 483, 509, 873, 1091

63   Rob 628

65   MHT I 231; Rob 1130

66   BDF §444(4); Moule 101; Rob 1179

67   DM 267; Moule 101; MHT III 96; Rob 1020, inset

68   DM 267; MHT III 96; Rob 1405, inset

69   MHT III 89

70   BDF §441(3); MHT I 86; MHT III 183; Rob 678, 695, 915

71   Moule 121; MHT III 233; Rob 519, 649

Chapter 23

1   MHT II 453; Rob 404, 412, 1390

2   BDF §406(1); MHT II 455; MHT III 147; Rob 339, 1039, 1041bis, 1094, 1123, 1425

3   MHT I 86; MHT III 183

4   BW 71; MHT II 341; Rob 786

5   BDF §225; Moule 181; MHT I 45, 240; MHT II 89, 454; MHT III 155; Rob 413, 548, 1126, 1203

6   MHT III **336**; Rob 916; Zer §402

7   Rob 561

8   DM 188; MHT II 452; Rob 597, 884

9   Zer §229

11   Moule 37; MHT II 72, 111, 408, 458; Rob 483, 628

12   BDF §64(1), 287; Moule 119; MHT II 180, 348; MHT III 41, 43, 159, 227; MHT IV 53; Rob 226, 289, 405, 625, 686, 690, 888, 1103, 1121; RD §461(a); Zer §210, 360n

13   MHT III 55

14   BDF §425(3); MHT II 111, 341; MHT III 158; Rob 511, 560, 720, 750, 966, 1141; RD §429

15   BDF §191; BW 45; DM 161(2); Moule 204; MHT II 459; MHT III **240**; Rob 534, 542, 794, 820, 903, 1186; RD §346(f), 347(g); Zer §59

16   BDF §5(1b)

18   BDF §122; Rob 170, 348, 530, 760; RD §346(d)

19   BDF §355; DM 231; Moule 19, 76; MHT III 89; Rob 323, 375, 860; Zer §360n, 362

21   Rob 695

22   BDF §5(1b); MHT II 341

23   BW 134; Rob 805

26   BDF §170(2); BW 21; MHT III 232; Rob 517, 645; RD §344(d)

28   BDF §449(1); DM 302; MHT I 125; MHT III 338; Rob 475, 1173

29   Rob 219

30   Rob 338

31 BDF §366(1); MHT II 114, 447; MHT III 99, 293; Rob 195, 587, 588, 929, 934, 1416; Zer §2, 297

32 BDF §306(5); Rob 749

33 MHT III 36; Rob 696, 792, 794

35 MHT II 194; Rob 1009

36 BDF §443(1)

37 MHT III 183; Rob 1009; Zer §306

38 BDF §5(1); Rob 159, 604; RD §363

39 MHT II 181; Rob 409

40 BDF §87; MHT II 198

41 Moule 122; Rob 720

42 BDF §198(2); MHT II 464; MHT III 241

43 MHT II 92

44 BDF §442(4); MHT II 421; Rob 1183

45 MHT III 225; Rob 775

47 BDF §5(1); Rob 700; RD §379

48 BDF §474(5a); MHT II 194

49 BDF §270(3); Moule 101; MHT III 185; Rob 366, 560, 778; Zer §291

50 BDF §282(3); MHT II 424; MHT III 40, 45; Rob 176

51 BDF §97(2); Rob 434, 529

52 MHT II 424

53 BDF §97(2), 352; Moule 157; MHT II 452; Rob 316, 375, 906, 1165; RD §470(j)

54 BDF §323(4); Rob 493, 885; RD §343(b)

55 Moule 101; MHT III 137; Rob 726, 729, 1032, 1043

56 BDF p.5 n.1

Chapter 24

1 BDF §186(2), p.5 n.1; BW 36; Moule 39; MHT II 160; MHT III 187, 235; Rob 274, 495, 522, 672, 718, 841; RD §345(c)

2 Moule 91, 92; Rob 575

3 MHT II 100; Rob 225

4 BDF §140; MHT II 133, 426, 450; MHT III 56; Rob 267, 1423; RD §410(a); Zer §390

5 Rob 611

6 MHT II 454; MHT III 137; Rob 1032; RD §424(b), 451(a)

7 BDF §476(3); MHT III 24, 325; MHT IV 47; Rob 649, 1049

10 BDF §162(3); BW 9; MHT II 194; MHT III **168, 206**; Rob 214, 501, 767; RD §343(g)

11 BDF §157(5), 214(6); DM 165; Rob 404, 540, RD §347(g); Zer §282

12 Moule 119; MHT II 453

13 BDF §353(1); Moule 34, 93; MHT II 424, 452; MHT IV 53; Rob 263, 424, 469; RD §163 A

14 MHT II 432; Rob 529, 625, 680, 883; RD §369

15 BDF §260(1); BW 124; MHT II 426, 450; MHT III **167**; Rob 1423; Zer §390

16 Rob 518, 765, 1061, 1171, 1425; RD §344(e), 455(d), 470(1); Zer §352, 386

17 DM 99; MHT II 432; Rob 572, 625, 703, 735, 835, 1202; RD §357; Zer §282

18 BDF §125(2); Rob 172, 235, 549, 656, 657, 1183; RD §350; Zer §455e

19 DM 273; MHT II 150, 465; MHT III 166, 185; Rob 399, 419, 651, 735, 740bis, 1046; RD §325

20 BDF §300(1), 443(1); DM 295; MHT III 49; Rob 731, 732, 985, 1045, 1177; RD §430(b), 448(d)

21 BDF §129, 221, 277(3), 439(2), 448(6); BW 43, 166; DM 111; Moule 27, 81; MHT II 105; MHT III 66, **291**; Rob 216, 244, 392, 424, 628, 679, 701, 771, 884, 978, 1029, 1035, 1148bis, 1185, 1186; RD §420(a), 451(a)

22 MHT I 51; MHT II 213, 358; MHT III 225, 335; Rob 550, 657, 1186

23 DM 296, 298; Moule 153; Rob 489, 1028, 1038, 1039; RD §451(b)

24 Rob 968, 1413, 1414; RD §424(b)

25 BDF §146(2), 187(6), 400(8); Moule 50; MHT III 33, 141; Rob 487, 658, 659, 680, 716, 1061,

1077; RD §374, 455(d); Zer §35

26 BDF §358(1); MHT II 422; MHT III **90**; Rob 887, 919; Zer §455g

27 Moule 63, 106, 181; MHT II 190; MHT III **15**, 43, 155; Rob 367, 566; RD §461(b)

28 Moule 90; MHT III 138; Rob 297, 298

29 Moule 53; MHT III 52, 179; Rob 625, 765, 792, 1065, 1088

30 BDF §404(2); MHT II 426, 450; Rob 1039, 1423; Zer §390

31 BDF §211; Moule 168; MHT II 461; MHT III 39, 251, 349; Rob 575, 680, 682, 1213; RD §374

32 MHT II 83, 432, 452, 472; MHT III 23; Rob 367, 888, 974, 1212

33 MHT II 453; MHT III 146; MHT IV 53

34 MHT I 135; Rob 334, 842; RD §348

35 MHT III 137; Rob 534, 587, 726

38 BDF p.3 n.4; Moule 183; MHT III 23; Rob 587, 739

39 Moule 121; MHT II 121; MHT III 232, 350; Rob 203, 260, 1041

41 BW 26; MHT II 461; Rob 580, 743; RD §358

42 MHT II 343; Rob 159

44 MHT III 217

45 MHT III 139; Rob 315, 1036, 1212

46 BW 95; DM 202; Rob 858, 1080bis, 1081; RD §456

47 BDF §137(3), 207(1), 419(3); Moule 69, 181; MHT I 182; MHT II 450, 454; MHT III **78**, 155, 316, 343; Rob 413, 491, 535, 946, 1126, 1203

49 MHT I 182

50 BDF §239(3); Moule 85; Rob 643, 683, 1205

51 BW 124; MHT II 426, 450; Rob 561, 581, 1072, 1423; Zer §390

53 Rob 1406

John

216, 279; Rob 280, 434, 438, 473, 484, 516, 640, 662, 670, 801, 887, 895, 896, 964, 1034, 1111; RD §335, 344(c)

16 BDF §208(2), 442(9); BW 69; Moule 71, 72; MHT I 100; MHT II 436; MHT III **258**; Rob 407, 505, 574, 829, 1181, 1397; RD §330; Zer **§95, 452**

17 BW 69; Rob 1200

18 BDF §205; BW 96; DM 103, 118, 203; Moule 69, 116; MHT I 144, 235; MHT II 424; MHT III **254**; Rob 364, 536, 586, 593, 614, 656, 707, 708, 829, 893, 896, 906; Zer **§102**, 103, 372

19 BW 100, 105; Moule 92; Rob 704, 897, 905, 915; RD §448(g); Zer §80

20 DM 252; Rob 918, 1205; Zer §174

21 DM 264; MHT III **304**; Rob 233, 768, 1157

22 BDF §483; BW 131; Rob 619

23 BDF §462(1); BW 141

24 Rob 905; Zer §80

25 BDF §420(2), 445(1); DM 123; MHT III 156; Rob 1012, 1135, 1160bis, 1165, 1420; RD §444, 470(c)

26 BDF §73; BW 137; Rob 505, 550, 644, 720

27 BDF §379, 393(4); BW 162; MHT I 208, 237; MHT II 435; MHT III 139; MHT IV 21; Rob 503, 658bis, 961, 992, 996; Zer §410

28 BDF §353(1); BW 21; Moule 18; MHT II 452; MHT III 87; Rob 970; RD §423(c); Zer **§362**

29 BDF §321; BW 80; DM 185; Moule 31; MHT II 474; MHT III **151**, 231; Rob 391, 868, 1193; RD §448(h); Zer §372

30 BDF §62, 214(1), 231(1), 277(1); BW 14, 27; DM 112, 252; Moule 42, 65, 83; MHT II 421; MHT III 32, 37, **216**, 279; Rob 234, 629, 632, 677; Zer §96

31 Rob 904; RD §413

32 BDF §468(3); BW 97; Moule 14, 180; MHT II 429; MHT III 156, 161; MHT IV 69; Rob 408, 440, 602, 792, 893, 896, 897; Zer §375

33 MHT II 424, 435; MHT III 46, 135, 325; MHT IV 21, 66; Rob

440, 677, 707, 708, 724

34 Rob 893, 896

35 MHT II 113; Rob 366

37 MHT III 161; Rob 1042

38 BDF §465(2); DM 168; MHT II 152; MHT III 161; Rob 411, 416, 433, 465, 875, 1044, 1123

39 BW 36; Moule 52; MHT III 183; MHT IV 71; Rob 299, 470, 714, 813, 871, 949, 1044; Zer §102

40 MHT III 135, 273; Rob 519, 614bis, 762, 779, 785

41 BDF §286(1), 465(2); Moule 121; MHT I 90; MHT II 269; Rob 215, 416, 433, 549, 657, 691bis, 714, 762, 762bis, 770, 795, 881, 893, 896, 897

42 BDF §277(1); DM 123; MHT III 37; Rob 215, 255, 376, 411, 678, 835; RD §374

44 BDF §209(3); MHT III 259; MHT IV 77; Rob 578, 598

45 BDF §209(3); BW 22, 73; MHT III 259; Rob 578, 782

46 Rob 428, 478, 598, 720, 743, 875, 949

47 MHT III **75**; Rob 1100

48 BDF §232(1); BW 123; Moule 66; MHT III 275; Rob 621, 634, 635bis, 765, 858, 978, 1075; RD §451(a)

49 MHT II 431; MHT III 144, 183, **184**; MHT IV 69, 77; Rob 769, 781, 1126; RD §387(b)(2); Zer §175

50 BDF §416(1); Moule 66; MHT II 161; MHT III 161, 345; Rob 277, 396, 476, 634, 871, 1028, 1029, 1123; RD §451(a)

51 MHT II 161; MHT III 82; Rob 423

52 MHT II 441; Rob 364

Chapter 2

1 MHT III 27, 210; Rob 762

2 Rob 405, 428

3 BDF §180(5); Rob 700

4 BDF §299(3); Moule 32; MHT II 83; MHT IV 17, 68; Rob 539, 736; Zer §221n, 447

5 MHT I 186; MHT III **77, 106**; Rob 243, 729, 855; Zer **§338**

6 DM 99; Moule 67; MHT II 452; MHT III **77**, 87, 266; Rob 571, 855, 906; Zer §362, 362n

7 MHT III **77**; Rob 510, 855; RD §343(1)

8 DM 126; MHT III **77**; Rob 855

9 BDF §169(3); BW 160; Moule 36; MHT II 32; Rob 474, 506, 507, 841, 1184; RD §343(1)

10 BDF §61(1); BW 66; DM 118; Moule 97; MHT II 161; MHT III 31, 37, 113; Rob 218, 277, 643, 678

11 BDF §292; MHT II 105, 463; MHT III 192; Rob 216, 701, 702, 704, 771, 781; RD §387(e)

12 Rob 405, 470, 680, 681, 686

13 MHT II 422

14 Rob 265, 427

15 BDF §5(1b), 443(1); Rob 427

16 DM 302; MHT I 125; MHT III **76, 77**; Rob 855, 950; Zer §**246**

17 Moule 18; Rob 500, 903, 1029

18 BDF §456(2); MHT III 318; Rob 311, 433, 964, 1034; Zer §420

19 BDF §387(2); BW 117; Moule 56; MHT III 76; Rob 586, 856, 948, 1023; RD §407; Zer §115

20 BDF §200(2); BW 43; DM 196; Moule 11; MHT II 172, 191, 422; Rob 230, 283, 365, 367, 523, 527, 833, 1183; RD §320, 346(b), 401(a); Zer §253

21 DM 79; Rob 399, 498, 707, 708

22 BDF §294(1); DM 258; MHT II 474; Rob 715bis; RD §380

23 MHT II 463; MHT III 171; Rob 523, 760, 1184; RD §343(e), 360; Zer §206

24 BDF §61(1), 402(1); BW 55, 125; DM 275; Moule 119; MHT II 180; MHT III 41, 142, 148, 194; Rob 226, 287, 476, 584, 686, 688, 689, 765, 885, 966, 1071, 1186; RD §377, 428; Zer §210

25 BDF §330, 402(1); DM 296; MHT III 139; Rob 1029, 1043, 1176, 1392, 1421; RD §428, 452(b); Zer §346n, 410

27 Rob 230

Chapter 3

1 DM 70; Rob 395, 434, 460, 599, 782, 1185

2 BW 22; DM 77; MHT III 259; Rob 611bis, 793

3 DM 259; Rob 751, 857

5 Rob 751, 795

6 BDF §462(2); Rob 1200; Zer §141

7 BDF §337(3); BW 108; DM 302; MHT I 124, 126; MHT III **77**; Rob 852bis; Zer §246

8 BDF §323(3); MHT II 195, 199; MHT IV 76; Rob 299, 342, 548bis, 800, 1177; RD §448(d); Zer §69

10 BDF §273(1); DM 123; MHT II 422; Rob 678, 768, 1175; RD §387(c)

11 MHT II 469; Rob 407, 653; Zer §455a

12 Rob 654, 1012, 1160, 1420

13 MHT II 441; Rob 600, 859, 1183; Zer §274, 372, 471

14 MHT II 441; Rob 968

15 BDF §187(6); Moule 80f.; MHT III **237, 263**

16 BDF §391(2), 466(3); BW 68; DM 270, 286; Moule 141; MHT I 209; MHT II 139, 463; MHT III 136, 197; Rob 135, 437, 753, 758, 762, 770, 1000bis, 1413, 1414; RD §383, 435(c); Zer §**350**, 440n

17 BW 23, 72; DM 101; Moule 144; MHT IV 66; Rob 1166, 1400

18 BDF §428(5); BW 97, 161; Moule 155; MHT I 171, 239; MHT II 463; Rob 897, 898, 963, 1028, 1159, 1169; RD §426(a) and (b), 470 (a), (b), and (j)

19 BDF §185(2); DM 244, 295; MHT I 140; MHT II 469; MHT III 45, 216; Rob 426, 663, 666, 699, 789, 964, 1033, 1183, 1184, 1191; Zer §445

21 MHT II 193; MHT IV 68; Rob 364, 795

22 MHT III 87, 170; MHT IV 77; Rob 438, 884

23 DM 253; Moule 18; MHT II 452; MHT III 27, 87; Rob 392; RD §353; Zer §362n

24 DM 254; Rob 905

25 BDF §164(2); MHT III 208; MHT IV 69; Rob 433, 515, 598, 610

26   MHT II 424; Rob 539

27   MHT III 89; MHT IV 72; Rob 857, 907, 1019, 1162, 1388, 1420; RD §403(a)

28   BDF §470(1); BW 81; MHT III 46, 326; Rob 707

29   BW 55; Moule 32, 178; MHT II 444; MHT III 242; MHT IV 48, 69; Rob 94, 531bis, 550; Zer §60, 365

30   MHT III 46; Rob 218, 707, 708; RD §379

31   BW 68, 151; Rob 243, 598

32   BDF §342(2), 343(3); MHT I 143; MHT II 424, 469; MHT III 70, **85**; Rob 859, 901bis

33   Rob 859, 1034

34   MHT III 282; Rob 597, 1163

35   BDF §217(2); DM 69, 105; Moule 76; Rob 585, 643; Zer §103

36   BW 34; MHT II 463; Rob 540, 879

Chapter 4

1   BDF §185(2); MHT III 216; Rob 434, 438, 666, 684, 841, 1034, 1049, 1421

2   BDF §425(1), 450(3); MHT III 41; MHT IV 74; Rob 434, 680, 1129, 1148, 1149, 1154; RD §472(a)bis, 472(f)

3   BDF §327; MHT III 167, 170; Rob 434

4   BW 12; Moule 55; Rob 393, 582, 887, 919; RD §359, 405

5   BDF §207(1), 294(1); BW 13; DM 253; Moule 68, 86; MHT II 431; MHT III 167, 216, **256**, 324; MHT IV 69; Rob 428, 505, 547, 596, 646, 715; RD §343(k), 353; Zer §97

6   BDF §101; BW 26; DM 254; Moule 50; MHT III 260; Rob 367, 549, 599, 604, 778, 909bis, 1116, 1146; RD §403(a), 460(c)

7   Moule 127; MHT II 90; MHT III 135; Rob 343, 434, 598

8   BW 99; DM 243, 254; Rob 905

9   BDF §193(5); DM 108, 254; Moule 33; MHT II 49; MHT III 37, 169; Rob 204, 343, 371, 482, 530, 678

10   BDF §277(1); BW 130; MHT I 201; MHT II 90; MHT III 37, 135; Rob 418, 656, 678, 922bis, 1015, 1046, 1069, 1105, 1110, 1417; RD §460(b): Zer §455z

11   BDF §445(3); BW 66; DM 141; Rob 394, 656bis, 777, 778, 1105, 1106, 1166, 1179, 1182, 1185, 1189; RD §410(a), 460(b), 470(n)

12   DM 253; Rob 667, 680

13   Rob 599

14   BDF §266(3); BW 152; DM 126; MHT III 97; Rob 519, 520, 716, 813, 889, 1212, inset

15   DM 248; MHT II 74; Rob 201, 985, 1088, 1413; RD §410(a); Zer §117

16   BDF §336(1); MHT III 76; Rob 299, 856; Zer §117

17   MHT II 208; MHT III **269**; Rob 699; Zer §289n

18   BDF §292, 474(5c), 475(1); DM 126; MHT I 145; MHT III 225; Rob 657, 720, 790, 833, 843; RD §379

19   Moule 7; RD §451(a)

20   BW 105, 153; MHT II 469; Rob 426, 842, 843, 919, 1183; RD §360

21   BW 153; Moule 32; MHT II 469; MHT III 139; Rob 971, 1159; RD §419(f); Zer §428

22   Rob 233, 429, 678, 713, 1159

23   DM 241; MHT I 66; MHT II 365, 469; MHT III 139; Rob 234, 400, 476, 540, 566, 710, 971, 1186; RD §410(a), 419(f); Zer §428

24   Rob 919

25   Rob 215, 707, 708

26   Rob 778

27   BW 37; DM 149, 254; Moule 50, 61; MHT III 272; Rob 424, 604, 611, 756, 791, 1154, 1188; RD §388, 410(a), 472(d) and (f)

28   DM 254; Rob 433

29   BDF §427(2); DM 265; MHT I 170, 193; MHT III **283**; Rob 251, 917, 949, 1167, 1175; RD §448(b), 464(b)

31   BDF §215(3); BW 84; DM 113, 188; MHT II 195; MHT III 67, 156, 277; Rob 587, 645, 884

32   BDF §443(1); MHT III 135

33 BDF §427(2); DM 253; MHT III **283**; Rob 292, 743, 917, 1168

34 BDF §393(6); BW 112; DM 270, 294; Moule 120, 146; MHT I 208, 210; MHT III 139; Rob 685, 992, 1076; RD §375

35 BDF §323(2), 487; MHT I 12; MHT II 422, 469; MHT III **17**, 63, 76; Rob 422, 626, 678, 856, 870, 1168, 1180; Zer §207, 278

36 BDF §444(3); MHT III 335; Rob 299, 659; RD §386(b)

37 Rob 786

38 MHT III 135

39 BW 158; MHT II 463; Rob 709, 1123

40 BW 160; DM 253; Rob 762; Zer §102

41 MHT II 161; MHT III 29; Rob 1179

42 Rob 686; RD §376

43 BW 69; Rob 762

44 DM 131, 243; Rob 691, 1191

45 BW 44, 100; DM 227, 258; Rob 1128

46 MHT II 378, 380; Rob 970

47 DM 249, 254, 294; Rob 368, 597, 884

48 DM 254; MHT III 96; Rob inset

49 BW 123; DM 215; MHT II 210, 380; MHT III 140; Rob 977, 1091; RD §421(a)

50 BDF §294(1); MHT III 324; Rob 715bis, 841

51 BDF §423(1); MHT III 322; Rob 1212

52 BDF §328; BW 91; DM 93; Moule 10, 34, 161; MHT I 63, 245, 248; MHT III **65**, 72, 226, **248**; Rob 206, 470, 546, 665, 834; RD §342(c) and (f)

53 DM 153; MHT III 304; Rob 566, 680, 709, 721

54 Rob 1396

Chapter 5

1 Rob 782

2 BDF §241(6), 412(2); MHT II 85; MHT III **18**, **152**, 171; Rob 104, 169, 524, 604, 760

3 BDF §460(3); Rob 427

4 BDF §107, 218, 303; Moule 76; MHT IV 74; Rob 291, 585, 710, 719, 1149; RD §472(b); Zer §103

5 Moule 101; MHT II 172; MHT IV 68; Rob 892, 1115

6 BW 77; Moule 8; MHT III 62; Rob 428, 879

7 BDF §379; BW 76, 158; DM 109, 182; MHT I 219; MHT II 436; MHT IV 73; Rob 879, 960, 978, 1001, 1068; RD §419(a); Zer §410, 425

8 DM 300; MHT III **77**; Rob 681, 855bis, 950; RD §375, 401(a)

9 MHT II 190; MHT IV 68; Rob 681, 838, 855, 890; RD §375, 401(a); Zer §246

10 MHT II 422

11 BDF §251; BW 66; MHT II 73, 139, 424; MHT III 37, 46; Rob 258, 274, 275, 480, 481, 656, 695, 707, 769, 855; RD §174 b, 379

12 Rob 778, 1114

13 BDF §330; MHT I 210; Rob 841

14 Moule 208; MHT I 125; Rob 234, 890; RD §402(a)

15 MHT III 26; Rob 836, 859, 1035, 1112, 1114

16 Zer §420

17 Rob 681, 1388; RD §375; Zer §229

18 MHT I 90; Rob 396, 884, 1060, 1166

19 MHT II 424; Rob 190, 707, 708, 1018bis, 1094, 1181, 1388; RD §439; Zer §229, 471

20 MHT II 73, 202; MHT III **100**; Rob 188, 311, 325, 985

21 Rob 969

22 Rob 1397

23 DM 276; Rob 1137

24 MHT I 67; MHT III 175; Rob 453, 593, 897, 898

25 MHT II 469; MHT III 139; MHT IV 76; Rob 135, 234, 333, 356bis, 781, 859; RD §387(b)(2); Zer §69, 226, 428

26   Rob 1181

27   Moule 116, 177; MHT II 431, 441; MHT III 49, 56; MHT IV 69; Rob 781, 802

28   BDF §322, 393(3), 427(2); Moule 203; MHT II 469; MHT III 139; MHT IV 76; Rob 333, 859, 890; Zer §226, 428

29   BDF §166; MHT II 431; Rob 500, 859

30   DM 130; Rob 685, 828, 890, 1162

31   BDF §372(1a); MHT III 116; Rob 677, 890, 1010, 1018

32   BDF §306(3); Rob 479, 746, 764

33   Rob 896, 897

34   MHT III 64; Rob 110, 677, 866

35   BDF §273(1); DM 110; MHT II 225; MHT III 183; Rob 334, 625, 1212; RD §320

36   BDF §185(1), 270(1), 390(4); MHT I 49; MHT II 113, 161, 424; MHT III 135, 186; MHT IV 72; Rob 220, 265, 274bis, 516, 667, 686, 789, 894, 896, 1204; RD §376; Zer §186

37   BDF §342(2), 445(4); BW 96; DM 203; Moule 203; MHT I 144; MHT II 424; MHT III 183; MHT IV 76; Rob 893, 896, 1179, 1189; Zer §69

38   BDF §277(1); MHT I 67; MHT II 424; MHT III 37, 45, **283**; Rob 453, 678, 703

39   BDF §273(3), 277(1); MHT II 469; MHT III 37, 45; Rob 329bis, 678, 707, 941, 1183; RD §308, 407; Zer §198, 424

40   MHT II 469; Rob 878

41   Rob 110

42   Rob 499, 500; Zer §207

43   MHT II 469; Rob 707, 762; Zer §455a

44   BDF §277(1), 468(3); Moule 180; MHT II 429, 469; MHT III **13**, 37, **226**; MHT IV 69; Rob 437, 442, 678, 771, 857, 1128, 1135; Zer §375

45   BDF §336(3), 339(2b); MHT III **76, 80**; Rob 779, 853, 890, 895

46   BW 164; Rob 540, 1012, 1014

47   Rob 1009, 1012, 1160; RD §444

Chapter 6

1   Rob 44, 503

2   BDF §66(2), 134(1a); BW 12, 31; MHT II 189, 195; Rob 368, 404, 604, 774, 1218; RD §320

3   MHT II 32

5   Rob 774, 1035, 1399

6   BDF §330; DM 244; MHT III **41**; Rob 891, 950, 1029, 1043, 1421; Zer §346n

7   BDF §393(2); DM 286; Rob 745, 921, 998; RD §342(j), 378; Zer §207, 352

9   BDF §111(3), 247(2), 296, 299(1); MHT III 196; Rob 407, 674, 704, 713, 736, 762; RD §380

10   BDF §160; Moule 33; MHT I 63, 75; MHT III 221; Rob 486, 1391; RD §342(k); Zer §74

11   BDF §111(3); BW 69; Rob 732, 762, 967, 1181; RD §424(d)

12   Rob 618, 751, 974

13   BDF §172; MHT II 171; MHT III 186; Rob 598, 762, 777

14   DM 126; MHT III **26**; Rob 444, 718, 768; Zer §7n

15   DM 94(2); Rob 287, 480, 657; Zer §198n

16   DM 100; Rob 602, 841, 904, 974; RD §401(a)

17   BW 99; MHT III 179; Rob 361, 366bis, 904, 1214; RD §401(a), 402(b), 403(b)

18   BDF §443(1); MHT II 190; Rob 367, 1179, 1215; RD §320, 402(b)

19   BDF §233(1); BW 48, 139; DM 93, 258; Moule 50; MHT II 122; Rob 263, 469, 603, 904; RD §163 A, 342(e), 402(a)

20   DM 175; Rob 890, 947

21   MHT III 227; Rob 603, 857, 886, 919; RD §402(b)

22   BDF §330, 467; MHT III **67**; Rob 437, 444, 776, 887, 1029, 1034; Zer §365

23   BDF §467; MHT II 60; Rob 232, 1029

24   BDF §324, 467; BW 133; Moule 153; Rob 887, 1029, 1049

25 MHT I 146; Rob 896

26 MHT III **26**; Zer §7n

27 Moule 33; MHT II 441; Rob 471, 595

28 Rob 850, 880, 889, 923, 934, 1409

29 MHT II 463; Rob 400, 567, 706, 708, 720, 721, 850

30 MHT II 436; MHT III 37; Rob 850; Zer §425

31 MHT III 135; Rob 375, 903bis

32 Moule 14; MHT III 70; Rob 1187

33 MHT II 205; MHT III 217

34 Rob 300

35 BW 109; MHT II 463; MHT III 96; Rob 235, 349, 850, inset

36 MHT IV 65; Rob 889, 1182; RD §410(a)

37 DM 272; MHT II 437; MHT III 21, 39, 97; MHT IV 65; Rob 235, 409, 653, 682, 713, 773

38 MHT IV 65; Rob 895, 1166, 1187bis, inset; RD §470(n)

39 BDF §466(3); MHT II 424, 434, 437; MHT III 39, 95, 179, 197, 316; MHT IV 65; Rob 400, 437, 439, 653, 684, 713, 718, 753, 769, 773, 775, 992, 1413; Zer §31

40 MHT II 463; MHT III 139; MHT IV 65; Rob 400, 520, 522, 586, 708, 762

41 Rob 444, 561, 853, 859, 1201

42 Rob 697, 698

43 MHT III **76**; Rob 610, 853

44 BW 37; Rob 235, 520, 523, 586, 889

45 Moule 40 n.1; MHT II 459; MHT III 89, 234; Rob 235, 504, 516, 614, 859bis, 1097bis, 1429; RD §344(c)

46 MHT II 424; MHT III 45, 304; Rob 1034

47 Rob 653; RD §327

48 Rob 677, 1407

49 Rob 1183

50 BW 130; DM 225; MHT II 436; Rob 599, 768, 1413; Zer §425

51 DM 113, 149; Rob 234, 768, 872, 1185bis; RD §410(a)

52 DM 254; MHT III 135; Rob 444, 811

53 BDF §169(2); DM 254; MHT II 441; Zer §67

54 MHT II 129; Rob 586; RD §174 a

56 Zer §117

57 BDF §222; MHT I 105; MHT II 422; Rob 584bis

58 Rob 968

59 MHT I 236

60 Rob 444

61 Rob 587

62 BDF §482; MHT II 441; Rob 470, 487, 550, 1023, 1203; RD §351

63 MHT II 474; MHT III 151; Rob 768, 1206, 1430

64 BDF §351(2); DM 230; MHT III 86; Rob 374, 550, 597, 792, 878, 1118bis, 1159, 1214; Zer §282

65 MHT III 89; Rob 234, 1388, 1420

66 BW 18; DM 103; Moule 72f.; Rob 444, 597

67 MHT II 171; Rob 878, 917, 923, 1175; RD §448(b)

68 BW 59; DM 193; MHT I 83; MHT II 431; Rob 790, 791, 876, 924, 934; RD §401(c)

69 DM 118; Rob 423, 652, 763, 895, 1035

70 MHT II 469; MHT III 55; Rob 779; Zer §455a

71 BW 9; DM 77; MHT II 145, 171; MHT III 168; Rob 501, 884

Chapter 7

1 Rob 444, 885

2 DM 244; MHT III 214; Rob 399

3 BDF §369(2); Moule 139; MHT II 210, 476; MHT III **100**; Rob 308, 328, 1180; Zer §206

4 BDF §372(1a), 405(1); MHT I 212; MHT II 469; MHT III 115, 146; Rob 752, 764, 1009, 1038, 1100

5 MHT II 463; Rob 1185

6 DM 254; Rob 770bis, 777

8 BDF §323(3); MHT II 210; RD §375

9 BDF §332(1); Rob 833

10 Rob 429, 444, 764

11 MHT III 46; Rob 707bis

12 BDF §447(6); DM 261; MHT III 36; Rob 1394

13 BW 15; Moule 62; Rob 491, 500, 619

14 Rob 444, 838, 885

15 Rob 1172; RD §342(o)

16 DM 254; Rob 496; Zer §445

17 BDF §64(6); MHT II 369; MHT III 338; Rob 292, 551, 619, 741, 757, 878, 1019bis, 1045, 1177, 1188; RD §303, 381, 448(f); Zer §207

18 MHT II 424; MHT III 45; Rob 698, 762

19 DM 250; MHT II 469; Rob 1175

21 Rob 1397

22 Moule 14 n.3; MHT III 304; Rob 243, 434, 1166, 1187, 1202, 1429; RD §470(n)

23 MHT II 139; MHT III 199, 217; Rob 275, 418, 541, 656, 774, 965, 1175bis

24 BW 47; Moule 33, 135; MHT III 245; Rob 478

25 Rob 27, 444, 698, 703

26 Rob 135, 845, 917, 1168, 1415

27 BDF §382(4); DM 241; MHT III 112; Rob 1183

28 BDF §442(1), 444(3); DM 254; Zer §455a

30 MHT II 469; MHT III 173; Rob 231, 905, 1183; Zer §455a

31 BDF §294(4); MHT II 165, 194, 463; Rob 716, 720, 1175

32 DM 225; Rob 444, 1123

33 MHT II 422; Rob 659

34 BDF §99(1), 471(3); MHT II 60; MHT III 342; Rob 232, 233, 969; Zer §278

35 BDF §166, 480(6); DM 286; MHT III 212, 226; Rob 495, 501, 581, 917, 1001, 1205; RD §343(d), 359; Zer §420

36 BDF §99(1); MHT II 60; Rob 232, 233

37 MHT II 196, 474, 475, 476; Rob 234, 444; RD §320, 439; Zer §367

38 BDF §466(4); Moule 30 f.; MHT II 463, 474, 475; MHT III **316, 320**; MHT IV 74; Rob 333, 355, 356, 437, 459, 1130

39 BDF §294(1); MHT II 463; MHT III 324; Rob 368, 433, 795, 859bis

40 BDF §164(2); Moule 72; MHT III 208, 234; MHT IV 70; Rob 599bis

41 DM 243; MHT II 194; Rob 578, 1190

42 Moule 153; Rob 970; Zer §217

44 Rob 857

45 BDF §291(3); BW 70; MHT III **46;** Rob 444

46 MHT IV 72

47 DM 254; MHT III 335; Rob 917, 1175; RD §448(b)

48 BW 29; MHT II 463; Rob 599

49 Rob 404, 407; RD §327

51 MHT II 211; MHT III **283;** Rob 308, 917, 1168, 1214; Zer §325

52 BW 79, 118; MHT II 86; MHT III 63; Rob 866, 949; RD §448(h)

Chapter 8

2 MHT IV 67

3 Moule 89; Rob 1210

4 BDF §101; Moule 99; MHT II 193

5 Rob 405, 1402

7 MHT III 159, **226;** Rob 1102, 1121

9 BDF §216(3), 305, 419(3), 455(3); Moule 60 n.1, 89; MHT I 105; MHT II 454; MHT III 155, 198, 268, 276; Rob 282, 294, 602, 1210; Zer §10

12 MHT II 454; MHT III 96, 183; Rob 768, inset

13 BW 141, 148; DM 254

14 BDF §323(3), 372(1a), 446; MHT III 334; Rob 208, 866, 870, 1010, 1018, 1026, 1045

15 BDF §258(2); MHT III 177

16 BDF §475(2); BW 112; DM 244,
246, 292; Rob 208, 424, 1019,
1026; RD §443

17 BW 154; RD §375

18 MHT III 42, 151

19 BDF §360(2); DM 254; MHT III
92; Rob 922, 1015, 1417

20 MHT II 469; Rob 586, 905, 1159,
1165; RD §360; Zer §455a

21 Rob 870; RD §423(c)

22 MHT II 194; MHT III 259

23 MHT III **14**; Rob 547bis, 548,
765; Zer §134

24 MHT III **26**; Rob 356; Zer §7n

25 BDF §160, 300(2); BW 143; DM
254; Moule 34; MHT III **49**; Rob
244, 294, 419, 470, 487, 546,
550, 729, 730bis, 738, 917; RD
§342(k), 351; Zer §74, **222**, 459

26 BDF §448(3); DM 241; Moule 68;
MHT II 424; MHT III 135, 257;
Rob 698, 1186

27 BDF §151(1); Rob 473, 1029; RD
§342(h), 451(a); Zer §346n

28 MHT II 441; Rob 698, 837, 871

29 Rob 537, 549, 611, 659, 845

30 BDF §423(2); BW 137; MHT II
463; MHT III 322; Rob 1132

31 MHT I 67; Rob 234, 453, 1117;
Zer §278, 327

32 MHT I 149; Rob 871, 872

33 BW 96; MHT I 144, 149; Rob 872,
896

34 MHT IV 71

37 Moule 75; Rob 1159

38 BDF §278; DM 258; MHT I 85; MHT
III 38; Rob 614; Zer §102

39 BDF §360(1); MHT III **92**, 168,
208; Rob 921, 1015, 1016, 1022;
RD §441; Zer §42, 311

40 Zer §42

41 Zer §42

42 BDF §452(3); Moule 149, 205;
Rob 579, 708, 881, 1014; RD
§304; Zer §42

43 Zer §42

44 BDF §14, 73, 97(1), 268(2),
273(1), 282(3); Moule 112; MHT
II 100; MHT III **40**, 112, **177**,
206, 208, **227**; Rob 224, 551,
683, 768, 1219; RD §320; Zer
§42, 45, 117, 134

45 MHT II 436; MHT III 345; Zer
§424

46 DM 92

49 Rob 690

51 BW 165; MHT III 96; Rob 850,
1019, inset; RD §439

52 MHT II 469; MHT III 96, 233;
Rob 473, 507, inset, 1405

53 BDF §293, 293(2); MHT II 208;
MHT III 47; Rob 441, 728; RD
§337; Zer §**217**

54 Moule 116; Rob 1019, 1034; RD
§375

55 BDF §182(4); Moule 148, 149,
192; MHT III **216**, 321; Rob 505,
530, 1026

56 BDF §392(1a); Moule 146; MHT II
470, 474, 475; MHT III **102**,
138; Rob 993, 1212, 1405; Zer
§410, 413, 429

57 DM 254; MHT I 234; MHT II 221,
422; MHT III **168**; Rob 310, 337,
1183

58 BDF §395; MHT III 62, 140; Rob
394, 880, 977, 1091; RD §421(a)

59 BDF §471(4); MHT I 156, 161;
Rob 350, 581, 807, 817, 1136

Chapter 9

1 Moule 73; Rob 784

2 BDF §391(5); DM 249; MHT I 210;
MHT III **102**, 156; Rob 998; RD
§435(a); Zer §352

3 BDF §448(7); DM 165; Moule 145;
MHT III 95, 304; MHT IV 66; Rob
404; Zer §7n

4 DM 281; MHT III **110**, 321; Rob
976, 1081, 1159, 1431

5 MHT II 431; MHT III 112, 183;
MHT IV 69; Rob 684, 972

6 BDF §473(1); Rob 420, 681, 779;
RD §348, 374

7 BDF §205, 465(2); MHT II 32;
MHT III **77**; MHT IV 72; Rob 253,
592, 714, 855; Zer §103

8 BDF §330; Moule 206; MHT II
469; MHT IV 70; Rob 503, 768,

866, 887, 1115, 1139, 1421; Zer §274, 367, 429

9 BDF §291(6); DM 296; Rob 1028; RD §346(c)

10 DM 254; MHT II 194; Rob 339, 419, 420, 503, 1213; RD §374

11 BDF §291(6); Rob 253, 420, 681, 708, 779; RD §374

12 Rob 234, 707

13 MHT II 431; MHT III **41**; MHT IV 70; Zer §205

14 MHT III 324; Rob 368, 718, 1213

15 Rob 681

16 DM 101, 254; MHT II 194; MHT III **26**; Rob 710, 779; Zer §7n, 424

17 DM 254; Moule 62; MHT I 94; MHT II 83, 436; Rob 420, 964, 1213; RD §374

18 BDF §330; DM 258; Moule 121f., 176; MHT II 431; MHT III **67**; MHT IV 70; Rob 291, 841, 975, 1029; RD §451(a); Zer §205

19 Rob 768

20 DM 254(2); Rob 524

21 BDF §283(4); DM 254; Moule 121; MHT III 41; Rob 733; RD §380

22 BDF §97(2), 120(2), 347(1); DM 132, 155, 160, 206; MHT II 190; MHT III 86, 162; MHT IV 66; Rob 366, 480, 811, 816, 905, 993; Zer §290, 410

24 Rob 597, 697, 700

25 BDF §291(6), 339(3); BW 135; DM 154, 254; Moule 101, 154; MHT II 474; MHT III 64, **81**; Rob 708, 866, 892, 1045, 1115; RD §460(c); Zer §274

26 DM 254; MHT II 83; MHT III 231; Rob 420

27 BDF §338(2); MHT III 78; Rob 878

28 BDF §291(1); MHT III 46, 156; Rob 268, 473, 707bis; RD §379, 420(c)

29 Moule 154; MHT III 149; Zer §286

30 BDF §452(2); DM 243; MHT II 83, 449, 469; MHT III 331; Rob 420, 433, 1029, 1190; Zer §455a

31 Rob 698

32 DM 254; Moule 73; MHT II 83; Rob 597, 1029, 1213

33 BDF §358(1), 428(2); Moule 149; MHT III 90, 92; Rob 920, 1014, 1016; RD §470(c)

34 MHT II 422; Rob 656, 678, 768, 774; RD §387(e); Zer §7n

35 MHT II 441, 463; Rob 841, 1029

36 BDF §291(6), 442(8), 483; MHT II 435, 436, 463; Rob 960, 999, 1182; Zer §425

37 BDF §291(4); MHT III 46

38 DM 254

39 BDF §101

40 Rob 611, 779

41 MHT II 194; Rob 1013, 1014

Chapter 10

1 BDF §291(4); DM 128; Moule 105; MHT II 424; MHT III 46; Rob 300, 708; RD §474(a)

3 BDF §133(2); MHT II 75; MHT IV 76; Rob 428, 608; Zer §69

4 Moule 83; Rob 358, 404, 801

5 MHT I 190; MHT III 97; Rob 355, 356, 418, 889, inset; Zer §444n

6 BDF §291(6); Rob 500, 708, 736, 880

7 BW 9; MHT III **212**; Rob 501, 768

8 DM 109; Rob 507, 622

9 Rob 428

10 MHT III **180**; Rob 1025, 1387

11 BW 65; DM 116, 151, 152; Rob 398, 418, 429, 632, 656, 762ter, 776, 865, 1206; RD §324, 327, 334, 387(b)(1), 474(o)

12 BDF §430(1), 471(3); DM 264; Moule 105, 156; MHT I 231, 232; MHT III **285**, 342; MHT IV 77; Rob 428, 434, 764, 955, 1138, 1163; RD §469; Zer §440n

13 Moule 28; Rob 509

14 Rob 762

15 MHT III 63; Rob 632, 870; RD §401(b)

16 Moule 124; MHT III 48; MHT IV 76; Zer §226

17 Rob 965

18 BW 20; MHT III 139; MHT IV 67; Rob 420, 579, 845

21 MHT III **26**; Zer §7n

22 MHT III 27, 171; Rob 408, 760

23 MHT II 146, 190

24 Moule 209; MHT II 194, 400; MHT IV 67; Rob 1394

25 MHT II 424; Zer §455a

27 DM 165; Rob 762

28 BW 109; MHT III 96, 286; Rob 333, 356, 752, 875, 1164, inset; RD §470(j)

29 BW 96; MHT I 50; MHT II 74, 437; MHT III 39

30 MHT III 37; Rob 402, 677; RD §326

32 BDF §319; DM 186; Moule 8; MHT III **63**; Rob 740, 845, 880bis; RD §402(a)

33 Rob 480

34 Rob 1028

35 Moule 35; Rob 434, 480, 708, 1160, 1182, 1420

36 BDF §470(1), 478; DM 294; MHT III 183; Rob 425, 437, 442, 781, 952, 1015, 1028; RD §387(b)(2), 449; Zer §416n

37 MHT I 125; MHT III 284; Rob 1012, 1020, 1160, 1170; RD §439, 444

38 DM 195; Rob 425, 850, 983, 1026; RD §401(a), 402(a), 430(a)

39 BDF §140; MHT III 24; Rob 409, 885

40 BDF §332(1); BW 67; DM 119(2), 120; Moule 18; MHT II 452; Rob 487, 659, 833, 970; Zer §362n

42 MHT II 463

Chapter 11

1 Moule 72; MHT II 144, 452; MHT III 259; MHT IV 77; Rob 256, 578; Zer §362n

2 BDF §339(1); MHT I 132; MHT III **80**; Rob 859, 1114; Zer **§266**

3 MHT IV 68; Rob 1191; RD §412

4 Rob 632

6 DM 258; MHT III 324; Rob 470, 706, 718, 1152, 1153, 1191

7 BDF §484; MHT IV 19; Rob 931, 1205

8 MHT II 422; Rob 885

9 MHT II 171; Rob 587, 800, 1019; Zer §325

10 Rob 587

11 Rob 895, 905

12 BDF §372(1a); BW 163; Moule 148; MHT III 115; Rob 905, 1009, 1191, 1417

13 Rob 498, 905, 1029, 1398; RD §451(a)

14 BDF §459(2); Rob 1191, 1210bis, 1398

15 Rob 1398

16 Rob 580

17 MHT I 36; Rob 266, 800

18 BDF §161(1); MHT I 102; MHT III 172; Rob 283, 424, 469, 575bis, 760; Zer §70, 71

19 BDF §228; MHT III **16, 270**; Rob 619, 620, 905

20 BDF §101; MHT II 145; Rob 521, 791

21 DM 169; Moule 149; MHT I 201; Rob 313, 420, 841, 922, 1015; Zer §316

22 Rob 676, 684, 733; RD §373

23 Rob 420

24 Rob 669

25 MHT II 463; Rob 356, 768; Zer §226

26 BW 105; MHT II 434, 463; MHT III 96; Rob 915, inset; RD §405

27 BW 166; DM 262, 294, 298; MHT III 183; Rob 391, 781, 891, 1028, 1034, 1150; RD §322, 472(c)

28 BDF §420(2); MHT I 131; MHT II 211; MHT III 62, **156**; Rob 861, 881

29 Zer §367

30 MHT II 190; Rob 841, 905bis

31 BDF §102(2), 207(1), 390(4); MHT III 135; MHT IV 71; Rob

596; Zer §207

32 DM 290; MHT I 201; MHT II 145;
Rob 313, 420bis, 681, 706, 722,
779, 922, 1015

33 MHT II 476

35 BW 139; MHT III 72; Rob 391,
834

36 DM 188; Moule 207; MHT II 194;
MHT III 66, 68; Rob 302, 339,
741, 884

37 MHT II 83; MHT IV 73; Rob 698,
857, 920, 985, 993; Zer §352

38 BDF §207(1); MHT II 201, 476;
Rob 341, 559, 560, 593, 596,
604

39 MHT II 337; Rob 657, 856

40 Rob 1030

41 Rob 541, 856

42 MHT I 135; MHT III 268; Rob
477, 617, 843; Zer §112, 316

43 MHT III 304; Rob 328, 1193

44 BDF §159(3), 347(1); Moule 192;
MHT II 72, 190; MHT III 86; Rob
193, 197, 361, 366, 486, 856,
905, 910, 1117; RD §342(j)

45 MHT II 463

47 BDF §366(4); MHT III **98**; Rob
880bis, 923, 934; RD §405,
448(g)

48 BDF §323(1), 444(3), 473(1);
MHT II 422, 463; MHT III 63,
190; Rob 681

49 BDF §186(2); BW 10; DM 230; MHT
III 195, 196, 235; Rob 675, 742

50 DM 111; Moule 64; Rob 631bis,
993, 1034, 1413; RD §344(d),
371, 466; Zer §91, 145

51 BDF §186(2); MHT III 235; Rob
688, 709, 1029, 1034; Zer §346n

52 MHT II 473; MHT IV 66; Rob 581,
593, 1162; RD §468

53 Rob 709

54 BDF §241(1); BW 12; Moule 83;
MHT II 50; Rob 205, 640

55 BDF §390(4), 395; Moule 74; MHT
I 12; MHT III 135; Rob 517, 621

56 Moule 61; MHT I 191; MHT II
194; MHT III 96; MHT IV 68; Rob
905, 1217, inset, 1405; RD
§320; Zer §444

57 BDF §369(4); MHT II 190, 211;
MHT III **105**; MHT IV 74; Rob
134, 234, 308, 905, 986, 993

Chapter 12

1 BDF §213, 345; DM 254; Moule
74; MHT I 100, 101; MHT III
248, 260; Rob 110, 424, 598,
621, 622, 702, 762bis, 970,
1191; RD §410(a), 412; Zer §71

2 DM 111, 254; Rob 627

3 BDF §113(2); DM 254; MHT II
379; Rob 510, 598, 859

4 BDF §356; MHT III 89; Rob 111

6 BDF §119(4); Moule 28; MHT II
272

7 MHT I 175; Rob 932

8 MHT III 42

9 BDF §270(1); DM 254; Moule 107;
MHT I 84; MHT III **186**; MHT IV
66; Rob 656, 774, 777

10 DM 270; Moule 203; MHT III **54**;
Rob 811, 993, 994, 1180

11 MHT II 463

12 BDF §270(1), 412(3); Moule 107;
MHT III 153, 186; Rob 774

13 BDF §6; MHT I 14; Rob 243, 528,
595, 838; RD §346(a)

15 Moule 92; MHT III 35; Rob 264,
462

16 Rob 487, 550, 605, 653, 765,
905, 1029; RD §336; Zer §346n

17 DM 254; Moule 16, 206; MHT III
81; Rob 892

18 BDF §388; Rob 909, 1035, 1042,
1101, 1422; RD §461(c)

19 MHT I 135; Rob 243, 843, 941

20 BDF §390(4); MHT III 135; Rob
27

21 DM 254; Rob 243, 923; RD §405,
446

22 BDF §135(1d); Rob 405

23 MHT II 441, 470; MHT III 139,
155; MHT IV 74; Rob 895, 992;
Zer §411, 428

24 Rob 1019; Zer §325

25 Rob 317

26 Rob 870, 969, 1019

27 BDF §448(4), 496(1); Rob 598, 843, 895, 1187, 1399

28 Rob 462, 845

29 BW 98, 128; DM 254, 258; MHT III 291; Rob 908, 1047, 1081

30 MHT III 268; Rob 584

32 BDF §107, 138(1); BW 20; MHT III **21**; Rob 190, 597, 889, 1018; RD §439; Zer §322n

33 Rob 740bis, 1029

34 MHT II 423, 441, 469; Rob 697, 704, 735

35 BDF §455(3); Moule 197; MHT I 158; Rob 976

36 MHT II 463; Rob 133, 807, 974

37 MHT II 463; Rob 1129

38 MHT III 304

39 Rob 699, 875

40 BDF §308, 369(3); MHT I 117; MHT II 470; MHT III 23, 52, 70; Zer §342

41 MHT II 469; MHT IV 70; Zer §429

42 BDF §120(2); MHT II 463; MHT IV 66, 74; Rob 1155, 1188bis

43 BDF §107, 185(3); DM 112; MHT III 216; Rob 301, 633, 1150, 1154; RD §472(e); Zer §445

44 MHT II 463; Rob 1135; Zer §367, 445

46 MHT II 434, 463; MHT III 196; MHT IV 77; Rob 753

47 MHT III 234; MHT IV 66; Rob 234, 1400

48 MHT II 424; Rob 698; Zer §278

49 MHT II 424; Rob 698

Chapter 13

1 BDF §207(3), 464; Moule 121; MHT I 90, 135; MHT II 32, 470; MHT III 70, 139, 215, 266; MHT IV 74; Rob 435, 498, 691, 843; Zer §428

2 BDF §464; Moule 169, 209; MHT II 211; MHT III 139; Rob 309, 435, 799

3 BDF §464; MHT III 70; Rob 435, 562; RD §434(a)

4 BDF §464; MHT II 76; MHT III 27; Rob 188, 314, 435, 597; Zer §7n

5 BDF §464; MHT II 368, 455; Rob 435, 716, 757

6 BDF §319, 473(1); BW 78; MHT III **63**; Rob 418, 420, 880, 915, 1175

7 MHT II 83

8 BDF §365(2); DM 249; MHT I 177, 191; MHT III 96, 97; Rob 915, 933, inset, 1405; Zer §278, 296, 444

9 Rob 1162, 1172, 1173

10 BDF §393(5); MHT II 248; MHT III **139**; Rob 234

12 Moule 16; Rob 481, 1045

13 BDF §143, 147(3); BW 5; MHT I 235; MHT III 230; Rob 270, 416, 458bis, 466, 1028; RD §340(c), 449

14 Rob 399, 845

15 MHT III 70; Rob 633

16 DM 83; Rob 516; RD §344(c)

17 BDF §372(1a); Rob 850, 890, 1019, 1022, 1417; RD §439, 441

18 BDF §293(5), 448(7); Moule 145; MHT III 95, 304; MHT IV 66; Rob 560, 845, 1203, 1430; RD §155 d

19 BDF §12(3); Moule 72; MHT III 144; Rob 765, 978, 983, 1075

20 BDF §107; Rob 190, 956bis, 1018; RD §414

21 MHT III 156; Rob 675; RD §409

22 MHT III 56; Rob 739; RD §409

23 Moule 18; MHT II 452; RD §409; Zer §362n

24 BDF §328; MHT II 204; MHT III 46, 123, 130; Rob 703, 724, 1045; RD §409, 448(c)

25 Rob 602, 707; RD §409

26 MHT II 345, 435; MHT III 46; MHT IV 21; Rob 707, 708; RD §379; Zer §201, 367

27 BDF §244(1); DM 121; MHT I 236; MHT III **30, 63**; Rob 488, 664, 880, 1381; RD §410(a); Zer §150

28 Rob 626, 739

29 BDF §119(4); MHT II 211, 272;
    MHT III 195, 318; Rob 235, 442,
    595, 706, 720

31 DM 198; MHT I 135; MHT II 441;
    Rob 843, 847; RD §401(a)

32 Moule 119; Rob 1009; RD §401(a)

33 Rob 548

34 DM 249; MHT III 139, 225; MHT
    IV 73; Rob 845, 993; RD
    §424(b); Zer §415

36 Rob 857; Zer §201

37 Rob 879

38 Moule 133; MHT III 111; Rob
    inset

Chapter 14

1   MHT II 463; MHT III 23; Rob
    329, 941; RD §308, 407

2   BDF §323(3); MHT II 476; MHT
    III 63, 135; Rob 424, 869,
    1015, 1025; RD §442

3   BDF §323(1), 442(2); BW 80; DM
    185; MHT II 60, 247; MHT III
    63, 334; Rob 299, 353, 690,
    846; RD §303; Zer §322n

4   BDF §323(3); Rob 731

6   Moule 112; MHT III 178; Rob
    249, 583, 769; Zer §174

7   MHT II 190; Rob 923, 1181, 1417

8   Rob 393

9   BDF §201, 474(6); MHT III 62,
    244; Rob 419, 528, 879; Zer §54

10 Moule 104 n.1

11 Rob 287, 395, 856, 1016, 1025,
    1202

12 BDF §323(3); MHT II 424, 463;
    MHT III 63

13 DM 127; MHT II 424; Rob 243,
    727, 729, 850, 956; RD §414;
    Zer §278

15 Rob 1019; Zer §320

16 BDF §306(5); MHT II 422, 436;
    Rob 613, 747, 1023; Zer §425

17 MHT II 60; Rob 233, 614,
    709bis, 857; Zer §102

19 DM 274; Rob 395, 963

21 BDF §291(4); MHT II 424; MHT
    III 41, 46; MHT IV 66, 68; Rob

635, 688, 707, 708bis, 769; RD
§377

22 BDF §299(4), 442(8), 456(2);
    MHT II 181; Rob 739, 916, 965,
    1001, 1034, 1415; RD §381,
    448(e); Zer §420

23 MHT III **56**; Rob 802; Zer §320

24 Rob 685

25 MHT III 26

26 BW 87; DM 94, 192; MHT II 424;
    Rob 418, 482, 483, 509, 634,
    708bis, 709, 795; RD §342(i)

27 BDF §270(3); MHT III 23, 185;
    Rob 315, 777; Zer §192

28 BW 80, 164; Rob 234, 817, 923,
    1015; RD §438; Zer §278, 317

29 BDF §442(15); DM 282; MHT III
    140; Rob 109, 709bis

30 Zer §455b

31 Moule 144; MHT I 177; MHT II
    211, 476; MHT III 94, **95**; MHT
    IV 66; Rob 308

Chapter 15

1   Rob 777

2   BDF §101, 466(3); Moule 104,
    206; MHT II 424; MHT III 39,
    157, 316; Rob 243, 437; Zer §31

3   Rob 584

4   MHT I 103, 241; Rob 586, 587;
    Zer §117

5   BDF §468(3); Moule 157; MHT II
    424; MHT III 45; Rob 437, 442,
    1165

6   BDF §333(1); BW 92, 94; Moule
    12, 29, 148, 181; MHT I 59,
    134, 247; MHT II 448; MHT III
    73, **74**; MHT IV 70; Rob 392,
    820bis, 828, 836, 837bis, 847,
    850, 1020, 1204, 1418; Zer §257

7   BDF §107; Rob 850

8   BDF §333(2), 369(3), 394; BW
    94; DM 197, 295; Moule 146; MHT
    I 208; MHT III 73, **74, 139**; Rob
    324, 699, 837, 843, 984, 992,
    1076; RD §434(a); Zer §257,
    342, 410, 461

9   Rob 856, 968

10 Rob 779

11 Rob 699, 784, 1204

12 BW 112; DM 270, 295; Rob 393, 699, 992, 993; Zer §410

13 BDF §394; MHT I 208, 211; Rob 272, 401, 429, 699, 992; RD §434(a); Zer §410

14 Rob 681; RD §375, 387(e)

15 DM 94; Rob 480, 769, 845; RD §342(i)

16 MHT I 55; MHT II 211; MHT III 129; Rob 309, 327, 729, 993, 1214; Zer §198

17 MHT IV 73; Rob 699

18 MHT I 79, 245; MHT III 32; Rob 28, 670, 1008; Zer §287

19 BW 107; DM 289; MHT III 345; Rob 559, 598, 921, 1013, 1014; Zer §134

20 BDF §284(1); BW 158; DM 272; Rob 509, 716, 1009; RD §437; Zer §17, 303

21 BDF §448(3); Moule 69; MHT III 256; Rob 484

22 BDF §84(2), 428(2); DM 289; MHT I 52; MHT II 194; Rob 336, 339, 887, 921, 922, 1013, 1014, 1015, 1016, 1147, 1169, 1417, 1429; RD §11, 302, 405, 438; Zer §317

24 BDF §84(2), 360(1), 428(2), 444(3); MHT I 52; MHT II 194; MHT III 92; Rob 336, 339, 887, 921, 922, 1013bis, 1014, 1015, 1016, 1147, 1417, 1429; RD §11, 302, 405, 438; Zer §287

25 BDF §397(3), 448(7); Moule 145; MHT III 95, 304; Rob 1033, 1203, 1430

26 Moule 92; Rob 561, 708, 795, 970, 1181; RD §344(d)

27 BDF §322; BW 77; DM 183, 186; MHT I 119; MHT III 62; Rob 879, 1185

Chapter 16

2 BDF §120(2), 382(1), 448(6); MHT II 470; MHT III 139, 321, 330; MHT IV 66, 74; Rob 859, 998, 1114, 1186; Zer §410, 428

3 BDF §448(3); MHT III **71**; Rob 834, 845

4 BDF §448(3); Rob 1049

5 MHT II 469

6 MHT III 23, 345

7 Rob 1019bis, inset; Zer §408

8 BW 133; MHT III 154; Rob 566, 964, 1126; RD §462(a)

9 Moule 147; MHT II 463; Rob 964

10 Moule 147; Rob 964

11 Moule 147; Rob 964

12 MHT III 135; Rob 857

13 Rob 698, 708, 709, 1109, 1397

14 MHT IV 70

15 MHT IV 70

17 MHT I 102; MHT III 209; MHT IV 70; Rob 393, 515, 599, 698, 703, 719; RD §343(i); Zer §80

18 Rob 738

19 BDF §324; BW 67; MHT III 64; Rob 610, 659, 699, 857, 1029

20 MHT II 462; MHT III 253; MHT IV 70; Rob 458bis, 595, 871

21 MHT III 112; Rob 866

22 MHT III 23; Rob 424bis, 871

23 BDF §107; DM 127; MHT I 66; Rob 190, 482bis, 708, 709, 1018; RD §439

24 MHT II 247, 421; MHT III 89; Rob 325, 360, 375, 848, 907, 1388; RD §403(a)

25 MHT II 469; MHT III 139; Zer §428

26 DM 109; Rob 618, 709

27 Moule 121; MHT III 41, 259; Rob 579, 614; RD §366

28 BW 22; Rob 598

30 BDF §219(2), 393(5); MHT II 463; MHT III **139**, 253, 259; Rob 579, 589, 699; Zer §119

31 BDF §440; Rob 1175

32 BDF §305; DM 249, 250; MHT II 204, 470; MHT III 198; MHT IV 74; Rob 657; Zer §410, 428, 455a

33 MHT III 151; Rob 135, 677

Chapter 17

1 BW 59; Rob 462, 801; RD §341(b)

2 BDF §95(1), 138(1), 282(3),

369(2); BW 142; MHT II 218, 424, 437, 441; MHT III 21, **40**, 70, 100, 317; Rob 193, 309, 348, 409, 411, 437, 500, 713, 718, 876, 963, 984; Zer §12, 31

3   MHT I 113, 206; MHT II 75; MHT III 139, 324; Rob 203, 699, 718, 776, 984, 985, 992bis, 1079; RD §434(a); Zer §410

4   Rob 234, 418, 677, 682, 843; RD §374

5   BDF §403; Moule 44; MHT III 144; Rob 418, 461, 462, 678, 682, 716, 765, 891, 978bis, 1074, 1075; RD §374, 421(b); Zer §102, 108

6   BDF §162(7); BW 95; Moule 120; MHT II 221; Rob 337, 598, 894, 895; RD §304, 403(a)

7   DM 112, 162; MHT II 215, 221; Rob 310, 337bis, 820, 1419; RD §11

8   MHT II 215; Rob 234, 337, 423

9   BDF §294(4); Rob 566, 567, 618, 619, 720, 721, 1388; Zer §96

10   DM 144; Moule 120; Rob 685, 770, 898

11   BW 116; DM 176; Moule 32; MHT II 437, 469; MHT III 35; MHT IV 69; Rob 462, 464, 716, 948, 1390

12   BW 29, 149; Moule 175; MHT II 437; MHT III 208; MHT IV 69; Rob 599, 1188; RD §362

13   Rob 902

14   BW 22; Rob 598; Zer §134

15   BW 20, 156; MHT IV 66; Rob 598bis

16   Rob 598

17   BW 147; Moule 44, 112; MHT III 177; Rob 768

18   Rob 439

19   MHT III 89; Rob 360, 908, 983

20   BDF §339(2b); MHT II 463; MHT III 87; Zer **§283**

21   Moule 32; MHT III 35; Rob 234, 264, 395, 461, 462, 1366; RD §172 c

22   Rob 898

23   BDF §205; MHT I 234; MHT II 473; MHT III 89; Rob 360, 593, 677, 908, 983, 1049, 1116, 1388

24   Moule 32; MHT I 179, 245; MHT II 60, 424, 437; MHT III **21**, 35, **100**; Rob 264, 462, 653, 713, 933, 969, 1048; RD §341(a), 423(c); Zer §206

25   DM 71; Moule 32, 167; MHT I 113; MHT III 35, 335; Rob 264bis, 419, 461, 462, 464, 843, 1128, 1391; RD §341(a); Zer §33

26   BDF §153(2); MHT II 419; MHT III 245, 304; Rob 478bis, 482

Chapter 18

1   BDF §56(3); MHT II 121, 149; MHT III 172; Rob 213, 275, 627, 680

2   Rob 859

3   BDF §418(5); MHT III **154**; Rob 548, 1127

5   Rob 859, 888

6   Rob 521

8   Rob 1028

9   Moule 145; MHT II 435; MHT III 58, **95**, 304, 325; MHT IV 21

10   BDF §111(3); MHT III 217, 296; Rob 457, 762

11   BDF §365(4); DM 258; MHT I 189; MHT III 39, 96; Rob 459, 683, 850, 934, 1161, 1174, inset; RD §470(g)

12   RD §425

13   BDF §186(2); MHT III 235; Rob 255

14   MHT III 149; Rob 529, 1035, 1058, 1084

15   MHT III 89; Rob 405, 529, 537, 707bis

16   BW 98; DM 110, 206; Moule 54; MHT III 274; Rob 746, 747bis, 775, 777

17   MHT III 210; Rob 708

18   MHT II 424, 452; Rob 909bis, 910, 1116, 1406; Zer §365

20   Moule 13 n.2; MHT I 236; MHT III 70; Rob 589

21   Rob 726

22   Rob 1116

23   DM 254; Rob 1009bis

24 DM 253, 254; Rob 841

25 MHT II 452; MHT III 156; Zer §362n, 365

26 DM 101; Rob 575, 706, 720; RD §358

27 DM 258

28 Moule 7; MHT III 226; Rob 1183, 1413

29 Rob 500

30 BDF §353(1), 355, 428(2); Moule 18, 122; MHT II 452; MHT III 87, 89, **92**; Rob 1015, 1016, 1429; RD §444; Zer §362n

32 BDF §198(6); Moule 145; MHT II 444; MHT III **95**, 304; Rob 531, 740, 1029, 1043

33 MHT II 32; MHT III 37, 183; Zer §175

34 BDF §64(1); MHT I 87; MHT II 181; MHT III 42; Rob 288, 688

35 Rob 1172

36 BDF §260(2, 3), 361; MHT III **92**; Rob 922, 993; Zer §314

37 BDF §107, 277(2), 441(3), 451(1); Moule 165; MHT I 86; MHT II 60; MHT III 37, 337; Rob 233, 599, 915, 917, 1165, 1175, 1192; RD §448(d); Zer §69

38 MHT III 37; Rob 411, 736

39 BDF §366(3), 392(1a); MHT I 210; MHT II 421; MHT III 99, 139; Rob 430, 541, 876, 878, 924, 935, 980, 992, 1399; RD §430(a); Zer §411

40 Rob 1172, 1173

Chapter 19

1 BDF §459(2); BW 100; Rob 801; RD §396

2 BW 35; DM 94; Moule 90; Rob 408, 483, 883; RD §342(i), 345(b)

3 BDF §147(3); BW 73, 85; DM 189; MHT I 70; MHT II 202; MHT III 66; Rob 311, 465, 884, 969, 1214; RD §302

6 BDF §276(2), 459(2), 493(1); MHT III **182**; Rob 1190, 1200; RD §425, 474(h)

7 Rob 480

8 Zer §69

11 BDF §360(1), 428(2); MHT I 148; MHT III **92**; Rob 885, 887, 906bis, 921, 923, 1014, 1015, 1016, 1417; RD §438; Zer §317

12 BDF §420(2); DM 99; Moule 72f.; MHT III 156; Rob 521, 542, 573; Zer §327

13 BDF §101; MHT II 409; MHT III 234; Rob 104, 367; Zer §69, 104

14 Rob 501, 793

15 BW 108

16 MHT III 135

17 BDF §132(2), 188(2); MHT II 148; MHT IV 32; Rob 104, 539

18 BDF §104(1); MHT III 225; Rob 300, 775

19 BDF §5(1); MHT III 88; Rob 362, 375, 603

20 BDF §5(1); BW 154; Rob 28, 104, 205

21 Moule 21; MHT I 125; MHT III 46, **76**, 183; Rob 707bis; Zer §175, 246

22 BDF §342(4); MHT III **85**; Rob 358, 801, 895

23 MHT II 67, 170; MHT III 27; Rob 212, 408, 1184

24 BDF §229(2), 310(2); BW 108; DM 302; Moule 63, 145, 162; MHT I 157; MHT III 54, **95**, 304, 337; Rob 619, 690, 811, 931, 943; RD §406(a), 407; Zer §233

25 BDF §125(2), 162(4), 238; Moule 38, 52; MHT I 106; MHT III 169, 273; Rob 235, 255, 501, 614, 767, 904; RD §345(e), 366

26 Moule 31; Rob 525

27 Moule 31; Rob 502, 586, 691

28 BDF §478; MHT III 344; Rob 425, 898

29 Rob 214, 254

30 Moule 16

31 BDF §478; MHT II 189, 226; MHT III 313, 344; Rob 365, 392, 1212; RD §320

32 MHT III 187; Rob 530, 746, 747, 775, 1212; RD §320

33 Rob 546, 602, 909, 910, 963, 1041, 1042, 1118

35 BDF §291(6); MHT III **46**; Rob
    707, 1118; RD §379

36 Rob 260, 704

37 Rob 293, 594, 706, 720, 721,
    772, 871

38 MHT II 32; MHT IV 68; Rob 578

39 DM 77; Moule 56; MHT II 106;
    Rob 495, 1127

40 Rob 533, 1076

41 BDF §97(2); Rob 316, 762, 905

Chapter 20

1 BW 157; MHT I 222; MHT II 439;
   MHT III 187; MHT IV 72; Rob
   522, 762, 868, 1097

2 Moule 29; MHT I 59; MHT II 448,
   474; MHT IV 70; Rob 392, 566,
   747, 845, 1202

3 BDF §207(1); MHT II 237; Rob
   746, 747, 775, 838; Zer §97

4 BDF §484; Rob 278, 401, 549,
   656, 662, 669, 747; RD §336,
   350; Zer §97

5 Rob 868; RD §401(b); Zer §97

6 Rob 868; RD §401(b); Zer §97

7 Moule 68, 87; Rob 593, 603,
   648, 868; RD §401(b); Zer §97,
   103

8 BDF §459(2); Rob 868; RD §336;
   Zer **§97**

9 Rob 1165

11 Moule 54; MHT III 274; Rob 525,
    624bis; RD §345(e), 369

12 BW 36; DM 110; Moule 54, 96;
    MHT II 438; MHT III **17**, 274;
    MHT IV 70; Rob 589, 624, 653,
    868, 906, 1202

13 Rob 868

14 MHT III **167**; Rob 133, 443, 868;
    Zer §7

15 BDF §282(3); Rob 443, 683, 869,
    1009; Zer §7

16 Rob 259, 416, 443, 462, 465,
    714, 869; Zer §7

17 BDF §323(3), 336(1, 3), 470(1);
    DM 302; MHT I 125; MHT II 476;
    MHT III 63, **76**; Rob 443, 561,
    853, 869; Zer §7, 247, 476

18 MHT II 474; Rob 259, 438, 443,
    869, 1028, 1212; Zer §7

19 BDF §205; Moule 68; MHT I 183;
    MHT II 439; MHT III 27, 187;
    MHT IV 72; Rob 522, 593, 653,
    708, 722, 779; Zer §103

20 BDF §415; BW 134; MHT III 160;
    MHT IV 69, 77; Rob 1128

21 Rob 429

22 Rob 207

23 BDF §107, 323(1), 473(1); Moule
    152; MHT II 206; MHT III 63;
    Rob 190, 315, 1019, 1418, 1419;
    RD §320, 408; Zer **§249**

25 Moule 14; MHT I 49, 191; MHT II
    129; MHT III 97; Rob 258, 259,
    inset, 1405; RD §174 a; Zer
    §444

26 BDF §205; Moule 68; MHT III 27;
    Rob 593; Zer §103

27 MHT I 125; Rob 882, 1201, 1387

28 BW 73; Moule 116, 117; Rob
    261, 461, 466bis, 779; RD
    §341(c), 387(f)

29 DM 250; MHT II 469; MHT III
    345; Rob 859, 895, 1028

30 DM 251, 253, 255; Moule 162;
    MHT II 465; MHT III 88, **337**;
    MHT IV 69, 77; Rob 362, 655,
    1181

31 Moule 166, 205; MHT III 88,
    183; Rob 540bis; Zer §250

Chapter 21

1 BDF §233(1); Rob 603

2 BDF §162(1); MHT III 207; Rob
   405, 501, 767

3 MHT I 204; MHT III 135; Rob
   353, 627, 882, 923, 990, 1062

4 Rob 593; Zer §103

5 BDF §123(1), 427(2); MHT I 170;
   Rob 155, 623, 917, 1168

6 BW 26; DM 101; MHT II 461; MHT
   IV 67; Rob 408, 580, 593, 652

7 BDF §109(8); Rob 716, 810

8 BDF §161(1); DM 87; Moule 34;
   MHT I 102; MHT II 141; Rob 268,
   469, 499, 520, 521, 533, 543,
   575, 802; RD §345(b); Zer §71

9 BDF §111(3); Rob 841

10 BDF §111(3), 336(3); BW 93;
    MHT I 135; MHT III 75; MHT IV

70; Rob 519, 577, 716, 843, 845

11 MHT II 469; Rob 672, 1129

12 Rob 437, 885, 949, 1128

13 BDF §111(3); Rob 1205

14 Rob 702, 843

15 BDF §185(1); BW 9; DM 77; Moule 198; MHT II 165; Rob 187, 255, 501, 516, 659, 667, 1201

16 Moule 198; Rob 255, 1201

17 Moule 198; Rob 255, 1028, 1201

18 MHT II 203; Rob 314bis, 802, 884, 969bis, 971, 1159; RD §402(b)

19 BDF §349(2); MHT II 444; Rob 531, 740, 876, 891, 1029, 1043, 1110

20 BW 145; MHT IV 67; Rob 724

21 BDF §299(2), 459(1); MHT III 304; Rob 395, 411, 697, 705, 736bis, 1202; RD §448(e)

22 BDF §127(3), 299(3), 373(1), 383(1); Moule 133; MHT III 37, **111**, 303, 304, 321; Rob 395, 736, 976, 978; RD §419(b)

23 BDF §127(3); DM 103; MHT I 114; MHT III 45, 63, **111**; Rob 593, 703, 870, 1216

24 MHT I 9; Rob 137, 406, 416, 785

25 BDF §294(5), 305, 350, 429; MHT I 205; MHT II 216, 219; MHT III 86, 137, 285; Rob 234, 369, 729, 877bis, 891, 1030, 1040, 1082bis, 1162, 1205, 1210; RD §451(b), 456, 474(k); Zer §102

Acts

Chapter 1

1 BDF §62, 260(1), 464; DM 126, 230; Moule 31, 181; MHT I 79; MHT II 9, 455; MHT III 32, 56, 167, 227; Rob 121, 280, 419, 440, 463, 663, 669, 716, 954, 1152, 1179, 1193, 1203; RD §21, 472(d), 474(f); Zer §35, **151**, 227

2 Moule 57, 169; MHT III **350**; Rob 121, 841, 1412

3 BDF §186(2), 223(1), 313; BW 124; DM 216, 282; Moule 56; MHT III 143, 148, 267; Rob 121, 147, 581, 820, 1039, 1074; Zer §115

4 BDF §396, 470(2); BW 21; DM 82; MHT III 137, 233, 326; Rob 121, 442, 475, 507, 519, 578, 618, 688, 715, 717, 1029; RD §344(e), 454; Zer §486

5 BDF §195(1d), 226, 433(3); BW 100; DM 252; Moule 60f., 168; MHT I 21; MHT III **193**, 240, 282, 286; Rob 110, 121, 389, 418, 420, 533, 612, 656, 702, 1158, 1205; RD §360, 470(m), 474(m)

6 BDF §251; DM 128, 246; MHT II 195; MHT III 333; MHT IV 54; Rob 316bis, 523, 695, 916, 1151; RD §442, 448(d); Zer §401

7 BDF §162(7), 446; BW 142; Moule 38; MHT III 27; Rob 497

8 Rob 418, 787; Zer §267

10 DM 206; MHT II 133, 452; MHT III 335; Rob 267, 904; Zer §457

11 BW 158; DM 277; Moule 132; Rob 398, 701, 718, 771; Zer §365

12 MHT I 49, 69, 235; MHT II 152; MHT III 152, **218**; Rob 154, 232, 267, 269, 458, 469, 640, 778, 780

13 BDF §444(4); DM 77; MHT II 452; MHT III 168; Rob xii, 501, 629, 760; RD §371

14 MHT II 452; MHT III 174; Rob 623

15 BDF §162(4), 443(1), 447(7); DM 105; MHT I 107; MHT II 473; MHT III 338; Rob 283, 434, 602

16 Moule 57; MHT III 33, 45, 185; Rob 399, 651, 859; Zer §267

17 DM 105; MHT IV 45; Rob 509

18 BDF §29(3); DM 254; Moule 162; MHT II 49, 246, 323, 440; MHT III 213; Rob 472, 510, 599, 775, 834, 1151, 1217; RD §472(d)

19 MHT II 49, 153; MHT III 151, 191; Rob 28, 219

20 BDF §384; MHT II 157; Rob 272, 939, 1116, 1214

21 BDF §479 (2); Moule 13 n.2, 94f., 99 n.1, 181; MHT III 71; Rob 721

22 BDF §294(2); BW 15; Moule 181; MHT II 454; MHT III 155; Rob 413, 639, 717, 974, 1126

23 Rob 214, 215

24 BDF §339(1), 390(3), 420(3); BW 73; MHT III 80, 135; Rob 678, 706, 861

25 BDF §442(16); Moule 92; MHT I 90; Rob 561, 692, 1396; RD §377

26 Moule 92; Rob 215, 562

Chapter 2

1 Moule 8, 129 n.1; MHT I 233; MHT II 426, 450, 473; MHT III **145**; Zer §387

2 MHT II 452; MHT III 158; Rob 261, 376, 966, 969, 1105, 1140; RD §424(b), 429, 462(d)

4 BDF §257(2), 480(3); MHT II 455; MHT III 176; Rob 748

5 BDF §205; Moule 68; MHT II 452; Rob 212, 593

6 BDF §173(1); MHT III 161, 233; Rob 1042

7 Moule 168, 183; MHT II 98, 100; Rob 224

8 Moule 45; MHT I 88

9 BDF §261(4), 444(4); MHT III **170**; Rob 186, 788

10 DM 107; MHT III **170**

11 Moule 45; Rob 770, 1123; RD §375

12 BDF §287, 386(1); MHT III 44, **123**; MHT IV 62; Rob 692, 747, 883, 1031

13 BDF §474(6); BW 136; Moule 18; MHT II 381; Rob 749, 903, 1127

14 BDF §123(2), 480(1); MHT III 33; Rob 1107

15 Rob 793, 1158

16 DM 128

17 BDF §198(6); Moule 95; MHT I 16; MHT II 443; MHT III 241; Rob 393, 531, 577, 1042; RD §303; Zer §60

18 BDF §439(2); Moule 97; MHT III 185; Rob 1148

19 BW 87

20 DM 215; Moule 115; MHT III 140, 174; Rob 561, 1091bis

21 Moule 31; MHT I 16; Rob 720, 744, 1042

22 Moule 31; Rob 399, 427, 534, 579, 698, 716; RD §379

23 BDF §140; MHT II 462; MHT III 24; Rob 317, 339, 698, 1113; RD §379

24 MHT III 139; Rob 122, 1058; RD §426(a)

25 DM 103; MHT II 190; Rob 234bis, 367, 594; RD §275

26 BW 38; MHT II 191; Rob 224, 604

27 BDF §162(8), 205; DM 103; Moule 68; MHT III 43; Rob 502, 591, 593, 792

28 BDF §159(1); Rob 510

29 Moule 75; MHT III 88, 304; Rob 234, 587, 612, 881, 1119, 1130, 1182; RD §462(c)

30 BDF §198(6); MHT II 443; Rob 531, 877, 1205

31 BDF §162(8); DM 103; Moule 68; Rob 502, 593

32 Rob 701, 714

33 BDF §199; DM 256; Moule 203; Rob 448, 498, 652, 781, 1179; RD §347(a); Zer §57

34 Moule 204; Rob 652; Zer §473

35 BW 163

36 BDF §275(4); Moule 95; MHT III 200; Rob 772; Zer §190

37 BDF §443(3), 474(6), 480(1); MHT III 23; Rob 350, 1179

38 BW 56; DM 104; Moule 70; MHT III 214, 266; Rob 389, 592, 595, 780, 781, 782, 795; RD §361; Zer §45

39   BDF §189(2), 205; Moule 68, 70; MHT III **15**, 239, 254; Rob 541, 593, 733; RD §347(b)

40   BDF §244(3); Moule 45; MHT III **30**; Rob 666, 813, 1396

41   Moule 107, 162; Rob 283, 1151

42   DM 110; Moule 90; MHT II 452; Rob 542

43   Rob 541

44   BDF §447(9)

45   BDF §325; DM 276; MHT I 167; MHT III 67, 93, 125; Rob 581, 722, 884, 922, 958, 967; RD §419(g), 424(c), 426(a); Zer §358

46   BDF §444(1); DM 107; Moule 62, 78; MHT II 195; Rob 508, 519, 608bis, 609, 1179

47   BDF §202; MHT I 107; MHT II 173, 473; Rob 318, 891, 1115, 1116

Chapter 3

1   MHT III **179**; Rob 602, 905

2   BW 85; DM 189; Moule 29, 125, 167; MHT II 202, 447; MHT III **41**, 55, **93**, 180, 195; Rob 318, 392, 429, 480, 884, 891, 905, 990, 1088; RD §302, 320, 342(i)

3   BDF §99(1), 328, 409(5); MHT III 65; Rob 313, 559, 877, 884, 905; RD §303

5   DM 134; Rob 538, 828, 905, 1036, 1127

6   Moule 58; MHT II 100; Rob 698, 905

7   Moule 36 n.2; MHT II 112; Rob 210, 508, 905; RD §351

8   BW 86; DM 190; MHT I 161; Rob 423, 905, 1116bis, 1136

9   Rob 905, 1103, 1390

10   BDF §277(3), 330, 408; BW 55; Moule 92; MHT II 126; MHT III 33, 41, 149; MHT IV 47; Rob 262, 626, 885, 887bis, 905, 1111, 1117, 1179, 1390

11   MHT II 146; Rob 269, 407, 604, 655, 1390

12   BDF §425(3); Moule 128; MHT I 217; MHT III 33, 141, **158**; Rob 334, 423, 818, 1065, 1068, 1078, 1140; Zer §229, 386

13   MHT II 466; MHT III 45; MHT IV 49; Rob 649, 707, 1151; RD §472(d)

14   MHT III 185; Rob 399, 651, 785, 818

15   BDF §458; Rob 714

16   BW 21; Moule 58, 82, 109; MHT II 465, 473; MHT III 221, **267**; Rob 517, 639, 644

17   BDF §417; DM 113; MHT I 230; MHT III **154**; Rob 609, 1128

18   BDF §140; MHT III 25; Rob 409, 858, 877, 1036, 1080

19   MHT I 218; MHT II 227; MHT III 27, 52, 144; Rob 649, 986, 1049, 1075

20   Moule 138; MHT II 466; MHT III 105; RD §430(b)

21   BDF §140; MHT III 25, 174; Rob 716, 1151; RD §472(d); Zer §390

22   Rob 733, 1151; Zer §226

23   BDF §107; MHT I 16; MHT II 71; Rob 189, 598, 727, 959; RD §417

24   DM 244; Rob 732

25   BDF §491; BW 58, 74; MHT III 208; Rob 625, 716; RD §380

26   BDF §404(3); BW 30, 133; DM 226, 285; MHT II 450, 451; MHT III 146; Rob 538, 549, 800, 891bis, 991, 1072, 1073bis, 1116, 1128; RD §433

Chapter 4

1   BDF §423(1); MHT III 322

2   Moule 77; Rob 587, 966, 1071, 1428

3   Rob 538

4   Moule 132; MHT II 173; MHT III 315; RD §301

5   BDF §205; MHT I 16; MHT II 426, 427; Rob 1047, 1423

6   Rob 214

7   BDF §277(1); MHT III 37, 65; Rob 648, 655, 678, 740

9   BDF §163; BW 17; MHT II 260; MHT III 212, 258; Rob 500, 703, 780; RD §343(f)

10   BDF §491; Rob 656, 698, 705, 715, 1421; Zer §**214**

11   DM 149; MHT II 112; MHT III 44;
     Rob 698, 703, 769

12   BDF §412(4); Moule 66, 76, 77,
     103, 106 n.1; MHT III 153, 264;
     Rob 635bis, 749, 751, 778,
     1107; RD §383

13   BDF §408, 447(7); MHT I 158;
     MHT III 55, 149; Rob 127, 415,
     691, 812, 887, 1035, 1197,
     1421; RD §24, 475

14   Rob 1087, 1179

16   DM 244, 261; MHT I 236; MHT III
     30, 304; Rob 656, 880, 1152

17   BDF §198(6); DM 103; Moule 208;
     MHT II 443; MHT III 241; MHT IV
     47; Rob 531, 538, 1094, 1425;
     Zer §60

18   BDF §399(3); MHT III 141; Rob
     546, 550, 607; RD §351

19   BDF §245a(1); MHT II 453; MHT
     III 216; Rob 516, 666, 1045;
     Zer §445

20   BDF §431(1); Rob 312, 677,
     1094, 1164, 1171bis, 1173,
     1174, 1214; RD §468

21   DM 106; MHT I 212, 230; MHT III
     117, 182; Rob 766, 905, 966,
     1031, 1046, 1128

22   BDF §233(2), 347(3); Moule 38,
     42; MHT II 190; MHT III **216**;
     Rob 268, 498, 602, 666, 905

23   MHT I 90; Rob 733

24   Rob 419, 1214

25   BDF §254(3); Moule 169; MHT II
     474; MHT III 181; Rob 739, 1397

27   MHT III 181; Rob 905

29   BDF §275(3); Moule 91; MHT III
     200; Rob 224, 560, 765, 772;
     Zer §188

30   BDF §404(3); Moule 58, 77; MHT
     II 450, 451; MHT III 146, 148;
     Rob 1072, 1073

31   BW 153; Rob 905

32   DM 230; MHT III 191; Rob 688,
     691, 751; RD §383

33   BDF §473(2); Moule 169; MHT II
     202; MHT III **350**; Rob 311; RD
     §302

34   BDF §339(3); DM 244; Moule 206;
     MHT III 67, **81**; Rob 587, 884,
     891, 892, 1115, 1116; RD
     §402(a), 422, 460(c); Zer §473

35   MHT I 167; MHT II 202, 206; MHT
     III 93, 125; Rob 190, 312, 318,
     922, 967, 1214; RD §320,
     419(g), 424(c), 426(a); Zer
     §358

36   DM 225; Moule 46, 73; MHT I 75;
     MHT II 441; MHT III 208, 220,
     221, 258; Rob 487, 530, 579bis,
     714; RD §346(d)

37   Moule 206; Rob 891, 1116; RD
     §402(a), 422, 460(c)

Chapter 5

1   Rob 215, 256bis, 457

2   MHT I 237; MHT II 408; Rob 256,
     319, 517, 627, 810, 1116; RD
     §155 c

3   BDF §391(4); BW 122; DM 215,
     285; Moule 43 n.1; MHT II 408;
     MHT III 136; Rob 1001, 1089,
     1090; RD §435(d), 457(c)

4   BW 91; DM 132, 197; Moule 43
     n.1, 102, 120f., 209; Rob 541,
     739, 965, 1166

5   DM 196; Rob 833, 1116

6   MHT II 453

7   BDF §144, 442(5); MHT I 16, 70,
     233; MHT II 426; MHT III 231,
     335; Rob 460, 581bis

8   BDF §101; Rob 308, 510, 710,
     810

9   BDF §202; Moule 50, 115; MHT
     III 149, 174; Rob 529, 601,
     739, 1084; RD §363, 381

10   Moule 53

12   BDF §133(3); Moule 57; MHT II
     146; MHT III 24; Rob 269bis

13   BDF §465(1); MHT IV 50; Rob 529

14   BDF §187(6), 465(1); BW 130;
     MHT I 67, 68; MHT II 206; MHT
     III 237; Rob 435, 453, 1106,
     1390

15   BDF §465(1); Moule 138; MHT I
     35; MHT II 102; MHT III **100**;
     Rob 194, 214, 984, 1091

16   BDF §474(8); MHT III 58; Rob
     404, 412, 617, 928

17   Moule 103; MHT I 228; MHT II
     126; MHT III 151, **152**, 154; Rob
     261, 1107, 1108

19   BDF §223(1); DM 148; MHT III
     27, 179; Rob 408, 581, 791

20   MHT III 57; Rob 497, 706; Zer
     §231, 363

21   BDF §232(1), 390(2), 392(4); BW
     50; Moule 66; MHT I 237; MHT
     III **138**, 275; Rob 635, 1086;
     Zer **§455z**

22   Moule 206; MHT III 52; Rob 800

23   BDF §213, 447(5); MHT III 27;
     Rob 601, 603, 621; Zer §184

24   BDF §299(2), 386(1); BW 114,
     160; MHT I 198; MHT III 123,
     130; MHT IV 62; Rob 405,
     736bis, 789, 938, 940, 1021,
     1044, 1408

25   DM 224; MHT III **88**; Rob 233,
     881, 1389; Zer §365

26   BDF §327; Rob 531, 995; RD
     §434(c)

27   MHT III **66**

28   BDF §291(1); BW 95; DM 203;
     Moule 178; MHT II 443; MHT III
     172, 241; MHT IV 48; Rob 224,
     253, 510, 531bis, 697, 760,
     878, 895; Zer §60

29   BDF §245a(1), 306(5); MHT II
     453; MHT III 216; Rob 405, 747;
     Zer §445

30   Rob 317, 603, 1127

31   BDF §199; BW 35; Moule 203; Rob
     480, 526, 1088; Zer §57

32   MHT III 218

33   Moule 89

34   BW 45, 149; MHT III 210; Rob
     653

35   BW 30; Rob 605

36   BDF §283(4), 301(1); DM 134;
     MHT II 96, 462; MHT III 147,
     216, 253; Rob 172, 233, 411,
     540, 542, 581, 732, 743, 1038,
     1113; RD §347(g), 382; Zer §393

37   Rob 732, 835

38   BDF §372(1a); Moule 150; MHT
     III 115; Rob 547, 963, 1018,
     1019, 1418; RD §439; Zer **§307**,
     308

39   BDF §370(2); Moule 150; MHT I
     193; MHT II 92; MHT III 99; Rob
     995, 1009, 1096, 1415; Zer §303

41   BDF §327; Moule 162; MHT II
     466; MHT III 37, 66; Rob 632,
     884, 1151; RD §472(d)

42   Rob 1102, 1109, 1121; RD
     §461(b)

Chapter 6

1   BDF §113(3); DM 110; MHT II
     158; MHT IV 8; Rob 104, 626,
     782, 1043; RD §369; Zer §347

2   Rob 348

3   DM 261, 284; MHT I 50; MHT II
     162; MHT III 315; Rob 816, 989,
     1149; RD §431; Zer §11, 343

4   BDF §353(3, 7); MHT III 89

5   BDF p.3 n.5, §187(2), 214(6),
     316(1); Moule 94; MHT I 50; MHT
     II 129, 162; MHT III 315; Rob
     173, 235, 275, 276; Zer §11

7   BDF §134(1c); MHT II 473; MHT
     III 312

8   BDF §418(6); MHT III **159**; Rob
     788

9   BDF §209 (2, 3); MHT III **15**,
     170; MHT IV 8

11   DM 103; MHT II 440; MHT III
     213, 315; Rob 594, 634, 801,
     897, 1042, 1113

13   MHT III 315; Rob 1102

14   Rob 701

15   BDF §101

Chapter 7

1   MHT IV 54; Rob 546, 800, 916

2   MHT II 102; MHT III 140; Rob
     215, 419, 1091

3   Rob 464, 957; RD §353

4   BDF §205; Moule 68; MHT III
     143; Rob 561, 566, 721, 979,
     1074

5   BDF §430(2); DM 250; MHT I 231,
     232; MHT III 285; Rob 1036,
     1131, 1138, 1139; Zer §440n

6   Rob 889

7   BDF §107, 380(3); MHT II 75;
     MHT III **110**; Rob 203, 959

8   MHT III 168; Rob 522, 760

9   BDF §101; Rob 308

10   MHT II 465; MHT III 206; Rob
     339, 480, 481, 640, 1100

11 BDF §261(7); MHT I 107; MHT II 151, 192; MHT III 171

12 BDF §62, 205; BW 137, 167; DM 298; Moule 207; MHT I 235; MHT II 122; MHT III 161, **254**; Rob 262, 536, 1042, 1103; RD §451(c)

13 BDF §191(2); DM 115; Rob 537, 587

14 BDF §220(2); BW 43; Moule 79; MHT I 103; MHT III 241, **265**; Rob 589bis; Zer §363n

16 BDF §162(3), 179(1); Rob 367, 510, 561, 716

17 BDF §187(4); Rob 716, 968, 974

18 DM 281; Rob 639, 748, 975, 1412; RD §420(b)

19 BDF §400(8); DM 215; MHT II 309; MHT III 136, 141, 143; Rob 477, 703, 1068, 1090bis; RD §435(d); Zer §383, 392

20 BDF §192; Moule 46, 184; MHT I 104; MHT II 78, 443; MHT III **239**; Rob 537, 671, 718; RD §347(c); Zer §56

21 BDF §157(5), 278, 423(2); DM 94, 124; MHT II 309, 462; MHT III 39, 322; Rob 339, 401, 482, 680, 811

22 Moule 95; Rob 772; Zer §231

23 BDF p.3 n.4, §130(1); Moule 27, 183; MHT II 58; Rob 207, 392

24 BDF §316(1); Rob 805, 1204

25 Rob 315, 885, 1036, 1049

26 BDF §191(1), 326; BW 85; DM 189; Moule 9; MHT I 129; MHT II 325; MHT III **17**, **65**; Rob 522, 739, 861, 885, 1397

27 Rob 367

28 Rob 206, 718

29 BDF §219(2); Moule 78f.; MHT II 463; MHT III 253; Rob 589; Zer §119

30 BDF §165; DM 138; MHT II 172; MHT III 213; Rob 760

31 MHT I 117; Rob 474

32 BDF §128(2)

33 MHT III 56

34 BDF §422; Moule 22; MHT II 214, 444; MHT III 94, 157; Rob 187, 430, 932, 1110, 1147, 1399; RD §406(a); Zer §369

§369

35 BDF §217(2), 270(3), 343(2), 420(2), 491; Moule 14f.; MHT I 144; MHT II 123; MHT III 70, **156**, 185; Rob 253, 268, 649, 698, 778, 860, 863, 1113; Zer §192

36 BDF §261(7); MHT I 133; MHT II 151; MHT III 171; Rob 698, 794

37 Rob 698, 778

38 Rob 698

39 MHT III 23; MHT IV 45; Rob 537

40 BDF §261(7), 466(1); DM 70; Moule 90, 176; MHT I 69; MHT II 429; MHT III 45, 316; Rob 436, 459, 541, 697, 698, 701, 703, 960; RD §340(d); Zer §25

41 MHT II 384; Rob 367bis, 532

42 BDF §147(3); DM 218; MHT III 52; Rob 463, 800, 1087

43 BDF §141(2), 184; BW 21; Moule 85, 198f.; MHT III 26; Rob 244, 355, 517, 550, 642, 647; RD §344(d)

44 MHT II 146; Rob 268

45 BDF §140; MHT II 189, 266, 466; MHT III 25; Rob 367, 409, 582, 716

46 BDF §409(5)

47 MHT II 146, 191

48 BDF §433(1); MHT III **287**; Rob 424

49 Rob 735, 740

51 Moule 114; MHT III 23, 220; Rob 300, 523, 542, 573

52 MHT III 209; MHT IV 53; Rob 502

53 BDF §206(1), 293(2); DM 103; Moule 70, 204; MHT II 463; MHT III **255**, 266; Rob 482, 728; Zer **§101**

54 Moule 89; MHT III 23

56 MHT II 83, 302, 441; MHT III 25; Rob 1123, 1213

57 Rob 339, 789

58 DM 161; MHT III 38; Rob 256, 811

60 BW 91; DM 300; Moule 10f., 192; MHT I 125; MHT III 72, **77**; MHT IV 29; Rob 834

Chapter 8

1   MHT II 453; Rob 581, 782, 787;
    RD §353

2   MHT III **56**; Rob 802

3   MHT III 166; Rob 174, 419, 473

4   BDF §251; DM 128; Moule 162;
    Rob 695, 696

5   MHT III 40; Rob 684

6   DM 282; MHT II 450; MHT III 52;
    Zer §387, 390

9   BDF §301(1), 406(1), 414(1);
    MHT III 148, 159, 195; Rob 316,
    743bis, 888, 1038, 1121

10 MHT II 194, 474; Rob 704, 769,
    1113

11 DM 90; MHT III 243; Rob 523,
    527, 533, 906, 909, 966, 1060,
    1070, 1071, 1407; RD §346(b);
    Zer §54

12 Rob 1179

13 MHT II 452

14 Rob 728

15 BW 166; MHT III 106, 146; Rob
    367, 995; RD §434(b)

16 MHT I 107; MHT III 159; Rob
    375, 560, 906, 1103, 1121; RD
    §361

17 BW 141; MHT II 194, 202; Rob
    318bis

18 BDF §257(2); Moule 57; MHT III
    176, 255; Rob 1113

19 DM 260; MHT III 139; Rob 706

20 BDF §205, 384; BW 113; DM 173;
    Moule 23; MHT I 195; MHT III
    122; MHT IV 62; Rob 327,
    939bis, 940, 1408; RD §406(b),
    447

21 BW 13; DM 248; MHT II 465; Rob
    541, 640; RD §410(a)

22 BDF §375; DM 242, 298; Moule
    154, 158 n.1; MHT III 251; Rob
    430, 576, 1024, 1027; Zer §402

23 BDF §205; DM 228; Moule 69,
    204; MHT I 71, 235; MHT II 440;
    MHT III 64, 161, 213, 253, **254**;
    Rob 458, 536, 593, 865, 1041,
    1123bis; RD §451(c)

24 Moule 65; MHT II 301, 453; MHT
    III 159; Rob 630, 706, 720,
    1217

25 DM 253, 254; Moule 162; Rob
    474, 696, 1151

26 BDF §290(1), 419(5); MHT II
    157, 464; MHT III 44, 156; Rob
    328, 602, 608, 698, 703, 792,
    1205

27 BDF §6, 418(4); BW 133; DM 285;
    Moule 103, 140; MHT II 453; MHT
    III 87, 154, 157; Rob 374,
    877bis, 991, 1118, 1128; RD
    §401(c), 433, 460(c), 462(a);
    Zer §282

28 MHT II 452; Rob 562

30 BDF §488(1b); DM 241; Moule
    158, 164; MHT III 330; Rob 571,
    916, 1148bis, 1176, 1201; RD
    §356, 448(b) and (d), 472(a),
    474(d)

31 BDF §328, 373(2), 385(1),
    452(1); BW 113; DM 174, 243,
    245; MHT I 198; MHT II 71; MHT
    III **65**, 116; Rob 194, 628, 890,
    938, 1010, 1021, 1022bis, 1214,
    1408, 1421; RD §406(b), 440,
    441; Zer §329

32 BW 160; MHT II 465; Rob 715,
    968; RD §424(b)

34 MHT II   453; Rob 748

35 MHT III 155; Rob 367, 474; Zer
    §363n

36 Rob 602, 743, 974, 1094, 1171,
    1425

38 Rob 578, 597

39 DM 102; Rob 349, 479; RD §362;
    Zer §473

40 BDF §205, 313, 403; BW 125;
    Moule 68; MHT III 58, 144, 148;
    Rob 218, 593, 643, 695, 975,
    979, 1060, 1074, 1092, 1427; RD
    §421(e), 457(d)

Chapter 9

1   BDF §174, 251, 260; Moule 37;
    MHT III 166; Rob 216, 507; RD
    §343(1)

2   BDF §107, 416(2); Moule 152;
    Rob 190, 482, 497, 1018, 1041,
    1419

3   BDF §260; DM 216; Moule 90; MHT
    II 427, 450; MHT III 145, 171;
    Rob 538, 1072, 1423; RD
    §347(d); Zer §387

4   BDF §416(1), 493(1); MHT III
    161; Rob 506, 762, 1042

5   BDF §480(5); MHT III 27

6 BDF §99(1), 300(1); DM 298; MHT III 49, 154, **330**; Rob 310, 313, 729, 731, 739, 1044, 1045, 1176, 1215; RD §380bis

7 Moule 36; MHT I 66; MHT III **233**; Rob 213, 449, 472, 506, 529, 762; RD §342(h); Zer §69

8 Moule 89; MHT II 83; Rob 1213

9 BDF §353(1); Moule 105; MHT II 452; MHT III 88; Rob 1138, 1172, 1406

10 Moule 183

11 BDF §336(1), 480(5); MHT II 210; MHT III 154, 155; Rob 310, 762

12 Moule 138; MHT III 105, **315**; Rob 189, 864, 1114, 1116; Zer §268

13 MHT III 233; Rob 484, 733

15 BDF §165, 190(1), 444(4); BW 8; DM 72, 115, 215; Moule 38; MHT I 217; MHT II 440; MHT III 141, 213, 239; Rob 496, 704, 1179; Zer §40

16 BDF §304; MHT III 50

17 BW 163; Moule 75; Rob 716, 721, 762

18 Moule 26, 91; MHT III 57; Rob 559

19 DM 254; Moule 88

20 MHT III 183, 325; Rob 698, 885, 1034

21 BDF §205, 347(3); BW 99; DM 206; Moule 68; Rob 699, 769, 860, 905, 1107, 1108, 1123

22 Moule 88; Rob 213bis, 891, 1127, 1220

24 Moule 138; MHT III 55, 235; Rob 820

25 BDF §223(5)

26 BDF §101; Moule 153; Rob 1128

27 BDF §170(2); Moule 153; MHT III 232; Rob 244, 367, 1035, 1047

28 BDF §479(2); Moule 13 n.2, 68, 99 n.1; MHT II 452

31 BDF §225; BW 12, 148; DM 188, 254, 261; Moule 60, 162, 185; MHT III 241; Rob 524, 607, 787; RD §345(d)

32 MHT II 147, 427; Rob 1043, 1085, 1423

34 BDF §320; DM 184; Moule 7; MHT I 119; MHT II 60; MHT III **64**, 154; Rob 310, 866, 986; Zer §390

35 MHT II 147; Rob 269

36 Rob 714, 716; RD §315(b)

37 MHT II 427; Rob 1043, 1423

38 BDF §184; BW 36; Moule 83; MHT I 125; MHT II 147; MHT III 171, 216; Rob 256, 505, 538, 568, 640; RD §343(k), 347(f), 353

39 BDF §316(1); DM 153; MHT II 108, 453; MHT III 55, 154; Rob 311, 529, 542, 732, 810; Zer **§234**

40 Moule 192; MHT IV 29

42 BDF §225; DM 107; Moule 49; MHT III 171, 237; Rob 607, 1423

43 MHT II 427; Rob 1043, 1423

Chapter 10

1 BW 130, 150, 151; DM 224; Moule 167; Rob 258; RD §155 c

2 BW 150, 151; DM 145; MHT III 315; Rob 772

3 BW 150, 151; Moule 206; MHT III **248**; Rob 471, 864; RD §342(c)

5 DM 108; Rob 609

6 MHT III 206, 273; Rob 615; RD §366

7 Moule 206; Rob 272, 892

9 Moule 34, 62; Rob 538, 793

10 DM 110; Rob 623

11 Moule 50; MHT II 171; Rob 315, 603, 1213; RD §320

14 MHT II 434; MHT III 196; Rob 752, 1173; Zer §446

15 MHT I 125; MHT II 67; MHT III 37; MHT IV 19; Rob 396, 1202, 1205

17 BDF §153(3), 386(1); Moule 150, 151; MHT I 198; MHT III 123, 130, 335; MHT IV 62; Rob 579, 602, 890, 910, 938, 940, 1021, 1031, 1408

18 Moule 154; MHT III 65, 152; Rob 1043, 1045, 1105, 1107, 1108

20 BDF §154, 448(3); MHT II 210, 453; MHT III 154, 155, 330; Rob 571

21   Rob 735

22   Rob 561, 614, 833, 1179

23   MHT II 453; Rob 809

24   MHT II 452; MHT III 55

25   BDF §233(2); Moule 129, 174; MHT I 16, 217; MHT II 427; MHT III 142; Rob 98, 393, 996, 1002, 1040, 1043, 1059, 1060, 1065, 1068, 1423; RD §435(d), 455(d); Zer §386

26   Rob 686

28   MHT I 236; MHT II 100, 164; MHT III 30, 137; Rob 314, 665, 967, 1032, 1036, 1045; RD §451(a); Zer §455b

29   DM 254; Rob 212, 739, 1043, 1044, 1113; Zer §142

30   BW 10; Moule 34, 73; MHT II 452; MHT III **248**; Rob 471, 645, 793

31   MHT III 58; Rob 233

32   DM 254; Rob 399, 792, 794, 1105, 1108

33   BDF §339(1); DM 256; MHT I 131, 228; MHT III 80, 135, 159; Rob 861bis, 990, 1080, 1088, 1113, 1121

34   DM 298; Moule 199; MHT III 55; RD §451(a); Zer §363n

35   DM 225(2); Rob 1108

36   MHT III 324; Rob 438, 718, 723; Zer §19

37   BDF §137(3), 225, 474(5a); Moule 181; MHT I 240; MHT II 454; MHT III 316; Rob 413, 458, 607

38   BDF §209(3), 332(1); Moule 33; MHT II 149; MHT III **72**, 137, 240; Rob 219, 533, 1032, 1045

39   BDF §444(5); Rob 339, 1113

40   Rob 537, 794, 1095

41   DM 272; MHT III 143; Rob 612, 752, 833, 960, 979, 1074, 1162, 1163

42   BDF §491; MHT II 57; Rob 419, 1035

43   MHT II 463; MHT III 151; Rob 1036

44   BDF §257(2); MHT III 176; Rob 891

45   BDF §345; BW 153; Rob 578, 782, 897, 1181

46   BDF §480(3); MHT IV 50

47   Moule 124, 157 n.1; Rob 231, 728, 960, 1061, 1094, 1171, 1425; RD §380, 468; Zer §386

48   BDF §328; MHT III 65, 149, 256; Rob 1084; RD §361

Chapter 11

1   BDF §225; DM 107; MHT III 313; Rob 608, 1181

2   Rob 599, 766, 885

3   BDF §300(2); Moule 132, 159; RD §448(d)

4   BDF §308, 419(3); MHT II 454; MHT III 155; Rob 1102, 1126

5   BDF §153(3); BW 12; Moule 38, 82; MHT II 171, 452; Rob 315, 498, 639

6   Rob 787, 838

7   MHT III 154, 161; Rob 1042; Zer §69

9   MHT II 67

11   Rob 188

13   MHT III 137; Rob 1032, 1041, 1049

14   MHT III 37; Rob 402; RD §326 §326

15   BDF §404(2); MHT II 450; Rob 566; Zer §387, 390

16   BDF §195(1d); Moule 76, 77; MHT III 240

17   BDF §194(1), 298(5), 453(4); BW 164; Moule 49; MHT III 89, 237, 335; Rob 658, 736, 968, 1008, 1181, 1417; RD §437

18   DM 242; Moule 13; MHT III 72; Rob 1190

19   BDF §234(8); BW 13, 32; MHT II 210, 461; MHT III 225, 271; Rob 605, 657, 696

20   Rob 1181

21   BDF §412(4); Rob 1107; Zer §192

22   Rob 643

23   BW 41; DM 90; Rob 530

24   BDF §202; Rob 405

25   BDF §205; MHT I 235; Rob 990

26   BDF §102(5), 332(2); DM 103; MHT II 72, 163, 427; MHT III 72, 149, 199; Rob 160, 192, 298, 659, 774, 833, 1043, 1423; RD §312, 387(e); Zer §253

27   MHT IV 53

28   BW 10; DM 106; MHT I 60, 92; MHT II 123, 474; MHT III **21**, 86; Rob 253, 410, 603, 728, 877bis, 891, 1036, 1082; RD §163 A, 303, 402(c)

29   Rob 367

30   Moule 57, 184; Rob 714, 861, 862, 1113

Chapter 12

1   BDF §209(2); Moule 59, 62; MHT III **15**, 268; Rob 578, 608

2   BW 39; DM 162; MHT III 240; Rob 533, 534; RD §346(f)

3   BDF §435(a), 447(7), 465(1); DM 275; Moule 177; MHT II 445; MHT III 27, 227, 311; MHT IV 48; Rob 411, 434, 551

4   MHT II 176; MHT III **56**; Zer §234

5   Moule 162; MHT II 452; MHT III 337; Rob 629

6   BDF §213; BW 20; Moule 74; MHT I 114; MHT II 452; MHT III 27, **79**, 260; Rob 408, 620, 621, 878; RD §343(k), 368

7   DM 113; Moule 72, 91; MHT II 210; Rob 310, 328, 559, 597

8   MHT III **77**; Rob 314, 807, 811, 855, 950

9   BDF §153(3); MHT III 331; Rob 855, 1153

10   BDF §62; MHT II 83, 158, 432; MHT III 178, 225; Rob 477, 550, 728, 762, 777, 794, 1107, 1213

11   BDF §275(3); Moule 75; MHT III 200; Rob 339, 772

12   BDF §268(1); MHT III **206**; Rob 255

13   Rob 990

14   BDF §213; Moule 74; MHT II 461; MHT III 331; Rob 231, 319, 358, 580, 621, 908, 1036, 1039, 1040, 1081; RD §304

15   BDF §424; MHT III 148, 322; Rob 695, 1036, 1084, 1186

16   MHT III 159, 226; Rob 551, 1102, 1212

17   MHT I 240

18   BDF §299(2); DM 242; Moule 35; Rob 224, 411, 484, 736, 739, 916, 1131, 1177; RD §33 b, 448(e), 462(b)

19   Rob 1061

20   BDF §119(1); MHT II 452; Rob 235, 906

21   Rob 522, 603

23   Moule 71

24   BW 140; MHT II 87, 191

25   BDF §205, 268(1); Moule 100 n.1, 204; MHT I 133; MHT III **206**; Rob 235, 431, 835, 859bis, 862ter, 1099

Chapter 13

1   BDF §268(1), 444(4), 474(5c); DM 107; MHT I 228; MHT II 88, 91, 474; MHT III 151, **152**, 206; Rob 608, 1107bis

2   DM 261; Moule 90; MHT III 333; Rob 566, 816, 1149bis; RD §472(b); Zer §21

3   MHT III 39; Rob 682, 862

4   Moule 162; Rob 440, 686

5   BW 48, 141; Moule 35; MHT II 128; MHT III 246; Rob 214, 258, 269, 480, 828, 862, 885

6   BW 12; Moule 82; Rob 639; RD §343(k)

7   Rob 574

8   BDF §60(2); MHT I 236; MHT II 83, 165; MHT III 31; Rob 279, 433

9   DM 142; Moule 106; MHT I 83; Rob 734, 761

10   BDF §146(1b), 387(3); MHT I 177; MHT II 441; MHT III 208; MHT IV 49; Rob 264, 330, 463, 464ter, 791, 874, 917, 942, 1157, 1162, 1193; RD §341(a); Zer §42

11   DM 109; Moule 82; MHT III 51, 89, 216; Rob 639, 800

12   MHT II 255; Rob 218

13   BDF §228; DM 109; Moule 62, 106; MHT III **16**, 170, **270**; Rob 620, 766, 836; RD §367

14   MHT III 27, 171

15 Rob 234

16 BDF §412(5); MHT III 35, 153; Rob 1107

17 BDF §261(7); Rob 611

18 BDF §201; MHT II 58, 109, 390; Rob 165bis, 219, 528

19 BW 101; MHT II 391; MHT III 53

20 BDF §201; MHT II 172; MHT III 243; Rob 523, 527; RD §346(b)

21 BDF §201, 316(2); MHT III 168

22 BDF §157(5), 162(2); DM 77, 103; Moule 70; MHT I 71; MHT II 462; MHT III 28, 156, **168**, 247; Rob 458, 482, 501, 780, 1114, 1136; Zer §70

23 BDF §284(3); MHT III 190

24 BDF p.3 n.2, §217(1); Moule 74; MHT II 466; MHT IV 49; Rob 94, 621

25 BDF §298(4), 299(2); Moule 124, 132; MHT I 93; MHT II 434; MHT III 49, 137; Rob 720, 736, 738, 916, 996, 1036; RD §381, 448(c)

26 Rob 497

27 Rob 608, 858; Zer §473

28 BDF §409(5); MHT III 149; Rob 1085, 1086, 1129

31 BDF §458; Moule 56, 101; MHT II 161; Rob 429, 602, 728

32 BDF §152(2), 474(5b), 476(3); MHT III 246, 325; MHT IV 47; Rob 423, 474, 483, 1035, 1107

33 MHT III 80, 206; Rob 861, 1113

34 DM 244; Rob 392

36 BDF §200(4), 202, 286(2); DM 243; MHT III 243; Rob 560, 1153; Zer §474

37 Rob 706

38 BDF §491; Moule 56, 58; Rob 1421; Zer §21

39 MHT III 151, 217; Rob 566, 720, 721

40 Rob 409, 430, 933, 996

41 MHT III 96; Rob 597, 849, 1019, inset, 1418

42 BDF §99(1), 206(1), 215(3); Moule 68f.; MHT III 277; Rob 313, 314, 409, 594, 645; Zer §252

43 BDF §458

44 Moule 94; Rob 990

45 Rob 261

46 BDF §135(1d), 420(3), 462(1); MHT III 42; Rob 810, 965

47 BDF §157(5); MHT II 450, 462; Rob 221, 482

48 MHT II 157

49 Rob 582

50 DM 106; MHT III 259; Rob 578, 788bis

51 Rob 197

Chapter 14

1 MHT II 427; Rob 197, 502, 710, 789, 1000, 1423; RD §343(b)

3 BDF §332(1); Moule 50, 162, 163; MHT III 24, **337**; Rob 649, 833

4 BW 44, 71; DM 128, 147; Moule 81; MHT III 36; Rob 695, 1394; RD §379, 385

5 BDF §276(2), 393(6), 444(5); MHT III 139; Rob 424, 628bis, 1052; RD §457(b)

6 MHT I 48; MHT III 182; Rob 257; RD §163 B b

7 MHT II 388, 452

8 MHT I 48, 221; MHT III 180, 220; Rob 257, 521, 523, 1096; RD §163 B b, 345(b)

9 BDF §400(2); MHT III 141; Rob 1042bis, 1066, 1076; Zer §384

10 BDF §270(1), 484; MHT III 186, 225; MHT IV 9; Rob 423, 549, 656, 659, 789, 838

11 Rob 28, 104, 428; RD §346(c)

12 BDF §177; MHT II 129, 142; MHT III 41; Rob 258, 428; RD §201 B d

13 BDF §213, 474(5a); Moule 74; MHT I 228; MHT III 151, **152**; Rob 428, 621, 1107; RD §201 B d

14 BDF §135(1d); MHT I 157; MHT II 102; MHT III 42; Rob 212; Zer §208n

15 BDF §299(1), 392(3); Rob 482, 736bis, 738, 789, 1036

16 BDF §200(4); MHT III 241; Rob 521; RD §345(b)

17 BDF §425(1), 442(16), 450(3); MHT II 91, 106; MHT III 23, 41; Rob 204, 210, 300, 1129, 1154; RD §472(f); Zer §210, 460

18 Moule 157 n.1; MHT I 217, 220; Rob 606, 800, 1061, 1094, 1102, 1425; RD §461(b), 468

19 BDF §327; MHT II 194, 240; MHT III 66; Rob 319, 489, 859, 908, 1030, 1039, 1040, 1081, 1216; RD §403(a), 451(b), 456

21 BDF §148(3), 339(2a); Moule 101, 101 n.1; MHT II 400; MHT III 53, 80; Rob 475, 892bis; Zer §66

22 BDF §397(6), 479(2); Moule 90; Rob 524, 562, 1035, 1036, 1047, 1113

23 BDF §345; BW 99; MHT II 190, 463; Rob 905

25 BDF §205

26 BDF §347(1); Rob 905

27 BDF §227(3), 304, 347(2); Moule 61, 102, 184; MHT II 466; MHT III 50, 158, **212**; MHT IV 50; Rob 611

28 BDF §332(1); Rob 224, 1205; RD §474(m)

Chapter 15

1 BDF §196; DM 160; Moule 45, 125; MHT III **242**; Rob 530, 760, 780

2 BDF §301(2); MHT III 149, 181; Rob 515, 788, 1084, 1205

3 BDF §327; Moule 73 n.1, 162; MHT III 66; Rob 696, 787, 1191; Zer §227

4 DM 101; Moule 73, 184; MHT II 148, 466; MHT III 258; MHT IV 50; Rob 788, 789, 818; Zer §90

5 BDF §209(2); Moule 27; MHT III **15**, 217

6 Rob 788, 1419

7 MHT II 474; Rob 475, 1035, 1041

8 Rob 861, 1113, 1396

9 Moule 92; MHT II 111; MHT III 23; Rob 219, 282, 580, 645, 750, 861, 1113; RD §359

10 BDF §392(1a); DM 218; Moule 127; MHT III 37, 136; Rob 1089; Zer §392

11 BDF §160; DM 145; MHT III 137; Rob 487, 531, 718

12 BW 90; DM 196; Moule 13; MHT III **71**; Rob 834

13 DM 196; MHT III 143; Rob 834, 857, 1074

14 BDF §53(2), 453(2); MHT III 181; Rob 968, 1045

15 Rob 529

16 MHT III 52; Rob 1219

17 DM 126; Moule 138; MHT I 237; MHT II 435; MHT III 40, 105, 325; Rob 683, 713, 723, 986; RD §430(b); Zer §201

19 BW 69; DM 143; MHT III **242**; Rob 613

20 Moule 110; MHT I 217; MHT II 387; MHT III 181; Rob 518, 788, 789, 1068, 1078, 1080, 1082; Zer §386

21 Moule 8; MHT III 62

22 BDF §316(1), 410, 468(3); Moule 109 n.3; Rob 173, 214, 413, 439, 628, 655, 808, 1039, 1084, 1127; RD §328, 474(c); Zer §394

23 BDF §140, 272; BW 126; DM 102, 107; MHT I 179; MHT III 24, 78, 305; MHT IV 48; Rob 582, 649, 696, 787, 944, 1093, 1205; RD §457(e), 474(c) and (r); Zer **§184**

24 BDF §464; Rob 432, 897

25 BDF §316(1), 464; Rob 432, 1039, 1084

26 BDF §464; Rob 432

27 BDF §223(3), 339(2c); DM 226; Moule 206; MHT I 230; MHT III 267; Rob 686, 891, 991, 1128-29; Zer §114

28 BW 21; DM 218; MHT II 69, 70, 165; MHT III 139; Rob 186, 187, 518, 646, 1059, 1061, 1078, 1085, 1187; RD §457(b); Zer §473

29 BDF §101, 102(3), 346, 414(5), 428(4); BW 20; DM 227; Moule 41, 110; MHT I 171, 176, 228; MHT II 193; MHT III 85, 157, 181; Rob 212, 299, 318, 330, 360, 364, 808, 908, 962, 1121, 1160; RD §403(a)

30 Moule 162; Rob 696, 1191

32 Moule 57; MHT II 259; MHT III 267; Rob 349, 686ter

34 BDF §103

35   DM 165; Rob 477, 655

36   BDF §296; DM 134(2), 261; MHT III 333; MHT IV 47; Rob 546, 714, 1149; RD §388

37   MHT I 130; MHT III **79**; Rob 565, 857, 884, 1081; RD §401(a); Zer §249

38   BDF §328; MHT III **65**; Rob 576

39   BDF §391(2); MHT I 209; MHT III 136; Rob 1000, 1091

41   BDF §327; Rob 788

Chapter 16

1   Rob 863

2   Rob 566

3   BDF §330, 408; BW 101; MHT III 149; MHT IV 47; Rob 394, 428, 801, 887, 1029, 1035, 1421; Zer §346n

4   Moule 91; MHT II 195, 202; MHT III 52; Rob 311, 476, 562, 788, 1214

5   MHT II 192; MHT III 220, 239; Rob 524bis; Zer §53

6   Moule 100; MHT I 133, 134; MHT III 80; MHT IV 47; Rob 788, 862bis, 863, 1110, 1113, 1425; RD §460(c); Zer **§265**, 265n

7   MHT II 194; MHT III 282; Rob 781, 863, 1156

8   MHT II 129; MHT III 171

9   BDF §223(1); Moule 56; MHT II 452; Rob 561, 581, 1065, 1406; Zer §115

10   BDF §153(3); Rob 1034

11   BDF §115(2); MHT II 100, 151, 278; MHT III 171; Rob 159, 244, 257, 367, 652, 1202; RD §333

12   BDF §164(3), 353(3); Moule 111; MHT II 452; MHT III 178, 210; Rob 263, 412, 497, 728, 729bis, 954

13   BDF §397(2); BW 21; MHT I 82; MHT III 27; Rob 792, 1039

14   BDF §167, 392(3); Moule 38; MHT III 139, **215**; Rob 498, 1036

15   BDF §278, 328, 442(10); MHT III 39, **65**; MHT IV 52; Rob 537, 1009, 1417; RD §347(e)

16   BDF §242, 316(3); BW 135; DM 228; MHT II 100, 427; MHT III **22**, 56, 185; Rob 442, 728, 810, 1043, 1128, 1423; Zer §389n

17   MHT III 40, 53; MHT IV 55

18   BDF §320; BW 49, 81; DM 184; Moule 7, 49, 93, 122; MHT I 119, 240; MHT II 432; MHT III **64**, 194; MHT IV 53; Rob 578, 884

19   BDF §170(2), 278; DM 103; MHT III **22**, 232

21   BDF §410; Rob 1039, 1084

22   BDF §328, 338(2), 392(4); MHT II 102; MHT III **65**, **78**, 138; Rob 212, 609, 618, 628, 883

23   MHT III 221; Rob 861, 863; Zer §265n

24   Rob 278, 710

25   MHT III 225; MHT IV 52; Rob 507, 608

26   MHT II 121, 122, 190; MHT III 27; Rob 262bis, 367, 1213; RD §163 A bis

27   Rob 431, 909, 1040, 1081, 1213

28   BDF §157(1); DM 131; MHT I 125; Rob 299, 484, 688

29   MHT III 55

30   Rob 880, 924

31   Moule 49; MHT III 237; Rob 402

33   BDF §266(3); Rob 518, 576bis, 771

34   BDF §122, 187(6); MHT I 67, 235; MHT III 160, 237; Rob 170, 453, 530, 1122; RD §346(d)

36   BDF p.3 n.5; DM 243; Moule 79; MHT I 52; MHT II 221; Rob 336, 993, 1219; RD §320

37   BDF §452(2); BW 41; DM 90, 244; MHT II 453; MHT III 18; Rob 339, 530, 653, 659, 686, 1120, 1187, 1190, 1213; RD §346(d), 425; Zer §473

39   BDF §209(1), 224(1), 328; MHT II 195, 453; MHT III **15**, 65, 259, 268; Rob 578

40   Moule 92

Chapter 17

1   BDF §261(2); MHT I 230; MHT III 171; Rob 1126; Zer **§217**

2 BDF §189(1), 327; Rob 408, 576; Zer §70, 125

3 Rob 442, 1034bis, 1035; Zer §486

4 MHT III 282; Rob 224, 669, 1163

5 MHT II 57, 194, 389; Rob 165, 885

6 BDF §322; BW 82; MHT II 129, 194; MHT III 62; Rob 258, 572, 1035, 1137, 1172, 1396; RD §463

7 BDF §214(4); BW 27; Moule 82; MHT II 465; Rob 639

8 Rob 258

9 BDF §5(3b); Moule 192; MHT I 20; MHT IV 30; Rob 763

10 BDF §99(1), 223(1); Moule 124; Rob 313, 314, 728, 760; Zer §115, 133

11 BW 114; DM 174; Moule 124; MHT III 48, 127, 131; MHT IV 62; Rob 487, 890, 1408

12 Moule 162; Rob 1151

13 BDF §205; MHT III 159, 171; Rob 760; Zer §346n

14 BDF §453(4); Moule 85; MHT III **321**; Rob 643; Zer §50

15 BDF §60(2), 99(1), 207(1), 244(1), 453(4); BW 160; DM 121; MHT II 165; MHT III 31, 139; Rob 279, 313, 314, 316bis, 339, 488, 669, 760, 968, 974; RD §424(b)

16 BDF §120(2); DM 108; MHT III 161, 171; Rob 121, 169, 224, 408, 613, 760, 885, 1041, 1123, 1131, 1204

17 Moule 103, 163; MHT III **151**

18 BDF §119(1), 290(6), 385(1); DM 174; Moule 150, 151; MHT I 198; MHT II 73, 275; MHT III 36, 147; MHT IV 62; Rob 201, 529, 695, 787, 788, 890, 938, 940, 1021, 1025, 1031, 1044, 1082, 1085, 1394, 1408; RD §381, 382, 402(a), 406(b), 408, 440, 448(g), 452(c); Zer §339

19 MHT II 151; Rob 187, 701, 785, 879

20 BDF §126(2), 299(1), 385(1); MHT III 123, 130; MHT IV 62; Rob 559, 736, 742, 878

21 BDF §244(2), 392(3); MHT II 191; MHT III **30**, 169, 200; Rob 749, 751, 773, 1087; RD §383; Zer §**150**

22 BDF p.2 n.4, §244(2), 416(1); DM 71; Moule 7; MHT II 151; MHT III **30**, 57, 161; Rob 187, 399, 464, 665; RD §341(b); Zer §**148**, 231

23 Moule 91, 92; MHT III 88; Rob 362, 561

24 MHT III 174, 175

25 Moule 41; Rob 518

26 Moule 95, 143; MHT I 133; MHT II 466; MHT III 27; MHT IV 49, 50; Rob 772, 863, 1113, 1391; Zer §191, 265n

27 BDF §386(2), 425(1); BW 135; Moule 143; MHT I 230; MHT II 196, 211, 216; MHT III **127**, 157, 232; Rob 244, 327, 508, 939, 1021, 1027, 1030, 1044, 1045, 1086, 1129bis, 1138bis, 1139, 1140, 1148, 1149, 1190bis, 1408; RD §307, 440, 452(c), 472(a); Zer §403

28 BDF §160, 249, 487; BW 56, 150; DM 136; Moule 123; MHT I 81; MHT II 9, 73, 244; MHT III **36**, **165**, 221, 268; Rob 195, 422, 608, 694, 1200, 1215; Zer §130

29 BW 106; Rob 920

30 Moule 90, 163; Rob 487, 629, 1084, 1152; Zer §74

31 BDF §219(1, 4); BW 34, 45; Moule 77, 78, 130; MHT I 240; MHT III **262**; Rob 550, 589, 590, 716, 860, 963; Zer §117

32 DM 147; Rob 333, 1394; Zer §226

34 DM 111; Rob 187

Chapter 18

2 BDF §261(1); Moule 54; MHT III **85**, 171; Rob 236, 459, 487, 530, 909, 910bis, 1040, 1047, 1049, 1116, 1407

3 DM 243; MHT III 221, 345; Rob 367, 471, 486, 1039, 1215, 1428

4 BDF §356, 444(2); MHT III **65**; Rob 885

5 DM 88; MHT III 220; Rob 529, 808, 1037; Zer §275

6 BDF §480(5); MHT III 24, 27; Rob 810, 1202

7 BDF §353(3); MHT II 386, 452; MHT III 27; Rob 263, 529

8 BDF §187(6); MHT I 67, 235; MHT III 67, 237; Rob 453, 884

9 DM 102; MHT I 125; Rob 583, 792, 890, 1173bis

10 BDF §400(8); BW 122; DM 215, 285; MHT III 141, 318; Rob 477, 1002, 1090

11 BDF §192, 332(1); MHT III **72**; Rob 672, 833; Zer §253

12 MHT II 398; Rob 269, 510; RD §343(m)

13 BW 58; DM 108; Rob 616; RD §366

14 BDF §360(4); Moule 149, 163; MHT II 189; MHT III 33, 89; Rob 368, 877, 1014, 1015bis, 1153, 1193; Zer §35, 317

15 BDF §224(1), 362; MHT III **86**, 268; Rob 110, 608, 686bis, 766, 1038

17 BDF §170(2), 176(3); Moule 28; MHT II 139; MHT III 232; Rob 256, 539

18 BW 137; MHT II 105; Rob 342, 1127, 1406; Zer §275

19 BDF §103, 327; MHT III 41, 66

20 Rob 1131

21 BDF §205, 484; MHT III 52; MHT IV 19

22 BDF §421; MHT III 158; Rob 1136

23 BDF §339(2a), 421; MHT III **80**, 158; Rob 788, 891, 892, 1113, 1136

24 BDF §125(1); Moule 46; Rob 172, 189bis; RD §341(b)

25 BW 50; DM 95, 115, 155; Moule 63, 106; MHT III 15, 220; Rob 485, 524, 619, 816, 1136; RD §367, 398

26 MHT II 212, 455; MHT III 30; Rob 665; RD §397

27 BDF §392(1d); MHT II 160; MHT III 80; Rob 818, 1036; Zer **§262**

28 MHT II 205, 301; Rob 311, 529, 582, 1036

Chapter 19

1 BW 69; DM 143; MHT II 121, 427, 450; MHT III 145; MHT IV 47; Rob 189, 233, 260, 1047, 1423; RD §162 c, 387(d); Zer §387, 389, 390

2 DM 241, 246; MHT IV 54; Rob 207, 234, 537, 816, 916, 1024, 1045, 1113, 1179, 1186; RD §410(a)

3 BDF §258(1); MHT III 255; Rob 739, 1179; Zer **§101**

4 Moule 169; MHT II 463; MHT III 325; Rob 399, 416, 993

5 MHT III 255

6 BDF §480(3)

7 Moule 94; MHT II 171, 172; MHT III **201**; Rob 773; Zer §188

8 Rob 431, 811

9 Moule 102; Rob 891

10 DM 106

11 Moule 105; Rob 253, 1138, 1139, 1205

12 Moule 192; MHT II 72; Rob 192

13 BW 53, 68; DM 95, 142; MHT II 365; MHT III **166**; Rob 475, 484, 617, 759, 762, 791; RD §387(d)

14 BDF §125(2); MHT I 80, 246; MHT II 194; Rob 236, 255, 742; Zer §153, 362

15 Moule 198; MHT I 131; MHT III 155, **166**; Rob 736, 762, 777, 791

16 BDF §64(6), 421; Moule 91; MHT I 80; MHT III 158; Rob 252, 559, 560, 607, 745bis; RD §111, 378; Zer **§153**

17 BDF §472(2); MHT IV 50; Rob 418

19 MHT III **17**; Rob 674, 828

20 Moule 169; MHT III **350**

21 BDF §276(3), 392(3); Moule 209; MHT III 139, 143, 148; Rob 310, 476, 688, 787, 1074; RD §342(h)

22 BDF §205; DM 103; Moule 68; MHT III 52; Rob 586, 593, 800

23 Rob 224, 1205

24 BDF §316(3); Moule 105; MHT III 56, **152**; Rob 224, 810

25 Moule 62; MHT II 110; Rob 620, 710

26 BDF §186(1), 216(3), 303; BW 11; DM 78, 196; Moule 39; MHT I 73; MHT III 196, 235; Rob 295, 494, 643, 697, 701, 1035, 1166, 1187; RD §343(d)

27 BDF §44(2), 180(1); MHT I 60; MHT II 111, 462; MHT III 22,

138, 235; Rob 219, 253, 257, 410, 518, 750, 1162bis; RD §163 B a, 464(a)

28 Moule 115; MHT I 50; MHT II 162; MHT III 316; Rob 395, 1202; Zer §11

29 MHT II 124, 369; Rob 510

30 BDF §423(2); MHT III 322; Rob 423, 885

31 BDF §190(1); MHT II 124, 369; MHT III 239; Rob 258, 537

32 BDF §306(5), 345; BW 26; Moule 83; MHT I 236; MHT II 67, 161; MHT III 30, 31, 198; Rob 301, 425, 641, 665, 692, 747, 898, 1029, 1176; RD §378

33 BDF §164(2); MHT III 209; MHT IV 46; Rob 515

34 BDF §466(4), 493(1); DM 100; Moule 31, 115; MHT III 316; MHT IV 30; Rob 436, 439, 1130, 1200, 1202; RD §474(h)

35 BDF §241(7), 431(1); DM 244; Moule 115; MHT III **17**, 162; Rob 68, 253, 260, 653, 726, 892, 1041, 1123, 1159, 1190; RD §162 b

36 Moule 102, 150; MHT III 88, 157, 159, 322; Rob 212, 375bis, 881, 909, 1119bis, 1120, 1130, 1389, 1396; RD §462(c); Zer §142

37 BDF §44(2), 418(6); DM 243; MHT II 125; MHT III 157, **159**; Rob 253bis, 257, 410; RD §163 B a

38 BDF §5(3b); Moule 163, 192; MHT II 57; MHT III **26**; Rob 541, 1153

39 Rob 545, 618, 1009, 1154

40 BDF §178; DM 251; Moule 39; MHT II 341; MHT III 138, 231; Rob 229, 511, 547, 815-16, 820; RD §343(1)

Chapter 20

1 MHT III 143; Rob 1074

2 MHT III 170

3 BDF §162(7), 356; DM 82, 285; Moule 38, 129; MHT I 217; MHT III 89; Rob 497, 877, 1002, 1060, 1068, 1076; RD §344(e); Zer §242

4 BDF §99(1); MHT III 168; Rob 173, 205, 235ter, 236, 501,

529, 639, 813; RD §346(a)

5 BDF §148(1); MHT III 171; Rob 471, 475; RD §342(h), 353

6 Moule 205; MHT III 171, 225; Rob 657

7 BDF §99(1); MHT II 439; MHT III **17**, 179, 187; Rob 313, 529, 653, 672, 792, 877; RD §343(k)

8 MHT II 328; Rob 969

9 Moule 73; MHT II 286; MHT III 258; Rob 235, 579, 580, 835, 891

10 MHT I 125; RD §363

11 BDF §425(6); MHT III 154; Rob 1140, 1179

12 MHT III 282; Rob 116

13 BDF §261(2), 425(3); MHT III 171; Rob 235, 1140

14 BDF §261(2); MHT II 72, 79; Rob 199

15 BDF §21, 214(3); BW 12; Moule 82, 92; MHT II 113, 362; MHT III **17**, 171, **277**; Rob 199, 214, 221, 505, 573, 638, 653, 748, 1202; RD §343(k)

16 BDF §161(3), 205, 385(2); DM 93, 243; Moule 139; MHT I 17, 63, 196; MHT II 148, 392; MHT III 127, 149, **248**; Rob 470, 472, 613, 905, 986, 1021, 1030, 1058, 1085, 1408; RD §366, 442; Zer §403

17 Rob 508

18 BDF §103, 434(2); Moule 30, 92, 94; MHT I 56; MHT II 203; MHT III 179, 201, 226; Rob 299, 312, 334, 561, 566, 717, 721, 773, 793

20 MHT III 137; Rob 1032, 1061, 1094, 1102, 1171, 1174, 1205, 1425; Zer §383

21 DM 148; MHT III 86; Zer §184

22 BDF §323(3); MHT I 151; MHT III 63; MHT IV 53; Rob 374, 523, 765, 878, 1118, 1172, 1213; Zer §282

23 BDF §148(1), 449(1); MHT II 121, 122; Rob 262, 475, 646, 1430; RD §163 A

24 BDF §157(3), 391(1, 3); BW 122; DM 159; Moule 52 n.1, 138 n.1; MHT III 56, **105**, 246; Rob 480, 499, 811, 990, 1089; RD §424(b), 430(c)

25 Moule 13; MHT IV 53

26   BDF §182(3); Moule 164; MHT III 215, 222, **333**; Rob 515, 576, 765, 987, 1035

27   MHT I 217; MHT III 253; Rob 807, 1061, 1089, 1102, 1171, 1174, 1205, 1425

28   BDF §390(3); Moule 121; MHT I 90; MHT III **78**, 135; Rob 480, 510, 589, 810; RD §387(b)(2)

29   Moule 41, 89; MHT I 26

30   BDF §288(1); MHT III 194; Rob 687, 689

31   Rob 419, 1035, 1041

32   MHT III **264**

33   BW 19; DM 81; MHT II 111; MHT III 232; Rob 282, 474, 508

34   Rob 441

35   BDF §245a(1), 425(6); MHT III 31, 154, 216; Rob 573, 663, 666, 679, 708, 1034; RD §374

36   Moule 192; MHT IV 29

37   DM 82; Rob 515

38   Rob 488, 659, 670, 716, 905

Chapter 21

1   BDF §261(2); MHT II 67, 101, 121, 427; MHT III 171; MHT IV 47; Rob 183, 235, 260, 263, 522, 547, 653, 836, 1038, 1202, 1423; RD §162 e

2   BDF §339(2b); MHT III 87; Rob 891; Zer §283

3   BDF §103, 159(4), 261(2), 309(1), 327, 339(2b), 353(3); MHT II 452; MHT III **66**, 171; Rob 299, 486, 548, 817, 883, 1115

4   BDF §103; BW 167; DM 298; Moule 57; MHT III 149; Rob 1046; RD §453(a)

5   Moule 85, 174, 192; MHT II 427; MHT III 174; MHT IV 29, 47; Rob 548, 643, 1423; Zer §275

6   Rob 691

7   BDF §126(1); MHT II 129; Rob 205, 582

8   MHT III **16**; Rob 339, 614; RD §342(h)

10   MHT II 161

11   BDF §284(2); MHT III 190; MHT IV 55; Rob 289, 690

12   Moule 129; MHT III 149; Rob 1065, 1066, 1068, 1085, 1088; Zer §386

13   Moule 161; MHT III 52, 139, 226; Rob 593, 657, 1077, 1121, 1162, 1181

14   BDF §420(2); MHT I 134; MHT III 156, 315; Rob 862, 863, 1214; Zer §265n

15   BDF §327; MHT III **216**; Zer §275

16   BDF §164(2), 294(5), 339(2c), 378; DM 87, 126, 284; Moule 130 n.1; MHT I 73, 223; MHT III **80**, **109**, 206, 209, 210; MHT IV 46; Rob 393, 502, 515, 519, 599, 614, 719, 721, 891, 955, 989, 1202; RD §343(i), 431, 474(i); Zer §18, 343

17   BDF §99(1), 205, 423(2); MHT III 322

18   BDF §99(1); Moule 92; MHT III **17**; Rob 313, 314, 561

19   Rob 746

20   BDF §327; MHT III 50, **66**; Rob 741

21   BW 38; DM 87, 298; Moule 33, 45; MHT III 241; Rob 482, 521, 524, 773, 950, 1034, 1046, 1082, 1084; RD §345(d), 453(a)

22   MHT I 52; MHT II 221; Rob 310, 337, 356; Zer §226

23   BDF §205, 353(2); MHT III 154; Rob 1127

24   BDF §369(3); Moule 139; MHT II 74; MHT III 24, 57, **100**; Rob 201, 324, 342, 412, 720, 809, 816, 984

25   Moule 110; MHT III 181; Rob 476, 483

26   BDF §99(1); Moule 64; MHT III **17**, 57; Rob 313, 314, 522; RD §387(a)

27   BDF §73, 209(3); MHT II 91, 188, 195, 265; Rob 339, 1213, 1220

28   BDF §103, 342(4), 488(1a); MHT I 143; MHT III **26**, **69**; Rob 330, 526, 769, 783, 844, 894, 897, 901, 1107; RD §346(b)

29   DM 232; MHT III 66; Rob 323, 362, 375, 883, 905, 906

30   BDF §327; MHT III 27, **66**; Rob 774, 1179; RD §387(e)

31 BDF §397(3), 423(6); BW 76; Moule 203; MHT I 74; MHT III 199; Rob 213, 256, 774, 879, 1033, 1132, 1202; RD §155 c; Zer §50

32 BDF §418(5); MHT III 154; Rob 835, 1126, 1127

33 BDF §386(1); MHT I 198, 199; MHT III 65, 123, 130; MHT IV 62; Rob 251, 375, 736, 938, 1031, 1044bis, 1389, 1408; RD §403(a)bis, 452(c)

34 BDF §306(5), 423(4); Moule 43; MHT III 198, 322; Rob 692, 747, 884

35 MHT II 427; Rob 392, 1043, 1085

36 BDF §134(1b); DM 116; MHT III 312; Rob 404, 407, 412, 655, 1104

37 MHT IV 54; Rob 915, 916, 1175

38 BDF §440(2); MHT III 183; Rob 769, 917, 1157, 1176; RD §387(c)

39 MHT III 171, 282; Rob 1151, 1163, 1205

40 MHT I 7; Rob 104, 770

Chapter 22

1 BDF §473(1); BW 59; Rob 507

2 BDF §324; MHT I 7; MHT III 64; Rob 28bis, 29, 104, 542, 653, 1029

3 MHT II 144; MHT III 171, 185, 210; Rob 495, 497, 615, 1105

4 BW 11; Moule 82; Rob 639

5 BDF §103, 418(4); BW 133; Moule 103; MHT I 149; MHT III 87, 157; Rob 299, 374, 548, 877, 1118, 1128; Zer §275, 282

6 Moule 62, 90, 91; MHT II 427; MHT III 149; Rob 536, 539, 560, 617, 620, 792, 1085, 1423

7 BDF §493(1); MHT III 161; Rob 506, 1042; Zer §69

8 MHT III 39; Rob 235; RD §102 G

9 Moule 36; MHT I 66; MHT III 233; Rob 449, 472, 506; RD §342(h); Zer §69

10 BDF §336(1); MHT II 453; MHT III 39, 75, 149, 154; Rob 716bis, 795, 1084

11 Moule 89; MHT II 461; Rob 580, 1159

12 RD §344(d)

13 Moule 93, 122; MHT II 432; MHT III 194; MHT IV 53; Rob 235

14 MHT III 13, 233; Rob 763, 1033

15 BDF §342(2); MHT III 70, 85, 200; Rob 720, 773

16 BDF §317; BW 102; DM 162; Moule 26; MHT I 163; MHT III 154; Rob 329, 332, 808bis, 1110; RD §308, 397; Zer §232

17 BDF §278, 409(4), 423(4); Moule 43; MHT I 74; MHT II 427; MHT III 149; Rob 1039, 1085, 1132, 1423; Zer §49

18 Moule 135; Rob 784

19 BDF §353(3); Moule 49; MHT I 227; MHT II 452; MHT III 237; Rob 608

20 MHT II 452; Rob 213, 1220, 1406

21 BW 49; Moule 135; Rob 469, 593

22 BDF §358(2); BW 11; Moule 82; MHT III 90; Rob 393, 639, 920, 1014; RD §438

23 MHT II 129; Rob 799

24 BDF §392(4), 420(2); MHT I 133; MHT III 138, 149, 156; Rob 308, 718, 726, 861, 863, 1084; Zer §265n

25 MHT II 407; MHT IV 54; Rob 258, 533, 916, 1181

27 BDF §441(2)

28 DM 251(2)

29 Rob 1029, 1033, 1034; RD §451(a)

30 DM 161; MHT III 58, 182, 273; Rob 615, 766, 815, 820, 1046; RD §398

Chapter 23

1 MHT III 200

3 BDF §100, 488(1c); MHT II 206; MHT III 138; Rob 314, 340, 616, 678, 1201, 1216

4 Rob 473

5 BDF §487; Rob 234, 422, 473, 484, 874, 1041, 1200

6 BDF §442(16); Moule 39; Rob 511, 791; Zer §156, 460

7 Rob 787

8 BDF §275(8), 445(2); MHT I 80; Rob 745, 1094, 1189; RD §378; Zer §153

9 BDF §482; MHT II 389; Rob 582, 1023, 1203, 1417; RD §474(e)

10 MHT III 99, 138; Rob 564, 995, 1214

11 BDF §205; Rob 221, 593; Zer §473

12 MHT II 89, 90; MHT III **56**; Rob 531, 802, 1040, 1046, 1048; Zer §227

13 MHT II 161; MHT III **56**; Rob 666, 802; Zer §227

14 BDF §198(6); Moule 178, 178 n.1; MHT II 443; MHT III 42, 233; MHT IV 48; Rob 473, 531, 689; RD §377; Zer §60, 209

15 BDF §425(3); Moule 52; MHT III 30, 141, 144, 158; Rob 490, 546, 659, 978, 1061, 1068, 1075, 1077, 1082, 1141

16 MHT II 125

17 Rob 231, 1087, 1397

18 Moule 102, 139, 163; MHT III 65, 157; Rob 696, 1087, 1151, 1397

19 DM 113; MHT III 18, 65; Rob 736, 738, 1087

20 BDF §425(3); MHT II 212; MHT III 30, 158; Rob 547, 968, 1002, 1066, 1068, 1141; RD §424(b)

21 MHT I 125; MHT II 89, 90, 161; Rob 474, 517, 579, 976

22 BDF §470(2); Moule 52; MHT III 326; Rob 235, 442, 1047, 1113; RD §454

23 BDF §119(1), 301(1), 470(3); Moule 126; MHT II 272; MHT III **195**; Rob 168, 232, 442, 742, 793, 1047

24 BDF §215(3); Moule 126; Rob 1179, 1204

25 Rob 1113

26 BDF §60(2); BW 126; MHT I 179; MHT III **78**, 305; MHT IV 48; Rob 944, 1093

27 Moule 100; MHT I 117; MHT III 187; Rob 243, 339, 431, 433, 778, 1035, 1099

29 Moule 39; MHT I 239; Rob 511

30 BDF §101, 346, 424; BW 92; DM 198; Moule 12, 53; MHT I 74, 176; MHT II 219; MHT III 73, 85, 86; Rob 330, 594, 603, 846, 877, 908, 1040, 1049, 1082, 1113, 1130

31 BDF §223(1), 261(2); Moule 163; MHT III 171; Rob 1151; Zer §115

34 BDF §209(3); Rob 578, 740, 1035

35 BDF §465(2); MHT I 133; Rob 434, 861, 863; Zer §265n

Chapter 24

1 Rob 607

2 Moule 57; MHT I 106; MHT II 354, 455; MHT III 267; Rob 236

3 BDF §60(2), 103, 488(1a); MHT III 232; Rob 300, 530; RD §346(d)

4 Moule 45, 119; MHT II 89; MHT III 344

5 BDF §190(3), 467; MHT I 224; Rob 782, 1135

6 Rob 288, 438, 724, 1181

7 Moule 92; MHT III 24

8 Rob 1181

9 MHT II 212; Rob 319, 705, 1084

10 Moule 24, 73, 101; MHT I 229; MHT III 162; Rob 597, 619, 811, 892, 1041, 1103, 1115, 1123

11 BDF §189(1), 390(1); Moule 31 n.2, 103; MHT II 161, 172; MHT III **17**, 87, **135**, 157; Rob 374, 666, 714, 717, 877, 978, 991, 1111, 1118, 1128; Zer §282

12 BDF §445(2); DM 107, 248; Rob 1165, 1189; Zer §227

13 Moule 130; Rob 511bis, 720

14 BDF §187(4); Rob 699, 703

15 MHT III 86; Rob 686, 700, 705, 877, 1039, 1076, 1082, 1179

16 BDF §219(2); Moule 79, 132, 197; MHT II 463; MHT III 253; Zer §119

17 BDF §418(4); BW 133; Moule 56, 69, 103, 140; MHT III 87, 157, **236**; Rob 374, 535, 581, 594, 877, 991, 1118, 1128; Zer §51, 282

18   BDF §209(3); Rob 578, 612, 1123

19   BDF §385(2); BW 109; DM 169; Moule 149, 150; MHT I 196; MHT III **90**, 126; MHT IV 62; Rob 235, 920, 1014, 1021, 1022, 1408; RD §405, 440, 441; Zer §356, 467

20   Rob 439, 686, 700, 705

21   BDF §292; MHT III 193; Rob 348, 363, 701, 702bis, 716, 1379; RD §301, 379

22   BDF §244(2); MHT I 133, 236; MHT III 30; Rob 235, 580, 619, 665, 810, 1128ter; Zer **§148**, 265n

23   MHT I 90; Rob 540, 810, 828, 861, 863, 1171, 1425

24   MHT I 88, 90; Rob 810

25   BDF §169(1); Moule 36, 62, 160; Rob 470, 487, 547, 551, 800, 810, 1109, 1126; Zer §74

26   BDF §244(1), 425(2); BW 44; Moule 82; MHT III **30**, 154; Rob 284, 529, 546, 637, 638, 665, 1139bis; RD §346(a), 462(d)

27   Moule 134; MHT II 19, 132; Rob 221, 265, 1123; RD §176 C e

Chapter 25

1   MHT II 157; Rob 836

3   DM 298; MHT III 56; Rob 995, 1046; RD §434(b), 453(b); Zer §227

4   BDF §205, 396, 406, 470(2); DM 256; Moule 68, 78, 153, 163; MHT III 137, **147**, 326; Rob 586, 593, 1036, 1038, 1422; Zer §486

5   Rob 233, 234, 534, 742

6   Moule 134, 203; MHT II 161; Rob 666

7   BDF §109(2), 423(2), 442(11); MHT III 322; Rob 153, 477, 619, 655

8   BDF §262(1); MHT III 169; Rob 742, 1028

9   MHT I 131; MHT II 132, 453; MHT III 155; Rob 265, 603, 878

10   BDF §244(2), 352; Moule 18; MHT I 236; MHT III **30, 88**, 169; Rob 277, 362, 375, 482, 484, 603, 665, 881, 895, 1116, 1389; RD §460(c); Zer §360

11   BDF §322, 399(1); BW 96, 102, 127; DM 256; Moule 127; MHT III 62, 140; Rob 472, 511, 720, 742, 765, 809, 881, 896, 1059, 1066, 1078, 1417, 1424

12   Rob 429, 816

13   BDF §339(1), 418(4); Moule 89, 100, 140; MHT I 132, 133; MHT III **80**, 157; Rob 412, 812, 861, 862, 863, 877, 979, 1113, 1128; RD §359, 422, 433, 460(c); Zer **§264**

14   Moule 58; MHT II 161; MHT III 15, **268**; Rob 197, 234, 542, 608, 1048; Zer §130

15   BDF §205; Rob 429, 787, 1048

16   BDF §217(1), 386(4), 458; DM 280, 297; Moule 133; MHT I 169; MHT II 466; MHT III 58, 113, 130, 140; MHT IV 59; Rob 792, 939, 970, 977, 1030, 1035, 1048, 1091, 1408, 1422; RD §406(b), 420(e), 451(a), 454; Zer §346

17   MHT III 56; Rob 603

18   BDF §458; Rob 619, 718bis, 719; Zer §18

20   Moule 154; MHT III 55, 127, 131; MHT IV 62; Rob 472, 890, 940, 1021, 1031, 1045, 1408

21   BDF §406(2); Moule 139; MHT III 42, 148; Rob 580, 976, 1039

22   BDF §480(5); BW 106; DM 169, 190, 256; Moule 9, 151; MHT III 65, 91, 120; Rob 233, 394, 886, 919, 923; RD §405, 445; Zer §356

23   BDF §444(5); Moule 59; MHT III 15, **268**; Rob 254, 424, 608; Zer §192

24   BDF §134(1c); MHT III 312; Rob 233, 404, 530, 1036, 1047, 1085, 1173

25   BDF §429; MHT I 239; MHT III 55; Rob 908, 1036, 1040; RD §451(a)

26   DM 138; Rob 742, 743, 760, 875, 879, 996bis, 1030, 1045; RD §452(c)

27   Rob 1039

Chapter 26

1   BDF §229(1), 312(2), 320; BW 81, 86; Moule 7; MHT III 58, **64**; Rob 367, 885; Zer §272

2   BDF §341; Moule 24; MHT I 148;
    MHT III 169; Rob 690, 811, 895;
    Zer §15n

3   BDF §137(3), 409(5); BW 54, 56;
    DM 95(3); Moule 37 n.1; MHT III
    149, 162, 169, 221, **316**; Rob
    439, 490, 608, 1130; RD
    §342(m), 462(c); Zer §15n

4   BDF p.2 n.4, §99(2); Moule 163;
    MHT II 221; MHT III 169, 200;
    Rob 319, 773, 782, 792, 1107,
    1152, 1215; RD §304, 320

5   BDF p.2 n.4, §60(1); MHT I 78;
    MHT III 31; MHT IV 47; Rob
    280bis, 670, 1418; RD §335

6   Rob 1107, 1152

7   BDF §263(3), 350, 458, 474(6);
    MHT I 70; MHT II 216, 219; MHT
    III 33, 86, 169; Rob 463, 465,
    522, 550, 718, 763, 877, 1082,
    1213

8   Moule 52, 151; Rob 430, 614,
    1024; Zer §404

9   BDF §405(2); Moule 163; MHT III
    42, 147; Rob 231, 688, 1038,
    1039, 1049, 1085bis

10 BDF §444(4), 458; Moule 197;
    Rob 432, 714, 1113; Zer §274

11 BDF §60(3), 326; BW 85; Moule
    9, 85; MHT I 128; MHT III **65**;
    Rob 432, 885

12 BDF §458; Moule 131, 197; MHT
    III **218**; Rob 432, 714, 780

13 BDF §186(2); DM 112; Moule 32;
    MHT III 225, 235; Rob 432, 550,
    633, 775, 864

14 BDF §416(1), 493(1); MHT III
    27, 161, 304; Rob 28, 104, 506,
    1042

16 BDF §444(1), 448(3); MHT III
    330, 339; Rob 427, 432, 700,
    720, 724, 819, 871, 1048, 1078;
    Zer §466

17 BDF §339(2b), 400(6); Moule 91;
    MHT III 87, 142; Rob 432, 559,
    713; Zer §283

18 DM 284; Moule 109; MHT III 221;
    Rob 432, 566, 1088, 1392, 1415

19 BDF §458; MHT II 157; Rob 272,
    537, 962; RD §347(e), 440

20 BDF §161(1), 205; DM 298; Moule
    169, 210; MHT I 225; Rob 585,
    1047, 1135, 1179; Zer §394

21 BDF §35(3), 101, 392(1a); MHT
    II 67; MHT III 169; Rob 183

22 BDF §430(2); BW 21; Moule 83,
    109, 130, 169; MHT I 231, 232;
    MHT III 221; MHT IV 61; Rob
    520, 640bis, 720, 1138, 1139,
    1179

23 BDF §65(3); Moule 73 n.2, 151;
    MHT III **260**; Rob 372bis, 656,
    1024, 1097

24 BDF §473(1); Rob 418, 420, 656,
    661, 683, 774, 789; RD §387(c)

25 BDF §60(2); MHT III 31; Rob
    233, 812

26 BDF §352, 429; Moule 19 n.1,
    167f.; MHT II 111; MHT III 137,
    285; Rob 219, 313, 323, 750,
    903, 1094, 1162bis, 1165

27 BDF §258(1); Rob 538, 915

28 BDF §195, 405(1); BW 79; Moule
    78; MHT III **63**, **147**, **262**; Rob
    192, 653, 880, 1079, 1081,
    1084; RD §402(a); Zer §395

29 BDF §195, 359(2), 385(1),
    442(13); BW 21, 114; Moule 78,
    151; MHT I 198; MHT II 192; MHT
    III 46, 91; MHT IV 62; Rob 291,
    566, 646, 653, 660, 710, 732,
    854, 886, 919, 923, 938, 1021,
    1025, 1162, 1182, 1408; RD
    §379, 406(b), 440, 447; Zer
    §121, 356

30 BDF §276(2); MHT III 182; Rob
    314, 529, 786, 789

31 BDF §322; MHT II 454; MHT III
    62

32 BDF §358(1), 360(3), 428(2); BW
    106; DM 169, 289; MHT II 190;
    MHT III 90, **91**, **92**; Rob 886,
    887, 906, 909, 920, 1014, 1015,
    1016, 1080, 1081, 1417, 1429;
    RD §403(a), 438bis, 456

Chapter 27

1   BDF §143, 327; DM 213, 285;
    Moule 129; MHT I 69, 217; MHT
    II 202; Rob 256, 311, 342, 459,
    743, 1002, 1060, 1068, 1424; RD
    §11, 155 c

2   BDF §472(1d); MHT II 106, 199;
    Rob 210, 223, 469

3   BDF §410; MHT III 149; Rob 476,
    532, 861, 1084

4   BDF §443(3); MHT II 427; Rob
    469, 634, 1039, 1428

5   BDF §223(1); MHT II 101, 128;
    MHT III 171; Rob 257, 263, 476,
    563, 608, 787

6 BDF §104(1); MHT III 86, 149; Rob 235, 585

7 Moule 101, 101 n.1; Rob 477, 634

8 BDF §184; BW 36; MHT III 216; Rob 186, 214, 538, 568, 613, 640; RD §347(f); Zer §153

9 BDF §328; DM 251; MHT III 345; Rob 261, 884, 909, 1071, 1081, 1407

10 BDF §397(6); Moule 154; MHT I 213; MHT IV 52; Rob 162, 438, 877, 1036bis, 1047, 1082; RD §454

11 Zer §445

12 BDF §386(2); DM 247; Moule 95, 154; MHT I 194; MHT III 30, **127**; Rob 244, 608, 792, 1021, 1024, 1027, 1030, 1044, 1045, 1214, 1408; Zer §403

13 BDF §61(1), 244(2), 308; MHT III **30**, 52, 172, 232; Rob 235, 634, 665, 799, 909, 1060

14 BDF §308, 433(3); BW 22; Moule 60; MHT III 52, **268**, 282; Rob 166, 205, 606, 702, 799, 834, 1163; RD §364

15 BDF §241(5); MHT III **17**; Rob 312, 572, 1214

16 Rob 211, 263, 477, 618, 634, 834

17 BDF §425(6); MHT II 205; MHT III 53, 99, 154; Rob 235, 314, 476, 633, 799, 802, 995; RD §372

18 MHT III 56; Rob 855; RD §402(b); Zer §227

19 MHT II 193; MHT III **17**; Rob 212, 886

20 BDF §253(1), 445(3); DM 109; Moule 161; MHT II 96; MHT III 52, 140, 172; Rob 205, 224, 618, 765, 1061, 1076, 1179bis; RD §455(d), 470(n)

21 MHT III 33; Rob 464, 886, 920, 1014, 1151, 1152

22 BW 21; MHT I 241; MHT III **138**; Rob 475, 517, 886, 1204; RD §344(d), 387(a)

23 Rob 497, 724, 758

24 MHT IV 50, 53; Rob 1058

25 BDF §160; Rob 487, 718

26 DM 103; MHT III 53; Rob 802

27 MHT II 71, 175, 324; MHT III 51, 137, 172, 225; Rob 184, 284, 550, 581, 648, 672, 775, 1036

28 Rob 231, 800

29 DM 263; MHT I 36; MHT II 192, 324; MHT III 53, 99; Rob 244, 266, 802, 886, 919, 995, 1173

30 BDF §425(3); MHT III 158; Rob 256, 476, 966, 1141; RD §155 c

31 Rob 1419

33 BDF §161(3), 414(1); DM 93; Moule 62; MHT II 111, 175; MHT III **65**, 159; MHT IV 50; Rob 219, 244, 282, 471, 672, 877, 1102, 1121, 1173, 1412; RD §420(b)

34 BDF §240(1); BW 17; DM 110; Moule 54, 62; MHT I 106; MHT II 111; MHT III 226, **274**; Rob 451, 517, 570, 623; RD §344(d), 369

35 MHT II 455; MHT IV 49; Rob 367

36 BDF §169(2); Rob 508, 519

37 MHT III **201**; Rob 773; Zer §188

38 BDF §101; Moule 33; MHT III **233**; Rob 508, 810, 818

39 BDF §386(2); Moule 150, 151, 154; MHT I 117, 196; MHT II 108, 309; MHT III 127; Rob 940, 1021, 1031, 1214, 1408; RD §39, 440, 442

40 BDF §241(6), 425(2); MHT II 321; MHT III **17**, 154; Rob 157, 265, 309, 638, 653, 1140

41 BDF §47(4), 326; Moule 60; MHT II 9, 118, 243, 294; MHT III **65**; Rob 145, 232, 256, 264, 580, 885; RD §155 d, 201 A a

42 MHT III 139; Rob 432, 828, 987

43 BDF §99(1); BW 20, 91; Moule 41, 203; MHT III 52, 72, 235; Rob 212, 313, 518, 797, 800, 835; RD §344(e); Zer §123, 252

44 Moule 49; MHT III 36, 272; MHT IV 47; Rob 601, 604, 696, 1395, 1423

Chapter 28

1 MHT II 359

2 BDF §316(3); Moule 54, 105; MHT II 194; MHT III 56; Rob 339, 1205

3 DM 101; MHT III 56; Rob 256

4   MHT IV 54; Rob 317, 365, 579bis, 697

5   DM 256; Moule 163

6   Moule 101, 101 n.1, 153; MHT I 239; MHT II 60, 106, 194, 197, 207, 254, 384; MHT III 89; Rob 210, 233, 318, 1036

7   Moule 46, 62; MHT II 276; MHT III **15**; Rob 516, 617

8   MHT II 125, 342, 427; MHT IV 47; Rob 162, 257, 1423

9   Rob 1396

10 Moule 134

11 BDF §198(7); MHT II 88, 271; MHT III **243**; Rob 199, 235, 613, 836

12 BDF §201; MHT III 244; Rob 836

13 MHT III 172, 225; Rob 189, 200, 298, 550, 657, 836; RD §336

14 BDF §261(1), 327; MHT III 72, **171**; Rob 836, 1113; Zer §252

15 MHT I 14; MHT II 109; Rob 528, 836

16 MHT II 124; MHT III 58; Rob 167, 258

17 BDF §271, 413(3), 423(2), 430(2); Moule 103; MHT I 228, 231, 232; MHT II 427; MHT III 24, 55, 151; Rob 562, 789, 1107, 1108, 1132, 1138, 1139, 1423

18 MHT II 188

19 BDF §425(3), 430(2); MHT I 231, 232; MHT III 158; Rob 1140bis

20 BDF §409(5); MHT II 67, 319; Rob 316, 485, 562, 613, 815, 816; RD §342(j), 366; Zer §73

21 Rob 428, 752, 1139, 1164

22 BDF §447(4); MHT III 89; Rob 1151

23 BDF §444(5); MHT III 217; Rob 548, 792, 892, 1116; RD §343(k)

24 MHT III 36; Rob 1394

26 BDF §336(1); MHT II 58; MHT III 97; Rob 333, 356, inset; RD §301; Zer §61, 226

27 BDF §369(3); MHT III 23; Rob 204, 819, 988, 1415

28 Moule 96; MHT III 14; Rob 1421; Zer §226

30 BDF §332(1); Moule 13; MHT III **72**; Rob 774, 833

Romans

119

20 DM 119, 286; Moule 44, 73; MHT
I 117, 219; MHT III **14**, 143,
148, 240; MHT IV 85; Rob 272,
606, 654, 763, 787, 1002, 1038,
1072, 1090, 1182, 1201; RD
§435(d); Zer §352

21 DM 245, 274; MHT II 191, 395,
463; MHT III 23; Rob 1129, 1188

22 MHT II 402; MHT III 23, 146;
Rob 319, 457, 489, 891, 1038,
1084; RD §342(1), 451(b); Zer
§393

23 BDF §179(2); Rob 1212

24 BDF §400(2); BW 129; DM 105,
245; MHT I 217; MHT II 463; MHT
III 141, **262**; Rob 585, 996,
1002, 1067, 1076, 1087; RD
§410(a)

25 BDF §236(3); BW 56; DM 108;
Moule 51; MHT III 89; Rob 396,
561, 585, 616, 960

26 BDF §444(1); DM 108, 146, 245;
MHT II 440; MHT III 213, **339**;
Rob 496, 561, 585, 651, 1179;
Zer §40

27 MHT II 104, 309; Rob 350

28 BDF §430(3), 453(2); BW 129; DM
219; Rob 968, 1041, 1086, 1087,
1138, 1155; RD §424(b), 457(b)

29 BDF §488(2); Rob 427, 510, 533,
794, 1155, 120lbis; RD §346(f),
474(b); Zer §394

30 Moule 40; MHT II 273; MHT III
234; Rob 232, 427, 629, 794,
1155, 1201; RD §474(b)

31 BDF §488(2); MHT I 222; Rob
372, 427, 1097, 1201

32 MHT I 230; Rob 710, 960, 1129,
1166

Chapter 2

1 BDF §146(1b), 219(2), 281,
451(5); BW 59; DM 129; Moule
31, 103; MHT III 35, 151, 253;
Rob 402, 463, 464, 721, 748,
978, 1107, 1193; RD §341(b),
419(a), 423(d)

3 BDF §146(1b); Moule 31; MHT III
35, 37; Rob 402, 459, 464,
678bis, 699, 1177

4 BDF §263(2); DM 119; Moule 8;
MHT III **14, 63**; Rob 654, 763,
880, 1035; Zer §140

5 BW 8; DM 105; MHT II 440; MHT
III 213; Rob 497

6 BDF §469; DM 125; Rob 441, 714

7 BDF §163; Moule 58; MHT III
153, 212; Rob 500, 1200

8 Moule 58; MHT III **317**; MHT IV
86; Rob 100, 599, 764

9 Moule 169; Rob 549, 757, 1179

11 BW 38; Moule 52; Rob 1106

12 BDF §120(2); BW 38; DM 272;
Moule 113 n.1; Rob 598; RD §388

13 BDF §258(2); DM 108; Moule 113
n.1; MHT III **117**; Rob 424, 757,
796; RD §386(b)

14 BDF §188(2); DM 148; MHT III
40, 112, 185, 313; Rob 537,
704, 778, 796, 972

15 BDF §465(1); BW 21; MHT II 206;
MHT III 23; Rob 311, 645, 728,
1097bis

16 BDF §382(3); Moule 130; Rob
590, 718, 721, 763, 971

17 BDF §454(3), 460(3), 467; MHT
III 39, 115, 253, **343**; Rob 341,
796, 1417

18 BDF §454(3); Moule 153; MHT III
151; Rob 500, 764

19 BDF §454(3); DM 298; MHT III
137, 148; Rob 489, 801, 1038,
1082; RD §343(j), 451(b)

20 BDF §454(3)

21 BDF §490; DM 258; Moule 106;
Rob 915

22 Moule 106; MHT II 450; Rob 915

23 DM 150; Moule 106; MHT III 253;
Rob 712, 796, 915

25 MHT IV 93; Rob 796, 1019, 1418

26 BDF §282(2); MHT II 463; MHT
III **40**; Rob 481, 683, 819, 1019

27 BDF §223(3); Moule 57; MHT III
187, 267; Rob 583bis, 778, 782,
1022, 1129; RD §442, 462(a);
Zer §114

28 Rob 590, 766, 962

Chapter 3

1 BDF §139, 496(1); BW 67; MHT
III **22**; Rob 395, 408, 739, 763,
1198

2 BDF §447(4); BW 67; DM 163, 244, 261; Rob 413, 485, 659bis, 816, 1152

3 BDF §299(3); Rob 395, 739, 1190

4 BDF §98, 369(3); BW 113; DM 276, 277; Moule 138; MHT II 450; MHT III 105, 145, 148; Rob 193, 940, 986, 1170, 1413; RD §424(a), 430(b), 467, 472(e)

5 BDF §465(2), 495(3); BW 88; Moule 103; MHT III 98, 152, **211**; Rob 315, 761, 876, 1108, 1199

6 BDF §385(1), 456(3); BW 88; DM 193, 248; MHT III 318; Rob 940, 965bis, 1022, 1025, 1170; Zer §356

7 BDF §442(8); Moule 167; Rob 433, 678, 739, 1145; Zer §459

8 BDF §427(4); MHT III **14**; Rob 234, 319, 678, 763, 1028, 1033, 1036, 1039, 1047, 1049

9 BDF §433(2); Moule 168; MHT II 322, 385; MHT III 56, **287**; MHT IV 86; Rob 391, 419, 423, 621, 739, 812, 816, 1036; RD §470(m); Zer §234

10 Rob 751, 1164

11 BDF §413(1); MHT II 60, 202, 205; MHT III 151; Rob 315, 764, 1106, 1216; RD §320

12 BDF §353(2); Moule 81; MHT II 81; Rob 187, 643, 751

13 BDF §108(1); Moule 66; MHT I 52; MHT II 108, 195; Rob 336, 343, 635, 1213; RD §302

15 Rob 1062, 1080, 1220

18 BDF §214(6); Moule 82; MHT II 465; Rob 500, 639

19 DM 144; MHT IV 92; Rob 771

20 BDF §258(2); MHT II 434; MHT III **177**, 196, 287; Rob 752, 962; Zer §177

21 DM 161; Rob 523, 781, 1062

22 BDF §447(8); MHT III **211**, **212**; Rob 500, 567, 1184; Zer §38, 467

23 BW 92; DM 197, 208; Moule 41; Rob 476, 518, 814, 837, 847; RD §344(e)

24 Moule 109; MHT III 190, 221; Rob 175, 401, 779, 782; RD §387(b)(3), 387(e); Zer §132n

25 BDF §219(3), 284(3), 474(5a); Moule 35, 54, 56, 78, 81, 115, 207; MHT III 180, **190**, **253**, **263**, **268**; Rob 154, 401, 480, 567, 584, 589, 595, 600, 624, 781, 783, 784, 810; RD §325; Zer §117, 473

26 BDF §402(2); Moule 115; MHT III 15, 143, **212**, 222, **260**; Rob 547, 599, 766, 781, 1071; Zer §38, 134

27 BW 140; Rob 498, 582, 740, 780

28 MHT III 137, 240

29 BDF §254(3); MHT III 181

30 BDF §107, 456(3); DM 103; Moule 195; Rob 301, 1025, 1027, 1154; RD §442

31 Rob 307, 316bis, 940, 1170

Chapter 4

1 BDF §480(5); MHT III 98, 168; Rob 1175

2 Rob 739, 1009; Zer §303

3 MHT II 463; MHT III 253; Rob 393, 458; Zer §473

4 BW 52; MHT III 58; Rob 523, 609, 757, 759

5 MHT II 139; MHT III 58; Rob 258, 274; RD §212 A b

6 Rob 394, 722; Zer §134

7 MHT II 190; MHT III 296; Rob 367, 720, 724; RD §275

8 BDF §365(3); MHT III 96; Rob 1399, inset

9 BDF §481; Rob 394, 1202; Zer §473

10 BDF §496(1); BW 133; DM 227, 256; Rob 1198; Zer §117

11 BW 16; DM 79; Moule 38, 57; MHT III 143, **211**, **214**, **267**; Rob 498, 780, 781, 782, 1066; Zer §114, 352

12 DM 115; Moule 110; Rob 423, 521, 548, 1095, 1162; RD §345(b), 468, 474(j)

13 BDF §399(1); Moule 57; MHT III 140, 175, **211**; Rob 400, 499, 796, 1059, 1066, 1078, 1188, 1424

14 MHT III **15**, 260; Rob 599, 766, 1023, 1416; RD §387(a); Zer §134

15   MHT III 344

16   BDF §107; DM 146, 245; MHT III **15**, 47, 143, 260; Rob 423, 1066, 1095, 1162; RD §468; Zer §112

17   BDF §294(2); Moule 130; MHT II 465; MHT III 246; MHT IV 93; Rob 644, 717, 719, 1028; Zer §18

18   BDF §434(1); MHT III 143, 226; Rob 224, 616, 1066

19   BDF §103, 427(1); DM 263; Moule 105; MHT II 58; Rob 207, 215, 299, 674, 1114, 1146; Zer §376

20   BDF §187(6), 196; DM 88, 103; Moule 204; MHT III 242, **266**; MHT IV 93; Rob 334, 532, 594, 861; Zer §170

21   Rob 724, 816, 964, 1035, 1114

23   DM 102

24   DM 102; Moule 49; MHT III 58, 237; Rob 602

25   Moule 55, 194, 195; MHT III **268**; Zer §36, 112

Chapter 5

1   Moule 15; MHT I 35, 110, 247, 248; MHT II 74; Rob 200, 583, 598, 823, 850, 859, 889, 928, 931, 1192; RD §402(a), 406(a), 410(a)

2   BDF §343(2); MHT I 145; MHT III 70, **262**; Rob 224, 900bis

3   BDF §493(3); Moule 117; MHT II 463; MHT III 173, 253; Rob 394, 1187, 1200; RD §470(n)

4   Moule 117; Rob 1200

5   BW 95, 148; DM 203; Moule 117; MHT III 23, 173; Rob 499, 500, 583, 896, 1200; Zer §38, 105

6   BDF §255(3), 476(1); Moule 166; MHT IV 85; Rob 567, 632; RD §371

7   BDF §102(2), 349(1), 385(1); BW 89; DM 193; Moule 64, 111; MHT III **86**, 173, **180**; Rob 530, 652, 653, 763, 876; RD §346(d), 348; Zer §473

8   BDF §394; Moule 64; Rob 315, 594, 784, 964, 1034

9   BDF §219(3); DM 119, 256; Moule 77, 195; MHT III 253; Rob 518, 659; Zer §113

10   DM 227, 293; Moule 195; MHT IV 89; Rob 529

11   Moule 179; MHT I 224; MHT III 253; Rob 394, 1134bis

12   BDF §235(2); DM 106(2), 113; Moule 50, 58, 132; MHT I 107; MHT III 272; Rob 348, 434, 438, 604, 773, 833, 963; RD §401(a), 473; Zer §**127**

13   BDF §258(2); MHT II 190, 196, 198; MHT III **177**; Rob 342, 796; Zer §177

14   BDF §488(3); BW 90; DM 106; Rob 348, 605, 833, 860; RD §301

15   BW 67; Moule 44; MHT III 240; Rob 660, 774, 1159, 1417

16   BDF §488(3); Rob 348, 860

17   Moule 44; MHT III 220, 240

18   BDF §481; BW 55; Moule 44, 70; MHT II 463; MHT III 214; Rob 394, 438, 458, 1190, 1202; RD §473; Zer §45

19   MHT IV 85; Rob 394, 660, 969, 1201; RD §473

20   Moule 143; MHT I 207; MHT III 344; Rob 613, 722, 998; RD §473; Zer §**353**, 414n

21   Moule 143; RD §473

Chapter 6

1   Moule 143; MHT III 72; Rob 850, 876, 934, 1192, 1394; Zer §251, 414n

2   BW 87; DM 85, 192, 272, 275; Moule 10, 124; Rob 539, 728, 889, 940, 960, 996; RD §347(g), 414; Zer §226

3   Rob 592, 784

4   BDF §272, 337(1); MHT I 83; MHT III 213, 221; Rob 493, 496, 651, 850, 969; RD §343(h), 387(b)(3); Zer §40n

5   BDF §194(2); MHT III **220**; Rob 528, 1417; RD §410(a)

6   BDF §400(8); BW 8, 121; DM 76; Moule 38; MHT I 218; MHT II 440; MHT III 141; Rob 496, 699, 990, 1002, 1067, 1088bis, 1128; RD §343(h)

8   Rob 529, 872

9   Rob 1128

10 BDF §154, 188(2); Moule 36, 46, 131; MHT III **238**; Rob 479, 539, 541, 715; RD §347(g); Zer §56

11 BDF §157(3), 188(2), 406(1); MHT I 103; MHT III 137, 148, 246, **264**; Rob 481, 537, 587, 588, 1038, 1181; RD §451(b)

12 BDF §337(1); BW 116, 122; DM 207; Moule 38; MHT III **76**; Rob 1090, 1097, 1192

13 MHT I 125, 129; MHT III 42, **76**; Rob 316, 689, 855, 950, 968, 1140

14 BDF §258(2); BW 88; DM 192; Moule 66; MHT III **177**; Rob 207, 635, 793, 796, 889

15 BDF §75, 299(3); Moule 66; MHT III 72; Rob 850, 940, 1192, 1399; RD §381, 401(a); Zer §251

16 MHT III 334; Rob 316, 720, 1150, 1154, 1188; RD §410(a), 472(f)

17 BDF §294(5), 327; DM 126; Rob 461, 719, 721, 792, 1422; Zer §452

18 Rob 518

19 Moule 97; MHT III 185; Rob 537, 650, 856

20 Moule 46; MHT III 238; Rob 313, 523, 537

21 BDF §284(3); DM 106; Moule 132; Rob 714, 721bis, 722

23 MHT III 27; Rob 587

Chapter 7

1 Rob 602, 733bis, 978; RD §419(d)

2 BW 110; DM 290; MHT III **212**; Rob 500, 529, 1019, 1190, 1419

3 BDF §182(3), 189(2), 349(1), 400(8); BW 89, 122; DM 215, 285; Moule 128; MHT I 217; MHT III 141, **215**, 239; MHT IV 93; Rob 425, 515, 876, 996, 1002bis, 1087, 1090, 1190; RD §435(d), 455(d); Zer §352, 383

4 BDF §188(2), 189(2); Moule 144; MHT III 143, 239; Rob 539, 1071, 1190

5 BDF §269(2); MHT III 187; Rob 312, 782

6 Moule 143; MHT III **213**; Rob 721, 1091, 1095, 1162bis, 1164;

RD §468

7 BDF §281, 360(1), 428(2), 443(3), 452(3); MHT III 39, 92, 339; Rob 402, 678, 768, 874, 915, 921, 940, 1014, 1016, 1192

8 BW 149

9 MHT II 194; MHT III 39; Rob 341, 1160

10 BW 150; MHT II 60; Rob 232, 398, 539, 680, 698, 782; RD §323bis

12 Moule 144; Rob 1152; RD §324

13 Rob 537, 550, 609, 1102, 1121

14 MHT II 378; Rob 158

15 MHT II 61; MHT III 45; Rob 698, 1158

16 MHT III 115; Rob 319, 1422

17 MHT III 37; Rob 677

18 BDF §399(1); BW 4, 127; DM 217; MHT III 140; Rob 158, 234, 399, 416, 431, 705, 890, 1058, 1059, 1424; RD §455(c)

19 Rob 718, 1158

20 MHT III 115; Rob 683, 698

21 DM 241; Rob 539, 778, 1035, 1041, 1190

22 Rob 529, 780; Zer §110

23 Rob 295, 530, 551, 748, 780, 796, 1109

24 DM 71; Moule 38, 187 n.1; MHT II 440; MHT III **214**; MHT IV 83, 90; Rob 461bis, 497, 518, 706, 1203; RD §340(d); Zer §41

25 BDF §281; BW 34; Rob 287, 537, 540, 770, 780bis, 1190, 1378; RD §376

Chapter 8

1 DM 140, 241; MHT III 187; Rob 425, 1190; RD §23, 387(b)(3)

2 BDF §281; MHT III 39; Rob 402, 780, 784, 788

3 BDF §219(2), 263(2), 480(6); BW 28; DM 95; Moule 35, 63, 131; MHT I 221; MHT III **13**, 253; MHT IV 86, 87; Rob 372, 419, 459, 491, 618, 654, 763, 780, 784, 978, 1096; RD §324, 342(m), 367, 387(b)(3), 419(a), 427; Zer §96, 119

4 MHT III **285**; Rob 778; Zer §441

5 Rob 767

6 Rob 780bis

7 BDF §452(3); Rob 962

8 BW 34; Rob 540; RD §347(g)

9 BDF §219(4); Moule 38; MHT I 171; Rob 234, 589, 698, 761, 780, 795, 1008, 1154, 1160, 1186; RD §470(c), 472(e); Zer **§117**, 183

10 BDF §372(2b); Moule 195; Zer §303

11 BDF §372(2b); Moule 38; MHT III 115; Rob 584, 1009

12 BDF §190(1), 400(2); BW 33; DM 85; MHT I 217; MHT III 141, 238; Rob 341bis, 537, 996, 1067, 1076, 1087, 1095, 1162, 1192; RD §410(a); Zer §352

13 BDF §372(2a); Moule 44; MHT III 240

14 DM 91, 112; Moule 44; MHT III 240; Rob 533, 698, 732

15 Moule 131; MHT I 10; Rob 29, 465, 595; RD §341(c); Zer §34

16 BDF §463; DM 130; Rob 529, 1035

17 DM 262; MHT III **335**; Rob 395, 1023bis; RD §442

18 BDF §239(8), 474(5a); BW 56; DM 120, 232, 243; Moule 53, 169; MHT I 114; MHT III **79, 350**; MHT IV 94; Rob 535, 626, 661, 777, 875, 877, 878, 1035, 1107, 1191; RD §402(c), 425

19 Rob 1191

20 BDF §222; MHT I 105; MHT II 98; Rob 224, 298, 349, 550, 1100, 1139, 1191; RD §33 b

21 Moule 175; MHT II 440; MHT III 213; Rob 503, 770, 780, 964, 1191

22 Moule 94; MHT III 200; Rob 639, 772, 1191

23 MHT III 24, 41, 42; Rob 498, 503, 577, 687, 1191; Zer §132n

24 BDF §442(14); DM 136; Moule 45; MHT III 241; Rob 448, 531, 533, 543, 742, 1105, 1191; RD §339(d), 346(f); Zer §459

25 Moule 58; MHT III 267

26 DM 130, 146, 276, 277; Moule 59, 111, 200; MHT II 200; MHT III 182, 194, 268, 320; Rob 529, 560, 565bis, 573, 629, 722, 739, 766, 770, 967, 1046; RD §357, 374, 424(a)

27 Moule 59; MHT III 268; Rob 609, 1046

28 BDF §148(1), 413(3); MHT I 65; MHT III **151**; Rob 477

29 BDF §182(1), 493(3); MHT III 143, 215; Rob 480, 504, 528, 621, 841, 991, 1071; RD §343(j), 432

30 Rob 837, 841

31 BDF §496(2); Moule 53; Rob 432, 630, 1192, 1198

32 BDF §439(3); DM 260; MHT III 331; Rob 244, 291, 424, 509, 623, 724, 725, 773, 812, 960, 965, 1001, 1148ter; RD §343(1), 435(e), 472(a)

33 BDF §490; Rob 504, 607, 652, 764, 779, 795, 916, 1118, 1175

34 BDF §351(2), 495(3); Moule 103; MHT II 219; MHT III 17, 26, 86, 151; Rob 652, 781, 878, 1119, 1199; Zer §282

35 BW 14; DM 78; MHT III **211**; Rob 793, 1188

36 BDF §157(5); BW 78; DM 184; Rob 481, 501

37 Moule 78, 87; MHT III **265**; Rob 629

38 Rob 427, 895, 1118, 1189

39 BDF §269(2); DM 152; MHT III 187, 197; Rob 749, 779, 782

Chapter 9

1 BDF §463; Rob 434, 444, 588, 886, 1035, 1132

2 MHT IV 97

3 BDF §211, 272, 359(2); BW 86; DM 169, 190; Moule 9, 64, 72; MHT I 212; MHT III **65**, 91, 146; Rob 367, 575, 812, 886, 919, 1038bis, 1148; RD §405, 445, 451(b); Zer §356, 393

4 BDF §141(8), 460(3); Moule 124; MHT III 27; Rob 409, 427, 724, 954, 1182

5 BDF §266(2); Moule 58, 59, 111; MHT I 228; MHT III **15**; Rob 486, 604, 608, 766, 795, 1108; RD §387(b)(2)

6 BDF §304, 480(5); MHT III **47**; Rob 698, 724, 732, 752, 1034

7 MHT II 463; MHT III 345; Rob 207

8 MHT II 23, 441, 463; MHT III 58, 313; Rob 701, 1158

9 DM 76, 127; Rob 394

10 BDF §479(1); Rob 394

11 BDF §446, 478; MHT III 268, 334; Rob 425, 434, 566, 782, 1173, 1188; Zer §130

12 BDF §61(1); Rob 218, 277, 394, 663

13 Rob 760, 967

14 Rob 876, 917, 934, 940

15 Rob 474; Zer §74

16 MHT II 197; Rob 342, 519

17 BDF §290(4); MHT III 45, 105; Rob 686, 699, 705, 986, 1413

18 MHT II 195; Rob 342

19 BDF §475(2); Rob 423, 739, 812

20 BDF §146(1b), 434(2), 450(4); Moule 156, 163; MHT III 33, 153, 226, 338; Rob 402, 423, 464, 545, 678bis, 1148, 1149, 1151; RD §435(a), 472(d)

21 BDF §393(3); Moule 156; MHT III 36; MHT IV 94; Rob 503, 693

22 BDF §165, 263(2), 467; Moule 96, 151; MHT III 14, 213; Rob 438, 496, 654, 763, 1129, 1417; Zer §40, 140

23 BDF §165; Rob 713

24 BDF §477(2); Moule 168; Rob 438, 718

25 BDF §219(1), 426, 430(3), 477(2); Moule 105; MHT I 281; MHT III 261, 282; Rob 438, 1138, 1139bis, 1156, 1163; RD §469

26 BDF §477(2); MHT I 16; Rob 1042; RD §410(b)

27 BDF §477(2); Moule 65; Rob 166, 474, 632; Zer §96

28 BDF §477(2); DM 138; RD §320

29 BDF §477(2); MHT II 190; Rob 367

30 BDF §163, 272, 447(8); MHT III 221; Rob 782, 1184; RD §469;

Zer §467

31 Rob 965

33 BDF §187(6); Moule 50; MHT III 237

Chapter 10

1 BDF §272, 447(4), 463; DM 130; Moule 70; MHT III 191; Rob 685, 1151

2 Moule 40; Rob 500

3 MHT I 163; Rob 781, 817, 818; Zer §38

4 DM 103; Moule 70

5 BDF §474(5c); Rob 1035; Zer §226

6 MHT I 124; MHT III 135; Rob 499, 606, 1399

8 BDF §130(3); Rob 394, 505, 649

9 MHT III 162; MHT IV 92; Rob 1123

10 Moule 27, 70; MHT III 291; Rob 392, 820

11 BDF §187(6); Moule 50; MHT III 237

12 BW 20; Rob 514, 594, 687; RD §344(b)

13 Moule 151

14 BDF §77, 366(1), 493(3); DM 171, 193, 258; MHT I 185; MHT II 463; MHT III 99; Rob 506, 648, 706bis, 720, 721bis, 820, 934bis, 1106, 1158, 1200, 1399

15 BDF §470(1); Rob 302, 395, 741, 917, 967bis, 1032, 1193, 1419; RD §424(b), 448(h)

16 BDF §448(3); MHT II 61; Rob 752bis, 753

17 DM 241; MHT III 283, 330; Rob 1169

18 BDF §427(2), 448(3), 450(4); Moule 163; MHT III 338, 347; Rob 425, 506, 652, 918, 1151, 1158, 1174, 1175; RD §470(j) and (k), 472(a) and (d)

19 MHT III 252, 282; Rob 355, 657, 760, 1158, 1163, 1174

20 BDF §191(3), 220(1); MHT III 58, 156, **264**; Rob 551, 820

21 DM 110

Chapter 11

1   BW 143; DM 258; Rob 810, 917, 940, 1168, 1175, 1191; RD §448(b), 470(g)

2   BDF §219(1); BW 34, 44; DM 91; MHT II 123; MHT III 261; Rob 529, 739, 1168, 1390; RD §470(g)

3   MHT IV 85; Rob 634

4   BDF §53(4), 448(3); Moule 183; MHT I 59; MHT II 152, 173; Rob 254, 411, 739; RD §118 d

6   BDF §456(3); DM 248; MHT III 318; Rob 1025, 1159

7   BDF §171(2); BW 4; Moule 37; Rob 509

8   BDF §109(4), 393(6), 400(2); MHT II 450; MHT III 141; Rob 1061, 1076, 1424; Zer §384

9   BW 32

10   BDF §400(2, 4); MHT II 124, 450; MHT III 141; Rob 262, 1061bis

11   BW 110; DM 249, 286; MHT I 207; MHT III 190; Rob 940, 998bis; RD §435(a); Zer §353

12   MHT III 175, 181; Rob 218

13   BDF §474(4); MHT III 149; MHT IV 94; Rob 440, 602, 1151

14   DM 263; Rob 1017, 1024, 1421; Zer §403

15   MHT III 175; Rob 395, 411

16   Rob 1023, 1181

17   BDF §120(3), 488(2); MHT III 115; Rob 402, 418, 678, 1201, 1417

18   BDF §483; Moule 90; MHT I 125; Rob 1158, 1204

19   BDF §488(2)

20   BDF §119(4), 196; BW 40; Moule 44; MHT I 125; MHT III 99, 242; Rob 532, 1199; RD §346(e); Zer §58

21   BDF §370(1); Moule 59; MHT III 221; Rob 609, 1012bis, 1160; RD §470(c)

22   BDF §456(3), 469, 475(2), 477(2); DM 247, 248; MHT III 318; Rob 441, 524, 965bis, 1025

23   Rob 418, 524

24   BDF §120(3); DM 108; Moule 91, 92; MHT III **18**; Rob 524, 525, 559, 561, 616

25   BDF §188(2), 275(4); Moule 82; MHT II 113; MHT III 111, 238; Rob 550, 791, 1412

26   Moule 91, 94; MHT III 200; Rob 324, 559, 772; Zer §190

27   MHT III 221; Rob 615, 704, 782

28   DM 102; Moule 195; MHT III 268; Zer §112

30   BDF §196; BW 40; DM 90; Moule 44; MHT III 243; Rob 532; RD §474(b); Zer §58

31   BDF §196, 284(2); Moule 44; Rob 532, 685; Zer §58

32   DM 104, 111; MHT III **266**; Rob 627, 773

33   BDF §146(2); BW 7; DM 71; MHT III 33; Rob 302, 395, 432, 461, 463, 795, 1032, 1200

34   Rob 432

35   MHT II 422; Rob 432; Zer §455g

36   BDF §223(2), 275(7); Moule 68, 72; MHT III 267; Rob 432, 567, 583, 595, 759, 773; RD §361; Zer §113

Chapter 12

1   BDF §223(4), 480(6); Moule 35f., 58; MHT II 378; MHT III 28, **267**; Rob 443, 444, 583, 1205

2   DM 99; Moule 44, 100; MHT III 57, 240; MHT IV 85, 90, 94; Rob 530, 609, 891

3   BDF §223(4), 488(1b); DM 230; Moule 51, 58, 70, 92; MHT I 219, 237; MHT III 143; Rob 562, 583, 616, 629, 633, 1003, 1072, 1090, 1201; Zer §473

4   Rob 967

5   BDF §305; DM 132; Moule 60 n.1; MHT I 105, 183; MHT III **15**, 198, 268; Rob 244, 282, 294, 450, 460, 487, 568, 606, 673, 675, 692, 766, 774; RD §348; Zer §78

6   BDF §454(3); MHT I 183, 225; MHT III 333; Rob 433, 439, 581, 946, 1134, 1135, 1390

7   BDF §258(1), 446; MHT I 183; MHT III 177, **302**; Rob 433, 758, 1390

8 Moule 62, 114; MHT I 183; Rob
433, 561, 609, 1390

9 BDF §258(1), 468(2); BW 138; DM
229; Moule 179; MHT I 180, 182;
MHT III 177; MHT IV 89; Rob
396, 439, 758, 946, 1133; RD
§332, 462(e); Zer §373

10 BDF §150; Moule 46, 114, 180;
MHT III 239; Rob 439, 523bis,
1133

11 Moule 114, 156, 180; Rob 439,
523bis, 1133, 1172

12 BDF §196; Moule 114; Rob 439,
523bis, 524, 1133; RD §345(e)

13 Moule 114; Rob 439, 523bis,
1133

14 MHT I 180; Rob 439, 1133; Zer
§373

15 BDF §389, 488(3); BW 125; DM
216; Moule 126; MHT I 179, 180;
MHT III 78; MHT IV 89; Rob 440,
944, 946, 1092, 1106, 1201; RD
§407, 457(e)

16 BW 38, 138; Moule 52; MHT I
180, 182; Rob 440bis, 594, 614,
946; RD §407, 462(e)

17 DM 100; Rob 440, 573; Zer §92

18 Moule 33f., 111, 160; MHT III
14; Rob 486, 598, 611, 766,
1416; RD §342(m)

19 MHT I 180; MHT III **173**

20 MHT II 196, 440; Rob 342bis,
484, 1019

21 MHT II 199; MHT III 62; Rob
534, 763, 881

Chapter 13

1 MHT I 228; MHT III 52, 152; Rob
444, 579, 1108

2 BDF §188(2); Moule 144; Rob 807

3 BDF §471(3); MHT II 75; MHT III
14, **22**, 319, 342; Rob 201, 204,
763

4 Moule 70; Rob 1019

5 BDF §127(2); MHT III 148; Rob
1084, 1162, 1181

6 BDF §290(4); Rob 705bis, 941

7 BDF §481; BW 69; Rob 758, 1202;
RD §386(c)

8 BDF §399(1); MHT III 140; Rob
243, 748, 897, 898, 1066, 1078,
1424; RD §470(j)

9 BDF §64(1); DM 247; MHT I 87;
MHT III 42, 182, 197; Rob 288,
688, 748, 758, 766, 874; RD
§387(a)

10 BW 147; DM 145

11 BDF §442(9), 480(5); DM 219;
MHT I 182, 183; MHT III 45,
139, 335; Rob 298, 640, 666,
705, 1059, 1076, 1134, 1140

12 MHT II 212; MHT III 52; Rob 901

13 BDF §200, 337(1), 425(4); Moule
155; MHT III **76**, **158**, 243; Rob
261, 792, 850, 1140

Chapter 14

1 Moule 44, 46; MHT III **22**

2 BDF §397(2); MHT III 36, 137;
Rob 695bis, 1060, 1395

3 Rob 810

4 BDF §73, 188(2), 412(5); BW 33;
MHT II 390; MHT III **57**, 153,
238; Rob 402, 423, 539, 541,
678, 694, 738; RD §374; Zer
§231

5 Moule 51, 125; MHT I 89, 246;
MHT III 36; Rob 290, 616, 695;
Zer §473

6 BDF §188(2); MHT III 238; Rob
539

7 BDF §188(2), 272; Rob 539

8 DM 248; MHT II 74; Rob 201,
1010, 1019, 1027, 1179, 1189;
RD §410(a)

9 BW 91; Moule 10, 195; MHT III
71; MHT IV 81; Rob 699, 834

10 Rob 423, 678, 694, 738

11 BDF §188(2), 454(5); MHT III
333; Rob 1034

13 BDF §399(3); BW 128; Moule 127,
155; MHT III 140; Rob 1059,
1078, 1094, 1424; RD §457(b)

14 BDF §291(4); MHT III 46, 137;
Rob 588, 743; Zer §470

15 Moule 44; MHT II 205; MHT III
46, 242; Rob 317, 708

16 MHT III 189

17 Moule 112; MHT III 176, 221;
Rob 419, 784

19　BDF §266(3); MHT II 74; MHT III **16**; Rob 325, 767, 1176

20　BDF §223(3); Moule 58; MHT I 125; MHT III 267; Rob 583, 1152, 1153; Zer §114

21　BDF §338(1), 399(3), 480(1); MHT II 89, 90, 140; MHT III 141, 253; Rob 268, 706, 721, 858, 978, 1059, 1066, 1424; RD §179 a, 419(a), 423(d)

22　DM 107; MHT II 180; MHT III 265; Rob 721bis, 1175; RD §423(d)

23　BDF §344; BW 97; DM 202; MHT I 134; Rob 897, 898, 1019, 1419; Zer §257

Chapter 15

1　MHT I 221; Rob 1096

2　BDF §332(1); BW 52; DM 103, 110; Moule 53; MHT III **72**; Rob 746

3　Rob 1191

4　BW 21; DM 82; MHT I 115; Rob 563, 685

5　BW 113; MHT I 195; MHT II 211; Rob 326, 939, 940, 1214

6　MHT III **252**; MHT IV 92

7　BW 102; MHT III 335; Rob 372, 809, 1181

8　Rob 499, 632, 757, 909, 1040, 1049, 1060

9　DM 285

12　BDF §254(3); MHT III 181

13　BDF §404(1); DM 82; MHT I 195; MHT II 450, 451; MHT III **145**, 265; MHT IV 90; Rob 939, 940

14　Rob 686, 909

15　BDF §334; MHT III 30, 73; Rob 298, 583, 665, 846

16　MHT III 211; Rob 474, 498, 587, 594, 681

17　BDF §160; Rob 486, 626

18　Rob 720, 1158, 1164

19　BW 13; Moule 85, 109 n.1; MHT III 221; Rob 644, 645, 681, 909, 1414

20　Rob 710, 748, 1162bis, 1414; RD §378, 468

21　Rob 720, 1159

22　BDF §400(4); BW 84; DM 188, 213; Moule 108; MHT I 217; Rob 470, 487, 762, 765, 774, 884, 996, 1061, 1067, 1089, 1094, 1171, 1425; RD §468; Zer §74, 386

23　BDF §109(5); MHT I 217; MHT III 141; Rob 152, 434, 996, 1061, 1067, 1076; Zer §70

24　BDF §455(2); BW 160; Moule 88, 133; MHT I 167; MHT III 112; Rob 324, 434, 974, 1403; RD §410(b), 419(g)

25　DM 226; Rob 434, 891, 1129

26　BDF §452(2); BW 29; Moule 43; MHT III 170, 209; Rob 367, 434, 502, 528, 782, 891

27　BDF §113(2); DM 90, 243; MHT II 378; Rob 434, 529, 1009

28　Moule 55; Rob 434, 582

29　Moule 134; Rob 589; Zer §117

30　BDF §223(4); Rob 688

31　Moule 204; Rob 166, 783

32　Rob 529

33　DM 259; Rob 396

Chapter 16

1　BDF §93; Moule 145; MHT II 202; MHT III 187; Rob 315, 782

2　BDF §277(3); Moule 130, 145; MHT II 60; MHT III 41, 265; Rob 505, 680, 687, 718, 721; RD §343(k)

3　BDF §293(4); MHT III 47

4　Rob 633, 728

5　Rob 235, 728

6　DM 93; MHT II 144, 446; MHT IV 93; Rob 442, 488

7　BDF §125(2), 293(4); MHT I 52, 141, 144; MHT II 17, 221; Rob 172, 337, 622, 728

8　BDF §125(1); Rob 172

9　Rob 236

10　BDF §162(5); Moule 38; MHT III 169; Rob 172, 255, 759, 783

11　BDF §162(5); Moule 38, 106; MHT II 139; MHT III **15**, 169; Rob 259, 274; RD §174 b

12　MHT II 446; MHT IV 93

13　BDF §284(2); MHT III **77**; Rob 682

14　Rob 172, 173, 235, 255bis

15　Moule 93 n.3; MHT II 350; MHT III 221; Rob 173, 773

16　MHT III 212

17　BW 58; Rob 616, 758, 778, 783, 800, 954; RD §324, 386(c)

18　MHT III 23; Rob 771; RD §387(e)

19　BDF §447(5); BW 34, 52; DM 103; Rob 221, 487, 605, 813, 919; RD §347(f)

20　BDF §384; Rob 611

21　BDF §268(1); MHT II 88; Rob 173, 504

22　MHT II 485; MHT IV 83

23　Rob 235, 236bis

25　BDF §201; BW 15, 42; DM 78, 90; MHT I 75; MHT III 243; Rob 230, 439, 527, 696, 1117; RD §346(b); Zer §54

26　MHT II 379; Rob 439, 772

27　BDF §467; MHT III 343; Rob 437, 438, 439, 776

I Corinthians

1200bis; Zer §140

Chapter 3

26   BDF §490; MHT III 282; Rob 962,
     1163, 1207

27   BDF §138(1), 263(4), 490; Moule
     138; MHT III **14**, **21**, 55; Rob
     409, 411, 757, 762, 763; RD
     §386(b)

28   BDF §490; Moule 138; MHT II
     112; MHT III 55, 151; Rob 654,
     1109

29   BDF §369(4), 490; Moule 138;
     MHT III **105**, 196; Rob 752, 986,
     987ter; RD §383, 430(d)

30   BDF §444(4); Moule 72; Rob 539;
     Zer §230

31   BDF §481; Moule 139; Rob 949,
     985, 1202

Chapter 2

1   Moule 105; MHT II 444; Rob 85,
     677; Zer §40n

2   BDF §442(9); Moule 156, 168,
     168 n.1; MHT III 335; Rob 85,
     1181

3   MHT III 37; Rob 85, 677

4   BDF §47(4), 112, 474(4); Moule
     78, 79; MHT II 78, 143; Rob 85,
     157,   566,   1206;   R D
     §201 D, 387(b)(2), 474(n)

5   Moule 205; MHT III 253; Rob 566

6   BDF §447(8); BW   30, 142;
     MHT III 264; Rob 1186; Zer §467

7   BDF §220(2); DM 153; Moule 74,
     79; Rob 418, 586, 589, 621,
     724, 784, 1107, 1110, 1117; RD
     §460(b)

8   BDF §360(4); MHT III 70, 99;
     Rob 1015, 1417

9   BDF p.3, n.4; Moule 183

11   Rob 782

12   Rob 325, 983, 1388; RD §306,
     430(a)

13   BDF §183; BW 23, 24; Moule 40;
     MHT II 459; MHT III **211**, 234;
     MHT IV 90; Rob 504, 516, 654;
     RD §333

14   BDF §190(1); Rob 159

15   BDF §488(1a); Rob 159, 208

16   BDF §259(3); MHT II 187; Rob
     724

1   BDF §113(2); MHT II 378; Rob
     158bis; RD §316(b)

2   BDF §448(6), 460(1), 479(2);
     MHT III 246, 330; MHT IV 82;
     Rob 484, 1201; RD §474(t)

3   BDF §113(2), 456(3); DM 241;
     MHT II 378; Rob 158, 159, 267,
     1186bis, 1411; RD §316(b)

4   BDF §113(2); DM 135; MHT II
     378; MHT III 112; Rob 743, 750

5   BDF §442(9), 448(8); MHT IV 94;
     Rob 583

6   BDF §101, 448(2); BW 84, 100;
     DM 156(2), 188; Rob 838

7   BDF §101; DM 134; Moule 144;
     Rob 743, 1189

8   BDF §276(2); MHT I 90; MHT II
     247; MHT III 182, 191; Rob 691,
     786

9   BDF §109(7), 474(4); MHT II
     341; RD §387(b)(2)

10   Moule 96; MHT III **13**

11   BDF §236(3); Moule 51; Rob 616

12   BDF §460(3); Rob 427, 560, 983,
     1178; Zer §301

13   DM 273; Moule 77; MHT III 49;
     Rob 590, 731, 732bis, 1176

14   BDF §372(2a); MHT II 60, 191;
     Rob 233, 1008, 1417; Zer §301

15   MHT III 41; Rob 350, 582, 1008,
     1417; Zer §301

16   Zer §183

17   Moule 131; Rob 412, 728, 729,
     960; Zer §301

18   DM 112; MHT III 147; Rob 658,
     1038

19   BDF §170(2); BW 7; DM   70;
     Moule 52; MHT I 65; Rob 474

20   MHT IV 93

21   BDF §454(3); BW 8; Moule 144;
     MHT III 265; MHT IV 81; Rob
     497, 685, 949, 1000; RD §343(g)

22   DM 248; Rob 793, 1189; RD §388

23   Rob 1027

Chapter 4

1 DM 276; MHT II 433; MHT IV 91;
   Rob 481, 710, 968; RD §424(b)

2 BDF §451(6); DM 270; Moule 161,
   162; MHT III 265; MHT IV 92;
   Rob 992, 993

3 BDF §145(2), 393(6); BW 154; DM
   241, 294; MHT I 210, 236;
   MHT III 31, 139; Rob 458, 537,
   670, 992, 1186; RD §347(c)

4 Moule 51, 90; MHT III **42**, 253;
   Rob 319, 627, 688

5 Moule 133, 144; MHT III **14**,
   111; Rob 752, 757, 763

6 BDF §247(4), 305, 384, 481;
   Moule 64, 77, 111, 120; MHT II
   70, 75, 121, 200, 463; MHT III
   182, **271**; MHT IV 70, 93; Rob
   203, 260, 325, 342, 561, 587,
   607, 622, 630, 675, 721, 749,
   984, 987, 1202bis; RD §162 c,
   371, 470(e); Zer §96, 341

7 Rob 341, 1184

8 BDF §359(1), 361, 439(2),
   495(2); BW 44, 106; DM 91, 169;
   Moule 11, 137; MHT I 200;
   MHT III 72, **91**; MHT IV 81, 83;
   Rob 428, 529, 818, 841, 923bis,
   1004, 1148, 1149, 1199; RD
   §405, 445bis, 472(a); Zer §184,
   355n

9 BDF §461(2); MHT II 369; Rob
   480, 481, 769, 788

10 BDF §477(2); MHT II 307

11 MHT II 72; Rob 148, 191

12 Moule 150; Rob 1121

13 Moule 13; MHT III 321; Rob 618

14 Rob 845, 1138, 1139

15 BDF §372(1a), 448(5); DM 240;
   MHT III **115**, 330; Rob 233, 283,
   582, 1018, 1187; RD §439

17 BDF §351(1), 378, 418(4); DM
   272; Moule 33; Rob 483, 712bis,
   724, 782, 960, 989; Zer §322

18 BW 93; DM 198; MHT III 158

19 Rob 356, 871

20 Moule 79; MHT III **265**; Rob 1202

21 BDF §443(2); DM 105, 133;
   Moule 79; MHT I 12; MHT II 23;
   MHT III 241; Rob 394, 456, 534,
   589, 737; Zer §117

Chapter 5

1 BDF §322, 442(9), 473(1); Moule
   140; Rob 710, 727, 770, 803,
   881; RD §379; Zer §219

2 BDF §5(3b); MHT III **95**; Zer
   §352, 415

3 DM 244; Rob 705, 1152

4 Rob 628

5 MHT III 46

6 DM   151;   Rob   776;   RD
   §387(b)(1)

7 BDF §452(3); MHT II 112; Rob
   219, 349, 399

8 DM 130; Moule 144; Rob 498,
   931, 955, 999, 1414; RD §435(c)

9 BDF §334; BW 30, 103; DM 84;
   Moule 12; MHT III **73**; Rob 317,
   423, 757, 811, 846, 1047, 1170

10 BDF §239(8), 358(1), 433(2),
   456(3); Moule 149; MHT III 318;
   Rob 272, 887, 920, 947, 963,
   965, 1014, 1026, 1162, 1163; RD
   §426(b), 465

11 Moule 12; MHT II 60; MHT III
   73, 149; Rob 232, 317, 846,
   1047, 1060, 1185

12 BDF §299(3); MHT III 240;
   MHT IV 92; Rob 547, 736, 944,
   1202

13 BDF §288(1); MHT II 181;
   MHT III 194; Rob 689; Zer §209

Chapter 6

1 BDF §239(5); Moule 53; MHT III
   274; Rob 603, 811

2 BDF §219(1); MHT I 103, 236;
   MHT II 60, 343; MHT III 31,
   253; Rob 233, 504, 516, 587,
   652, 670; RD §344(c)

3 BDF §427(3); Moule 164; MHT I
   240; MHT II 379; MHT III 283;
   Rob 751, 1149, 1173bis; RD
   §472(a)

4 BDF §450(4); Moule 163; MHT II
   343; MHT IV 94; Rob 423, 698,
   941

5 BDF §98, 139; DM 99; Moule 92,
   188; MHT I 99; MHT III **23**; Rob
   232, 313, 409, 561, 648, 718,
   726, 1001

6 BDF §442(9); Moule 61; MHT III
   45; Rob 460, 487, 610, 705

7 BDF §314, 450(4); DM 132, 160,
   255; Moule 61, 163; MHT I 162;
   MHT II 354; MHT III 43, 57; Rob
   218, 293, 690, 808, 816, 1421;
   RD §378

8 BDF §442(9); MHT III 45, 51;
   Rob 487, 704, 705

9 BDF §445(1); BW 116; DM 175;
   MHT II 104, 377; Rob 947, 1160,
   1164; RD §470(j)

10 BDF §442(9); Rob 1164, 1189

11 BDF §131, 317, 448(2); MHT I
   163; MHT II 397; MHT III 53;
   Rob 411, 654, 701, 704, 807,
   809

12 BW 33; DM 85; Moule 27 n.2,
   196; Rob 1158

13 Moule 196; Rob 703, 704

14 Rob 582

15 MHT III 24; Rob 860, 940

16 BW 89; Moule 29; MHT III 253;
   Rob 233

18 BW 21; Moule 83, 196; MHT III
   216; Rob 471, 640; RD §344(d)

19 MHT III 23; Rob 497, 716

20 BDF §179(1), 451(4); BW 11; DM
   261; Moule 39; MHT III 333; Rob
   511, 1149bis; RD §472(b)

Chapter 7

1 BW 14; Moule 63; Rob 619, 720,
   721, 722

2 Moule 121; MHT I 89; MHT III
   28, 191; Rob 408

3 Moule 193; MHT II 203

5 BDF §98, 376; Moule 53, 96,
   145, 148; MHT I 169; MHT II
   203; MHT III 13, 95, 321; Rob
   597, 751, 1010, 1023, 1025

6 Moule 59; MHT III 268; Rob 609,
   1199

7 BDF §448(2); BW 71; DM 128;
   Moule 153 n.1; MHT III 36, 191;
   Rob 545, 688, 691, 695, 923,
   968, 1181, 1394

8 MHT III 321; Zer §440n

9 BDF §372(2b); MHT II 309;
   MHT III 79; Rob 218, 1012

10 MHT III 95; Rob 518, 794

11 Rob 1419

12 BDF §460(1); MHT II 60, 203,
   325; MHT III 37; Rob 232, 680

13 BDF §469; MHT II 429; MHT III
   325; MHT IV 101; Rob 440, 442,
   724, 956

14 BDF §456(3); MHT II 463;
   MHT III 262, 313, 318; Rob 587,
   1026

15 DM 176; Moule 79, 205; MHT I
   172; MHT III 262, 263, 265; Rob
   429, 948

16 Moule 154, 159 n.1; Rob 264,
   462, 1387

17 BDF §376, 448(8); BW 30;
   MHT III 75, 262, 264; MHT IV
   94; Rob 1025; Zer §470

18 BDF §494; MHT III 264; Rob 740,
   1198

19 DM 116; Rob 394, 654, 751

20 MHT II 419; Rob 716

21 BDF §494; Moule 21, 28, 167
   n.3; MHT I 49, 165; MHT III
   76; Rob 430, 1023; RD §320

22 MHT III 264; Rob 795

23 BDF §179(1); Moule 39; Rob 429

24 MHT III 264

25 BDF §425(3); BW 134; Moule 63,
   127; MHT III 158; Rob 1128,
   1140

26 BDF §399(1); MHT II 433;
   MHT III 140; MHT IV 91; Rob
   320, 545, 1059, 1205, 1424

27 BDF §464, 494; MHT I 125; Rob
   432; BDF §101, 190(3)

28 BDF §101, 190(3); Moule 202;
   MHT III 74, 219, 238; Rob 536,
   710, 846, 923, 1020, 1022,
   1027, 1419; RD §301, 401(a),
   408, 439, 441; Zer §257

29 BDF §387(3); DM 249; Moule 34,
   145, 161; MHT III 95, 303;
   MHT IV 92; Rob 319, 487, 994,
   1127, 1140

30 Moule 145

31 BDF §152(4); MHT I 64; MHT III
   51; Rob 476, 477, 533; RD
   §342(c), 346(f)

33 MHT II 156; Rob 767

34 BDF §101; MHT III 220; Rob 523,
   993; Zer §414n

35 BDF §117(1), 202, 263(2),
   413(3); Moule 96; MHT III 14,
   151; MHT IV 81; Rob 287, 504,
   537, 546, 547, 687, 689, 763,
   1109; RD §221 b, 377; Zer §140

36   BDF §336(2), 372(1a); BW 117; MHT II 352; MHT III 75, 115, **116**; Rob 489, 629, 1204

37   BDF §468(3); DM 118; MHT I 224; MHT III 45; Rob 440, 549, 656, 700; Zer §375

38   BDF §101, 102(3); Moule 120, 144; MHT II 409; Rob 218, 299

39   BDF §364(3); BW 97, 128; DM 219; Rob 291, 716, 720, 733, 897, 1019, 1076, 1080, 1082; Zer §325

40   BDF §471(1); Rob 1019

Chapter 8

1   Moule 63; Rob 435

2   Rob 435, 1038

3   Rob 435, 698, 845; Zer §342n

4   BDF §475(2); DM 247; MHT III 175; Rob 424, 435; RD §388

5   BDF §454(2), 477(2); DM 247, 274; MHT III 175; Rob 793, 1025, 1026, 1181

6   BDF §223(2), 297; Moule 72; MHT I 106; MHT III 325; Rob 440, 583, 724; Zer §342n

7   BDF §196, 269(2); BW 40; MHT III **187**; Rob 500, 532, 743

9   Rob 537, 995; RD §434(c)

10   MHT II 342; MHT III 143, 153; Rob 778, 1072

11   MHT II 206; Rob 317

12   BDF §442(9); MHT III 189

13   BW 100; DM 156, 245, 267; Moule 164; MHT I 191; MHT II 140; MHT III 96; Rob 268, 962, 1154, 1399, inset, 1416; RD §179 a, 427, 472(e)

Chapter 9

1   BW 143; MHT II 193; MHT III 283; Rob 364, 587, 917, 1157; RD §448(b)

2   BDF §439(2), 448(5); DM 241; Rob 244, 537, 1012, 1148, 1160, 1187; RD §444, 470(c), 472(a)

3   Rob 537, 703, 704

4   Moule 156; MHT II 90; MHT III 139, 283; Rob 918, 1158, 1169, 1174; RD §470(g)

5   Moule 156; MHT III **246**; Rob 477, 480, 918

6   BDF §431(1); MHT I 220; Rob 402, 1068, 1164, 1177; RD §470(j)

7   Rob 478, 532, 770, 1147; RD §387(e)

8   BDF §427(2), 440(1); MHT III **283**; Rob 208, 917bis, 1158, 1174, 1177; RD §448(f), 470(g)

9   Moule 28; MHT II 395; Rob 223, 508, 541

10   BDF §452(2); MHT I 217; MHT III 141; Rob 224, 996, 1061, 1067, 1076

11   BDF §113(2), 372(1c); MHT II 378; MHT III **115**, 190; Rob 681, 1009, 1017, 1022; RD §441; Zer §329

12   Moule 62; MHT III 211, 231; Rob 500, 533, 681, 1187, 1417

13   MHT II 399; Rob 521, 542, 623; RD §345(b)

14   Rob 598

15   BDF §369(2), 393(2); Moule 77; MHT III **100**, 135, 139, 265; Rob 439, 533, 587, 704, 845, 984, 996, 1058

16   BDF §58; Moule 149; Rob 270, 1012

17   Moule 32, 149; MHT III 225, 247; Rob 485, 550, 816, 1100; RD §342(j)

18   BDF §369(2), 394; DM 295; Moule 139; MHT II 200; MHT III **100**, 143; Rob 477, 656, 759, 784, 984, 992, 1078; Zer §408, 411

19   BDF §244(3); BW 31; Moule 102; MHT I 230; MHT III 30, 157, **215**; Rob 516, 539, 540, 597, 660, 665, 775, 843, 1129, 1217

20   BDF §262(1); Moule 66; MHT III 169; Rob 843, 1217

21   BDF §182(3); Moule 42, 102; MHT I 236; MHT II 60, 243, 307; MHT III **100**, 215; Rob 232, 349, 504, 516, 1216, 1217; RD §320, 343(j), 344(c)

22   BDF §275(7); Moule 160, 202; Rob 742, 773, 843, 1199

23   Rob 504, 843; Moule 132

24   Moule 132; Zer §352

25 BDF §154; BW 52; DM 93, 254; Moule 163; MHT III 46; MHT IV 81; Rob 148, 478, 707, 880, 1153

26 BDF §425(4); BW 78, 136; MHT I 231; MHT III 158, 285; Rob 880, 1127, 1138, 1139, 1140, 1154, 1159, 1163; RD §472(f)

27 BW 78; MHT II 75; Rob 201, 244, 633, 988; RD §430(d)

Chapter 10

1 DM 243; Rob 419; Zer §473

2 BDF §317; MHT I 163; Rob 808 bis

3 BDF §269(5); MHT III 186; Rob 776, 883

4 BDF §269(5), 327; BW 84; DM 188, 190; MHT II 208; MHT III 67; Rob 201, 339, 418, 838

5 BDF §327; Moule 108; MHT III 30, 253; Rob 418

6 BDF §327; MHT III 67, 143; Rob 488, 500, 704

7 BDF §327; MHT II 90; MHT III 135; Rob 403, 931, 1088, 1185

8 BDF §327; MHT III 262; Rob 403, 931, 1088, 1185

9 BDF §327; MHT II 206; Rob 317, 403, 635, 931, 1088, 1185, 1218

10 BDF §327; MHT II 71, 206, 365; Rob 189, 403, 967, 1088

11 BDF §133(3), 327; MHT III 25, 46, 67; MHT IV 86; Rob 404, 626, 703, 707

12 Moule 199; MHT IV 96; Rob 320, 430, 933, 1000

13 BDF §400(2); MHT I 217; Rob 598, 632, 996, 1060, 1067, 1076, 1087

14 DM 245; Moule 164; MHT III 173; Rob 471, 1154; RD §472(e)

16 BDF §295, 490; MHT III 324; Rob 429, 488, 718, 880bis; RD §342(n), 380; Zer §19

17 DM 274; Moule 62; MHT III 231, 303; Rob 509, 773, 774, 962, 1397; RD §426(a)

18 BDF §169(2), 272; MHT III 215; Rob 760, 783

19 Rob 233, 234, 743, 1035, 1036

20 BDF §460(1); Moule 29; MHT II 448; MHT III 215, 313; MHT IV 89; Rob 886, 1214

21 BDF §259(3); DM 81; Moule 62; Rob 509, 791, 1183

22 MHT II 196; Rob 325, 516, 923

24 BDF §479(1); MHT III 197; Rob 394, 1203

25 Rob 263

27 MHT III 151; Rob 1018; RD §439

29 BDF §283(3); DM 249; Moule 120; MHT I 87; MHT II 181; Rob 688bis, 694, 739; Zer §467

30 BDF §281, 372(2c); BW 41; DM 90; Moule 62, 130; MHT III 40, 241; Rob 402, 509, 530, 609, 632, 678, 720, 721; RD §365

31 BDF §454(3), 480(1); Rob 1189; RD §410(a)

32 BDF §444(2)

33 BDF §154, 245(1), 283(3), 413(3); Moule 35; MHT III 151, 190; Rob 479, 487, 504, 652, 660, 690

Chapter 11

2 BDF §154; Moule 35; Rob 479, 482, 487, 506, 881, 895, 1035; RD §426(a)

3 BDF §493(3); Rob 769, 781

4 BDF §225; Moule 60; Rob 477, 606

5 BDF §131, 194(1), 270(1); DM 90, 152; MHT III 21, 186, 220; Rob 342, 530bis, 656, 687, 789; RD §346(c) and (d)

6 BDF §372(2a), 399(1); BW 102; DM 160, 243; MHT II 199, 200, 250; MHT III 57, 140; Rob 342, 371, 809, 948, 1012, 1059, 1218, 1424; RD §320

8 Rob 793

9 BDF §452(3); Rob 565, 584

11 Rob 1187

12 DM 102; Rob 565, 582, 584, 773

13 MHT III 88, 149, 253; Rob 541, 687, 689, 890, 1086; RD §377

14 BDF §190(1), 466(1); MHT III 239; Rob 686; RD §376

15 BDF §190(1); DM 100; Moule 71; MHT III 239; Rob 574

16 BDF §483

17 BDF §244(2), 430(3); Rob 218 bis, 277, 663; Zer §213

18 BDF §322, 447(4); DM 182; MHT II 473; MHT III 62; Rol 174, 487, 550, 585, 803, 881, 893, 1042, 1103, 1152, 1422

19 DM 243

20 BDF §113(2); DM 256; MHT II 473; Rob 234, 562, 1152

21 BW 78, 82; DM 128, 184(2); MHT II 195, 450; MHT III 36; MHT IV 90; Rob 342, 695, 854, 880, 1395

22 BDF §427(2); DM 171, 244; Moule 156; MHT II 226; MHT III 143; Rob 918, 928, 934, 1072, 1090, 1169, 1174

23 Moule 52 n.1, 72, 92; MHT I 237, 246; MHT II 206; MHT III 37, 259; Rob 190, 312, 561, 579, 838, 1049, 1214, 1399

24 BDF §272, 284(2); DM 104; Moule 63, 64; Rob 234, 595, 685

25 BW 124; MHT III 143; Rob 612, 974, 1074, 1181

26 BDF §383(2); BW 78; MHT III 111, 175; Rob 880, 975, 1412

27 Moule 144; Rob 504, 787, 1188

28 MHT II 433; MHT IV 91; Rob 519; RD §344(e); Zer §68

29 BDF §488(1b); MHT I 230; Rob 880, 1023, 1129, 1201

30 Rob 880

31 BDF §360(4); MHT III 42; Rob 1015; Zer §209

33 BDF §364(3); Rob 562, 1000

34 BDF §364(1), 455(2); MHT I 167; MHT II 195; MHT III 94, 112, 261; Rob 521, 791, 974; RD §419(g)

Chapter 12

1 Moule 63

2 MHT I 115, 167; MHT III 93, 125; Rob 407, 412, 563, 922, 974, 1033; RD §419(g); Zer §358

3 Rob 116, 1034; Zer §451

6 BDF §275(7); MHT III 265; Rob 476, 773

7 Moule 53

8 BDF §306(2); MHT III 36, 197, 267; Rob 696, 746, 770, 1395; Zer §113

9 Rob 747bis, 758; RD §386(c)

10 Rob 166, 746, 749, 758; RD §386(c)

11 BDF §286(1); MHT III 18, 191; Rob 530, 580, 653, 758, 773, 1199; RD §346(d), 386(c)

12 BDF §272; Rob 419

13 BDF §452(3); DM 251, 252; MHT III 247; Rob 485, 757, 793, 1189, 1397; Zer §72

15 BDF §236(5), 431(1); Moule 51; MHT III 210; Rob 550, 616, 1164; RD §470(j)

16 BDF §236(5); Moule 51; MHT III 210

19 BDF §360(4); Rob 1015, 1023

22 BDF §474(5a); MHT III **31**; MHT IV 94; Rob 663, 664, 777, 1107

23 MHT III 30, 137; Rob 668; Zer §146

24 BDF §448(3); MHT III 56

25 Rob 1413

26 Rob 1179

27 BDF §212, §442(9); Rob 550, 597, 792

28 MHT III 36, 55; Rob 300, 488 bis, 574, 696, 793, 1152, 1395

29 Rob 757, 774

31 BDF §272; MHT II 202; MHT III **221**; Rob 311, 551, 777, 784

Chapter 13

1 MHT III 246; MHT IV 94; Rob 129, 358, 758, 1105, 1420; RD §23, 386(c), 474(p)

2 BDF §131, 275(3), 372(1a); DM 215, 285; Moule 144; MHT II 111, 205; MHT III 116, 200; Rob 219, 316bis, 609, 750, 751, 758, 772bis, 1090, 1163, 1388, 1420; RD §464(a)

3 BDF §28, 369(2); MHT II 74, 111, 219; MHT III **100**; Rob 201, 324, 484, 504, 758, 764, 876, 984, 1216; RD §320; Zer §340

4 BDF §108(5); BW 69; DM 142; MHT II 400; Rob 148, 758, 1178; RD §329

5 Rob 1178; RD §329

6 Rob 1178; RD §329

7 Rob 476, 477, 774, 1178; RD §329

8 BDF §454(3); BW 101; DM 159; Rob 357, 758; RD §461(b)

10 Rob 766

11 BDF §382(1); BW 160; Rob 900, 971

12 MHT I 113; Rob 208, 564bis, 582, 600, 625, 649, 792, 827; RD §311, 369, 398

13 BDF §244, 258(1); DM 121, 165; MHT I 58, 78; MHT III 177; Rob 281, 405, 668, 758; Zer §148

Chapter 14

1 Rob 993; Zer §415

2 Moule 195

3 Moule 195

4 MHT III **176**

5 BDF §185(2), 252, 376; DM 120; Moule 83; MHT I 187, 208, 248; MHT III 135, **138**, 216, 321; Rob 548, 640, 1017, 1039, 1188; Zer §332, 336

6 DM 244, 246; Moule 79; Rob 483, 1188, 1189

7 BDF §366(1), 450(2); MHT II 60, 204, 409; MHT III 151, **337**; MHT IV 85; Rob 233, 357, 423, 581, 778, 871, 876, 1109, 1140, 1155, 1188, 1189bis; RD §474(j)

8 BW 101; DM 252; MHT I 156; MHT II 108; Rob 807

9 MHT III 89, 151; Rob 323, 353, 582, 871, 876, 889, 1110, 1115; RD §402(c), 460(c)

10 BDF §385(2); BW 115; DM 290; MHT I 196; MHT III 125, 127, 175; Rob 392, 1021, 1408; Zer §323

11 BDF §220(1); Moule 46, 76; MHT I 103, 104; MHT III 264; 'Rob 272, 588, 1388, 1420; RD §360; Zer §120

12 DM 270

13 Moule 164; Rob 950, 955

15 Moule 44; MHT III 241; Rob 261, 533, 874

16 DM 259; MHT III **14**; Rob 460, 691, 759, 765, 876, 965bis, 1026, 1159

17 Rob 1152, 1153; Zer §74

18 BDF §415, 471(1); MHT II 473; MHT III **160**

19 BDF §245(3), 480(4); DM 251; MHT II 442; MHT III 32; MHT IV 92; Rob 233, 261, 661, 792, 1188; Zer §145

20 BDF §258(1); BW 37; DM 87; MHT II 405; MHT III 177, 220, 239; Rob 524, 1378, 1383; RD §345(d); Zer §53

21 BDF §64(2); Rob 207, 591, 748

22 BDF §145(1); DM 103; Moule 70, 144; Rob 458, 537

23 MHT II 473; Rob 917, 1157

24 Rob 427

25 Rob 546

26 DM 111; MHT III 112; Rob 626, 1378

27 BDF §60(2), 442(9); BW 49; DM 93, 99, 107; Moule 67, 98; MHT I 79; MHT III 31; Rob 170, 279, 470, 487, 550, 571, 670, 791, 1379; RD §356; Zer §74

28 BDF §188(2), 252; MHT III **116**; Rob 166, 1418

29 Rob 775

31 BW 49; Moule 60; Rob 606, 608

32 MHT III 313

33 Rob 497

34 BDF §312(2), 479(2); MHT III 58; MHT IV 82; Rob 1220

35 MHT III 261; Rob 792; RD §388

37 BDF §162(7); Rob 845, 1038

38 MHT II 70; Rob 948, 1011

39 BDF §399(1); MHT I 125; MHT III 140; Rob 765, 1059, 1061, 1094, 1424, 1425; RD §468

Chapter 15

1 Rob 427, 724, 954; RD §23, 380, 474(p)

2 BDF §376, 478; Moule 83; MHT I 171; MHT III 321; Rob 425, 530,

640, 738, 954, 1008, 1011, 1018, 1169, 1188, 1205

3   BDF §342(1); BW 52; Moule 59; MHT III **5**, **69**; Rob 525, 550, 1034bis, 1035; RD §401(a); Zer §287

4   Moule 15; MHT I 137, 141; Rob 844, 894, 896, 1182; RD §401(a), 403(a)

5   RD §401(a)

6   BDF §185(4); MHT I 136; MHT II 315; Rob 511, 548, 642, 666, 674, 848

7   BDF §275(5); MHT III **200**; Rob 820

8   BDF §433(3); DM 276; Moule 111; MHT II 60; MHT III 321; Rob 233, 244, 516, 669, 757, 969, 1025, 1154; RD §424(b), 442, 472(e)

9   BDF §60(2); DM 121; MHT I 79, 236; MHT II 166; MHT III 31; Rob 279, 658, 669, 713, 779, 962; RD §326

10 Moule 80; Rob 411, 654, 712, 713, 720, 791, 1166, 1379; RD §380

11 MHT III 46; Rob 707

12 MHT III 210; Rob 658, 820, 1008, 1034bis, 1085

13 BDF §372(2b); Rob 1008, 1012

14 Rob 1008, 1417

15 BDF §254(2), 454(2); DM 242, 247; Rob 607, 817, 1012, 1154; Zer §306

16 BDF §254(2); Moule 148; Rob 1008, 1012; RD §437

17 MHT II 157; Rob 1008, 1012, 1417

18 Moule 164; MHT III 330; Rob 783

19 Moule 170, 205; MHT II 92; MHT III 228; Rob 204, 1008, 1389, 1417

21 DM 142; Rob 395, 794

22 Moule 80; MHT I 114; MHT III **262**; Rob 587, 827, 872

23 Moule 38; Rob 767; Zer §**39**

24 MHT II 204; MHT III 112; Rob 312, 851, 1214

25 MHT III 111; Rob 1412; RD §420(b); Zer §210

26 MHT III 63; Rob 870; Zer §210

27 BDF §275(7); MHT II 49; Rob 244, 395, 658, 1034, 1106; Zer §210

28 Moule 75, 160; MHT I 149, 163; MHT III 265; Rob 357, 657, 809, 819bis, 872; Zer §210

29 BDF §254(2), 442(14); BW 89; Moule 64; MHT I 58; Rob 630, 632, 876, 963bis, 965bis, 1012, 1025, 1180; RD §426(b); Zer §91, 94, 459

30 DM 93; Rob 470, 677

31 BDF §107, 149; DM 184, 262; MHT I 114; Rob 487, 685, 827, 1150; RD §472(c)

32 BDF §254(2), 323(1); Moule 7; MHT I 114, 120; MHT III 63, 239; Rob 539, 869, 931, 1416; RD §277

33 BDF §17, 487; MHT I 45; MHT II 9, 61, 63; MHT IV 96; Rob 207, 422, 1200

34 DM 150; Rob 626

35 BDF §298(2), 385(1), 448(3); Rob 740, 1022, 1184; Zer §356

36 BDF §475(1); Rob 264, 423, 463, 678

37 BDF §351(2), 385(2); BW 115; DM 230, 290; MHT I 151, 196; MHT III 86, 125, 127; Rob 374, 878, 892, 1021, 1106, 1119, 1187, 1213, 1408; RD §440; Zer §323

38 BDF §442(9); MHT III **191**

39 BDF §253(1); MHT III 196; Rob 687, 747, 747bis, 748, 749, 752bis, 770, 1153, 1163, 1187

40 BDF §127(5); Rob 748, 749bis

41 BDF §253(1); MHT III 172, 265; Rob 747bis, 748, 794

42 BDF §490; MHT III 180, 291; MHT IV 97; Rob 392, 429, 866

43 Rob 1178

44 Rob 234bis

45 Moule 204; MHT III 253; Rob 669

47 BDF §253(3); MHT III 175

48 BDF §490; DM 273; Rob 429, 710, 731bis

49 BDF §451(4); MHT II 74; MHT III 333; Rob 200, 349, 678

50 MHT I 58; Rob 405, 699, 1036

51 BDF §433(2); Moule 168; MHT III
    287; Rob 334, 423, 753, 819,
    876, 1212, 1397; RD §311,
    470(m)

52 BDF §254(2); Moule 186; MHT II
    335; Rob 392, 587

54 MHT II 126; Rob 258, 429, 778,
    1200; RD §163 B (b)

55 MHT II 22, 119; Rob 1200; RD
    §156 B (c)

56 DM 149; MHT II 126; Rob 1200

57 MHT II 126; Rob 461, 1106,
    1116, 1200

58 MHT III 265

                Chapter 16

1   BW 57; Moule 63; Rob 197, 594,
    619

2   Moule 155; MHT I 54; MHT II
    191, 200, 203, 238, 439;
    MHT III 187; MHT IV 91; Rob
    243, 325, 343, 672, 729

3   BDF §351(1); Moule 57, 133;
    MHT I 58; MHT III 27, 135, 267;
    Rob 408, 409

4   BDF §400(3); Moule 129, 148;
    MHT I 216, 217; MHT II 204;
    MHT III 139, 141; Rob 992, 996,
    1059, 1061, 1066, 1067, 1077

5   BDF §323(1); Moule 7; MHT I
    120; MHT III 63; Rob 434

6   BDF §424; DM 95; Moule 53;
    MHT I 74; MHT II 467; MHT III
    322; Rob 488, 490, 551, 722,
    969, 1109, 1121, 1127, 1130; RD
    §342(m), 423(b), 462(c)

7   BDF §475(2); Moule 53; MHT II
    467; Rob 877

9   MHT III 82; Rob 364, 800

10 BW 68; Moule 148; Rob 795, 993;
    Zer §322

11 BW 108; DM 171; Moule 22; MHT I
    178; MHT II 112; Rob 244, 853,
    856, 933, 943, 1399

12 MHT II 446; MHT IV 86, 92; Rob
    235, 423, 488, 619; RD §162(c);
    Zer §455

13 BDF §73

15 BDF §134(1a); MHT III 325; Rob
    173, 1034; Zer §415

16 BW 101; DM 158; Rob 233, 627

17 BDF §284(2); MHT III 190; Rob
    173, 205, 235, 288, 685

18 BDF §284(2); Rob 685; RD §375

19 MHT II 446; MHT IV 92; Rob 488

20 DM 132; Rob 692; RD §378

21 MHT III 186; Rob 416, 496, 685;
    RD §375

22 MHT II 154, 204; MHT III 122;
    Rob 313, 939, 945, 1012, 1160
    bis; RD §308

II Corinthians

23 BDF §397(3); DM 295; Moule 119,
    185; MHT III 191; Rob 602, 678,
    1033, 1034, 1035

24 Moule 119; MHT III 303; Rob
    510, 1429

Chapter 2

1   BDF §399(3); BW 31; DM 85;
    Moule 168; MHT III 45, 141,
    238; Rob 401, 539bis, 700,
    1059, 1078, 1424

2   BDF §442(8); DM 289; MHT III
    45; Rob 1014, 1182; Zer §459

3   BDF §290(4); Rob 686, 699, 705,
    706, 720, 721, 846, 887, 920

4   BDF §223(3); Moule 57; MHT III
    267; MHT IV 94; Rob 423, 583,
    598, 846; Zer §114

5   Rob 1008, 1417

6   Moule 108, 144; MHT II 165; MHT
    III 30, 46, 311; Rob 411, 537,
    782

7   DM 90; Moule 144; MHT I 193;
    MHT III 46, 242; Rob 208, 532,
    1090

9   MHT II 72; Rob 194, 699, 846,
    1045

10 DM 247, 272; Moule 130, 184;
    Rob 720, 956, 1417

11 MHT III 282; Rob 474, 1156

12 BDF §261(1); DM 104; MHT III
    82, 171; Rob 364, 513, 595,
    1213

13 BDF §190(3), 343(2), 401,
    406(3); BW 98, 125, 133; DM
    205, 213, 216, 218, 227; Moule
    14, 44; MHT I 145, 220; MHT III
    70, **142**, 146, **148**, 219, 238,
    242; Rob 235, 490, 532, 536,
    539, 688, 765, 900bis, 901,
    966, 1061, 1091, 1112, 1171,
    1427; RD §403(a), 455(b)

14 BDF §5(1), 148(1); MHT II 400;
    MHT III 53; MHT IV 85; Rob 407,
    474, 498; RD §347(e)

15 BDF §190(1); MHT III 239; Rob
    537

16 MHT III 36; Rob 626, 696, 1395

17 BDF §425(4); DM 225, 231; Moule
    17; MHT II 465; MHT III 158;
    Rob 644, 881

Chapter 3

1   BDF §488(1c); DM 131; Moule
    158; MHT II 205, 379; MHT IV
    85; Rob 307, 316bis, 1175

2   Moule 89, 91; MHT II 295; MHT
    III 23; Rob 217, 560, 778, 828,
    1201

3   BDF §113(2); MHT III **214**, 287;
    Rob 404, 658, 1034, 1085-86,
    1120, 1163, 1166

5   BDF §488(1d); MHT III 303; Rob
    423, 1429; Zer §209, 348, 464

6   MHT II 245; Rob 367, 480, 1213

7   Moule 15; Rob 1204, 1417

8   Rob 1136; Zer §38

9   BDF §172; Rob 1136

10 DM 251; Moule 15; MHT II 67;
    MHT III 151; Rob 1109, 1136

11 Moule 58; MHT III 267; Rob 583;
    Zer §114

12 Rob 532; RD §346(f)

13 BDF §482; MHT III 144; MHT IV
    85; Rob 318, 394, 883, 1003,
    1075, 1159, 1171, 1203; RD §320

14 BDF §424; Rob 244, 729

15 BDF §105, 455(1); DM 241, 281;
    MHT III 23, 112; Rob 300, 602,
    971; RD §419(e)

16 MHT II 61, 321; MHT III 113;
    Rob 207, 392, 617, 618, 971; RD
    §367, 419(e); Zer §169

17 Moule 115; MHT III 174, 344;
    Rob 769; Zer §169

18 BDF §159(4), 474(4); DM 112,
    162; Moule 115; MHT III **218**;
    Rob 486, 503, 530, 789, 810,
    820, 891, 967, 968, 1154; RD
    §342(j), 365, 424(b); Zer §47,
    72, 73

Chapter 4

1   Rob 1128

2   MHT II 205, 212; Rob 316, 338,
    771, 810

3   BDF §220(1); BW 32; DM 232,
    251; Moule 18; MHT III 264; Rob
    234, 587, 1417; Zer §120

4   BDF §168(2); Moule 143 n.2; MHT
    III 218; Rob 503, 779, 1094,
    1171; RD §343(b); Zer §47

5　Rob 584, 1187

6　Moule 184; MHT II 105; MHT III 23; Rob 764, 962

7　BW 22; DM 82; Rob 497, 514, 1413; Zer §414n

8　BDF §430(3), 488(1b); DM 102; Moule 105; MHT I 231, 237; MHT II 310; MHT III 56; Rob 596, 1138, 1139, 1201

9　Moule 105; MHT I 231; Rob 1139

10　BDF §271; DM 251; MHT III 24, 167

11　DM 251; MHT III 217

12　Moule 144

13　DM 129, 245; MHT III 194; Rob 1134; RD §374

15　Moule 108; MHT III 30

16　BDF §184, 200(1), 448(5); DM 124; MHT II 439; MHT III 190, 243; Rob 522, 681, 750, 766; Zer §110

17　BDF §263(2); Moule 186; MHT III **14**; Rob 297, 551, 654, 763

18　BDF §423(5); MHT III 323; MHT IV 99; Rob 891, 1132

Chapter 5

1　BW 16; DM 79; MHT III 214, 218; Rob 399, 418, 498, 762, 779, 882, 1019, 1419; RD §343(h), 402(a), 439; Zer §47, 322n

2　DM 251; Rob 563bis, 600

3　MHT I 115; Rob 244, 563bis, 1027

4　DM 106, 251; Moule 132; MHT I 107; MHT III 272; Rob 604, 722, 762, 963; Zer §127

5　BW 16; MHT III **214**; Rob 498, 595

6　Rob 217, 440, 474, 560, 1135

7　MHT III 267; Zer §114

8　Moule 53; MHT II 467; Rob 217, 625

10　BDF §239(8), 275(7), 286(1); BW 53; Moule 53; MHT III **201, 302,** 333; Rob 582, 773

11　BDF §350; MHT III **63**; Rob 500, 877, 880, 909

12　BDF §430(3), 468(1); Moule 179; MHT III 343; Rob 316, 439, 626, 792; Zer §96, 374

13　BDF §188(2), 342(1), 479(1); BW 31; DM 85; Moule 195; MHT III **238**; Rob 394, 539, 845, 1203

14　BDF §275(7), 451(2d); DM 78, 112; Moule 41; MHT III **211**; Rob 499, 699, 833, 1035; RD §343(f); Zer §**36**, 91

15　BDF §188(2), 442(9); BW 31; DM 112; Moule 64, 164; Rob 517, 539, 631, 773; RD §371; Zer §91

16　Moule 144; Rob 1417; RD §364

17　Moule 144; Rob 654

18　Moule 72; Rob 774

19　BDF §282(3), 396; DM 252; Moule 17, 116; MHT I 212, 227; MHT II 452; MHT III **40**, 89, **137**, 175; Rob 683, 964, 1033, 1406; RD §451(a)

20　BDF §396, 425(3); MHT III 158; Rob 1140, 1141

21　Zer §91

Chapter 6

1　Rob 440

2　BDF §465(2); Moule 29; MHT II 440; Rob 440, 497, 507

3　BDF §468(2); Moule 79, 155; MHT III 343; Rob 440, 442; Zer §374

4　BDF §157(4), 468(2), 491; Moule 78, 79, 196; MHT II 205; MHT III 28; Rob 316, 442bis, 454, 481, 591

5　BDF §468(2); Moule 79, 196; Rob 442bis

6　BDF §468(2); Moule 79, 196; Rob 442bis

7　BDF §468(2); Moule 58, 79, 115, 196; MHT III 180, 186, **207**; Rob 442bis, 582, 777

8　BDF §468(2); Moule 58, 79, 196; MHT II 287; MHT III 267; Zer §114

9　BDF §468(2, 3); Moule 196; MHT I 114; Rob 440, 442, 827, 1136, 1140; Zer §375

10　BDF §468(2); Moule 196; Rob 523, 828; RD §345(c)

11　BW 95; MHT III 23, 82; MHT IV 92; Rob 895

13 BDF §154, 159(4), 465(2); Moule
    34, 36, 160f.; MHT III **245**; Rob
    486, 487

14 BDF §189(1), 354; BW   44; MHT
    II 390; MHT III 89; Rob 330,
    375bis, 528bis, 529, 625, 890,
    1051; RD §308, 346(a)bis

15 Rob 217, 1184

16 Rob 216, 528

17 MHT III **76**; Rob 853

18 BW 59; MHT II 463; MHT III 253;
    Rob 458, 595

Chapter 7

1   Rob 576, 1399

3   BDF §495(3); MHT III 23

4   BDF §195(2)

5   BDF §343(2), 468(1); DM 252;
    Moule 14, 179; MHT I 145, 182,
    225; MHT III 28, 70, 343; Rob
    415, 439bis, 897, 900bis, 1135;
    RD §473; Zer §374

6   RD §473

7   BDF §244(2); Rob 665, 1091; RD
    §473

8   DM 153, 292; Moule 7, 167; Rob
    962, 1008, 1027, 1417; RD §443,
    473

9   Moule 59; MHT III 72, 260, 268;
    Rob 599, 834, 1166; RD §473

10 Moule 59; RD §473

11 BDF   §197,   399(1),   406(1),
    448(6); DM 107; Moule 59; MHT
    III 50, 140, 148, **220**, 239,
    268, 330; Rob 427, 481, 523,
    686, 700, 705, 741, 1038, 1059,
    1078, 1215, 1424; RD §163 B b,
    410(a), 473; Zer §53

12 BDF §216(1), 403; BW 28, 125;
    DM 216; Moule 83, 140; MHT II
    100; MHT III 144; Rob 225, 429,
    641, 846, 1060, 1073, 1080,
    1091, 1417, 1427; RD §457(d),
    473

13 BDF §60(3), 246; DM 101, 107;
    MHT III 29, 258; Rob 663, 1205;
    Zer §90

14 DM 247; Rob 603, 632, 962, 968,
    1008, 1417; Zer §96

15 BDF §60(3); BW 14; MHT III 211;
    Rob 612; Zer §64

16 Rob 217, 474

Chapter 8

1   BDF §220(1); Moule 76; MHT III
    264; Rob 587; Zer §120

2   BDF §225; DM 115; Moule 60; MHT
    III **268**; Rob 262, 607

3   BDF §236(2), 465(2); Moule 51,
    59, 167; MHT III **268**; Rob 434,
    609, 616; RD §366

4   Moule 179; Zer §184

5   Rob 1152, 1159

6   BDF §402(2); Moule 141; MHT I
    219; MHT III 143; Rob 968,
    1003, 1072, 1090; RD §435(d)

7   BDF §212, 387(3); BW 113; DM
    249; Moule 144; MHT I 179; MHT
    III **95**, 259; Rob 195, 598, 933,
    994; Zer §415

8   BDF §263(2); Moule 96; MHT III
    14, 217; Rob 763

9   DM 196; Moule 11; MHT III **71**,
    72; Rob 708, 834bis; RD §401(a)

10 BDF §399(1); Moule 124; MHT III
    140; Rob 221, 425, 523, 703,
    1059, 1066, 1158, 1162, 1424;
    RD §345(c)

11 BDF §400(2), 403; BW 127; DM
    217; MHT I 217; MHT III 141,
    144; Rob 395, 600, 996, 1061,
    1067, 1073bis, 1076, 1403,
    1413, 1424, 1427; RD §457(d)

12 DM 277; Moule 59; MHT III 268,
    320; Rob 957, 967; RD §424(a);
    Zer §335

13 Moule 145; MHT III **95**; Rob 395

14 BDF §369(4); Moule 138; MHT III
    46, **105**; Rob 707, 986

15 BDF §263(1), 481; MHT III **13**;
    Rob 218, 660, 763, 774, 1202

16 Moule 76; Rob 396, 585

17 BDF §244(2); BW 93; Moule 12;
    MHT III 30, 73; Rob 657, 665

18 BDF §258(1), 468(1); BW 72, 93;
    DM 148; Moule 12, 92; MHT I 68;
    MHT III 73, 343; Rob 433, 562,
    582, 770, 1134ter; RD §328, 473

19 MHT III 217; Rob 431, 433, 439;
    RD §328, 473; Zer §184, 374

20 Rob 431, 433, 699, 1039, 1134,
    1136; RD §328, 473

21 BDF §176(2), 264(2); Rob 433;
    RD §473

22 BDF §416(2), 488(1a); Moule 12;
    MHT III 29, 73, 162; Rob
    488ter, 530, 659, 664, 1041,
    1103, 1123bis; RD §336, 342(k)

23 BDF §454(3); BW 14; DM 112;
    Moule 65; MHT I 105; Rob 395,
    441, 504, 632; RD §371; Zer §96

24 MHT I 181; MHT III **343**; MHT IV
    89; Rob 946; Zer §184

Chapter 9

1   BDF §399(2); MHT III 140; Rob
    782, 1059, 1066, 1387, 1424

2   BDF §212, 284(2); Moule 108;
    MHT II 126; MHT III 30, 170,
    190, 259; Rob 221, 261, 475,
    548, 550; RD §163 B b; Zer §96

3   BDF §269(2); Moule 12; MHT III
    73, 89, 187; Rob 375, 983, 988,
    1388, 1406

4   BDF §471(3), 495(1); Moule 139;
    MHT III **95**, 99; Rob 988, 1199,
    1419; RD §430(d)

5   Moule 12, 141; MHT III 73; Rob
    996, 1086, 1182

6   BDF §481; DM 113; Rob 295, 604,
    1202

7   BDF §481; BW 79; DM 183; Moule
    8; MHT II 191, 366; MHT III 63;
    Rob 394, 597, 1202, 1390

8   BDF §488(1a); MHT II 390; Rob
    1201

9   Rob 272

10 BDF §101, 471(4); Rob 799

11 BDF §187(8), 468(2); Moule 31,
    179; MHT I 181, 182; MHT III
    219, 343; MHT IV 89; Rob 439,
    946, 1136; Zer §374

12 BDF §187(8); Moule 17; Rob 323,
    376, 435, 439, 536, 565, 881

13 BDF §272, 468(2); Moule 31,
    179; MHT I 181; MHT III 343;
    MHT IV 89; Rob 439, 781, 783;
    Zer §184, 374

14 BW 31; Rob 562, 605; RD
    §347(f), 363

15 Rob 605

Chapter 10

1   BDF §217(1); DM 69; Moule 58,
    205; MHT II 466; Rob 217, 407,
    424, 457, 474, 686, 688; RD

    §340(b); Zer §8

2   BDF §399(3), 405(1), 409(5),
    488(1b); DM 244; MHT I 212; MHT
    II 102; MHT III 140, 146; Rob
    217, 401, 407, 474, 481,
    490bis, 519, 743, 1035, 1038,
    1059, 1060, 1083, 1123, 1424

3   Moule 59, 102; MHT III 157; Rob
    407, 792bis

4   BDF §113(2), 192; Moule 46,
    184; MHT II 71, 443; MHT III
    238, 274, 343; MHT IV 89, 91;
    Rob 537, 626; Zer §56, 374

5   Rob 500, 593

6   MHT III 139; Rob 1417

7   Moule 58; MHT III **15**, 137, 268;
    Rob 407, 497, 699

8   BDF §373(2), 443(3); MHT III
    339; Rob 407, 716

9   BDF §223(3), 453(3), 483(3);
    Moule 145, 152; MHT I 167; MHT
    III 267, 321; Rob 407, 597,
    959, 969, 1025, 1040, 1091,
    1095; RD §320, 457(c)

10 BDF §130(3), 465(2); Moule 29;
    MHT II 112; MHT III 293; MHT IV
    81; Rob 233, 392, 434, 1206

11 BDF §280; Rob 291, 407, 678,
    699, 710bis, 731; Zer §114

12 BDF §94(2), 283(4), 416(2); MHT
    III 42, **160**; Rob 315, 316, 401,
    529, 687, 1201; RD §320; Zer
    §209, 473

13 BDF §294(5); Moule 71; MHT III
    324; Rob 407, 716, 719, 1078

14 BDF §433(3); Moule 92; MHT I
    68; MHT III **285**, 287; Rob 477,
    561, 629, 1159

15 Moule 71; MHT III 343; Zer §374

16 BW 21; Moule 86; MHT III 216;
    Rob 244, 297, 517, 547, 550,
    629bis, 647; RD §344(d), 353

18 MHT III 45; Rob 315, 316, 707

Chapter 11

1   BDF §359(1), 448(6), 495(3); BW
    106; DM 251; Moule 137; MHT I
    200; MHT III **91**, 330; Rob 368,
    486, 543, 886, 923bis, 1004,
    1186, 1199; RD §405, 446; Zer
    §355n

2   BDF §316(1); Moule 184; MHT I
    160; MHT III 55; Rob 261, 349,
    1088; RD §446

3   BDF §211; MHT I 248; MHT III
    99; Rob 782, 995

4   BDF §306(4); MHT III **197**; Rob
    747, 748, 1151, 1186; RD
    §472(d); Zer §311

5   BDF §429; MHT I 239; MHT III
    137, 250; Rob 297, 395, 519,
    548, 550, 629; Zer §473

6   BDF §128(2), 448(5); Moule 119,
    180; MHT III 343; Rob 129, 395,
    1202; Zer §8, 374

7   BDF §440(1)

8   MHT II 111; MHT III 27; Rob
    219, 1165

9   Moule 53, 157, 206; MHT II 467;
    MHT III 187; Rob 750, 778

10 BDF §397(3); DM 295; Moule 112;
    MHT III 178; Rob 1034

14 BDF §127(4); Moule 175; MHT III
    300

15 MHT III 321; Rob 1180

16 BDF §336(3), 473(1), 495(3); DM
    283; Moule 22, 151; MHT I 178;
    MHT III 137; Rob 208, 234, 743,
    853bis, 933, 1023, 1025, 1199,
    1399; RD §406(a)

18 BDF §258(2); MHT III 177

19 BDF §495(2); MHT IV 83; Rob
    1199

20 Moule 37; MHT III 256; Rob 606,
    802

21 BDF §396, 465(2), 495(3); MHT I
    212; MHT III 70, 137, 268; Rob
    434, 964, 1033, 1199; RD
    §451(a)

22 BDF §496(2); Rob 1198

23 BDF §102(6), 230, 462(2),
    495(3); DM 96; Moule 64; MHT II
    326; MHT III 28, **250**, 271; Rob
    244, 293, 297, 442, 450, 551,
    555, 558, 629bis, 784, 1109,
    1199; RD §352(a), 371; Zer §78

24 BDF §236(4); Moule 51; MHT II
    173; MHT III **18**; Rob 615, 635;
    Zer §253

25 BDF §121, 332(2), 343(2); DM
    196; Moule 14; MHT I 144, 145,
    148; MHT II 193, 269; MHT III
    70, 72; Rob 212, 793, 833, 897

26 BDF §166, 253(2); MHT III 181,
    212; Rob 501

27 MHT II 125; Rob 258, 784

28 BDF §202; Moule 86; Rob 244,
    537, 547, 646

29 MHT III **38**; Rob 677bis

30 Moule 79; Rob 475, 1416

31 BDF §413(3); MHT III 151

32 Rob 255, 258, 498

33 BDF §223(5); MHT IV 92

Chapter 12

1   BDF §353(5); MHT I 248; MHT III
    88; Rob 1092, 1130, 1149

2   BDF §213; Moule 74, 114; MHT I
    101, 229; MHT II 172; MHT III
    25, 46, 162, 178, 221, 260; Rob
    349, 408, 622, 778, 793, 1035,
    1041, 1045, 1103; RD §353

3   Moule 114, 197; MHT III 46; Rob
    710

4   MHT III 88; Rob 212, 225bis,
    349, 491, 881, 1139

5   MHT I 239; MHT II 463; MHT III
    46; Zer §96

6   BDF §145(2); Rob 519, 988; RD
    §430(d)

7   BDF §190(3), 378; DM 111; MHT
    IV 94; Rob 532, 536, 538, 629,
    960, 985

8   BDF §231(1); Moule 65

9   BDF §60(2), 246; BW 77; DM 183;
    Moule 15, 79, 91; MHT I 130;
    MHT II 165, 463; Rob 279, 488,
    541bis, 602, 664, 670, 879,
    897, 923; Zer §414n

10 MHT III 28, 112; Rob 973

11 BDF §154, 358(1), 495(3); BW
    106; MHT III 90, 250; Rob 478,
    920, 1003, 1014, 1160, 1416; RD
    §445

12 MHT III 58; Rob 408, 757, 772,
    1151

13 BDF §34(1), 154; Moule 131; MHT
    II 396; Rob 218, 341, 479, 512,
    1025, 1199, 1216; RD §320

14 BDF §154; Moule 161; MHT III
    52, 139, 226; Rob 702, 1077

15 BDF §60(2, 3), 61(1); MHT II
    165; Rob 218bis, 277, 279, 596

16 Moule 103; MHT III 157; Rob
    392, 476, 856, 948

17   BDF §343(2), 466(1); DM 203; Moule 36, 176, 202; MHT I 144; MHT III 70; MHT IV 86; Rob 436, 474, 488, 718, 720, 744, 893bis, 896; RD §403(a); Zer §29

18   DM 70; Moule 156, 202; MHT III 173, 283; Rob 684, 770; RD §375

19   BDF §322; MHT I 119; MHT II 465; MHT III 62, 190; Rob 297, 644, 696, 879

20   BDF §428(6); Moule 155, 157; MHT III 28, 58, 99, 283, **302**; Rob 267, 408, 534, 539, 731bis, 929, 995ter, 1159, 1161, 1174, 1403; RD §346(f), 466, 470(f)

21   BDF §423(2); MHT III 322; MHT IV 99; Rob 193, 475, 621, 716, 910, 995, 1117, 1173

Chapter 13

1   BDF §154, 234(4); Rob 478, 674, 702

2   BDF §206(1); Moule 69; Rob 674, 1035; Zer §322n

3   DM 246; MHT II 390

4   BDF §448(5), 457; MHT III 260; Rob 598; Zer §226

5   BDF §376; Moule 120; MHT I 171; MHT III 321; Rob 751, 1011, 1025, 1045, 1169

7   BW 66; Rob 394, 423, 656, 763, 886, 919, 1162, 1173; Zer §415

9   MHT III 45, 112, 195; Rob 698, 703

10   Moule 12 n.1; Rob 699, 845

11   BDF §451(6); Moule 21, 161, 162; MHT IV 92

12   Moule 21; MHT III 75; Rob 773bis

13   DM 113; Moule 41; MHT III **211**

Galatians

Chapter 1

1 BDF §223(2); BW 23; DM 102;
   MHT III 267; Rob 567, 582, 778,
   795

2 Rob 773, 780

4 BDF §229(1), 269(5); BW 163;
   MHT III 186; Rob 232, 618, 629,
   778

5 MHT I 183; MHT III 25; MHT IV
   91; Rob 408

6 BDF §306(4); BW 76, 82; DM 182;
   MHT I 80, 246; MHT III 197; Rob
   747bis, 748, 749, 879bis, 965;
   RD §378

7 BDF §376, 412(4), 448(8); DM
   247; Moule 106 n.1; MHT I 171;
   MHT III 153, 321; Rob 764, 778,
   785, 1011, 1107, 1169, 1420;
   Zer §470

8 BDF §135(4), 236(3); DM 292;
   Moule 51; MHT III **122**; Rob 313,
   402, 406, 616, 939, 1010, 1026,
   1419; Zer §306

9 BDF §236(3); Moule 51;
   MHT III 115; Rob 483, 968; RD
   §424(b), 447

10 BDF §360(2, 4), 440(1), 477(2);
    DM 289; MHT III **92**; Rob 922,
    1015

11 BDF §477(2); BW 81; DM 184;
    Moule 7; MHT IV 93; Rob 474;
    Zer §473

12 BDF §445(2), 477(2); Rob 582,
    1189; RD §410(a)

13 BDF §477(2); BW 83; MHT III
    186, 191; Rob 783, 885

14 BDF §60(3); Rob 298, 620, 633,
    779

15 Moule 73

16 BDF §220(1); Moule 76;
    MHT III 264; Rob 587bis; Zer
    §120

17 MHT IV 19

18 BW 90; Moule 53; MHT II 387,
    467; Rob 561

19 MHT II 468; Rob 224, 1025; Zer
    §470

20 Rob 538, 1034

21 RD §349

22 BW 131; DM 224, 232; Moule 17,
    80; MHT I 227; MHT II 452;
    MHT III **212**, 221; Rob 376, 412,
    487, 530, 888

23 BDF §134(2); BW 67; Moule 17,
    206; MHT II 452; MHT III **81**,
    151; Rob 659, 892, 1115, 1139,
    1147

24 BW 41; DM 105; Rob 523

                    Chapter 2

1   BDF §223(1); BW 10; Moule 56;
    MHT II 172; Rob 255, 283, 581,
    636

2   BDF §361, 370(2); Moule 70;
    MHT I 193, 201; Rob 542, 636,
    923, 988ter, 995, 1403; RD
    §430(d); Zer §344, 467

3   BDF §448(6); Moule 102;
    MHT III **157**; Zer §467

4   BDF §369(2), 467; Moule 139;
    MHT II 75; MHT III **99, 100**,
    343; Rob 613, 802, 984; Zer
    §218, 467

5   Moule 45, 53; MHT II 191, 467;
    MHT III **220**; Rob 367, 434, 438;
    Zer §467

6   BDF §301(1), 303, 330, 467; DM
    134; Moule 209; MHT III 49,
    196, 343; MHT IV 86; Rob 130,
    438, 731, 732bis, 743, 751,
    1115; RD §380; Zer §467

7   DM 155; MHT III **211**, 247; Rob
    130, 208, 485, 540, 546, 550,
    816, 820; Zer §72

8   Rob 130

9   BDF §391(3), 447(5), 481;
    MHT III 37; Rob 130, 394, 1000,
    1085, 1202, 1203; Zer §410

10 BDF §297; Moule 144; MHT I 95,
    179; MHT III **95**; MHT IV 94; Rob
    703, 714, 719, 723, 933, 960

11 DM 107; MHT II 466; MHT III 58;
    Rob 608, 816, 1118

12 BDF §210(3); BW 123; DM 282;
    Moule 128, 169; MHT II 327;
    MHT III 144, 259; Rob 579, 978,
    1075

13 BDF §391(2); Moule 141; MHT I
    209; MHT III 136; Rob 334, 530,
    533, 1000bis, 1181, 1414; RD
    §346(f), 435(c); Zer §350

14 DM 298; Moule 53; MHT I 244;
    MHT II 100; MHT III **63**; Rob
    224, 626, 880, 1028, 1029

15 MHT III 181, 220; Rob 530, 598,
    1390

16 MHT I 241; MHT II 463, 468;
    MHT IV 91; Rob 752, 796, 1025,
    1204; Zer §470

17 BDF §440(2), 451(2d); Moule
    158 n.1, 164, 196; MHT II 60;
    MHT III 330; Rob 232, 916bis,
    940, 1176, 1417; RD §448(d);
    Zer §303

18 BDF §157(4), 281; Moule 35,
    196; MHT III 40, 115; Rob 316,
    402, 480, 678

19 BDF §188(2), 281; Rob 402, 539,
    796

20 BDF §154; Moule 131; MHT III
    246, 264; Rob 479, 632, 715,
    779

21 Moule 164; Rob 1190, 1416

                    Chapter 3

1   BDF §146(2), 297, 477(2); DM
    107; MHT III 33, 187; Rob 349,
    473, 608, 621, 723, 792, 1193;
    RD §368; Zer §35

2   BW 145, 157; Moule 158, 175;
    MHT I 117; MHT III 259; Rob
    579, 1060

3   Moule 90

4   Rob 710

5   BDF §479(1); Moule 175;
    MHT III 53; Rob 394

7   DM 241; MHT III 208, 260; Rob
    698; Zer §42, 134

8   Moule 24 n.2, 73; MHT III **260**;
    Rob 367

9   BW 149; Moule 144; MHT III 168,
    260; Zer §134

10 BW 129; MHT II 450; MHT III
    136, 260; Rob 598, 631, 720,
    744, 773, 1067, 1086, 1088,
    1159; Zer §134, 392, 472

11 Rob 395; Zer §226, 416, 418

12 Zer §226

13 BW 18; DM 111, 286; Moule 64;
    Rob 317, 631ter; RD §371; Zer
    §91

14 BDF §207; Moule 176; MHT III
    168, **253**; Rob 1049

15 BDF §450(2); Moule 59; MHT III
    337; MHT IV 85; Rob 423, 1155,
    1188; RD §410(a)

16 BDF §425(4); DM 270, 272; Moule
    29; MHT III 158; Rob 342, 604,
    712

17 BW 123; MHT I 219; MHT II 172;
    MHT III 143; Rob 580, 672, 699,
    1003, 1072, 1090; RD §359

18 BDF §342(5); DM 162; Moule 15;
    MHT I 248; MHT III 70; Rob 583

19 BDF §480(5); BW 26; Moule 57,
    184; MHT II 113; MHT III 58,
    111, 267; MHT IV 93; Rob 221,
    349, 411, 647, 736, 974, 975,
    1412; RD §311, 420bis

20 BDF §433(1); Rob 423

21 BDF   §360(4);   Moule   103,
    106 n.1; MHT I 67; MHT III 152;
    Rob 777, 778, 940, 1015, 1417

22 BDF §138(1); MHT III 21

23 BDF §474(5a); DM 213; Moule
    169f.; MHT I 114; MHT III **79**,
    144, 350; MHT IV 93; Rob 857,
    878, 978, 1074, 1075

24 Moule 144

25 Moule 66; Rob 635

27 BW 146

28 BDF   §98, 446; MHT II 104;
    MHT III 334; Rob 313, 419, 558

29 MHT III 168

Chapter 4

1 Rob 733, 751, 757

4 DM 112, 162; Moule 66; MHT II
   459; Rob 820

5 Moule 66; Rob 960, 987

6 Moule 147; MHT I 10, 233;
   MHT III 23, 345; Rob 26, 231,
   441, 465; RD §341(c); Zer §34,
   419

7 Moule 144; Rob 395

8 BDF §430(3); MHT I 231; Rob
   1172

9 BDF §495(3); MHT IV 19; Rob
   879, 1111, 1199

10 DM 108; MHT III 55; Rob 613,
    810

11 BDF   §370(1), 476(3); DM 265;
    MHT I 193, 248; MHT III 99,
    325; Rob 995, 1169; RD §434(c)

12 Rob 482

13 BDF   §223(3); Moule 98; MHT I
    106; MHT III **30, 267**

15 BDF §360(1, 4); DM 169, 274;
    MHT III 92; Rob 841, 921, 922,
    1014, 1048; RD §473; Zer §319,
    344

16 Moule 144; RD §473

17 BDF §288(1); BW 46; Moule 210;
    MHT II 75, 196; MHT III 194;
    Rob 203, 325, 342, 984, 1403;
    RD §473; Zer §341

18 BDF §399(1); Moule 25, 53, 210;
    MHT II 69,   200,   450, 467;
    MHT III 55, 145; MHT IV 90; Rob
    186, 1162; RD §473

19 BDF §296; Moule 53; MHT II 113;
    MHT III 111; Rob 713, 975; RD
    §420(d), 473

20 BW 86, 106; DM 169, 190; Moule
    9; MHT II 467; MHT III 56, 65,
    91, 120; Rob 368, 784, 886,
    919, 937, 1199; RD §445, 473;
    Zer §356

22 MHT II 438; MHT IV 70; Rob
    1377, 1394; Zer §289n

23 BDF §342(5); Moule 14, 202;
    MHT I 248; MHT III 70

24 BDF §293(4); DM 138; MHT III
    187; Rob 704, 727, 729bis, 750,
    760, 881; RD §474(a); Zer §156,
    218

25 DM 136; MHT III 182; Rob 254,
    398, 411, 530, 547, 759, 760,
    766; RD §118 d, 387(a)

26 BDF   §293(4); BW 147; MHT III
    47; Rob 398, 547, 727

27 BDF §101, 430(3); MHT I 127,
    231; MHT II 157; MHT III 31;
    Rob 663, 892, 1138, 1139

28 MHT II 23, 441; Rob 1379; Zer
    §43

30 BDF   §365(2);   MHT I 177;
    MHT III 96, 97; Rob 942; Zer
    §444n

Chapter 5

1 BDF §73; Moule 44 n.2, 178;
   MHT I 61, 125; MHT III 242

2 BDF §467; MHT I 162; MHT III
   246; Rob 399, 482, 484, 816,
   1418

3 BDF §393(6); BW 161; DM 219;
   Rob 1062, 1076

4   BDF §319, 333(2); BW 78, 94; DM
    186, 272; Moule 8, 90; MHT I
    247; MHT III **63**, 73, **74**; Rob
    518bis, 562, 880, 960; RD
    §344(e); Zer §257

5   Moule 44; MHT III **214, 317**; Zer
    §46, 472

6   Moule 26; Rob 583

7   BDF   §429, 488(1b); Rob 1094,
    1171, 1425

8   BDF §109(6)

10 BDF §107; DM 260; Rob 540, 727,
    746, 957

11 BDF   §372(3);   Moule 164;
    MHT III **92**; Rob 1008; Zer
    §306n, **311**

12 BDF §317, 384; BW 102, 106;
    Moule 137; MHT I 163, 201;
    MHT III 57; Rob 809, 819, 873,
    923, 940, 1004; RD §447; Zer
    §232, 355

13 BDF   §190(4),   235(4),   481;
    Moule 50; MHT III 239; Rob 605,
    692, 1202; Zer §129, 473

14 BDF   §64(1); DM 137, 144, 145;
    MHT I 87; MHT III 42, 182, 201;
    Rob 288, 419, 688, 766, 773,
    874; RD §387(e); Zer §188

15 Moule 152; MHT I 124; Rob 933,
    996

16 BW 109; Moule 44; MHT I 118,
    130, 191; MHT III 75; Rob 834,
    1399

17 BW 110; DM 249, 286; Moule 142,
    142 n.2; MHT I 249; Rob 698,
    850, 957, 994, 998; Zer §352

18 BW 45; DM 91, 289; Moule 44;
    MHT III 240; Zer §303

19 Rob 404, 729; RD §435(a)

20 MHT II 126, 131; MHT III 28;
    Rob 265, 267, 794

21 BDF   §476(3), 488(2); MHT III
    325; Rob 290, 771, 1035

22 Rob 428, 794, 1178

24 BW 9, 73, 92; DM 147, 198; Rob
    767; RD §343(g)

25 BW 164; Moule 44; MHT III 75;
    Rob 1009, 1416

26 MHT I 177; MHT III 94; Rob 541

Chapter 6

1   BW 112; DM 292; Rob 439, 995,
    1027, 1180, 1419

3   BDF   §119(2),   131,   301(1),
    454(2); Rob 411, 743, 751,
    1127, 1173; RD §382

4   BDF §416(2); Moule 53 n.3, 70;
    MHT III 190; Rob 690

5   BW 89; DM 193; MHT I 90; Rob
    692, 889

6   BDF   §159(1); MHT III 200; Rob
    486, 773; Zer §72

7   Rob 698

8   MHT III 190; Rob 779

9   BW 134; Moule 110f.; MHT III
    159, 182, **285**; Rob 1023, 1102,
    1121, 1129, 1170; Zer **§441**

10 BDF §455(2); DM 277; MHT I 248;
    MHT III **14**; Rob 658, 670, 762,
    763, 968, 974; RD §419(g),
    424(b)

11 BDF   §334; Moule 12 n.1; MHT II
    8; MHT III 50, **73**; Rob 292,
    533, 734, 741ter, 846bis, 917,
    1045, 1177, 1378; RD §381bis,
    448(h), 473

12 BDF §196, 319; BW 40, 78; Moule
    45; MHT I 247; MHT II 74;
    MHT III **63, 100**, 242; Rob 148,
    201, 325, 532, 698, 732, 880,
    885, 985; RD §346(e), 473; Zer
    §58

13 Moule 107; RD §473

14 BDF   §409(4); MHT III **149**, 175;
    Rob 401, 796, 854, 940, 1003,
    1170; RD §388, 401(a), 447, 473

15 Rob 234, 743; RD §473

16 BDF §380(4); MHT III **110**; Rob
    1381; RD   §473; Zer **§455**

17 DM   236; Moule 39, 161; MHT III
    235; Rob 295, 495; RD §343(e),
    383

Ephesians

Chapter 2

1 BW 54; Rob 789

2 DM 263; MHT II 441; MHT III 208; MHT IV 84, 90; Rob 497, 651

3 DM 263; Moule 174; MHT II 441; MHT III 28; Rob 419, 497, 503, 530, 788; RD §346(d); Zer §43

4 BDF §153(2); BW 90; DM 196, 244; Moule 13, 32; MHT II 419; Rob 478bis, 482, 584, 833

5 BDF §258(2); BW 54; Moule 44; MHT I 127; MHT III **176**, 240; MHT IV 85; Rob 529, 533; Zer §176

6 MHT II 409; MHT IV 85

7 MHT IV 91; Rob 262, 784

8 BDF §258(2), 442(9); BW 24; DM 142, 162; Moule 18f.; MHT I 127; MHT II 260; MHT III 45, **176**; Rob 533, 582, 704, 705, 1182; RD §346(f); Zer §176

9 Rob 744

10 BDF §235(4), 333(1); DM 151; Moule 50; MHT III 190; Rob 605, 681, 716, 776; Zer §129

11 BDF §272; DM 263; MHT I 84, 236; Rob 774, 777, 783

12 BDF §141(8), 200(4); DM 82; Moule 41; MHT III 27, 215, 235, 243; Rob 398, 516, 658, 782; RD §344(c)

13 DM 263; Moule 206; MHT III 226; Rob 1115, 1139

14 BDF §167; BW 4; DM 69; MHT III 215, **242**; MHT IV 84; Rob 433, 480, 498, 769bis

15 Moule 45, 79; MHT I 103; MHT III **265**; Rob 433, 589, 769, 783

16 MHT III **43**; Rob 433; Zer §211

17 MHT II 453, 485; MHT IV 89; Rob 433, 483, 547

18 Rob 433, 745, 769

20 BW 16; DM 153; Moule 110; MHT III 181; Rob 498, 560, 787, 1131

21 BDF §101, 119(1), 275(3); Moule 94, 95; MHT III 200; Rob 772; Zer §190

Chapter 3

1 Moule 198; Rob 435, 488, 505; RD §343(k), 353

2 Rob 424, 435, 1045, 1148bis

3 BDF §195; BW 91; Rob 435, 845

4 BDF §269(2); MHT I 117; MHT III **187**; Rob 783

5 Moule 43; MHT III 243; MHT IV 84; Rob 435, 523, 787

6 DM 295; Moule 61 n.3; MHT III 215; Rob 435, 1078, 1089

8 BDF §60(2), 275(1); DM 145, 295; Moule 98; MHT I 236; MHT II 166; MHT III 31, 139, **200**; Rob 262, 278, 435, 439, 474, 483, 516, 663, 670bis, 773bis, 1078; Zer §188

10 Rob 435, 654

11 MHT II 419; MHT III 25; MHT IV 91; Rob 435, 724

12 MHT III **263**; Rob 435, 784, 1387

13 DM 126; Rob 412, 435, 728, 729, 783, 784

14 Moule 198; Rob 433, 435; RD §330

15 Moule 94, 95, 145; MHT III 175; Rob 433, 772

16 Moule 145, 175; MHT I 55; MHT III 129, **256**; Rob 309, 327, 433, 593, 766, 1086; Zer **§110**

17 BDF §468(2); Moule 31, 105; MHT I 182; MHT II 193; MHT III 23, 230; MHT IV 89; Rob 212, 433, 1087, 1090

18 Moule 31; MHT II 310; MHT III 55; Rob 212, 433, 787

19 MHT II 419; Rob 401, 433, 519; RD §344(e)

20 BDF §185(1); BW 25; Moule 26, 42, 86; MHT II 419; Rob 517, 548, 629, 647bis; RD §344(d), 353

21 Moule 175; Rob 408, 660

Chapter 4

1 BDF §272, 337(1), 468(2); BW 104; DM 168; Moule 31; MHT I 84, 93, 236; MHT II 419; MHT III 37, 230, 343; MHT IV 85; Rob 478, 716, 783, 1201

2   Moule 31, 105; MHT I 181;   32   Rob 594
    MHT IV 89; Rob 440, 807, 946

3   Moule 31; MHT I 181, 182   Chapter 5

4   MHT II 419; MHT III **263**
                                         2   MHT III 75
6   Rob 567
                                         3   MHT III 75; Rob 541, 753, 1173
7   Rob 746
                                         4   BDF §358(2), 430(3); MHT III
8   MHT IV 84; Rob 392, 479   75, **90**, 282; Rob 714, 887, 920,
                                             1138
9   BDF §167; MHT II 166; MHT III
    182, **215**; MHT IV 84; Rob 278,   5   BDF §99(2), 132(2), 353(6),
    298, 499, 665, 668, 735, 766;   422; Moule 130; MHT I 245, 246;
    RD §387(a); Zer §45   MHT II 22f., 203, 222, 434,
                                             444; MHT III 47, 75, 85, **157**,
10 BW 21; Moule 86; MHT III **25**,   196, 287, **303**; MHT IV 84, 86;
    55; MHT IV 91; Rob 297, 550,   Rob 319, 330, 360, 406, 713,
    647, 806; RD §353   753, 786, 890; Zer §61, 185

11 BW 71; MHT II 485; MHT III 36;   6   MHT II   441;   MHT III   75;
    Rob 424, 694, 1152, 1394   MHT IV 84, 90

12 Rob 624   7   Moule 61 n.3; MHT III 75

13 BDF §383(2); DM 281; MHT III   8   Moule 174; MHT II 441; MHT III
    111, 218; Rob 503, 773, 975bis,   75; Rob 497, 651
    1396, 1397; RD §420(d)bis
                                         9   DM 150
14 Moule 53; MHT II 339, 408;
    MHT III 89; MHT IV 89   11   MHT III 39; Rob 529

15 BW 52; DM 70, 93; Rob 712   12   BDF §282(2); DM 135, 217;
                                             MHT III 40; Rob 530; RD §346(d)
16 BDF §119(1); Moule 94; MHT III
    190, 200; Rob 589, 745   13   Moule 25; MHT III 55

17 BDF §134(2); DM 295; MHT II   14   Moule 199; MHT II 210; MHT III
    485; MHT III 75; Rob 405, 407,   180; MHT IV 96; Rob 310, 328,
    412, 700, 1078; RD §327   422, 948, 1199

18 BDF §352; MHT III 23, 89, 235;   15   Rob 440, 1172
    Rob 412, 518, 523, 910, 1117;
    RD §344(e), 460(c)   16   MHT II 309; Rob 440

19 Moule 89   17   Rob 440

21 Moule 112; MHT III 167, 178;   18   Moule 21, 76, 77; MHT I 126;
    Rob 488, 507, 545, 1027, 1048   MHT III **76**, 240; Rob 440, 533,
                                             854, 890
22 BDF §62, 406(2); Moule 127,
    139; MHT II 440, 485; MHT III   19   DM 132; MHT III 23, 43; Rob
    148; Rob 280bis, 283, 662,   440, 690
    1038, 1089; Zer §130
                                        20   Rob 440
24 DM 150; Moule 59; MHT III 268
                                        21   BDF §468(2); Rob 440, 500
25 Rob 746
                                        22   MHT I 181; MHT IV 84; Rob 393,
26 BDF §101, 387(1); BW 118; MHT I   440, 757, 1946
    125; MHT III **76**; Rob 605, 854,
    949, 1023, 1173; RD §442   23   Rob 399, 416, 768, 781, 782,
                                             794
28 BDF §275(6), 339(3); BW 151;
    Moule 62, 206; MHT I 127;   24   DM 241; Rob 394, 794
    MHT III **81**, 151; Rob 892, 1116;
    RD §460(b); Zer §274   25   BW 72; Rob 757

29 MHT II 434; MHT III 25, 196,   26   Moule 78; MHT II 369; Rob 521,
    274, 287; MHT IV 84, 92; Rob   784, 811
    626, 753, 994, 1416; Zer §446
                                        27   MHT II 361; Rob 687, 1023

28 MHT III 24

29 DM 262; MHT II 311; Rob 1147

30 MHT II 121; Rob 260

31 BDF §208(1); BW 26, 89; DM 193;
    Moule 71, 91; MHT II 463; Rob
    560, 574, 623

32 BDF §277(1); DM 244; MHT III
    37; Rob 677

33 BW 112; BDF §387(3), 389; Moule
    60, 144; MHT I 179; MHT III **15**,
    95; Rob 330, 746, 766, 769,
    933, 943, 994, 1187; RD §407;
    Zer §415

Chapter 6

1 Rob 757

2 Moule 113; MHT IV 84; Rob 793

3 BDF §102(3), 369(3); MHT III
   100; Rob 299, 875, 984

4 MHT II 311; Rob 757

5 BDF §272; MHT III 23; Rob 757,
   782

6 Rob 792

7 BDF §425(4); MHT III 158

8 MHT III 333; Rob 355, 1419

9 MHT II 205; MHT III 25; Rob
   315, 502

10 Moule 39, 161; MHT III 235,
    336; MHT IV 92, 81; Rob 550,
    816

11 MHT II 339; MHT III 28, 144;
    Rob 502, 991, 1003, 1075

12 BW 58; MHT IV 81; Rob 566, 651,
    763

13 MHT I 115; Rob 563ter, 777

14 BDF §140; MHT III 24; Rob 409

16 BDF §235(3); BW 44; Moule 77,
    78; MHT II 347; MHT III 186;
    Rob 589, 605, 652

17 Moule 96; MHT III 14; Rob 412,
    712, 954

18 BW 17; Moule 57, 63, 76, 78,
    94; MHT III 267, **270**; Rob 618;
    Zer §96

19 BW 17; Moule 63; MHT II 485;
    MHT III **129**; MHT IV 84, 92; Rob
    1090

21 DM 107; MHT III 344; Rob 608,
    785, 1388

22 Moule 12; MHT I 135; MHT III
    23, 73; Rob 699, 846

23 DM 98

24 Moule 197

Philippians

Chapter 1

1 Rob 394, 628, 763, 783

2 Rob 795

3 BDF §275(3); MHT III 200, **207**; Rob 604, 772

4 MHT III 30

5 BW 65; MHT I 286; MHT III 179, 187, **256**; Rob 783; Zer §107

6 BDF §154, 290(4); BW 4, 88; Moule 10; MHT III 39, 45, 246; Rob 478, 686, 699, 705, 776, 889

7 BW 54; Moule 65; MHT III 23, 39, 143; Rob 491, 504, 566, 632, 658, 787, 966, 1131

8 MHT III 137; Rob 1032

9 BW 55, 162; MHT III 29; Rob 663, 699

10 BW 55; DM 286; MHT III 89, 143, **151**; Rob 594, 991, 1071; Zer §403

11 BDF §159(1), 168(2); MHT III 232, 247; Rob 483, 485, 510, 595, 694; RD §342(j); Zer §73

12 BW 157; MHT III 15; Rob 608, 665, 766

13 MHT II 122, 463; Rob 262, 1091; RD §163 A

14 Moule 45, 108; MHT III **222, 242**; Rob 279, 540, 784

15 DM 135; Moule 125; MHT II 54; Rob 235, 265, 743bis, 750, 1153, 1200; RD §378

16 MHT II 339; MHT III 36; Rob 1153, 1394; Zer §440n

17 MHT III 137; Rob 538

18 BDF §160, 299(3), 448(6), 449(2), 454(3); BW 41, 88; DM 192; Moule 10; MHT III 241, 330, 333; Rob 218, 487, 530, 646, 703, 871, 889, 1186, 1187, 1430; RD §346(d); Zer §60

19 Moule 70, 89; Rob 787; Zer §**184**

20 Rob 787, 794

21 BDF §399(1); BW 126, 145, 149; Rob 1059, 1065, 1424; RD §347(c), 434(e), 457(a); Zer §**173**, 174

22 BDF §368, 442(8); BW 102, 127; DM 133; MHT II 408, 422; MHT III **117**, 264; MHT IV 83; Rob 537, 698, 737, 810, 875, 1023, 1183, 1424; Zer §459

23 BDF §246, 402(2); Moule 80, 81, 98; MHT III 29, 143; Rob 130, 278, 442, 488bis, 532, 546, 628, 664, 858, 1066, 1072, 1076; RD §474(r); Zer §467

24 BDF §399(1); Moule 127; MHT I 115; MHT III 140; Rob 1059, 1424

25 Rob 613, 699, 787, 828, 1398; RD §320; Zer §184

26 Moule 53; MHT II 467; MHT III 191; Rob 588, 783, 784, 1398

27 BDF §73, 392(2); BW 134; DM 160; Rob 439, 505, 529, 637, 766; RD §302, 339(c)

28 Rob 412, 537, 729, 1392

29 BDF §339(1), 468(2); Moule 31; MHT II 463; MHT IV 89; Rob 487, 632, 777, 1059, 1066, 1162, 1424

30 BDF §304; Moule 31; MHT I 225; Rob 414, 439, 530, 731, 1135bis

Chapter 2

1 BDF §137(2), 475(2); MHT I 59; MHT III 316; Rob 130, 410, 744, 1019; Zer §**9**

2 Moule 145 n.3; MHT III 189; Rob 992; Zer §**170**, 410

3 BDF §150; MHT III 44, 52; Rob 519, 690, 692, 1123bis

4 BDF §306(2); MHT III **100**, 197; Rob 292, 746

5 Rob 699, 703; Zer §465

6 BDF §399(1), 434(1); BW 135; DM 217, 294; Moule 204; MHT III **21**, 140, 226; Rob 152, 407, 546, 1041, 1059, 1066, 1424; RD §434(e), 455(c)

7 BW 38, 136; MHT III 220; Rob 1114

8 BDF §447(8); Rob 523, 645, 1122; RD §345(d), 471(b); Zer §467

9 DM 111; Rob 629bis, 632; RD §387(b)(2)

10 Moule 78; Rob 503

11 BDF §369(2); MHT II 73; MHT III

256, 302; Rob 188, 795, 1034; Zer §108

12 Moule 144; MHT I 174; MHT III 42; Rob 564, 606, 634, 1162, 1173

13 BDF §231(2), 399(1); BW 127; DM 298; Moule 65, 91; Rob 560, 564, 632, 1059, 1182, 1424; Zer §66

15 BDF §296; BW 13; Moule 85; MHT III 175; Rob 488, 505, 550, 644, 713, 714, 775; RD §343(k), 353, 380

16 BW 51; Rob 550

17 DM 292; Rob 627, 787, 828; Zer §184

18 BDF §154; Moule 34; MHT II 61; MHT III 246; Rob 207, 487, 535; RD §346(h)

20 BDF §118(1), 379; DM 273; Moule 63; MHT III 270; Rob 960, 961, 996

21 Rob 767, 773, 1397

22 Rob 441, 1199

23 BDF §455(2); BW 52, 160; Moule 62, 63, 163; MHT I 167; MHT II 98; MHT III **15**, 43, **270**; Rob 224, 620, 687, 974, 1386; RD §33 b, 377

24 BW 95; Rob 895

25 BDF §125(1); BW 93; Rob 172, 418, 502

26 BW 161; MHT I 227; MHT II 452; Rob 888, 964, 1120, 1406; RD §426(a)

27 BDF §235(3); BW 13, 38; Moule 86; MHT II 173; MHT III 216; Rob 505, 601, 646; RD §343(k), 353

28 DM 198; Moule 12; MHT III 30, 73, 160; Rob 297, 298, 545, 665, 846; RD §401(a)

29 BDF §157(3); Rob 480, 481

30 BDF §108(5), 168(1); MHT I 64; MHT II 400; MHT III **218**, 239; Rob 148bis, 503, 781; Zer §53

Chapter 3

1 BW 59; DM 119, 293; Moule 161, 199 n.1; MHT IV 92; Rob 420, 487, 546, 550, 890, 1058, 1085, 1146, 1153; RD §336

2 BDF §149, 488(1b); MHT III 162; MHT IV 80, 85; Rob 471, 769, 949, 1100, 1178, 1200, 1201; RD §409

3 Moule 46; MHT I 231; MHT III 239; Rob 540, 769, 785, 1138, 1139

4 Moule 179; MHT I 230; MHT III 157; Rob 1129, 1154

5 BDF §197; Moule 46; MHT I 10, 102; MHT II 286; MHT III 220; Rob 523, 598, 657

6 MHT II 126; MHT III 151; Rob 261; Zer §371

7 BDF §341; MHT I 148; MHT III 246; Rob 396, 480, 481, 584, 698, 704, 1041

8 BDF §159(2), 263(2), 448(6); BW 121; DM 241, 251, 255, 261; Moule 163; MHT II 275; MHT III **14**, 52, 137, 338; Rob 396, 481, 485, 504, 652, 764, 812, 983, 1036, 1109, 1145, 1148, 1151, 1186; RD §471(b), 472(d); Zer §140

9 BDF §163, 272, 285(2); BW 121; DM 130; MHT III 191, 221; Rob 588, 598, 685, 782, 783, 784; Zer §**180**

10 BDF §400(8); BW 121; DM 284; Moule 128; MHT I 218; MHT II 396, 407; MHT III 136, 141, 142; Rob 150bis, 990, 1002, 1067, 1088, 1200; Zer §392

11 Moule 109; MHT I 187, 194; MHT III 221; Rob 1017, 1421

12 BDF §368, 375; Moule 50, 132; Rob 605, 811, 812, 845, 901, 916, 1017, 1024, 1030, 1429; RD §439; Zer §127, 129, 349, 403

13 BDF §203, 406(2), 481; MHT I 212; MHT III 137, 148, **250**; Rob 472, 489, 506, 509, 765, 807, 1038, 1060, 1202; RD §342(h), 343(1), 451(b)

14 Rob 146, 547, 608, 656, 782

15 DM 134; Rob 395, 749, 931

16 BDF §389; BW 125; DM 216; Moule 126; MHT I 179, 204; MHT III 75, 78; MHT IV 89; Rob 329, 944, 1081, 1092, 1187; RD §308, 457(e)

17 BW 131; Rob 221

18 ,BDF §151(1); Rob 413, 473, 718, 1107

19 MHT I 50

20 BDF §284(2); MHT III **190**, 206; Rob 714; RD §423(a); Zer §472

21 BDF §400(2); DM 192; Moule 129; MHT I 217; MHT II 440; MHT III 41, 141, **214**, 220; MHT IV 90; Rob 496, 528, 996, 1061, 1066, 1067, 1076; Zer §41, 210

Chapter 4

1 BDF §73; Moule 144

2 MHT II 150; Rob 235

3 BDF p.4 n.2, §442(13); MHT II 150; MHT III 180, 335; Rob 612, 728

4 RD §402(a)

5 BDF §263(2); Moule 96; MHT III 14, 226; Rob 546, 763, 1202; Zer §140

6 Moule 34, 45; MHT III 241

7 BW 130; DM 111; MHT III 23; Rob 477, 499, 629, 800, 1183

8 DM 247; Moule 161; MHT II 287; MHT IV 92; Rob 698, 724, 733, 765, 812, 1146; RD §380

9 Rob 698, 724, 1182

10 BDF §101, 235(2), 399(1); DM 251, 263; Moule 132; MHT II 390; MHT III 140, 270, 272; Rob 348, 476, 487, 604, 963, 965, 1049, 1059, 1066, 1147, 1212, 1424; RD §320; Zer §127, 129

11 BDF §405(1), 480(5); DM 107, 197, 294; MHT I 229; MHT III 37, 146, 303; Rob 677, 687, 721bis, 835, 845, 965, 1038, 1041, 1060, 1103, 1166, 1429

12 BDF §444(3); Moule 75; MHT II 197, 405; Rob 117, 342, 371, 1181

13 Moule 77, 88; MHT III 159, 189; Rob 478

14 MHT I 228; MHT III 159, 189; Rob 1121, 1187

15 DM 251; Moule 167; MHT II 337

16 Rob 1183

17 MHT III 303; Rob 594, 965, 1166, 1429

18 BDF §125(1); BW 22; Moule 52; MHT III **15**, 140; Rob 172

19 BDF §384; Rob 262, 586, 783

20 Rob 785

22 BDF §437; Rob 548, 599, 670

Colossians

158

267, 331; Rob 243, 437, 496, 644

23 MHT III 200; Rob 243, 717, 772, 1148; RD §472(a)

24 Moule 71; Rob 165, 565, 574, 712, 724, 784

26 BDF §468(3); Moule 180; MHT I 224; MHT II 429; Rob 243, 440, 1135; Zer §375

27 BDF §132(2); DM 72, 115; Rob 243, 262, 713

28 Rob 243, 724

29 MHT II 419; Rob 714

Chapter 2

1 MHT I 52; MHT II 193, 221; MHT III 50; Rob 116, 337, 364, 733, 886, 908

2 Moule 31, 105; MHT I 182; MHT III 23, 206, **211**, 230; MHT IV 89; Rob 243, 262, 439, 1382

3 Rob 243

4 Moule 145; MHT III **95**, **102**; Rob 987; Zer §415

5 BDF §448(5), 471(5); DM 247; Moule 46; MHT III 189, 239; Rob 651, 1026, 1187

6 MHT III 75, **167**

7 MHT II 193; Rob 212

8 BDF §412(4), 474(5c); DM 294; Moule 106 n.1, 139, 155, 168; MHT I 178, 192, 228; MHT III 153; Rob 764, 787, 933, 995bis, 1107, 1116, 1159, 1164, 1169; RD §343(c), 470(n); Zer §344

9 RD §387(b)(2)

10 BDF §132(2), 172; DM 125; Rob 712

11 MHT II 108, 310, 440; Rob 215; Zer §38

12 BDF §109(2); Moule 90; MHT III 180, 218; Rob 152, 529

13 Moule 91; MHT III 39; Rob 560, 658, 789, 1205; RD §474(r)

14 BDF §5(3b); Moule 45, 79; MHT III **219**, 242; Rob 524, 528, 634, 648, 783; RD §345(d)

15 BDF §5(1), 148(1), 316(1); MHT II 310, 400, 408; MHT III 40, 51, 55, **265**; Rob 226, 474, 589, 805; Zer §235

16 MHT II 91; MHT III 27; Rob 204, 1182

17 BDF §132(2); Rob 712

18 BDF §119(2), 148(2), 154, 369(2), 428(4); DM 265; Moule 183; MHT I 239; MHT II 273, 290; MHT III **246**; Rob 65, 164, 477, 500, 551bis, 585

19 BDF §101, 153(1); Moule 94; MHT I 231; Rob 478, 713, 1138, 1139, 1164; RD §470(n); Zer §440n

20 BDF §211, 314; DM 150; Moule 210; MHT III 57, **251**; Rob 559, 576, 792, 807, 1417

21 MHT I 124; Rob 853, 1399

22 BDF §145(1), 276(1); Moule 110; MHT III 181; Rob 714, 789

23 BDF §118(2), 353(4), 447(2); MHT II 290; Rob 375, 626, 742, 881, 1152bis

Chapter 3

1 BDF §89; Moule 92; MHT III **14**; MHT IV 89; Rob 529, 547, 881, 1417; RD §346(h)

2 BDF §89; MHT IV 89; Rob 1172

3 BDF §89; MHT IV 89, 97; Rob 588, 628bis; RD §370

4 BDF §89; MHT IV 89

5 BDF §132(2), 200(4), 258(1); DM 127; Moule 130; MHT III 47, 311; MHT IV 89; Rob 727, 728, 758bis, 960

6 BDF §89; MHT II 23, 441; MHT III 208; MHT IV 89, 90

7 Moule 79; Rob 971

8 DM 251; MHT III 25; MHT IV 92

9 BDF §364(3); Moule 21; MHT I 117, 126; MHT II 310; MHT III **76**, **94**; Rob 854, 890; RD §402(a)

10 Moule 59, 70

11 BDF §98, 477(2); Moule 75, 160; MHT IV 81; Rob 657, 712, 1188, 1411

12 MHT III 28

13 Moule 120; MHT III 44, 234; Rob 508, 690, 692, 742, 968, 1418

14 BDF §132(2), 163, 235(3); MHT III **212**, **317**; MHT IV 86; Rob

411, 605, 713, 1418; Zer §128

15 Moule 70; MHT III 23, **264**; Rob
    499

16 BDF §140, 468(2); DM 132; Moule
    31, 45, 75, 78, 91, 105; MHT I
    181, 182; MHT III 23, 43, 230;
    MHT IV 93; Rob 440, 560, 690,
    946, 1133

17 BDF §358(2); Moule 79; MHT I
    181, 183; MHT III 206; Rob 727,
    729, 957

18 Moule 117; MHT I 163; MHT III
    90; Rob 393, 757, 807, 887,
    920; RD §386(b), 405

19 BDF §238; MHT II 402

20 MHT III **263**

22 BDF §272

23 BDF §425(4); MHT III 158; Rob
    550, 1140

24 Rob 498

25 Rob 355, 1217

Chapter 4

1 Rob 788

2 MHT III **265**

3 BDF §166, 425(2); BW 17, 129;
   DM 215; Moule 82; MHT III 154,
   212; Rob 407, 638bis, 1086,
   1090, 1140

4 DM 251

5 MHT II 309; MHT III 75; Rob
   625, 810

6 MHT I 183; Rob 269, 396, 439,
   880, 1045, 1090, 1208

7 BW 93; MHT III **15**

8 BW 93; DM 198; Moule 12; MHT
   III 23, 73; Rob 699, 846

9 MHT II 232; Rob 355, 547

10 BW 165; Moule 148, 149; Rob
    255, 1419

11 DM 142; Moule 31

12 BDF §125(1), 172; MHT II 275;
    MHT III **57**; Rob 172, 630, 772,
    994; Zer §231

13 BDF §115(2); MHT II 151, 278;
    Rob 244, 257

14 Rob 172bis, 255

15 MHT I 48; MHT II 71, 118; Rob
    172, 257, 608

16 BDF §437; MHT III **95**; MHT IV
    90; Rob 600, 1204; RD §21

17 Rob 343, 983

18 MHT III 189; Rob 685

I Thessalonians

Chapter 1

1 Moule 80; MHT II 110; MHT III 206; Rob 173, 780, 796

3 BDF §163, 168(2); DM 72; MHT III 190, **211**, 218; Rob 498, 503, 779bis, 780

5 BW 42; Moule 78; MHT II 275; MHT III 50, **175**; Rob 566, 731ter, 1045; RD §380; Zer **§181**, 230

6 BW 18; MHT IV 94

7 BDF §276(3); MHT III 25, 182; Rob 787; Zer **§183**, 184

8 BDF §269(2); BW 123; MHT III 182, 187, 221, 286; Rob 782; RD §457(c), 470(j)

9 MHT III 49, 137; Rob 731, 732, 779, 795, 1032, 1045, 1177

10 MHT III 180; Rob 475, 778, 1107; Zer **§372**

Chapter 2

2 Rob 1077

3 MHT III 270; Rob 598

4 BDF §430(2); Moule 32; MHT I 231; MHT III 23, 147, 247; Rob 485, 1085, 1103, 1139

5 Moule 78, 79

6 MHT III **259**; Zer §87

7 BW 111; DM 168; Moule 78; Rob 505, 968, 1403; RD §424(b)

8 BDF §101; Moule 62, 202; MHT I 236; MHT II 251; MHT III 231; Rob 164, 198, 206, 225, 508, 722, 1162, 1215

9 BDF §207(1); Moule 69; MHT III 144; Rob 593, 1003, 1075

10 BDF §190(2), 434(2); MHT III 137, 226, 239; Rob 537, 545, 1032; RD §347(f)

11 MHT I 225

12 MHT I 219; MHT III 143; Rob 787, 997, 1002, 1072; RD §435(d); Zer **§184**, 372

13 BDF §442(12); DM 251; Moule 167; MHT IV 85; Rob 545, 560, 791; Zer §66, 183, 462

14 BDF §111(2), 194(1); MHT III 212; Rob 530

15 DM 153; Rob 1205

16 BDF §207(3); Moule 70; MHT I 219, 249; MHT III 143, 189; Rob 1220, 1425

17 Moule 46, 91, 156; Rob 559, 665, 778

18 BDF §447(2); Moule 119; Rob 407, 1151, 1152bis; RD §326; Zer §8

19 BDF §446; DM 251; MHT III 190; Rob 587, 1188

20 BDF §452(2); DM 69; Rob 1390

Chapter 3

1 DM 87; Moule 119; MHT I 231; Rob 521; RD §345(b)

2 Moule 65, 119; MHT I 68; Rob 1066

3 BDF §399(3); Moule 140; MHT III 141; Rob 186n., 686, 1059, 1424

4 DM 251; Moule 53; MHT II 467

5 BDF §207(3), 370(2), 442(12); BW 121; DM 215; Moule 119, 140, 167; MHT I 193, 201; MHT III 99, 143, 266; Rob 458, 988ter, 991, 1071, 1088, 1169; RD §430(d); Zer §344, 462

6 Rob 579, 1036, 1139

7 BW 34, 104; MHT III 190; Rob 605, 787; RD §347(f)

8 BDF §73, 372(1a), 382(4); DM 245; MHT I 168; MHT II 73; MHT III 116; Rob 188, 879, 973, 1010bis, 1421; RD §437; Zer §331

9 MHT II 419; MHT IV 69; Rob 716

10 BDF §402(2); DM 111; MHT III 143, 189; Rob 297, 629, 647, 1002, 1072; RD §435(d)

11 Moule 23, 136; MHT I 179; MHT III 41; Rob 327, 785, 854, 940, 943, 1092

12 BDF §172; Rob 327, 940, 1181

13 MHT III 23, 189; Zer §187

Chapter 4

1 BDF §160, 267(2); Moule 34, 91, 161, 162; MHT II 485; MHT III 182; MHT IV 92; Rob 439, 560, 739, 766, 1046

2 Moule 57; Rob 583; RD §301

3 DM 218; MHT III 139; Rob 400, 518, 698, 1059, 1078

4 Moule 78

5 Rob 1172

6 BDF §399(3); DM 111; MHT II 60; MHT III 141; Rob 233, 338, 629, 1059, 1078, 1424

7 BDF §235(4); Moule 50, 78, 205; MHT III **263**; Rob 605bis; Zer §129

8 Moule 167; Rob 1154; RD §472(f); Zer §372

9 BDF §393(5), 495(1); DM 130; MHT I 219; MHT III **139**, 143; Rob 686, 997, 1003, 1071, 1072, 1097; RD §435(d)

10 DM 252; Rob 774, 1066

11 Rob 1060

12 MHT III 75; Rob 751

13 Rob 985

14 Moule 57, 80; MHT I 149, 162; MHT III 167, **267**; Rob 355, 817; Zer §231

15 BDF §101; DM 149; Moule 79; MHT I 191; Rob 618, 778, inset

16 BDF §272; BW 42; Moule 57, 78, 80; MHT III 41; Rob 589, 783; RD §387(b)(3); Zer §39

17 BW 44; Moule 80, 81, 82; MHT I 14; Rob 357, 528, 628, 638, 778

18 Moule 144

Chapter 5

1 MHT III 27

2 Rob 550

3 DM 172; MHT I 191; MHT II 99; MHT III 112; Rob 225, 267, inset

4 BDF §391(5); DM 249; Moule 142; MHT I 210, 249; Rob 998; RD §435(a); Zer §352

5 BDF §162(6); BW 8; DM 149;
   Moule 175; MHT II   22, 441;
   MHT III 208; MHT IV 90; Rob
   496, 497; RD §343(h); Zer §43

6 Rob 497, 931bis, 1200

7 MHT II 383

8 BW 133; Moule 103; MHT III
   157; Rob 497, 498

9 MHT III 55

10 BDF §369(2), 372(3); BW 44;
   Moule 63, 80, 81, 82; MHT III
   100; Rob 534, 628, 638, 833,
   1017, 1027, 1403; Zer §250, 332

11 BDF §247(4); Moule 120; MHT I
   246; MHT III 187; MHT IV 70;
   Rob 293, 675, 692

12 Rob 319

13 BDF §287; MHT II 311; MHT III
   43; Rob 171, 647

14 BW 58; Rob 625

15 BDF §370(4); MHT II 211;
   MHT III 78, **98**; Rob 309bis,
   431, 573, 692, 933, 996

16 BW 115; DM 175; Rob 947, 890

17 BW 115; Rob 890

18 BW 115; Rob 890

19 BW 116; MHT II 106, 203, 257;
   Rob 218, 318, 890

20 BW 116; Rob 890

21 Rob 890

22 Rob 518, 890

23 BDF §384; BW 113; Moule 136;
   MHT II 217; MHT III 41; Rob
   940, 1003; RD §447

24 Zer §372

25 Moule 63; Rob 619

27 BDF §409(5); BW 53; DM 95;
   MHT III 149; Rob 484, 1085

II Thessalonians

816, 1045; RD §342(j)

16 MHT II 157; MHT III 41; RD §208(b), 332

17 MHT I 179; MHT III 23, 189; Rob 940, 943, 1092

Chapter 3

1 Moule 161; MHT IV 92

2 Rob 1205

3 MHT II 259; Rob 956, 961, 1219; RD §415

4 BW 87; DM 192; Rob 540

5 DM 173; MHT I 179; MHT III 23, 189, **211**, **212**; Rob 500, 940, 1092; Zer §**38**

6 BDF §84(2); BW 167; MHT I 52; MHT II 209; Rob 336, 560, 1047, 1172, 1217; RD §301

7 Rob 880, 964, 1205

8 MHT III 144; Rob 1003, 1075

9 MHT III 25, 303; Rob 965

10 BDF §397(3); Moule 53; MHT II 467; MHT III 190; Rob 699, 950, 1012, 1028, 1046, 1047; Zer §440n

11 BDF §322, 488(1b); BW 167; DM 298; MHT III 62, 161; Rob 564, 617, 1042, 1103, 1127, 1201; RD §461(c), 474(d)

12 Rob 1046, 1047

13 MHT I 124; MHT III 159; Rob 1102, 1121, 1399

14 BDF §269(2); DM 148; MHT II 207, 396; MHT III 187; Rob 317, 329, 529, 698, 944, 1047, 1170

15 BDF §416(1); MHT III 161; Rob 481, 1123

16 Moule 136; MHT II 211; MHT III 41; Rob 309, 326, 940, 1214

17 Rob 493, 685, 713

I Timothy

Chapter 2

2 Rob 582, 629

3 Rob 642

4 Rob 423

5 Zer §473

6 Moule 64; MHT I 105; MHT III
   42, 258, **271**; Rob 490, 573,
   631, 770; Zer §91, 94

7 Rob 242, 401

8 DM 294; MHT II 157; Rob 273,
   431, 489, 886, 919; RD §446

9 Moule 57, 80; MHT II 157; Rob
   272; RD §196

10 Moule 57, 80; MHT III **267**

12 BDF   §257(3); MHT II   278;
    MHT IV 82; Rob 510

15 Moule 56; MHT III **267**; Rob
    1419

16 Rob 1425

Chapter 3

1 BW 19; MHT III   232; Rob 508;
   RD §343(1)bis

2 BW   70; DM 144; MHT II   76,
   379; Rob 189

3 Rob 613, 1172

5 Rob 876, 1172, 1417

6 MHT IV   94; Rob 664, 1172

7 Rob 765

8 Rob 580, 1172

11 MHT II 76, 157

13 BW   72; DM 148; Moule 81;
    MHT III **263**; MHT IV 104; Rob
    811

14 MHT III 30

15 MHT III   303; Rob   729, 880,
    983, 1388

16 BDF §312(1), 488(3); BW 45;
    Moule 199; MHT II 47, 417;
    MHT III   57; MHT IV 96, 97,
    101; Rob 242, 295, 401, 422,
    428, 534, 546, 551, 713, 793,
    954, 1109, 1199; RD §330, 349,
    380, 474(p)

Chapter 4

1 BDF §62; Rob 499, 518, 668; RD
   §344(e)

3 BDF §479(2); MHT IV 82; Rob
   518, 785, 1121, 1201, 1425

4 BW 134; DM 291; MHT IV 1022,
   1129; RD §442

5 Moule 57; MHT III 189, 267

6 Rob 543, 717

8 BW 134; DM 227, 230; MHT III
   274; Rob 272, 535, 547, 1128

10 Rob 565

13 BDF §383(1); DM 281; MHT III
    111, 321, **344**; Rob 976; RD
    §419(b)

14 Moule 57, 61; MHT I   125;
    MHT III 76, 267; Rob   508,
    611, 854, 890; Zer §246

15 MHT I 184; MHT III **265, 303**;
    Rob 589

Chapter 5

1 MHT I   124, 125; Rob   1218,
   1399

2 Rob 772

4 MHT II 108; Rob 215, 1103

5 BW 147; Moule 57; Rob 302, 547,
   565, 623

6 MHT IV 102

8 Rob 509, 516, 691, 1012

9 BDF §61(1), 185(4); DM 138; Rob
   218, 277, 488, 516, 666

10 BDF §259(3); MHT II 392; Rob
    163, 800, 1417

11 BDF §101; Rob 512, 972

13 BDF §416(2); Moule 82; MHT I
    229; MHT II 158; MHT III 111,
    160, 322; Rob 232, 272, 273,
    477, 617, 618, 638, 1040,
    1103bis, 1121, 1122, 1172; RD
    §208 c

14 BDF §101; Rob 919

17 Rob 284, 511, 654

18 Rob 223

19 Moule 83; MHT III 321; Rob
    251, 603, 640, 1025, 1188; RD
    §111, 442

21 DM 172; Rob 621; RD §368

22 BDF   §337(2); MHT I   125;
MHT II   203, 207; MHT III   76;
Rob 854, 890bis; RD §320

23 MHT I   125; Rob 779, 789

24 MHT III 195; MHT IV 104; Rob
235, 620

Chapter 6

2 BDF §170(3); MHT III   39; Rob
508

3 BDF   §115(1), 428(1); Moule
148; MHT I   171; Rob   609,
1011, 1169, 1420

4 Moule 148; MHT III   270; Rob
167, 267, 405

5 BDF §116(4), 159(3); BW 20;
Moule 41; MHT II   303; MHT III
235; Rob 166, 483, 486, 518,
582; RD §342(j), 344(e)

7 Rob 1191; Zer §420n

8 BDF   §101; MHT III   58; Rob
324, 871, 889

9 RD §332

10 BDF §202; Rob 542, 617

11 Rob 476, 1186; Zer §35

12 MHT III   77; Rob 478

13 Rob 603

14 MHT III 77

15 BDF   §200(4); MHT II   443;
MHT III   243; Rob   495, 523,
660, 691, 776, 785

17 BDF   §119(4),   165,   474(4);
MHT III   193; MHT IV 102; Rob
163, 493, 496, 651, 783, 908

18 MHT II   91, 378, 388; Rob 163,
204

20 BDF §146(1b),   337(2); MHT II
69; MHT III   33, 77; Rob 186,
261, 810, 856; Zer §35

21 MHT III   235, 270; Rob 715

II Timothy

169

10　MHT III　232

11　BDF §372(2a)

12　Moule 149; MHT III　115; Rob 1008, 1416, 1417; Zer §329, 333

13　BW 70; Rob 1119, 1416

14　BDF　§235(4), 389; BW　126; Moule 37; MHT II　389; MHT III　78, 272; Rob 164, 605, 944, 947, 1162, 1163; RD §465

15　BDF　§119(1); MHT II　274; MHT III 77; Rob 856; Zer §142

16　MHT II　69; Rob 316, 890

17　Rob 235

18　Moule 62; MHT III　235, 270; Rob 620, 908

19　MHT I　113; Rob 262, 1154

20　DM 128; MHT III　36; Rob 1183, 1395

21　Moule 68; Rob 597, 1419

22　BDF §227(3); MHT III　**269**; Rob 890

24　MHT II　379

25　BDF §370(3); Moule 112, 157; MHT I　55, 193, 194; MHT III **98**, 99, **129**, 178; Rob 135, 309bis, 327, 565, 983, 988bis, 989, 996, 1044, 1214, 1415; RD §452(c); Zer §345

26　MHT III　**194, 266;**　Rob 707

Chapter 3

1　MHT III　179; Rob 699, 769

2　BDF §460(2)

3　Rob 162

4　MHT III　216; Rob 661, 663, 666; Zer §445

6　BDF §101, 108(5), 111(3); Rob 148, 155

7　Moule 112; MHT III　178; Rob 1173

8　BDF　§475(2); Moule　62; MHT III　270; Rob 255, 486

9　Rob 707, 708

11　MHT II　193; MHT III　50; Rob 212, 731bis

13　MHT II 127; RD §176 C c

14　Rob 721

15　BDF §108(3), 257(2); Moule 8, 81; MHT III　62, 176, **263**; MHT IV　104; Rob 879

16　Moule 95; MHT III　199; Rob 272, 772, 1097; RD §387(e); Zer **§142, 189**

17　DM 110; Moule 68

Chapter 4

1　BDF §442(16); BW 53; Rob 484

2　BDF §337(2), 460(1); MHT III 77; Rob 328

3　MHT III　139

5　BDF §337(2); MHT III　37, 77

6　MHT III　37

7　BDF　§342(1); DM　94, 203; Moule 16; MHT III　**84**; Rob 895; RD §403(a)

8　BDF　§243; Moule 161, 207; MHT III　**213**, 226; MHT IV 92, 104; Rob 498, 903

9　BDF §244(4); MHT III　30; Rob 759, 1205

10　MHT II　67; Rob 172, 184, 225, 547, 759, 858, 861; RD §349

11　DM 229; MHT IV　104; Rob 172, 535, 549, 759, 1127

12　Rob 759

13　MHT II　70, 106; MHT III　171; Rob 186, 221, 235, 255, 614, 759

14　BW 118; MHT II　85, 211; Rob 759

15　BDF　§458; BW 102, 118; DM 159(2); MHT III　227; Rob 419, 759, 949, 955

16　MHT II 217; Rob 759, 779, 854, 939, 940

17　BDF　§217(3); MHT II　193; MHT III 313; MHT IV 92, 104; Rob 212, 759, 818

18　Rob 759, 1204

19　Rob 235, 759

20　Rob 759

21　Rob 235, 255, 621, 759; RD §368

Titus

Chapter 1

1 DM 106; Moule 112; MHT III 178

2 BDF §469; MHT III 27, 325; Rob 224, 441

5 MHT II 395; MHT III 37

6 Moule 155; Rob 234, 1416

7 Moule 155; MHT II 139; Rob 1172

10 BDF §119(2), 442(11)

11 BDF §428(4); MHT I 171; Rob 774, 962, 1169; RD §417, 470(d); Zer §440n

12 BDF §487; MHT I 88, 233; MHT II 9, 137, 158; MHT III **192**; MHT IV 96; Rob 273, 422, 692, 1200; RD §208 c

13 Rob 955

14 Rob 472

15 BDF §447(2); MHT II 105, 223; MHT III 190; Rob 362

16 DM 110; MHT III 146; Rob 1036, 1038, 1103

Chapter 2

1 BW 130; Moule 126

2 BDF §389; BW 126; DM 216; Moule 126; MHT I 179; MHT II 76

3 BDF §389; Moule 126; MHT I 179; MHT II 278; Rob 166

4 BDF §389; Moule 126; MHT I 179; MHT II 75; MHT III 101; Rob 203, 762, 943, 985

5 BDF §389; Rob 126; MHT I 179; MHT II 273, 274

6 BDF §389; Moule 126; MHT I 179

7 BDF §316(3), 389; DM 109; Moule 62; MHT I 179; MHT III 270; Rob 480, 690, 811; RD §397

8 BDF §389; MHT I 179; MHT II 139; Rob 652, 1087

9 BDF §286(2), 389; MHT I 179; MHT III 192; Rob 691, 944

10 BDF §389; Moule 126; MHT I 179; MHT II 408; MHT III 217;

171

MHT IV 104; Rob 311, 780

11 BDF §269(3); Moule 108 n.2,
    114; MHT II 157; MHT III 186;
    Rob 272, 537, 653, 656

12 MHT III 193; Rob 788

13 BDF §276(3), 442(16); BW 70; DM
    115, 147; Moule 109, 109 n.4;
    MHT I 84; MHT III **181**; Rob 82,
    786, 787; RD §387(b)(2)bis; Zer
    §185

14 BDF §113(1); DM 111; Rob 518,
    618, 632; RD §371; Zer §91

                  Chapter 3

1   BDF §460(1); Rob 483

2   Rob 311

3   Rob 1202

5   BDF §284(3), 294(1); MHT III
    190, 324; Rob 261, 681, 715

6   Rob 716

7   Rob 224, 707, 779

8   MHT I 207; Rob 509, 537, 764,
    812

9   BDF §47(3); MHT II 131, 157;
    MHT III 28; Rob 265bis

10 MHT II 379

11 Rob 687

12 Rob 172, 235

13 Rob 172bis, 255, 260, 1217; RD
    §162 c; Zer §415

14 DM 104; MHT III **266**; Rob 1041

Philemon

2 MHT II 109; Rob 215

5 BDF §477(2); Moule 54, 68, 69;
   MHT III 189, **256**; MHT IV 97;
   Rob 624, 1200; RD §474(g)

6 Moule 41

7 MHT III 267

8 Moule 102; MHT III 157

9 Moule 102, 113; MHT II 86;
   MHT III 157; Rob 201, 710

10 BDF §488(1b); Rob 713, 718

11 MHT II 353

12 Moule 12; MHT II 435; MHT III
    73; Rob 399, 416, 846

13 BDF §359(2), 458; BW 86; DM
    190; Moule 9, 53, 64; MHT II
    188, 467; MHT III 65, 91; Rob
    631, 886, 919; Zer §91

14 BDF §263(1); MHT III **13**; Rob
    550, 763, 994

15 BDF §102(2); Rob 699; Zer §112

16 BDF §230; Rob 491, 632, 663,
    670; RD §342(o)

18 MHT II 196; Rob 342

19 BDF §495(1); BW 93; Moule 145;
    MHT III 95, 191; MHT IV 83; Rob
    623, 685, 846, 1199

20 BDF §169(3), 384, 488(1b);
    Moule 23, 136; MHT I 195;
    MHT II 213; Rob 310, 509, 784,
    939bis, 940bis; RD §320, 343(1)

22 BDF §425(3); Moule 82, 135; Rob
    638

23 BDF §125(1); Rob 172

24 Rob 172bis

Hebrews

Chapter 1

1 BDF §464; DM 106; Moule 114; MHT I 107; MHT II 25; MHT IV 107, 110, 111; Rob 422, 432, 545, 546; RD §349

2 BDF §234(8), 464; DM 102, 106; Moule 114; MHT III 25; Rob 408, 432, 480, 671, 775

3 BDF §464; MHT II 298, 368; MHT III **214**; MHT IV 110; Rob 422, 496bis, 586, 651, 781, 792, 845, 860, 1099; Zer §41

4 BDF §464, 473(2); BW 43; DM 90, 108, 273, 276; MHT III 46, 181; MHT IV 109; Rob 218, 420, 422, 532, 615, 663, 667, 710bis, 733bis, 966; RD §366, 379, 424(d)

5 BDF §473(2); DM 103, 262; MHT II 463; MHT III 209; Rob 420

6 Moule 90, 199; MHT III 200; Rob 773; Zer §188

7 DM 110; Rob 626, 1202

8 Moule 32; MHT IV 118; Rob 465

9 DM 108; Moule 33; MHT III 215; Rob 483, 528

10 Moule 32; Rob 234, 792

11 DM 101

13 MHT III 111, 209

Chapter 2

1 BDF §60(3); MHT III 52; Rob 212, 279, 298, 350, 613, 996, 1415; RD §366, 434(c)

2 Moule 57; Rob 432, 583, 1107; RD §474(s)

3 BDF §28; BW 134; DM 227; Moule 206; MHT IV 107, 109; Rob 432, 710, 828, 1023, 1129; RD §474(s)

4 MHT III 190; Rob 151, 432; RD §474(s)

6 BDF §103, 456(2); DM 286; Moule 177; MHT III 234, **318**; MHT IV 107; Rob 234, 299, 411, 736, 742, 781, 1001, 1146, 1219; Zer §420, 420n

7 DM 108; Rob 218, 484, 485, 602, 616, 743

174

8   BDF §404(3), 447(1); BW 124; Moule 77; MHT II 450; MHT III **145**, 146; Rob 1073bis, 1153

9   DM 111, 225; Rob 218, 473, 485, 632, 743, 1041, 1123; RD §371

10   BDF §223(2); Moule 58; MHT I 106; MHT III **80**, 149, 267; MHT IV 111; Rob 530, 565, 583bis, 861, 887, 1039, 1084, 1086, 1114, 1128; RD §359; Zer §113, **263**

11   Rob 718, 863, 1179

12   Rob 216

13   DM 233; Moule 18; MHT III 89; Rob 323, 361, 375, 460, 906; RD §270, 304, 403(c)

14   BW 19; Moule 62; MHT III 231, 232; Rob 412, 509, 687, 705

15   BDF §398, 403; DM 90, 209, 213; Moule 56; MHT I 215; MHT III 45, 140, 144; MHT IV 109; Rob 582, 1052, 1060bis, 1070, 1426; RD §455(c)

16   BDF §103, 107, 441(3), 491; DM 261, 263; MHT IV 107; Rob 1146, 1149, 1200; RD §472(b)

17   BDF §101, 160; BW 52; Moule 33; MHT III 143, 221; MHT IV 107; Rob 474, 486, 530, 658, 887, 920, 1072; RD §342(k), 426(c); Zer §74

18   BDF §219(2); BW 135; MHT III 253; Rob 721, 722, 963, 1128; Zer §119

Chapter 3

1   DM 274; MHT III 161; MHT IV 107; Rob 505, 722, 785, 955; RD §426(c)

2   Rob 661

3   DM 113; MHT IV 109; Rob 244, 511, 615, 661, 667, 722, 733, 967; RD §424(d)

4   DM 183; MHT II 49; Rob 742

5   BDF §351(2); DM 88, 230; MHT I 151; MHT II 220; MHT III 87; Rob 374, 878, 1119

6   BDF §135(3); MHT III **311**; Rob 413, 789, 792, 1419

7   Rob 722

8   DM 171; MHT I 124; MHT III 23

9   BW 48; Rob 717

10   BW 48; DM 88; MHT II 408; MHT III 193; RD §427

11   BDF §372(4), 454(5); DM 247; Moule 179; MHT II 468; MHT III 333; Rob 916, 968, 1000, 1024

12   BDF §180(2), 369(2), 404(3); BW 8; DM 78; Moule 77, 114; MHT I 74, 178, 193; MHT II 25, 450; MHT III 146, 213; MHT IV 107, 110; Rob 330, 496, 504, 872, 996, 1073bis, 1169, 1415; RD §434(c), 470(e); Zer §344

13   BDF §200(1); DM 281; Moule 205; MHT II 113, 439; MHT III 42; Rob 221n., 608, 744, 745, 974, 975, 1412; RD §420(b)bis

14   DM 262; MHT III 115; Rob 1027, 1154, 1419; RD §472(e)

15   MHT I 124; MHT II 25, 450; MHT III 23; MHT IV 109; Rob 439

16   BDF §448(4); DM 108; Moule 57; MHT I 36; MHT II 60; MHT III 267; Rob 233, 583, 613, 917

17   MHT II 60; Rob 233

18   DM 246; MHT I 205; MHT II 216, 219; MHT III 86, 137; Rob 877, 1032, 1082; RD §401(c)

19   BDF §442(2); Rob 1035, 1183

Chapter 4

1   BDF §337(1), 370(1), 393(6); MHT I 185; MHT III 99; Rob 814, 908n., 996, 1399, 1415; RD §434(c)

2   BDF §202; DM 72, 232, 276; Moule 175; MHT III 58; Rob 526, 903, 967, 1154; RD §472(e)

3   BDF §372(4), 412(5), 425(1), 454(5); DM 247; Moule 73, 151; MHT I 230; MHT II 468; MHT III 153, 157, 333; MHT IV 107; Rob 132, 778, 968, 1000, 1004, 1024, 1129, 1140, 1154, 1202; RD §472(f)

4   BDF §103; Moule 29; MHT III **17**, 52; MHT IV 107, 108; Rob 518, 575, 653, 800

5   BDF §372(4), 454(5); MHT II 468; Rob 1024

6   BDF §62; DM 293; Rob 474, 1058

7   BDF §219(1); MHT I 124; MHT III 23, 261

8   BDF §360(4); Rob 1015, 1417; RD §438

9   MHT II 351, 409; Rob 541

10 MHT III 52; Rob 518, 800; Zer §257

11 BDF §473(1); Moule 168; MHT III **257**; Rob 744, 1399

12 BDF §182(5); DM 112, 120; MHT II 83; MHT III 216; Rob 278, 504, 580, 633, 667

13 BDF §214(6), 239(5); Moule 54; MHT II 407, 467; MHT III 274, 331; Rob 625, 1153

14 DM 171; MHT III 232; Zer §250

15 BDF §101; Rob 530

16 MHT IV 110; Rob 261

Chapter 5

1   DM 110; Moule 63; MHT I 218; MHT III 221; Rob 315, 486, 630, 762

2   DM 247; Rob 316, 485, 541; RD §426(b); Zer §184

3   BDF §229(1); DM 109; Moule 63; Rob 618; Zer §96

4   DM 262, 276; Rob 393, 762, 968, 1154; RD §424(b), 472(e)

5   DM 218; Moule 127; Rob 1089

7   BDF §210(1), 211; DM 101; MHT I 102; MHT II 461; MHT III **18**, **251**; MHT IV 110, 111; Rob 580, 598

8   BDF §488(2); BW 135; DM 126, 262, 293; Moule 102; MHT III 157; Rob 720, 721, 1027, 1115, 1129, 1140, 1154bis, 1201; RD §443, 462(a) and (d), 474(q)

10 MHT II 399; Rob 485

11 BDF §393(6); DM 87, 219; MHT III 28, 220; Rob 523, 1076, 1081

12 BDF §155(1), 452(3); BW 47, 52, 135; DM 94, 213, 227, 228, 293; MHT II 60; MHT III 89, 139, 141, 146; MHT IV 109; Rob 233, 375, 482, 490, 584, 740, 903, 1038, 1039, 1061, 1076, 1082, 1392; RD §342(1), 451(b)

13 BDF §165; BW 13; DM 78; Moule 62; MHT III **213**; Rob 395, 516; RD §343(1), 344(c)

14 BW 20; Moule 204; Rob 497, 514, 580, 584, 757, 789, 902, 910, 1108, 1117, 1122; RD §344(b), 461(c)

Chapter 6

1   BDF §110(1); Moule 81 n.1; MHT III 28, 215; Rob 407, 498

2   BDF §109(2), 168(2), 444(4), 474(4); MHT III **218**; Rob 501

3   DM 290; MHT III 28, 114; Rob 407, 1027, 1154, 1418

4   MHT I **66**; MHT III **233**; Rob **449**, 473, 507

5   BDF §169(3), 443(2); Moule 36; MHT III **233**; Rob 474

6   Moule 70; MHT I 230; MHT II 394; Rob 539, 613

7   BDF §474(5c); DM 138, 149; Moule 62; Rob 584, 603, 708

8   Rob 640, 1134

9   Moule 167; MHT III 28, 247; Rob 218, 407, 485, 508, 637, 1416

10 BDF §339, 391(4); DM 195, 230; MHT I 204, 210; MHT III 136; Rob 506, 716, 860, 998, 1001, 1060, 1080, 1082, 1090; RD §343(1), 435(d)

11 MHT III 28; Rob 311, 407

12 MHT III 232, 331; Rob 1153

13 Moule 60; MHT III **80**, 268; Rob 475, 607, 1159; Zer §263

14 BDF §107, 422, 441(1); DM 261; Moule 178; MHT II 444; MHT III 157, **336**; MHT IV 107; Rob 192, 551, 1004, 1024bis, 1110, 1150bis; RD §461(d), 472(c); Zer §61, 369

15 MHT III 232

16 BDF §474(4); BW 18; MHT III 268; Rob 607

17 BDF §219(2), 263(2); Moule 132 n.1; MHT III **14**, 241, 253; Rob 148, 654, 763; Zer §64, 140

18 BDF §412(5); MHT III 72, 153, 232; MHT IV 112; Rob 778, 827, 828; Zer §250

19 MHT II 139; Rob 258, 259, 274, 298, 418, 715; RD §174 b

Chapter 7

1   DM 127; MHT I 224; MHT III 45, 168; Rob 697, 701, 1134

2   BDF §418(6), 459(4); MHT I 224; MHT III **159**; Rob 714, 1153

3 Moule 164; MHT II 191, 251, 276; Rob 594

4 BDF §123(1); MHT II 24; MHT III 50; MHT IV 107; Rob 258, 292, 399, 418, 741bis, 1177; RD §381

5 BDF §164(1); MHT I 53; MHT III 157; Rob 343, 371bis, 412, 705, 1076, 1129, 1154

6 Moule 14; MHT III 70, 168; Rob 896

7 BDF §61(1), 138(1); MHT I 246; MHT III **21**; Rob 218, 277, 409, 654, 752, 763; Zer §141

8 Moule 104f.; MHT I 114; MHT III **152**; Rob 1035, 1153

9 BDF §391a; BW 126; DM 284; Moule 14; MHT I 204; MHT III 70, 136, 151; MHT IV 107; Rob 208, 896, 967, 990, 1086, 1091, 1093; RD §424(b), 432, 457(c); Zer §371

11 BDF §234(8), 360(4), 429; DM 254, 264; Moule 163; Rob 604, 748, 896, 1015, 1027, 1095, 1151, 1162, 1164; RD §457(f)

12 Rob 1023, 1129

13 Moule 15, 62, 200; MHT I 143; MHT III 146; Rob 580, 721, 748, 896

14 Moule 15; Rob 719, 1034

15 BDF §60(3), 372(1a); MHT III 29, 115; Rob 279, 659, 663, 748

16 BDF §113(2); Moule 59; MHT II 378, 379; MHT III 268; Rob 158bis, 896

18 BDF §263(2), 284(3), 308; MHT III **14**, 190; Rob 763; Zer §140

19 Rob 218

20 BDF §250; MHT III 36; Rob 435, 695, 710, 733, 896, 963, 967, 1389; RD §379, 424(d), 427

21 BDF §198(3), 250; Rob 334, 710, 819, 1394; RD §379

22 MHT II 178; Rob 218, 710; RD §379

23 MHT III **30**, 36, 143; Rob 613, 695, 896, 1061, 1085, 1119, 1389, 1394, 1425

24 DM 131, 151; Moule 109; MHT I 212; MHT II 371; MHT III 148, 186; Rob 401, 656, 789, 1039, 1070, 1122, 1394; RD §334, 387(c); Zer §142

25 BW 128; DM 113; Moule 165; Rob 550

26 BDF §442(12); MHT III 147; Rob 667, 710, 1086, 1181

27 BDF §62, 459(4); Moule 59; MHT I 90; MHT III **191**; MHT IV 111, 112; Rob 280, 691

28 Rob 315, 418, 480

Chapter 8

1 BDF §235(3); MHT III 175; Rob 605, 705, 710bis; RD §379

2 BDF §294(1); DM 116; MHT III 27, 324; Rob 317, 408, 715bis

3 BDF §268, 379; DM 273, 284; Moule 139; MHT III **109, 117**, 143; Rob 928, 955, 956, 961, 989; RD §406(a), 414, 415, 431

4 BDF §360(4); DM 254; Moule 208; Rob 207, 1015

5 BDF §465(2); Moule 14, 29; MHT II 129; MHT III 70; MHT IV 108; Rob 233, 392, 874, 932, 949, 1214; Zer §187

6 BDF §101, 235(2); MHT I 56; MHT II 262; MHT III 232; Rob 218, 728, 733bis, 801, 967, 1220; RD §320, 424(d)

7 BDF §360(4); MHT IV 109; Rob 708, 1015; Zer §316

8 BDF §442(4); MHT II 422; Rob 255, 473, 475

9 BDF §261(7), 423(5); Moule 91; MHT I 74; Rob 514, 560, 1123

10 Moule 180; MHT I 107, 224; MHT II 429, 463; MHT III 23; Rob 440, 479, 1135

11 MHT III 30; Rob 361, 746, 906, 1215, inset; RD §270, 304, 320, 403(c); Zer §146

12 MHT III 96; Rob 260, inset; RD §162 b

13 BDF §404(3); BW 125; MHT II 450; Rob 895, 1073

Chapter 9

1 BDF §443(2); DM 254; Moule 163; MHT III 186; Rob 777; Zer §187

2 BDF §245(2); MHT II 60; MHT III 27, **31**, 47; MHT IV 109; Rob 232, 660, 714

3 BDF §226, 245(2); BW 50; Moule 60; MHT II 443; MHT III 27, 269; Rob 408, 612

4 MHT II 124; Rob 253, 348

5 BDF §230, 393(6); BW 21; DM 111; Moule 60, 63, 86; MHT II 152; MHT III **21, 270**; Rob 154, 409, 517, 550, 629, 632, 647, 792, 1058; RD §344(d), 371

6 BDF §99(1); Rob 313, 1131, 1153, 1215, 1396

7 BDF §186(2), 252; MHT III 235; Rob 441, 505, 637, 715, 769, 776, 955, 1131; RD §343(e), 414

8 BDF §163; MHT III **212**; Rob 700, 1036, 1039, 1040, 1049, 1078, 1131

9 Moule 59; MHT III 47, 268, 311; Rob 413

10 BDF §235(2); Rob 201, 413

11 BDF §351(2); Rob 399, 412, 416, 705, 1139; Zer §187

12 DM 159, 230; Moule 57, 100 n.1; MHT I 51, 132; MHT II 157, 213; MHT III 267; Rob 272, 339, 809, 861, 1114; RD §208 b, 327

13 MHT IV 111

14 MHT IV 109; Rob 355

15 BDF §235(2); Rob 501, 604, 1131

16 Rob 969; RD §423(c)

17 BDF §235(2), 428(5); Rob 604, 963, 971, 1159, 1169, 1173, 1415; RD §419(f), 426(b), 470(b)

18 MHT I 143

19 Moule 95; MHT II 193; Rob 212, 214, 254, 686, 1131

20 Rob 716

21 MHT II 193; Rob 212

23 Rob 218, 615, 667, 686

24 MHT III 27, 135; Rob 574

25 BDF §198(2); DM 105; Moule 57, 59; MHT III 241; Rob 207, 589; Zer §117

26 BDF §358(1); BW 37; DM 247; Moule 50, 73, 149; MHT III **90**, 272; Rob 604, 887, 920, 963, 965bis, 1026, 1085; RD §426(b)

27 DM 113, 293; Rob 733, 963, 967, 1058; RD §424(d)

28 Rob 871

Chapter 10

1 Moule 164; MHT I 58, 225; MHT II 82, 448; MHT III 293; Rob 187, 392, 439, 550, 716, 1135

2 BDF §360(2), 374; Moule 151; MHT II 67; MHT III **92**, 143, 159, 318; Rob 778, 963bis, 965bis, 1015, 1026, 1102, 1175; RD §426(b), 442

6 BDF §148(2), 229(1); Moule 63; Rob 474; Zer §96

7 MHT II 450; MHT III 141; Rob 895, 1088

8 BDF §148(2), 229(1); Moule 101; Rob 474; Zer §96

9 Moule 101; Rob 895, 909

10 MHT II 25, 463; Rob 719, 891

11 DM 109; Rob 617, 687

12 Moule 64, 164; MHT III 269

13 BDF §451(6); Moule 34, 161; MHT III 111; Rob 487, 495; RD §343(e)

14 Moule 164; MHT I 127; Rob 891, 895, 1111, 1116

15 BW 124; MHT III 143; Rob 439, 909, 979, 1074, 1407

16 BDF §234(3); Moule 180; MHT I 107, 224; MHT II 429; MHT III 23; Rob 440, 1135

17 MHT I 190; MHT II 72; MHT III 97; Rob inset

18 BDF §229(1); BW 28; Zer §96

19 BDF §163; MHT III **212**

20 Zer §20

21 MHT II 129

22 BDF §159(3), 211; MHT II 192, 248; MHT III 23; Rob 211, 225, 340, 362, 485, 486, 1217; RD §320

24 Rob 501

25 BDF §283(3), 284(2); MHT II 78; MHT III 42, 43, **190**; Rob 124, 532, 710, 733bis, 967, 1123; RD §346(g), 424(d), 460(b)

26 BDF §229(1); Moule 63, 64, 112; MHT III 143, **178**, 269; Rob 612, 1074; Zer §96

27 BDF §301(1); MHT III 195; Rob
743

28 BDF §235(2); MHT I 114; Rob
251, 566, 604

29 BDF §465(2); Moule 44; MHT III
220; Rob 434, 511, 859

31 BDF §399(1); MHT III 140; Rob
1059, 1424

32 BDF §62; MHT IV 107; Rob 470,
475

33 BDF §290(5); MHT II 407; MHT
III 45, **215**; Rob 487, 705, 1153

34 BDF §397(1), 406(2); Moule 90;
MHT II 75; MHT III 148; Rob
218, 1035, 1036, 1038, 1041,
1103; RD §451(b)

35 MHT I 124; Rob 728

36 Rob 998

37 BDF §127(2), 304; MHT II 265,
270, 442; MHT III **50**; Rob 395,
733, 978; RD §419(d), 424(d)

38 MHT III 43; Rob 1419; Zer §226

39 BDF §162(6); DM 76; MHT III
208; Rob 497, 515

Chapter 11

1 BDF §426, 430(3); MHT I 231;
MHT III 307; Rob 234, 1138,
1139

2 DM 155; MHT III 157

3 BDF §433(3), 491; DM 286; Moule
168; MHT I 219; MHT III 25,
143, 287; Rob 423, 909bis,
1003, 1036, 1049, 1070, 1072,
1090, 1407; RD §435(d), 470(m);
Zer §352

4 BDF §405(1, 2); DM 293; MHT I
224; MHT III 146; Rob 667, 724,
1038, 1085; RD §451(b)

5 BDF §312(1); MHT I 217; MHT II
192; MHT III 141; Rob 365, 371;
RD §284; Zer §352

6 Rob 234

7 Rob 334, 1173

9 Rob 593

10 ′MHT II 278; Rob 262

11 BDF §194(1); MHT II 85; MHT III
220; MHT IV 112; Rob 616, 686,
793

12 BDF §269(5), 425(1), 442(9);
MHT I 230; MHT III 45; Rob 524,
704, 705, 777, 1129, 1140, 1181

13 BDF §104(3); BW 90; DM 107,
196; Rob 533, 833, 1137

14 Rob 1034

15 BDF §360(4); MHT I 204; MHT III
46, 52, 139, 259; Rob 887, 921,
923, 1015, 1062, 1153; RD §438;
Zer §316

16 Rob 218, 399, 416, 508

17 BDF §327, 342(5); BW 85; DM
190; Moule 9; MHT I 129, 142,
143, 238, 247; MHT II 139; MHT
III **65**; MHT IV 109; Rob 359,
760, 885, 895

18 MHT II 463; Rob 1034

19 Moule 78; Rob 818

20 Rob 788

21 DM 282; MHT I 114; MHT III 225;
Rob 775, 827, 979, 1115

22 MHT II 121; Rob 260, 812

23 BDF §241(3), 243; MHT II 78;
MHT III **17**, 225; Rob 833

24 BDF §429; Rob 1036

25 Moule 204; Rob 529; Zer §445

26 Moule 204; Rob 480, 500, 575,
594, 1202

27 MHT III **320**; Rob 833, 1113,
1121

28 BDF §342(4); MHT I 144; MHT II
71; MHT IV 107; Rob 148bis,
189, 895

29 Moule 55; MHT III **17**; Rob 476,
563, 565, 582bis, 652, 800; RD
§396

31 MHT II 109; Rob 317, 529

32 BDF §444(4), 473(2), 475(2),
491, 494, 495(1); MHT I 237;
MHT II 103; MHT III 157; Rob
210, 420, 934, 1126, 1402, 1409

33 BDF §293, 491, 494; Moule 37;
MHT I 116; MHT III 47, 232; Rob
477, 509, 606; RD §343(1)

34 BDF §209(4), 491, 494; MHT I
116; MHT II 105, 286; MHT III
259; Rob 476, 748

35 BDF §46(2), 430(3), 491, 494;
MHT I 224, 231; MHT II 69, 83,
407; Rob 218, 1138, 1139

36 BDF §491, 494; MHT III **197**; Rob
    749

37 BDF §491, 494; MHT II 72; MHT
    IV 108; Rob 534, 590

38 BDF §491, 494

39 BDF §491, 494; Rob 833

40 BDF §316(1), 491, 494; MHT III
    55; Rob 218

Chapter 12

1   BDF §117(1), 473(2); BW 107; DM
    171; Moule 91, 167; MHT II 178,
    282; MHT III 347; Rob 168, 420,
    425, 432, 524, 542, 562, 583,
    653, 764, 810, 931, 1154; RD
    §410(a), 472(f)

2   DM 100; Moule 204; MHT II 365;
    Rob 154, 502, 512, 574, 575,
    764, 1106; RD §343(1)

3   BDF §342(5); MHT III 221; Rob
    524, 635, 1107, 1121

4   BW 11; DM 279; Moule 92; MHT II
    113, 189; MHT IV 109; Rob 368,
    645, 975

5   MHT II 108; Rob 508, 509; Zer
    §219

6   DM 275; Rob 966, 1184; RD §427

7   BDF §257(3); MHT I 82; MHT III
    174, **267**; MHT IV 112, 125; Rob
    738, 794, 1159; Zer **§179**

8   BDF §473(2); DM 242; Rob 420;
    Zer §179

9   BDF §447(6); MHT III 334; Rob
    480, 532, 546, 664, 1152; Zer
    §226

10 BDF §250; Moule 62; MHT III 36,
    151; Rob 625, 1109, 1394

11 MHT III 151; MHT IV 107; Rob
    448, 497, 515, 519, 625, 1109;
    RD §344(e)

12 BDF §97(3); Rob 315, 1200; RD
    §320

13 BDF §487; MHT II 440; MHT IV
    106; Rob 421, 1413

14 BDF §227(3), 487; Moule 87,
    199; Rob 422bis, 425, 648, 871

15 BDF §101, 165, 180(5), 370(1),
    487; MHT I 178; MHT II 258,
    264; MHT III 99, 213; Rob 496,
    774, 800, 934, 995; RD §434(c)

16 BDF §101, 128(4), 208(2); DM
    100; Moule 71, 204; MHT II 212;

MHT III **307**; Rob 190, 308, 573

17 BDF §99(2); MHT I 245; MHT II
    221, 222, 310; MHT III **85**, 157;
    Rob 319, 360, 611, 941, 1129,
    1154; RD §472(e)

18 BDF §51(2), 65(3); Moule 114;
    MHT II 127; MHT III 232; Rob
    262, 536, 542, 793, 1118; RD
    §347(d)

19 BDF §429; Moule 114; MHT II
    125, 126; Rob 261, 818, 1094,
    1171; RD §163 B b

20 Moule 114; MHT II 375, 399; Rob
    508, 581, 1419; RD §343(1)

21 Moule 114; MHT II 311; Rob 168,
    221

22 DM 138; Moule 114; Rob 536,
    542, 760, 793; RD §347(d)

23 Moule 114, 170; MHT III **350**;
    Rob 792

24 Moule 114; Rob 218, 422bis,
    615, 667

25 BDF §372(1b), 474(5c); MHT I
    124, 200; MHT III 175; Rob 430,
    472, 664, 791, 810, 922, 933,
    996, 1160

26 BDF §243; MHT III 225

27 BDF §65(3), 425(3); MHT III
    158, 182; Rob 766bis, 1140

28 BDF §377(3); Rob 934, 955bis,
    956, 989, 1402; RD §196, 414,
    415, 431

29 BDF §452(3)

Chapter 13

2   BDF §414(3); MHT III 159, 226;
    Rob 400, 472, 475, 509bis, 551,
    860, 1102, 1120; RD §342(h),
    461(b)

3   MHT III 234

4   Moule 180; MHT III 27; Rob 396

5   BDF §365(3), 431(3), 468(2);
    Moule 22, 157, 180; MHT I 182;
    MHT III 58, 96, 97, 343; MHT IV
    108, 111; Rob 207, 930, 946,
    1165, 1175; RD §470(1)

6   BDF §407; Moule 10, 144; MHT I
    150; MHT II 103; MHT III 148;
    Rob 217, 334, 819, 871

7   BW 21, 118; DM 82; MHT III 47;
    Rob 514, 949, 955

8 MHT II 154; MHT III 25; MHT IV 107; Rob 206, 395

9 MHT I 125; Rob 1095, 1162, 1166

10 MHT III 139; Rob 599

11 BDF §229(1), 284(3); Moule 204; MHT III 27, 190, 267; Rob 718, 719, 953; Zer §96, 113

13 MHT III 198, 340, 347; Rob 425, 1154; RD §472(f); Zer §84

15 Moule 57; MHT II 139; Rob 108, 203, 268, 399, 524, 541; RD §192 b

16 BDF §196; MHT III 57, 242; Rob 532, 816; RD §346(e)

17 BDF §425(3), 458; MHT III 87, 158; Rob 374, 634, 877, 1119bis, 1128, 1140, 1214

18 BDF §322, 336(3), 397(2); MHT III 28, 62, 75; Rob 407, 678, 1035

19 BDF §60(3), 244(1); MHT III **30**; Rob 279, 545, 664

20 BDF §118(2); DM 152; Moule 78; MHT II 25; MHT III 186; Rob 777, 778, 784

21 BDF §214(6), 384; MHT III 25; Rob 327, 940

22 Moule 57; MHT III 28, 267; MHT IV 108; Rob 407, 583, 845

23 BDF §244(1); Moule 207; MHT III 30, 162; Rob 664, 910, 1041, 1103, 1110, 1123, 1418; RD §461(c)

24 BDF §437; BW 71; DM 145, 147; Moule 72; MHT I 237; MHT III **15**; Rob 548, 578, 766

James

Chapter 1

1   BW 126; MHT I 179; MHT III **78**, 186;   MHT IV 48;   Rob 329, 394, 944, 1093; RD §308, 340(d), 457(e)

2   BDF §275(3); Rob 524, 772; RD §345(d), 387(e); Zer §188

3   BDF §23, 263(2); Moule 96; MHT III **14**; Rob 763

4   MHT III 89, 101; MHT IV 115

5   BDF §474(5a); BW 117; Moule 41; Rob 518, 1023; RD §344(e)

6   BW 95, 117; DM 202; MHT II 235, 407; MHT III 175; Rob 149, 478, 801, 895; RD §346(c)

7   BDF §336(3); MHT III **76**; Rob 1035

8   DM 101; MHT IV 120; Rob 580

11   BDF §221; BW 92; Moule 12, 209; MHT I 135; MHT II 27; MHT III 73; MHT IV 120; Rob 837

12   MHT II 247; MHT III **213**, 296

13   BDF §117(1), 182(3); BW 13, 23, 79; DM 78, 101; Moule 8, 41; MHT I 74; MHT III 63, **215**, 258; Rob 516, 579, 1034, 1186; RD §344(c)bis, 358

14   BDF §493(3); BW 79; Moule 8; MHT III 63

15   BW 79; Moule 8; MHT II 60, 246; MHT III 63; Rob 232; RD §320; Zer §40

16   MHT II 80; MHT IV 115

17   BDF §98, 487; Moule 17; MHT II 60; MHT IV 115, 118; Rob 153, 233, 413, 421, 501, 655, 772, 1200

18   BDF §301(1); DM 134; MHT III 195; Rob 742, 1071

19   BDF §99(2), 402(2); BW 117; DM 286; MHT I 245; MHT II 222; MHT III **85**, **143**; MHT IV 115; Rob 319, 328, 329, 360, 429, 658bis, 908, 941, 1003, 1052, 1071, 1072, 1076; RD §320, 403(a), 457(d)

21   BW 115; Moule 185; MHT II 105; Rob 216

22   BW 5; MHT IV 120; Rob 947, 1162; RD §465

182

14 Moule 91, 152; MHT III 23; Rob
    560, 1173

15 Moule 17; Rob 881

16 Rob 1411

17 BDF §447(2); MHT IV 115; Rob
    273, 424, 1152bis

18 BDF §191(4); MHT III **215**, 238;
    MHT IV 120

Chapter 4

2 BDF §494; BW 125; DM 159, 213,
   216; MHT I 160; MHT III 55,
   143, 147, 148; Rob 805bis, 966,
   1071, 1083, 1091, 1383; RD
   §428; Zer §234

3 DM 159; RD §428

4 MHT II 222; MHT IV 114; Rob 411

5 BDF §487; MHT II 407; MHT IV
   114; Rob 626

7 BW 117; MHT II 421; Rob 948,
   1023

8 BW 117; MHT II 234, 421; MHT
   III 23; Rob 355, 538, 1214

9 BDF §337(1); MHT II 393; MHT
   III **76**; Rob 561, 856

10 MHT II 421; MHT III **76**; MHT IV
   119

11 MHT III 177; MHT IV 120; Rob
   512

12 BDF §412(5); MHT III 153; Rob
   778, 1107

13 BDF §289; DM 128, 272; Moule
   123; MHT II 400; MHT III 192;
   Rob 289, 299, 328, 348, 474,
   696, 770, 799, 1193, 1217; RD
   §308, 379, 387(e)

14 BDF §266(3), 298(2), 459(4); DM
   272; Moule 124; MHT II 83; MHT
   III **16**; MHT IV 114; Rob 728,
   735, 740, 767, 961, 1158

15 BDF §289, 291(2), 442(7); Moule
   71, 128; MHT II 74; MHT III 45,
   114, 144; Rob 574, 697, 708,
   1060, 1069, 1070; RD §457(d)

16 MHT IV 114; Rob 710

17 BDF §264(2); MHT III 39; MHT IV
   117; Rob 764bis, 1106

Chapter 5

1 MHT IV 115; Rob 299, 391, 428,
   430, 763, 854, 949, 1106, 1116

2 Rob 405, 801, 898

3 BDF §145(1); Moule 70; MHT II
   395; MHT III 179, **264**; MHT IV
   120; Rob 769; RD §306

4 MHT II 221, 393; MHT III 258;
   Rob 337, 579

5 MHT III **23**; MHT IV 120

6 BDF §139; MHT III **23**; Rob 757

7 BDF §241(5), 337(2); MHT II
   353; MHT III **18**, 77, 111; Rob
   201, 652, 856

8 BDF §337(2); MHT III 23, **77**

9 BDF §213; Moule 74; MHT III 27;
   Rob 394, 621

10 BDF §442(16); BW 48; Moule 35;
   MHT III 246; Rob 480

11 Moule 115

12 BDF §149, 213; BW 27, 53; DM
   110; Moule 21, 32, 74; MHT I
   126; MHT II 204; MHT III 75,
   76; Rob 328, 427, 471, 475,
   484, 622, 853; RD §342(h), 368

13 BDF §298(4), 494; MHT III 210;
   MHT IV 114; Rob 430, 515, 740,
   1023

14 MHT III 210; Rob 124, 328

15 MHT III 89; Rob 208, 325, 360,
   375, 908, 1019, 1388, 1420; RD
   §306, 403(a)

16 Moule 26; MHT I 156; MHT III
   56, 106

17 BDF §198(6); Moule 27 n.1, 178;
   MHT I 217; MHT II 23, 444; MHT
   III 52, 142, 291; MHT IV 48,
   117, 118; Rob 392, 531bis, 802,
   1094; RD §346(d); Zer §60

18 BDF §75; Moule 32; Rob 348, 799

19 MHT III 115, 210

20 BDF §259(3); Moule 185; Zer
   §211

I Peter

125; Rob 127

20 BDF §264(5); MHT III 27; Rob 603, 1114

21 Moule 69, 143

22 BDF §337(2); MHT III 77; Zer §245

23 MHT IV 125

24 DM 197; Moule 12; MHT I 135; MHT III 73; Rob 837

25 Moule 69; MHT IV 129, 130; Rob 535, 778

Chapter 2

1 MHT III 28, 200; Rob 408, 773

2 BDF §269(5); MHT II 378; Rob 349; Zer §245

3 DM 105; Moule 36; MHT IV 124; Rob 192, 1035

4 Moule 91; MHT III 258; Rob 424

5 MHT II 211; Rob 338, 401, 941

6 BDF §187(6), 258(2), 308; DM 156; Moule 28, 50; MHT II 321; MHT III 97, 237, **292**; MHT IV 129; Rob 392, 772, 800, 802, 1399, inset; RD §388

7 BDF §473; Rob 418, 718

8 Rob 714

9 Rob xii, 101, 597

10 BDF §430(3); MHT I 231; Rob 910, 1117, 1138, 1139, 1163

11 BDF §113(2), 407; Moule 185; MHT I 91, 181; MHT II 378; Rob 518, 728bis, 1039, 1084

12 Moule 175; MHT I 181, 182; MHT II 440; MHT III 213, 260; Rob 497, 721, 789, 946, 1134; Zer §373

13 BDF §468(2); MHT III 52, 200; Rob 772, 1140; Zer §245

14 MHT III 267; Zer §113

15 BDF §407, 434(1); MHT I 53; MHT III 148, 226; Rob 343, 400, 700bis, 779, 1078

16 MHT III 52; MHT IV 125, 129; Rob 127, 1140

17 BDF §110(1), 337(2); Moule 21; MHT III 77; MHT IV 128; Zer §245

18 BW 138; DM 229; Moule 117; MHT I 181; Rob 946, 947, 1161; RD §465; Zer §373

19 BDF §372(1c); Rob 411, 500, 699, 704

20 BDF §372(1c); MHT III **115**; MHT IV 128; Rob 740, 1417

21 Moule 70; MHT IV 124; Rob 633, 784, 954

22 Rob 954; Zer §245

23 Rob 954

24 BDF §188(2), 297; Moule 44, 46; MHT I 237; MHT II 435; MHT III **22**; MHT IV 129; Rob 561, 723, 954

25 Moule 185; MHT II 452; MHT III 52; Rob 787

Chapter 3

1 BDF §28, 369(2); BW 21; DM 229; Moule 82; MHT I 90, 181, 182; MHT II 74; MHT III **100**, 192, 217; MHT IV 42, 128, 130; Rob 127, 324, 516, 638, 779, 946, 984, 1026, 1217; RD §306, 344(d); Zer §373

3 BDF §168(2); BW 118; DM 264; Moule 79; MHT I 236; MHT III 186; Rob 127, 498bis, 779, 947, 949, 1161; RD §465

4 Moule 57, 79; MHT II 160; Rob 200, 272, 274, 712, 779

5 MHT III 192

6 BW 47; MHT IV 129; Rob 479; RD §324(g); Zer §257

7 BDF §468(2); MHT I 181, 182; Rob 946, 1072; Zer §373

8 BDF §98, 468(2); Moule 34; MHT I 180; MHT III **218**; MHT IV 129; Rob 470, 487, 945; Zer §74

9 BDF §468(2); Moule 70; MHT I 182; Rob 208, 573bis, 699, 946; Zer §373

10 MHT II 450; Rob 1061, 1171; Zer §245

11 Moule 92; Rob 561; Zer §245

12 BDF §259(3); Moule 49; Rob 1106

13 BDF §252, 351(2); MHT III 87, 114; Rob 127, 374, 878, 1020, 1118, 1419

14 BDF §153(1), 282(3), 385(2); BW 115; DM 290; Moule 32, 40, 150;

MHT I 196; MHT III **212**, 245; MHT IV 48, 128; Rob 127, 327, 478, 683, 1021, 1023, 1027, 1408; RD §440; Zer §245, 323

15 MHT I 182; MHT II 299; Rob 482; Zer §245, 282, 373

16 MHT I 182; MHT IV 125; Rob 473, 721, 946

17 BDF §385(2); BW 115; MHT I 196; MHT IV 128; Rob 127, 218, 1021, 1023, 1039, 1084, 1408; RD §440; Zer **§323**, 324

18 BDF §229(1); BW 38; Rob 432, 532, 618bis, 757, 1114

19 Moule 131; MHT III **153**; Rob 432, 778

20 BDF §205; Moule 56, 68, 91; MHT III **153**, **254**, 267; Rob 399, 416, 432, 560, 656, 705, 779; RD §387(b)(2)

21 DM 79, 93; Rob 432, 714

22 Rob 432, 792

Chapter 4

1 Moule 41, 44, 46; Rob 518, 816

2 Rob 348, 479, 1070, 1071

3 BDF §405(2), 460(2); MHT I 11; MHT II 193; MHT III 28; MHT IV 126; Rob 127, 364, 909, 992, 1062, 1076

4 BDF §126(2); Moule 132

5 BDF §254(2); Moule 161; MHT III 139, 181, 226; Rob 793

6 BDF §369(2); Moule 59; MHT III **102**, **291**; MHT IV 129, 130; Rob 699, 792, 1031

7 MHT I 181; Zer §245

8 BDF §213, 468(2); BW 27; DM 110, 131, 151; Moule 74; MHT I 181; Rob 622, 789, 946

9 Moule 82; MHT IV 42; Rob 638

10 Moule 204

11 BDF §425(4); MHT I 181; MHT III 25, 101, 158; MHT IV 3, 121, 124, 125, 129, 130; Rob 396

12 BDF §126(2), 196; MHT I 125; MHT III 158, 242; Rob 532, 626; Zer §324

13 MHT III 320; MHT IV 129; Rob 967; RD §346(a), 424(a)

14 BDF §269(6), 442(16); BW 73; MHT III 126, 187; MHT IV 130; Rob 602, 767, 777, 779, 785; Zer §184

15 BDF §119(1), 336(2); MHT II 92, 272; MHT III 76; MHT IV 126; Rob 204

16 Moule 78, 79; Rob 192

17 MHT I 217; MHT III 126, 139, 217; MHT IV 125; Rob 395, 512, 1061, 1076

18 MHT I 150; MHT III **13**, **22**; Rob 357, 763, 871

19 BDF §257(3); Moule 144; MHT II 207, 365; Rob 231

Chapter 5

1 BDF §474(5a); MHT III 215, 217; Rob 587, 779, 857, 878

2 BDF §101, 337(2); BW 46; DM 94; MHT II 258, 386; MHT III 77; Rob 551; RD §470(n); Zer §245

3 MHT II 386; MHT III 139

4 BDF §118(2); MHT III 213; MHT IV 129; Rob 355, 498, 1217

5 Rob 808, 1397; Zer §245

6 Moule 65; MHT II 129; Rob 258, 635; Zer §245

7 Moule 28, 63, 91; MHT I 181; Rob 212, 539, 560, 946, 1392

8 BDF §268(2), 368; BW 118; MHT II 60, 89; MHT III **206**; Rob 740, 795, 1040, 1044, 1085; Zer §242, 245

9 BDF §110(1), 164(1); BW 118; Moule 168; MHT III 55, 238; MHT IV 128; Rob 502, 505, 523, 541, 542, 687, 949, 955; RD §407; Zer §245

10 BDF §384; MHT II 396; MHT III 39, 154, 186, 190; MHT IV 128; Rob 195, 606, 778, 1126

11 MHT III 25; MHT IV 129

12 BDF §125(2), 205; BW 118; MHT II 110; MHT III 256; MHT IV 99, 129; Rob 173, 415, 583, 593, 846, 949, 1036, 1039; RD §407; Zer §106, **111**

13 Rob 169

II Peter

Chapter 1

1 BDF §118(1), 194(1), 276(3); DM 147; Moule 109f.; MHT I 84; MHT III 181, 220; Rob 82, 127, 530, 785, 786bis; RD §387(b)(2); Zer §185

2 MHT II 217; Rob 127, 432, 940

3 MHT IV 141; Rob 101, 127, 432, 533, 778

4 BDF §60(2); DM 121; Moule 90, 91, 145; MHT II 165; MHT III 215; MHT IV 141; Rob 279, 432, 670, 783; RD §335, 387(b)(3)

5 BDF §290(4), 493(3); MHT III 45; Rob 126, 432, 460, 487, 686, 705bis, 1184, 1200

6 Rob 432, 1184, 1200

7 MHT III 192; Rob 432, 1184, 1200

8 MHT III 217; Rob 315

9 BDF §428(4); MHT I 171; MHT II 290; MHT III 190; Rob 127, 423, 542, 720, 962, 1169; RD §417, 470(d)

10 DM 262; MHT I 191; MHT III 160;

Rob 787, 985, inset

11 MHT II 157; Rob 127bis, 401, 785bis, 786; RD §387(b)(2); Zer §185

12 MHT I 230; MHT III 157; Rob 483, 656, 1129, 1154

13 DM 113

14 DM 82; MHT IV 141; Rob 127

15 Rob 127, 333, 356, 1191

16 BDF §442(16); MHT I 231; Rob 1139

17 BDF §289; Moule 69; MHT II 178; MHT III 174, **183**; MHT IV 143; Rob 290, 438, 636, 709, 842, 1135; RD §379

18 MHT I 222; Rob 778, 864, 1097

19 BDF §383(2); MHT I 47, 169, 228; MHT II 87, 379; MHT III 23, 52, 111, 159; MHT IV 142; Rob 185, 663, 1121

20 BW 22, 149; MHT II 434; MHT III 196; MHT IV 143; Rob 514, 518, 699, 772, 1039; RD §344(b) and (e)

21 DM 262; Moule 73; MHT III 258;

MHT IV 143; Rob 751, 1165

Chapter 2

1 MHT IV 142; Rob 127, 613, 1134, 1203

3 BDF §148(1), 297; MHT II 400; MHT III 325; MHT IV 140; Rob 297, 440, 474, 551, 724; Zer §342, 455

4 BDF §23; MHT II 78, 396; MHT IV 142; Rob 438, 1012, 1160

5 BDF §248(5), 253(4); MHT I 97; Rob 275, 348, 438, 672

6 BDF §195(2); BW 16; Moule 38; MHT II 147; MHT III 215, 240; MHT IV 142; Rob 257, 438, 498, 539; RD §343(h)

7 MHT II 193, 353; MHT III 217; Rob 212, 438, 783

8 BDF §161(2); Rob 126, 434, 438, 470, 597

9 Rob 438; Zer §284

10 BDF §415; MHT IV 142; Rob 127, 438, 1122

11 BDF §456(3); MHT IV 141; Rob 205, 665

12 BDF §152(1); Moule 36; MHT II 420; MHT III 158; MHT IV 141, 143; Rob 473, 721, 1125

13 BDF §351(2); Moule 36, 90, 91; MHT II 219, 420; MHT III 87, 158; Rob 355, 374, 485, 529, 560, 878, 1125; Zer §282

14 BDF §182(3), 474(4); Moule 41, 41 n.2; MHT I 47, 74; MHT II 87, 441; MHT III 158, 215, 233; MHT IV 142; Rob 162, 185, 497, 516, 1125; RD §344(c); Zer §43

15 BDF §165; MHT II 440; MHT III 158, 213; Rob 521, 1125

16 BDF §286(2); MHT III 192; Rob 127

17 Rob 186, 704

18 BDF §102(6); Moule 90, 91; MHT II 163

19 BDF §191(5); BW 45; MHT III

240; Rob 218, 533, 534; RD §346(f)

20 DM 147; MHT III 62; Rob 341, 476, 785, 786, 881, 1416; Zer §185

21 BDF §410; MHT III 90, 149; MHT IV 142; Rob 127, 219, 597, 887, 909, 920, 1014, 1039, 1058, 1084, 1094

22 BDF §111(3), 126(1), 266(3), 480(5); BW 7, 101; DM 70; MHT I 155, 156, 238; MHT II 5, 351, 354, 363; MHT III 16, 54; MHT IV 140; Rob 394, 502, 767, 807; RD §397; Zer §232

Chapter 3

1 BDF §296; Moule 168; MHT III 192; Rob 127, 701, 714

2 BDF §168(1), 474(5a); Moule 166; MHT III 217, 218, 349; Rob 503, 762, 779, 785, 786, 1086, 1107

3 BDF §264(5), 468(2); Moule 166, 178; MHT II 366, 420; MHT IV 143; Rob 699, 775, 1039

4 DM 186; MHT III 17, 62; Rob 653, 717, 880, 978

5 Moule 55; MHT III 175, 267; Rob 320, 582, 793, 794, 1035, 1134

6 MHT II 75; MHT III 222; Rob 201, 547

8 Rob 281, 699

9 BDF §180(5); Rob 518, 1128

10 MHT II 242, 395; MHT III 174; Rob 374

11 MHT III 48; Rob 705, 741, 1131, 1396

12 MHT II 261; Rob 374

14 BDF §192; MHT III 239; Rob 537, 542; RD §347(g)

15 MHT IV 141; Rob 117, 480

16 BDF §275(1); MHT I 38; MHT III 39; Rob 773bis

17 MHT II 353; Rob 518bis, 993

18 Rob 786; Zer §185

I John

Chapter 1

1 BDF §342(2); BW 96; Moule 34; MHT III 232; MHT IV 135; Rob 713, 724, 791, 896, 901

2 MHT II 467; MHT IV 71; Rob 777, 901

3 BDF §342(2); Moule 165; MHT I 143; MHT IV 133; Rob 528, 611, 713, 724, 901

4 BDF §280; Moule 119; MHT III 28, 89; Rob 406, 678, 907, 1388; RD §374

5 BDF §397(3); BW 161; MHT III 233; Rob 579, 699, 1033

6 MHT IV 68; Rob 528

7 BW 165; Rob 518, 528

9 BDF §391(5); DM 249; Moule 142; MHT I 210; MHT II 242; Rob 961, 998; RD §435(a); Zer §327, 352

10 Moule 148

Chapter 2

1 BW 147; DM 195; Moule 119; MHT III 72; Rob 406; Zer §251

2 BDF §475(2); BW 13; DM 244; MHT IV 66; Rob 424, 441, 618, 685, 1185, 1199; RD §367

3 BDF §394; BW 40; Moule 77, 198; MHT III 45, 139; Rob 590, 700, 850, 1079

4 Rob 904

5 BDF §344; BW 97; MHT III 88; MHT IV 77, 137; Rob 500, 897

6 MHT III 139, 146; Rob 708, 1038

7 BW 84, 147, 158; DM 188; Rob 884

8 BDF §308; BW 77; Moule 130f.; Rob 713, 879

9 MHT III 62, 146; Rob 879, 1038, 1183

12 BDF §282(3); Moule 12; MHT III 73; MHT IV 135; Rob 845; RD §374

13 Rob 694, 845

14 Moule 12; MHT III 73; Rob 845

15 BW 73

16 Moule 40; MHT III **213**; MHT IV 135; Rob 788, 963

17 BDF §308

18 MHT IV 133; Rob 573, 769, 794

19 BDF §360(3), 448(7); Moule 145; MHT I 148, 201; MHT II 190, 433; MHT III **91, 95**; MHT IV 66, 136; Rob 753, 906, 922, 923, 1015, 1086; RD §438

20 Rob 230

21 Moule 182; MHT II 434; MHT III 196, 287; MHT IV 73; Rob 753, 845, 1166, 1397

22 BDF §429; Moule 157 n.1; Rob 1035, 1094, 1164, 1205; RD §470(i) and (1), 474(r)

23 Moule 182

24 BDF §451(1), 466(1); MHT I 69; MHT II 424; MHT IV 72, 137; Rob 437

25 MHT II 157; Rob 400, 416, 479, 538, 704, 718, 777

26 MHT II 197; Rob 845

27 BDF §466(1); Moule 176; MHT II 208; MHT III 139; Rob 230, 339, 437, 1217; RD §320

28 MHT II 460; MHT IV 136; Rob 473, 1147, 1413; Zer §289n, 322n

29 BDF §372(1a); Rob 1388, 1420

Chapter 3

1 BDF §298(3), 394; MHT IV 66; Rob 135, 741, 992, 999; RD §381

2 BDF §299(2); BW 160; DM 246; Rob 233bis, 736

4 DM 152; MHT III 183; MHT IV 71; Rob 769; RD §387(c)

5 MHT IV 66

6 Rob 880

8 BW 80; DM 186; MHT III 62; Rob 699, 880bis; Zer §134

9 DM 195; Moule 168; MHT III 72; Rob 890, 1081; RD §402(a), 456; Zer **§251**

10 ΄MHT II 441; MHT III 313; Rob 404, 1164, 1173, 1174; Zer §134

11 MHT III 45, 139; Rob 699, 992, 1079, 1192, 1203

12 BDF §216(1); BW 26; Moule 86; MHT IV 133; Rob 425, 647, 652, 968, 1176; Zer §134, 452

13 BDF §454(1); DM 246; Rob 532, 965

14 MHT III 161; Rob 586, 1041

15 MHT III 196; MHT IV 66; Rob 753

16 BDF §394; MHT III 139; Rob 632, 1033, 1079

17 BDF §366(4); MHT III **98**

19 MHT III 23, 260; Rob 699, 871; Zer §134

20 BW 25; MHT III 23, 189; Rob 512, 667

21 MHT III 23; Rob 512

22 BDF §107, 187(2), 214(6); MHT II 465; MHT IV 69; Rob 850

23 MHT III 139; Rob 850, 992

24 Rob 442, 679, 699, 716

Chapter 4

1 MHT I 125; Rob 752

2 BDF §416(3); BW 137; Moule 101; MHT I 229; MHT III 162; Rob 480, 1103, 1116, 1123; RD §461(c)

3 BDF §428(4); Moule 155, 182; MHT I 171; MHT III 162; Rob 546, 724, 962, 964, 1149, 1169; RD §417, 470(d)

4 BDF §185(2); MHT III 216

6 DM 103; Moule 73; MHT III **260**; RD §470(d)

7 BW 107, 144; DM 132, 171; Rob 692, 931; RD §378

8 BW 5, 72; DM 69, 149; Rob 794, 845

9 BDF §220(1); Moule 202; Rob 584, 699, 777, 845; Zer §120

10 Moule 14, 202; MHT III 70; Rob 699, 845

11 Rob 1009

12 MHT III 88; MHT IV 77; Rob 1418

13 Moule 72; Rob 401, 519, 599, 699; Zer §117

14 Moule 14; MHT III 70; Rob 894

15 DM 149; MHT III 183

16 MHT I 68; Rob 768; Zer §105

17 Moule 61; Rob 611, 699

18 Rob 758; RD §386(c)

19 BDF §451(1); Rob 549

21 MHT III 139; Rob 699, 992, 1079

Chapter 5

2 BDF §394; MHT III 45, 112, 139; Rob 432, 700

3 BDF §394; DM 249; MHT I 211; MHT III **139**; Rob 400, 699, 704, 993, 1034, 1079

4 MHT II 126, 437; MHT III 21; Rob 258, 409, 698, 704; RD §163 B b

5 MHT III 183

6 Moule 57; MHT III 226, 267; MHT IV 66; Rob 583, 589, 657, 659, 1166

8 BDF §205; MHT II 462; MHT III 254; Rob 593; Zer §32

9 DM 294; Rob 393, 699, 704, 964, 993, 1034, 1049

10 Moule 155; MHT I 171; MHT II 463; MHT III 267; Rob 226, 963, 1159, 1169; RD §426(a), 470(b); Zer §211, 257

11 BDF §397(3); Rob 400, 699, 704, 993, 1033, 1034

12 Rob 1164

13 BW 142; MHT II 463; Rob 360, 401, 418, 699, 778, 845, 846, 983, 993, 1034, 1388

14 MHT III **55**; Rob 699, 805, 1033; Zer §336

15 BDF §372(1a); DM 245; MHT I 160, 168; MHT III 116; Rob 482, 805, 1010, 1421; RD §342(i); Zer §234, 331, 336

16 BDF §153(1); BW 47; Moule 32; MHT III **281**; MHT IV 76, 135; Rob 234, 392, 477; RD §342(g)

18 Moule 207; Rob 226, 763, 1117

20 DM 283; MHT II 74; MHT III **13**, **44**; Rob 201, 325, 652, 703, 707, 763, 776, 984; RD §430(a)

21 MHT II 460; MHT III 42, 77; MHT IV 136; Rob 476, 689, 856

II John

1 MHT III 178; Rob 273, 657, 713, 1116

2 BDF §442(6), 468(3); Moule 180; MHT II 429; MHT IV 137, 155; Rob 441, 1199; Zer §375

3 MHT III 178, 304

4 MHT III 178, 209; Rob 515, 902, 1041; Zer §80

5 BDF §425(3); MHT II 194; Rob 339, 1140bis

6 MHT III 45; Rob 699, 703, 992

7 BDF §412(4), 416(3); Moule 101; MHT I 229; MHT III **81**, 153, 162; Rob 480, 1036, 1041, 1103, 1107, 1123bis

8 BDF §137(1); Moule 145; MHT I 50, 116; MHT II 162; MHT III 316; Rob 403, 1413; Zer §11

9 MHT III 45, 51

10 Moule 149; MHT I 125; Rob 792, 1093, 1160, 1420

12 Moule 56; MHT II 188, 204; MHT III 267; Rob 368, 625, 846, 919, 1388

13 MHT III 313; Rob 273; RD §208 c

III John

1   DM 113; Moule 112; MHT III 178

2   BDF §229(2), 392(1c); Moule 63; MHT III 270; Rob 619

3   BDF §453(2); Moule 112; MHT III 178; Rob 968

4   BW 137; Moule 112; MHT I 236; MHT II 166; MHT III 29, 161, 191; Rob 277, 663, 685, 699, 704, 992, 1042; RD §217 b, 434(a)

5   BDF §107; MHT I 116

6   MHT I 228; MHT II 465; MHT III 80, 159; MHT IV 69; Rob 861, 1121

8   BDF §451(1); MHT III 178; Rob 134, 633

9   MHT II 399; MHT III **40**; Rob 235, 269, 846

10   BDF §445(3); MHT IV 68; Rob 1166, 1185, 1189

12   BDF §312(1); Moule 112; MHT III 57, 178; Rob 635

13   Moule 56; Rob 582

14   Rob 625

15   BDF §337(4); Moule 8; MHT III 304

Jude

1 BDF §162(4); Moule 47; MHT I 103; MHT III 174, 240, **264**; MHT IV 139; Rob 501, 588, 767

2 MHT II 217; MHT III 121; Rob 125, 940

3 MHT IV 139; Rob 1106

4 BDF §412(4); MHT II 132, 205, 209; MHT III 153; MHT IV 139; Rob 127, 265, 341, 613, 776, 786, 1107, 1214

5 BDF §261(7); MHT I 230; MHT IV 139; Rob 125, 1032, 1035, 1129

7 BDF §160, 194(1); BW 51; Moule 90; Rob 125, 263, 486, 748, 1032

8 BDF §450(1); DM 261

9 Moule 175; MHT III 121; MHT IV 140; Rob 125, 232, 529, 940

10 BDF §152(1); Rob 473

11 BW 11; Moule 39, 47; MHT III **234, 238**, 242; Rob 510

12 BDF §45; MHT II 279, 358; Rob 704

13 BDF §253(2); MHT II 162; MHT III 28, 175; Rob 272

14 BW 44; Moule 47, 167; MHT II 192; MHT III 238, 241; Rob 125, 589

15 Moule 35 n.1; MHT II 235; MHT III 56; MHT IV 139; Rob 716

16 BDF §148(2); Moule 209; MHT II 366; MHT IV 139; Rob 439, 474

17 MHT IV 139

18 Moule 166; MHT II 366; MHT III 27, 89; Rob 603

19 MHT IV 139

20 BDF §60(1); Rob 280, 670bis

22 BDF §482; MHT II 196; MHT III 36; Rob 342, 696, 1153

23 MHT II 196; Rob 342

24 BDF §117(1), 214(5); MHT II 465; MHT IV 96, 139; Rob 505, 644, 1200; RD §343(k)

25 MHT III 25

Revelation

Chapter 1

1 Rob 258, 349, 780, 793; Zer §363n

3 BW 131; Rob 764, 788, 1108

4 BDF §136(1), 143, 480(5); BW 6, 72; DM 38, 70; Moule 103; MHT I 9; MHT II 154; MHT III **230**; Rob 135, 270, 394, 414, 459, 574, 734, 735, 764, 777, 877, 1202; RD §328, 379bis, 380, 385, 475

5 BDF §136(1), 468(3); Moule 77, 180; MHT I 9, 12; MHT II 79, 429; MHT III **314**; MHT IV 155; Rob 136ter, 202, 414, 458, 764, 777, 779; Zer §13

6 MHT II 429; Rob 441

7 DM 106; Rob 475, 1150; RD §472(c)

8 BDF §143; MHT III 174; Rob 414, 734, 735, 769, 777, 785; RD §380, 385

9 BW 148, 150; DM 102; Rob 504, 785; RD §323, 387(b)(2)

10 BDF §113(2); MHT II 377; MHT IV 147; Rob 645

11 MHT II 106, 128; MHT III **314**; Rob 218, 257, 263

12 Rob 257, 1383

13 BDF §182(4); DM 110; Moule 54, 177; MHT II 110, 120, 139, 441; MHT III 274; MHT IV 150; Rob 216, 218, 219, 257, 258, 274, 485, 530; RD §174 b, 209 e

15 MHT II 280; MHT III 27, 158, 314; Rob 414, 1104

16 MHT I 36; Rob 266, 414bis, 1135

17 BW 146; DM 153; Rob 669, 762, 769bis, 777, 785

18 BW 131; Moule 10; MHT II 131, 429; MHT III 89; Rob 231, 265; RD §176 C d

19 MHT III 313; Rob 404

20 BDF §294(1); MHT I 9; MHT III 324; Rob 512, 715

Chapter 2

1 DM 128; MHT II 120, 121, 359; Rob 203, 216, 274, 289; RD §379

196

2   BDF §406(1), 468(3); MHT I 56;
    MHT II 34, 206, 230, 429; MHT
    III 325; Rob 135, 312, 440,
    857, 1214; Zer §375

3   DM 102; MHT I 52; MHT II 221;
    Rob 309, 337; RD §304

4   MHT I 52; MHT II 215; Rob 309,
    337, 1035, 1393; RD §301, 304,
    320

5   BDF §192, 480(6); Moule 46; MHT
    I 52, 75; MHT II 221; MHT III
    115, 238, 239; Rob 309, 337,
    538, 539, 1010, 1025, 1218

6   Moule 46; Rob 1034

7   BDF §297, 466(4); MHT I 85; MHT
    II 197, 250, 424; Rob 203, 341,
    414, 437; RD §302

8   Moule 10; MHT II 106; MHT III
    71; Rob 218, 775

9   BDF §272, 406(1), 468(3); MHT
    II 429; MHT III 148; Rob 440,
    1039; Zer §375

10 BDF §98, 186(2); MHT III 209,
    213; MHT IV 151; Rob 498; Zer
    §45

11 MHT III 96; Rob 599, 1175,
    inset

12 BDF §269(5); MHT II 151; Rob
    655, 777; RD §387(b)(1)

13 MHT I 12; MHT II 119; MHT III
    273, 314; MHT IV 147; Rob 172,
    235, 255, 614, 712, 969; Zer
    §13

14 BDF §155(1); MHT III 151, 232,
    246; MHT IV 152; Rob 474, 482,
    519, 1106, 1393; RD §342(c)

15 MHT III 232; Rob 1105

16 BDF §192; BW 32; Moule 46, 61;
    MHT I 75; MHT II 467; MHT III
    238, 239; Rob 534, 536, 538,
    539, 590, 610, 1025; RD §347(d)

17 BDF §169(2), 297, 466(4); MHT
    II 197, 250, 424; MHT III 325;
    Rob 203, 270, 341, 414, 437,
    441, 519bis; RD §344(e)

18 MHT II 280; Rob 263, 441

19 MHT III 190; Rob 789

20 BDF §136(1); MHT II 89, 202,
    429; MHT III 314; MHT IV 155;
    Rob 136, 315, 414, 1216, 1393;
    RD §302, 320, 391; Zer §13, 375

21 BW 162; MHT II 470

22 BDF §373(2); DM 246; MHT II 75,
    477; MHT III 116; MHT IV 154;

Rob 203, 593, 1010, 1421; Zer
§331

23 MHT II 429; Rob 871

24 MHT II 60, 128, 160; MHT III
    187; Rob 232, 392, 406, 654,
    775, 866bis

25 BDF §337(1), 383(2); MHT III
    77; Rob 720, 975bis, 1412; RD
    §320, 420(b)

26 BDF §466(4); MHT I 69; MHT II
    424; Rob 136, 414, 416, 437,
    683, 1130, 1430; RD §462(b) and
    (e); Zer §25

27 BDF §113(2); MHT I 145; MHT II
    379

28 MHT III 70; Rob 901

Chapter 3

2   BDF §98; MHT I 114; MHT II 452;
    MHT III **79**, 89; Rob 375bis,
    857, 878, 884, 890, 921, 960;
    Zer §242

3   DM 255; Moule 34; MHT I 63,
    143, 145; MHT III 69, 115, 248;
    Rob 470, 740, 901, 1045, 1405,
    1419, inset; RD §342(c)

5   MHT I 104; MHT II 30; Rob 475,
    483, 485, 589, 809, 819, 1213,
    inset; RD §342(i)

7   BDF §468(3); MHT II 83, 131;
    MHT IV 154; Rob 265, 762; RD
    §176 C d; Zer §375

8   BDF §473(1); MHT I 237; MHT II
    435; MHT III 325; MHT IV 21,
    60; Rob 94, 136, 420, 722,
    1213; Zer §201

9   BDF §369(2), 392(1e), 406(1),
    408, 468(3), 476(1); DM 249;
    Moule 23; MHT II 202, 429; MHT
    III **100**, 148, 325; MHT IV 151,
    152, 155; Rob 135, 307, 311,
    324, 873, 984, 992, 1039bis,
    1214; RD §391; Zer §375

10 MHT III 345; Rob 598

11 BW 158

12 BDF §136(1), 466(4); BW 6; DM
    124; MHT II 424; MHT III 97,
    171, 314; Rob 136, 243, 414bis,
    437, 459, 655, 760, 1104, in-
    set; RD §325, 340(c), 474(c),
    475; Zer §13

14 DM 136; MHT III **14, 210**; Rob
    759, 765, 777; RD §387(a)

15 BDF §359(1); Moule 137; MHT I
    200; MHT III **91**; Rob 886, 923,

1004, 1097; RD §446bis, 458

16 MHT I 114; MHT II 67; MHT III
    79, 345; Rob 184, 857, 878

17 BDF §154, 160; DM 153; MHT II
    92; MHT III 183; Rob 204, 487,
    751, 769, 777, 785

18 BDF §155(6); Moule 91; MHT II
    60, 78, 265; MHT III 101, 149;
    Rob 202, 216, 232, 483, 807,
    1036, 1220, 1413

19 MHT III **173**; Rob 148

20 BW 95; MHT II 422; MHT III 115,
    335; MHT IV 152; Rob 507,
    601bis, 895; Zer §457

21 BDF §466(4); MHT II 424; Rob
    414, 437, 459, 586, 1130; RD
    §340(d)

Chapter 4

1 MHT II 210, 421, 454; MHT III
   315; Rob 136, 307, 328, 396,
   412, 1042, 1105, 1135, 1193,
   1213; RD §308, 475

2 Rob 601, 1135; RD §363

3 BW 13; Moule 85; MHT II 157,
   359; MHT III 185; Rob 211, 272,
   530, 644, 1135; RD §353

4 BW 13; Moule 85; MHT I 36; MHT
   II 67, 121, 170; MHT III 23;
   Rob 266bis, 274, 396, 485,
   1042, 1135; RD §342(j), 475;
   Zer §10

5 BDF §132(2); MHT III 311; Rob
   412, 713, 1135

6 BW 13; Moule 85; MHT II 67,
   157, 170; Rob 216, 300, 505,
   640, 644; RD §343(k), 353

7 Rob 201, 412

8 BDF §143, 493(1); DM 99; Moule
   66, 85; MHT II 67, 170; MHT III
   266, 314; Rob 300, 412, 414,
   644, 675, 793; Zer §10

9 BDF §382(4); DM 280; Moule 133;
   MHT I 168; MHT III **86**, 112; Rob
   324, 348, 601, 872, 972; RD
   §419(f); Zer §281, 336

10 BW 13; Rob 601, 642

11 Rob 427, 466ter, 758; RD
    §386(c)

Chapter 5

1 Rob 565

3 BDF §445(1); Rob 427, 1189; RD
   §470(n)

4 BDF §445(1); DM 301; MHT II 81;
   Rob 1061; RD §470(n)

5 BDF §391(4); BW 91, 122; DM
   301; MHT I 125; MHT III 136;
   Rob 782, 835, 1001, 1088,
   1089bis, 1090; RD §435(d)

6 BDF §132(2), 136(3); Moule 202;
   MHT II 159, 222; MHT III 311,
   314; Rob 320, 412, 414, 712

7 BDF §343(1); BW 97; DM 204;
   Moule 202; MHT I 143, 145; MHT
   III 67; Rob 897, 899bis, 901;
   RD §403(a), 475; Zer §289

8 BDF §132(2); MHT II 120, 121,
   170; MHT III 311; Rob 274, 713;
   Zer §281

9 BDF §219(3); Moule 77; MHT III
   253; MHT IV 151, 156; Rob 510,
   589, 1061

10 BDF §177

11 BDF §164(1); BW 13; Moule 85;
    MHT II 168, 169, 173, 454; MHT
    III 210; Rob 231, 283bis, 502,
    644

12 BDF §460(3); MHT II 454; MHT
    III 315; Rob 427, 758, 794,
    1182, 1200; RD §386(c)

13 BDF §173(1); Rob 603, 714, 758,
    794, 1200; RD §386(c)

14 MHT II 170; Rob 1200

Chapter 6

1 BDF §247(1), 382(4); MHT II
   439; MHT III 187; Rob 367

2 MHT III 151

3 BDF §382(4); Rob 368

4 BDF §369(2); MHT II 75, 101,
   424; MHT III 39, **100**; Rob 203,
   213, 437, 984

6 BDF §141(8), 480(5); BW 11; MHT
   I 125; MHT II 81; MHT III 27;
   Rob 501, 511; RD §343(b)

8 BDF §232(2); BW 40; DM 105;
   Moule 66; MHT II 176, 424; Rob
   452, 590, 635; RD §346(h); Zer
   §119

9 MHT II 129; Rob 910, 1118

10 BDF §147(3); MHT IV 154; Rob
    465, 505, 1394

11 BDF §140, 369(2); MHT II 75, 245; MHT III 25, **100**, 111; Rob 201, 213, 409, 802, 992, 1213

12 MHT II 83

13 Rob 635

14 MHT II 236

15 MHT II 139; Rob 203, 268; RD §192 b

16 BDF §155(3); MHT II 466; Rob 338, 483

Chapter 7

1 BDF §233(1); MHT I 36; MHT III 101, 196; Rob 266, 752, 1413

2 DM 127; MHT I 237; MHT II 171, 435; MHT III 26, 172, 325; MHT IV 21; Rob 683, 722, 864, 1118; RD §374; Zer 201

3 MHT I 125; MHT III 111; Rob 609, 975

4 BDF §136(1); MHT II 172, 173; MHT III 314; Rob 672

6 MHT II 146; Rob 263

9 BDF §136(2); MHT I 237; MHT II 435; MHT III 314, 325; MHT IV 21; Rob 136, 413, 441, 485, 722, 816, 1135, 1390; RD §342(j); Zer §201

11 Moule 85; MHT II 190; Rob 319, 339, 366, 644

12 Rob 427, 758, 787, 794, 1182; RD §386(c)

13 BDF §247(2); MHT IV 150; Rob 485, 1396

14 BDF §113(2), 343(1); Moule 75; MHT I 145; MHT II 429; MHT III 69; Rob 349, 899, 902bis; Zer §289

16 BDF §445(1); MHT II 434; MHT III 97, 196; Rob 752, 1175, inset

17 DM 99; MHT III **218**; Rob 170, 262

Chapter 8

1 BDF §382(4); MHT I 168; MHT II 341; MHT III **93**; Rob 204, 958, 973, 1146; RD §408, 416, 419(f)

3 BDF §369(2); Moule 43; MHT II 218, 372; MHT III **100**; Rob 782, 876, 984

4 BDF §188(1); Moule 43; MHT I 75; MHT III **238**; Rob 529; Zer §55

5 BDF §343(1); MHT I 143, 145; MHT II 123; MHT III 69, 70; MHT IV 60; Rob 510, 899bis, 901; Zer §289

7 BW 28; DM 79; Rob 350, 412, 502, 653, 779

9 BDF §136(1); MHT III 312, 314; Zer §13

11 BDF §49(1); MHT II 123, 343, 462; MHT IV 70; Rob 253, 458, 598

12 MHT II 60, 262; Rob 341, 349, 350, 1220, 1413

13 BDF §190(2), 247(2); Moule 73; MHT II 278, 432; Rob 135, 391, 487, 537, 674, 1193; RD §347(f), 448(h)

Chapter 9

1 Rob 231, 864, 910, 1116bis, 1118, 1123; RD §403(a), 460(c)

2 BW 25

4 BDF §369(2), 445(1); DM 248; MHT II 129; MHT III **100**, 196; Rob 752, 992, 1159bis, 1169; RD §410(a), 434(a), 470(n)

5 BDF §369(2); MHT III **100**, 113; Rob 992, 1413

6 BDF §149, 365(2); BW 88; Moule 10; MHT I 190; MHT III 63, 97; Rob 324, 709, 870, 873, 889, 1405, inset

7 MHT III 24

8 MHT II 194; Rob 339

10 BDF §182(4), 194(1), 400(8); MHT III **220**; Rob 272

11 BDF §143; BW 5; DM 70; MHT I 69, 233, 235; MHT II 205, 476; MHT III **17**, 230; Rob 104, 458, 653, 1202

12 BDF §136(5), 248(3); MHT I 58; MHT III 188; Rob 270, 405, 410; Zer §154

13 MHT II 432; Rob 782

14 BDF §136(1, 3); MHT I 36; MHT III 314, 315; Rob 255, 266, 412, 414, 604, 760; Zer §13

16 MHT II 168, 173; Rob 580

17 MHT III 24

18   MHT III 312

19   MHT II 157; MHT III 24; Rob 273

20   BDF §369(2), 391(5); DM 249;
     MHT I 210; MHT II 75, 121; MHT
     III **100**, 209; Rob 203, 998,
     1159; RD §435(a); Zer §352

21   BDF §445(1)

Chapter 10

1   MHT II 476; Rob 485, 892

2   MHT I 225; MHT II 347; Rob 155,
     414, 828, 1135, 1213

3   BW 160

4   MHT I 125; Rob 853bis

5   Rob 593

6   BDF §149; Moule 60, 183; MHT II
     464; MHT III 137; MHT IV 153;
     Rob 1034

7   BDF §309(1); MHT II 422; MHT
     III 53, 112; MHT IV 152; Rob
     474, 799, 847, 1215

8   MHT II 347; Rob 155, 1213; RD
     §475

9   MHT II 208, 347, 402; Rob 155,
     339; RD §315(h), 475

10   MHT I 111, 115; Rob 155, 563;
     RD 315(h), 475

11   Rob 605

Chapter 11

1   MHT II 454; MHT III 315; MHT IV
     147; Rob 1135; Zer §14

2   BW 21; Moule 84; MHT II 172;
     Rob 642, 782

3   BDF §471(1); Rob 485

4   BDF §136(3); MHT III 314; Rob
     410, 412, 704, 786

5   BDF §372(3); MHT I 187; MHT III
     25, 116; Rob 1017, 1026

6   Moule 27 n.1; MHT III 101, 139;
     Rob 974

7   MHT II 467; Rob 802; Zer §228

8   MHT III **22**; Rob 727, 729

9   BDF §164(2); MHT II 178; MHT
     III 209; MHT IV 151; Rob 315,
     515, 599, 775; RD §302, 320bis

10   MHT II 264; Rob 565, 1220; RD
     §320

11   BDF §218, 460(1); Moule 75; MHT
     II 178; Rob 775, 1378

12   MHT II 210; Rob 307, 328; Zer
     §69

13   MHT II 210; Rob 502, 709; RD
     §343(i)

14   Rob 135, 270, 410

15   Moule 120; MHT II 454; MHT III
     315; Rob 412bis; Zer §13

16   Zer §281

17   BDF §143; MHT I 52, 145; MHT II
     221; MHT III 69; Rob 309, 337,
     414, 734, 801, 834, 901, 1217;
     RD §320, 380, 385

18   BDF §393(3); BW 128; DM 219;
     MHT I 118; MHT III 139, 313;
     Rob 414, 757, 1076

19   MHT II 476; Rob 782, 1213

Chapter 12

1   Rob 485

3   MHT II 101; Rob 213

4   BDF §73; MHT I 114; MHT III **79**;
     Rob 224, 315, 857, 878, 1219;
     RD §320

5   BDF §136(3); MHT II 104, 161;
     MHT III 315; MHT IV 153; Rob
     349, 413

6   BDF §297; BW 23; DM 101; Moule
     29, 74; MHT I 59; MHT II 75,
     435, 448; MHT III 46, 258; MHT
     IV 21, 150; Rob 203, 392, 579,
     723, 820, 985; Zer §202

7   BDF §400(8); BW 120; Moule 128;
     MHT I 106, 217, 218; MHT II
     448, 449, 467, 484; MHT III
     141; MHT IV 152; Rob 1066,
     1093, 1426

8   BDF §445(1)

9   MHT I 233; MHT III 152; Rob
     399, 777

10   MHT II 127; Rob 136, 262

11   BDF §222; Moule 55; MHT II 100,
     423; Rob 224, 584

12   BDF §190(2); MHT III 35; Rob
     537, 1193; RD 347(f)

13   MHT II 104, 129, 161; Rob 258,
     728; RD §174 a

14 BDF §297; Moule 72; MHT II 435, 466; MHT III 46, 101, 210; MHT IV 21; Rob 407, 502, 672, 723, 775; Zer §202

15 Rob 169

17 MHT II 467; Rob 781; Zer §228

Chapter 13

1 MHT II 440; MHT III 213, **272**; MHT IV 153; Rob 892

2 MHT II 112; Rob 210, 1414

3 BDF §196; MHT II 476; MHT III 175, **214**; MHT IV 153; Rob 334, 496, 818; Zer §41

4 MHT II 467; Rob 476

5 MHT II 172; MHT III 139

7 MHT II 467; Zer §228

8 BDF §136(3); Moule 73; MHT I 237; MHT II 435; MHT III 325; MHT IV 21, 152; Rob 476, 722; Zer §201

10 BDF §372(2a); DM 105; MHT II 449, 450; MHT IV 152; Rob 590, 787, 1417

11 BDF §136(3), 182(4), 194(1); MHT II 476; MHT III **220**, 315; Rob 892, 1203

12 BDF §369(2); MHT I 237; MHT II 435; MHT III **100**, 175; MHT IV 21; Rob 992, 1397

13 BDF §391(5); Rob 998, 1391; RD §435(a); Zer §352

14 BDF §136(3), 222; Moule 55; MHT II 129; MHT III **71**, 315; Rob 256, 258, 713

15 MHT II 75, 430; Rob 984; Zer §352

16 BDF §369(2); MHT III 24, **100**; Rob 401, 787, 984

17 Rob 984, 1169

18 MHT II 169; Rob 283bis

Chapter 14

1 DM 138; MHT II 160, 222; MHT III 315; Rob 320, 760, 1135

2 MHT II 429; MHT III 27; Rob 1135

3 MHT II 173, 429; Rob 672, 1135

4 BDF §339(3), 380(3), 428(4); MHT I 168; MHT III **110**; MHT IV 39, 150; Rob 958, 969; RD §416, 423(c)

6 BDF §309(1); MHT II 454; MHT III 53; Rob 474, 565, 747, 799, 892, 1215; Zer §13

7 BDF §156; MHT III 246, 315; Rob 414, 788

8 BDF §168(2), 493(1); MHT I 135; MHT III 218; Rob 747, 843

9 MHT II 422; MHT III **272**; Rob 565, 601; RD §363

10 BDF §165; MHT II 422; MHT III 213; Rob 317, 680

11 MHT III 25

12 BDF §136(1); Rob 414; Zer §13

13 BDF §12(3), 369(2); Moule 23, 145 n.1, 207; MHT I 114, 248; MHT II 74; MHT III **100, 102**; MHT IV 151; Rob 210, 518, 597, 992; Zer §**414n**, 415

14 BDF §182(4); Moule 177; MHT II 121, 441; Rob 135, 136, 391, 414, 530, 658, 1135; RD §337

15 BDF §400(8), 442(2); MHT III 334; Rob 590, 747

17 Rob 747

18 MHT III **215**; Rob 265, 747; Zer §45

19 BDF §49(1), 136(3); MHT II 123; MHT III 314; Rob 253, 410

20 BDF §161(1); BW 21; Moule 84; MHT I 102; MHT II 123, 173; Rob 469, 517, 575, 642; RD §344(d), 353; Zer §71

Chapter 15

1 DM 141; Rob 762, 1106

2 BDF §212; MHT II 67, 197; MHT III 240, **260**; MHT IV 155; Rob 341, 475, 529, 598, 881; RD §346(a)

3 BDF §147(3); MHT II 429; Rob 461, 464, 465; RD §341(c); Zer §33

4 BDF §187(2), 365(4); Rob 395, 930, 934, inset; Zer §444

5 BDF §471(4); MHT II 476; Rob 1213

6 DM 141; MHT II 476; Rob 485, 560, 620, 762

7   BDF §164(2); MHT III 209

8   DM 281; MHT III 111

Chapter 16

1   BDF §73; MHT II 91, 196, 265; Rob 339, 342, 352, 1220, 1411

2   MHT II 126; Rob 232, 342

3   MHT IV 153

5   BDF §143; Rob 414

6   MHT II 90; MHT III 27; MHT IV 150; Rob 339

9   BDF §153(1), 391(4); BW 50; MHT II 445; MHT III 136, 245; MHT IV 48, 152; Rob 478, 485, 998, 1001, 1088, 1089, 1090, 1430; RD §435(d)

10   BDF §212; BW 26; Moule 73; MHT III 89, 260; Rob 214, 375, 598, 903

11   Rob 598

12   MHT III 26, 172; Rob 255, 760

13   MHT III 313

14   MHT III 313

15   BDF §369(2); MHT III 101; Rob 1413

16   MHT II 149; Rob 104

18   DM 113; MHT III 46; Rob 221, 546, 710, 723, 731bis, 978; Zer §202

19   BDF §168(2); MHT II 462; MHT III 58, 218; MHT IV 21, 70; Rob 458, 503

21   Rob 599

Chapter 17

1   MHT III 27, 94; Rob 774, 777, 1399, 1407

2   BDF §297, 469; MHT III 325; Rob 441, 724; Zer §455

3   BDF §172; MHT I 65; MHT II 440; MHT III 213, 233, 315; Rob 412, 414, 455, 474, 506, 510; RD §343(1); Zer §13

4   BDF §136(1); MHT III 3**14**, 315; MHT IV 146; Rob 156, 485

5   MHT II 60; Rob 233

6   MHT II 476; MHT IV 152; Rob 478

7   Rob 532

8   Moule 73; MHT II 476; MHT IV 61, 151, 152; Rob 334, 719, 819, 1216; RD §443

9   MHT II 435; MHT III 46; MHT IV 21; Rob 683, 723; Zer §202

10   MHT III 178; Rob 234, 747, 750, 764

11   Moule 72; MHT IV 152

13   Rob 311, 1214bis

14   MHT II 467; MHT IV 153

15   MHT III 26, 27

16   MHT III 40; Rob 590

17   BDF §383(2); DM 281; MHT III 23, 111; Rob 872, 975, 1412; RD §420(b)

18   Rob 234, 604

Chapter 18

1   Rob 892

2   BDF §493(1); MHT I 134, 135; Rob 260, 269, 843, 1200

3   BDF §168(2); Moule 73; MHT II 127, 221, 381, 423; Rob 337, 599, 1218; RD §320

4   Rob 1390, 1413

6   MHT IV 152; Rob 317, 580, 716

7   Moule 207; MHT III 345; MHT IV 154; Rob inset

9   MHT III 112; Rob 1217

10   Rob 498, 1193; RD §448(h)

11   Rob 475

12   BDF §60(1); MHT II 72; MHT III **17**, 31; Rob 192, 280, 441, 670

13   BDF §5(1d); MHT II 155, 362; Rob 186

14   MHT I 190, 192; MHT III 97; Rob 348, 873, 1165, inset

15   BDF §284(3); MHT III 190

16   MHT III **17**; Rob 485, 653, 710, 771, 1193

17   Moule 202; MHT II 335; MHT III 335; Rob 474; RD §387(e)

19   MHT III 24; Rob 1193

20 MHT III 35; Rob 461, 464, 786; Zer §33

21 MHT II 432

22 MHT I 192; MHT II 434; MHT III 196; Rob 753

23 MHT II 60, 262; Rob 341, 349, 1220

24 MHT III 27; Rob 689

Chapter 19

1 Rob 205; Zer §69

2 MHT IV 154; Rob 1220

3 BDF §343(1); MHT I 145; MHT II 221, 423; MHT III 70; Rob 337, 902; RD §304; Zer §289

4 MHT II 170; Rob 283

5 MHT III 35; Rob 459

6 MHT III 315

7 BDF §101; Rob 1212

8 Rob 485

9 BDF §474(5c); MHT II 123; Rob 262, 1396

10 DM 30; MHT I 178; MHT II 54; Rob 949, 1399

11 BDF §219(4); Rob 1213

12 Rob 414

13 MHT II 192, 230, 256, 321; Rob 135, 211, 364, 374, 485, 533

14 Rob 407, 412, 485

15 BDF §168(2); MHT II 123, 436; MHT III 40, 218; Rob 503, 680, 960, 1001

16 MHT II 443; MHT IV 153; Rob 660

17 MHT II 123; Rob 262, 269, 949

19 MHT II 467; Zer §228

20 Rob 414; Zer §13

21 Rob 260, 269, 599; Zer §281

Chapter 20

1 MHT II 131; Rob 265, 892; RD §176 C d

2 BDF §136(1); MHT I 233; MHT III 314; Rob 414, 714; Zer §13

3 MHT III 111; Rob 528, 975; RD §420(b)

4 BDF §445(1); MHT I 130; MHT II 429; MHT III 24, **71**; Rob 833, 834

5 BDF §62; MHT III 111; Rob 975

8 MHT I 237; MHT II 171, 435; MHT III 325; MHT IV 21; Rob 722; Zer §201

9 MHT II 400

10 BDF §339(3); Moule 206; MHT III 81

11 BDF §149; MHT II 466

12 Rob 349, 714, 1213

15 DM 289; Rob 1008, 1012, 1417; Zer §303

Chapter 21

1 BDF §62; Rob 394, 413; RD §379

2 BW 31; DM 82, 85; MHT III 238; Rob 539

3 Rob 611

4 BDF §445(1); Rob 262

5 Rob 480, 1396

6 MHT II 221, 424; MHT III 39; Rob 337, 785

8 BDF §13; MHT II 349, 460; MHT IV 153; Rob 712, 1118

9 BDF §136(2); MHT III 94, 186, 314; Rob 777, 1399, 1407

10 MHT II 124

11 BDF §60(1), 108(3); MHT II 123, 407; MHT III 31; Rob 150, 280, 414, 670

12 MHT I 225

13 MHT I 73; MHT III 26; Rob 254, 494, 791bis, 1390

14 MHT I 225; Rob 262, 412

16 BDF §165; MHT II 173; MHT III 240; Rob 263, 405, 732, 967; RD §424(d)

17 BDF §165; MHT II 141; Rob 268, 672, 714

18 MHT II 67, 124, 307; Rob 201, 253

19 MHT II 122, 376; Rob 262

20 MHT II 79, 90, 124, 362; Rob
168, 199, 204

21 BDF §204, 305; DM 97, 99; Moule
60 n.1, 66; MHT I 105; MHT II
67, 303; MHT III 198; Rob 253,
282, 400, 555, 556, 568, 571,
673, 675, 746; RD §378; Zer §78

23 BDF §445(1); Rob 541

24 MHT III 313

25 BW 10; Moule 39; MHT III 325;
Rob 793, inset

27 DM 247; MHT I 241; MHT II 434,
468; MHT III 196; MHT IV 150;
Rob 753, 1187, inset; Zer §470

Chapter 22

1 MHT II 475

2 BDF §104(1), 248(3); MHT II
129, 205; MHT III 188, 198; MHT
IV 43, 157; Rob 258, 300bis,
311, 745, 1214

3 MHT II 434; MHT III 196; Rob
166, 753

4 Rob 871

5 MHT II 264; MHT III 172

6 Rob 1396

8 MHT II 205; Rob 214

9 MHT I 178; MHT II 54; MHT IV
152; Rob 932, 1203; RD §465

11 MHT II 395, 400; Rob 947; RD
§407

13 Rob 429, 777; Zer §109

14 BDF §369(2); Moule 207; MHT III
102; MHT IV 151; Rob 757, 984;
Zer §342, 352, **414**

15 BDF §13; MHT III 151

16 Rob 399, 762

17 MHT II 475

18 BDF §488(1c); MHT II 173; MHT
III 115; MHT IV 148

19 MHT III 115; Rob 356; RD §303

20 MHT II 154; Rob 105n.